Dimensions in Communication: Readings

Second Edition

Dimensions in Communication: Readings

Second Edition

edited by James H. Campbell
Wichita State University

and Hal W. Hepler
Michigan State University

Wadsworth Publishing Company, Inc.
Belmont, California

To Betty and Sheila, still

Preface

This book of readings represents a definite set of viewpoints toward communication. The underlying premise is that persuasion exists in all communication. When people interact, persuasion is one of the catalysts.

In the first edition of this book, we supported our contentions with a number of selections never before collected in a single volume. The selections were arranged both to emphasize their interrelatedness and to reflect our particular outlook. There are, of course, other viewpoints and many other articles that could have been chosen. But we believe that the collection served as a good starting point, a valuable means of hinting at some of the dimensions of persuasion and communication. We invited the reader to construct his own viewpoint (even if it differed from ours) and to venture even further into the literature on communication.

In this second edition, some readings have been deleted and some new ones added. These deletions and additions reflect changes in our thinking and in our emphasis. We feel that this collection, like the first, makes a good starting point for understanding some of the dimensions of persuasion and communication.

Our students and colleagues have aided us in making the decisions concerning this volume. We are pleased with the wide acceptance of the first edition and with the general upsurge of interest in communication. What area of human activity could be of more relevance in the coming years?

Our thanks go also to the reviewers of the first edition, whose comments were helpful to us in preparing the second edition: Richard Sandow, Michigan State University; Norman G. Shidle, Roxbury, Connecticut; Audrey J. Roth, Miami-Dade Junior College; Leland Brown, Eastern Michigan University; Charles S. K. Jameson, University of Southern California; and Walter F. Terris, Eastern Montana College.

Contents

Section Three: Message Systems and Sub-systems

General Introduction

One of the major premises of this book is the belief that all communication is persuasive. The importance of persuasion varies among communication situations, but persuasion is always present to some degree. The selections in this book provide reasons for undertaking careful analysis of communication situations as well as information and ideas that will aid in such analysis. Of course, analytic tools, like most other tools, can be used for ill as well as for good. The carpenter's hammer can also be a lethal weapon. And the Critical Path Method (CPM) can be used in the manufacture of nerve gases.

If you are interested in persuasion, you are interested in prediction. When you predict, you are dealing with probabilities—you are saying that one thing is more likely to occur than another. However, you are seldom satisfied only to predict. Frequently what you predict as most *likely* to occur is not what you would *prefer* to have occur. Therefore, you attempt to alter, manipulate, and persuade.

Sensitive writers, speakers, and other communicators are eager to predict the responses that may be made to their messages. Uncertainty about what the interpreter of the message will think and do haunts the thoughts of the poet, the sculptor, the diplomat, and the businessman. As the receiver's responses become more important to the sender, the message is likely to become more persuasive, and the sender is likely to become more eager to predict with confidence the outcome he prefers.

Implicit in these statements is a paradox that produces stress for anyone constructing messages. The communicator may think that his efforts should be sincere and spontaneous; at the same time, he recognizes the necessity for deliberate and careful calculation in his dealings with others. Being entirely spontaneous is often the same as being thoughtless, and no one wishes to be thoughtless; on the other hand, deliberate analysis is often considered cynical and ruthless, and no one wishes to be cynical and ruthless. Thus the paradox, or dilemma, arises. In our society, both spontaneity and thoughtfulness are highly valued, and of course one can to some extent be both sincere *and* deliberate. But whether you are sincere in your dealings with your fellows is a moral issue and beyond the scope of this book. We are concerned here with whether you are analytic.

What must a situation be in order to be persuasive? Before we attempt an answer, some terms need to be defined. The level of definition is general, not technical or operational.

> *Reward* is reduction of the difference between the situation as someone—either a source or a receiver—now perceives it and the situation as he would prefer it.
> *Contrient* refers to situations in which one and only one of the participants can be rewarded. If one obtains the reward, the other goes unrewarded—for example, the employment situation with a larger number of applicants than jobs.
> *Cooperative* refers to situations in which the rewards are obtained by both participants.
> *Probability* is the relative frequency with which one event occurs out of a set of events. The probability of getting a head on a flipped coin is ½. Two things can happen, and since they are equally likely to happen, the probability that one of them will happen is .5, or 1 in 2. The probabilities taken up in the rest of this discussion are not the result of formal calculation, any more than a man's estimate of the probability that he can cross the road before the oncoming truck hits him involves a formal calculation. But the probabilities dealt with here are just as useful as those considered by the pedestrian.

Bearing these definitions in mind, let us see when persuasion is likely to be attempted and when it is reasonable to say that someone has been persuaded. Of course, first there must be at least two people, and one of them must have some effect upon the other. In addition, there must be the possibility of interaction between them. Given these conditions, what goes into someone's decision to communicate?

> 1. Reward to the source must be *greater than* the effort required for production of a message.

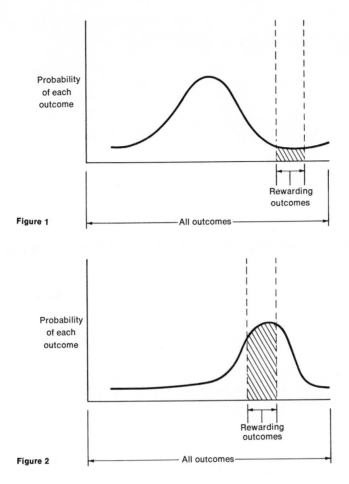

Figure 1

Probability of each outcome

Rewarding outcomes

All outcomes

Figure 2

Probability of each outcome

Rewarding outcomes

All outcomes

In other words, a man looks at a situation that involves himself and another and sees that, if he makes no effort at alteration, the result will be other than he would prefer. This situation can be represented as in Figure 1. However, before the source-to-be makes an effort to alter the situation and thereby to alter the outcome, he must be able to see the situation as represented in Figure 2. Further, he must think that the state of affairs shown in Figure 2 can be brought about with a sufficiently high probability. That is, the risk (probability) of expending effort without any gain must seem fairly small. The source-to-be, then, decides the probability that a given set of probabilities can be made to hold. If that first-mentioned probability is high enough, the source will risk his time and energy by making an effort to persuade.

Now let's look at what sorts of things affect the receiver's decision to respond as he thinks the source wishes.

2. (a) If the situation is perceived by the receiver as contrient, the reward to the source as perceived by the receiver must be *less than* the reward the receiver sees for himself, *and* the reward for the receiver must be *greater than* the effort required for the receiver to respond.

   (b) If the situation is perceived by the receiver as cooperative, the rewards combine—but probably not in a simple additive fashion.

Consider, for example, the plight of the politician. If he votes for a bill that is good for his constituents, but which was introduced by the other political party, he runs the risk of strengthening his opponents' position in the next election. Even though he also strengthens his own position, the question he considers is: "Whose position is strengthened most?" His decision about which way to vote certainly depends on many other factors, but this question is seldom disregarded entirely.

Finally, consider the source's idea of the relationship between himself and the receiver, and what effect this idea will have on the source's actions.

3. The source must believe that the relationship between himself and the receiver is such that the receiver will attend to and accept the position explicit or implicit in the message. If the source thinks the relationship between them is not of this kind, but might be made so, any effort he expends to change the relationship must be added to the effort required to produce a message.

We have looked at some of the things that make a situation "persuasive." However, here is the test: *The receiver must modify his behavior so that it more nearly conforms to the source's expectations.* Unless this modification occurs, persuasion has not taken place. And if persuasion has not taken place, the situation is not persuasive.

Suppose you know nothing, absolutely nothing, about a receiver of your message except, for example, that all of his possible responses to your message can be placed in seven categories. Into which of the seven categories will his response fall? Once you have guessed an answer to that question, what are the odds that you have made a correct guess and that his response will, in fact, fall into the predicted category? You have one chance in seven of guessing right. In other words, you have established two things about the receiver's responses: first, that you know they will all fall into one or another of seven categories; and second, that you cannot predict within which of the seven categories a given response will, in fact, lie. All categories, then, are equally likely to occur.

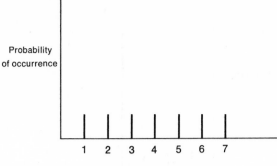

Figure 3　　　　　　　　　Response categories

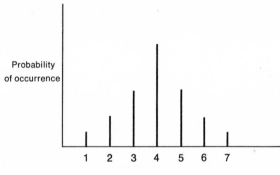

Figure 4　　　　　　　　　Response categories

When a speaker addresses himself to a particular audience for the first time, he is in the situation just described. As an aid in predicting the responses he will attempt to evoke in the future, the source of a message looks at the responses he has evoked in the past. He tries to make one response, or response category, more likely than another. If the situation is graphically represented, he tries to change the situation from that shown in Figure 3 to that shown in Figure 4. Ideally, he wants the situation shown in Figure 5. *This assumes, of course, that response category number 4, whatever it may be, is the one that he prefers.* He spent the effort necessary to communicate in the first place because he recognized that 4 might be made more likely to occur, with some benefit to him.

The responses that you have decided are available to the receiver have equal probabilities only when you know nothing about the receiver. But you never know nothing; you always know something. For example, one of the things you always know is that, other things being equal, most people will tend not to respond to a given message. Some will respond

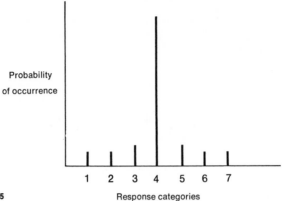

Probability
of occurrence

1 2 3 4 5 6 7

Figure 5   Response categories

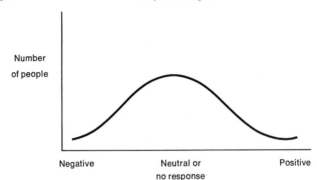

Number
of people

Negative   Neutral or   Positive
                  no response

Figure 6   Intensity of response

positively, with degrees of vigor ranging from just barely positive responses to quite emphatically positive responses. These last will be few in number, indeed. Others' responses also will vary in vigor, but they will be distributed in the direction of an emphatically negative response. The intensity of response, as measured by numbers responding, can be represented as in Figure 6. The same sort of curve can be used to show the distribution of probabilities of responses for a given individual. Instead of numbers of people responding, the curve would be drawn to show the probability of a given response, as in Figures 1 and 2. Figure 6, so modified, would then tell us that an individual's most probable response is his minimal response. Since any response costs something, and since everyone has priorities for the ways in which he spends his energies, the probability that the receiver will spend energy responding to the source's message, doing the source's bidding, is small. Therefore, the source must show the receiver that the course of action advocated by the source is worthy of the receiver's time and energy.

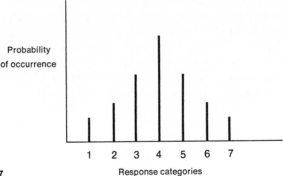

Figure 7

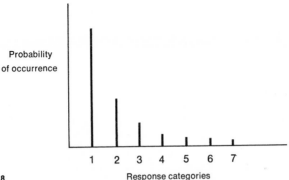

Figure 8

The source wishes to cause the probability of responses to alter in a fashion favorable to his purpose. Consider a set of possible responses that the source thinks can be fitted into the seven following categories:

1. Receiver buys a product and urges friends to buy, too.
2. Receiver buys a product.
3. Receiver considers reasons for buying a product.
4. Receiver does not consider buying a product.
5. Receiver considers reasons for buying a competitor's product.
6. Receiver buys a competitor's product.
7. Receiver buys a competitor's product and urges his friends to buy the competitor's product, too.

It is reasonable to suppose that the most likely action for the receiver to take is number 4. This distribution of the receiver's responses, with 4 the most likely, is shown in Figure 7. The source, in this case the advertiser of the product, wants to modify the probabilities of the receiver's responses so that response number 1 becomes the most likely. In other words, he wants to produce the situation shown in Figure 8.

How can this highly desirable state of affairs be achieved? That is what this book is about. All of the essays and all of the selections are here because they can aid the communicator in altering the probabilities of the receiver's responses in ways the communicator can predict and in ways that permit the communicator to reap rewards from his efforts. This book is designed to increase the sophistication with which its readers go about shaping the behavior of the people with whom they deal.

Section One

Conceptual Frames

We all use models. Little boys make model airplanes, and little girls play with dolls. The aircraft engineer makes models of wing sections to test in wind tunnels. The architect makes scale models of buildings. The physicist uses mathematical models of events in the real world (for example, with the famous $E = mc^2$). The businessman uses models of cash flow and of administrative lines of authority within his organization. The psychologist uses S R and S O R to indicate what he thinks happens in the learning process. Some *communication* models presented in this section can be used to analyze communication situations.

Why do we use models? The little boy makes model airplanes because it pleases him to construct them and to fly them. As the boy grows older, he may make model airplanes because they help him to understand the operation of real ones. The physicist constructs elaborate mathematical models because they help him to conceptualize the physical phenomena in which he is interested. This last is probably the primary reason adults construct and use models. That is, models help us to make predictions about the real world. Moreover, models are relatively inexpensive—for example, it is easier and cheaper to make a model of an airplane or a space capsule than it is to build the real thing. And models are easily manipulated. We can readily see, using an example of a mathematical model, that if $E = mc^2$ then m must be equal to E/c^2. Models allow us to isolate the parts of intricate reality that interest us and to examine the interrelationships of those parts. Models give us a way of structuring our world and of making predictions about what will happen in an "if X, then Y" sort of way. Models are, then, not good or bad, true or false, but *useful* or *not useful*.

In this section of the book, we look at the general problems, advantages, and disadvantages of models as well as at some models of model building. Bross's article clearly indicates the rationale for the use of models. Although he examines the bright and the dark sides of the construction and use of models, he does not question whether models should be used. One of the points he makes is that man *is committed* to the use of models in understanding and manipulating his environment and should, therefore, be conscious of the nature of these devices.

The first model presented in this section is Kenneth Boulding's. It is the most general and, at the same time, the most difficult. It reads so well that the complexity of the model Boulding offers may be minimized. The notion of the image is an all-encompassing one: Everything that impinges upon each of us is going to be an influence upon each of our images. More things affect our behavior and attitudes than many of us realize. In fact, there is a lot of hard thinking in store for anyone who tries to make Boulding's model into a device for manipulating environment.

The Westley-MacLean model is the most thoroughly worked out of those offered. It appears here because it can be used as a discussion basis for all the rest of the material in this book. It is also valuable because it deals with mediated communication—that is, with communication that passes through a third party.

The March and Simon discussion of uncertainty absorption in communications networks within organizations fits the Westley-MacLean model well. The uncertainty absorber is the intermediary through whose hands information must pass to the final consumer of information, the decision maker. The communicator in business, education, welfare work, and almost anything else finds that he is an organization man. Some of his communication problems derive from the way in which his organization is made up. Only by discovering how the structure and function of the organization affect communication within it can he hope to pursue effectively his goals and those of his organization.

The Toch-MacLean discussion of transactional psychology provides a way of looking at the world where all perception is seen as a transaction between the perceiver and the perceived. The total essay with its working assumptions is a thoroughly modern view of the relationship between man and his environment.

The Katz and Kahn selection on communication provides a comprehensive overview of topics within the broad area of organizational communication. Of particular interest is their discussion of communication up and down the line. This might profitably be compared with the Lloyd and Warfel discussion in Section III.

Models

Irwin D. J. Bross

Models provide us with a way of looking at and abstracting from the totality of communication. Bross's essay provides us with a model's model—a model for looking at and conceptualizing the uses of models. Bross describes how the decision maker chooses from a group of alternatives (that is, decides) on the basis of available information, values, and other criteria. We suggest that the effective communicator, like the decision maker, consciously chooses the ways in which human behavior may be shaped and changed.

The Symbolic World

The data refinery starts with raw data—the sights, sounds, and smells of the real world—and passes the information through several processes of abstraction. The end product, refined data, may then be pumped into the Decision-Maker.

The Decision-Maker itself operates in the symbolic world. A course of action is selected by a symbolic mechanism and then the process of abstraction is reversed—the recommendation is translated into physical action in the sensory world.

The effective use of a Decision-Maker requires some knowledge about both worlds, sensory and symbolic. Experience with data is needed for an appreciation of the symbolic mechanism. Similarly an understanding of the symbolic picture (i.e., the model) is required for an appreciation of data. This latter remark may strike you as curious. Perhaps it will seem less odd when you have finished this article.

Before I consider the rather elaborate *statistical* models, I want to devote some attention to the broad concept of a *model*. Models are vitally important in scientific work and, in my opinion, in any intellectual endeavor. An understanding of the nature and role of a model is prerequisite to clear thinking.

In ordinary language the word "model" is used in various ways. It covers such diverse subjects as the dolls with which little girls play and also the photogenic "dolls" who occupy the attention of mature men. I shall be concerned here with model in the sense of replica (as in a model airplane).

Physical Models

There are several kinds of model aircraft. Solid scale models resemble the actual planes in general appearance (shape, markings, etc.). The flying model aircraft not only resemble the originals in appearance but, to some extent, in *function* as well (i.e., they are capable of free flight). Some very elaborate models are essentially simplified versions of real aircraft; they have gasoline engines, operable controls, and may even have radio-control mechanisms which allow the plane to be directed from the ground.

A boy who is interested in aviation can learn about the subject from the construction and operation of such flying models. In much the same way a scientist who has constructed a model of some natural phenomenon may learn about this phenomenon from a study of his model.

The model aircraft is easier to study than a full-sized aircraft for various reasons. It is more convenient to handle and manipulate. It is also simpler than the original, and principles of operation may be more apparent. There is some danger of oversimplification, of course, and some characteristics of a real aircraft would be overlooked if all attention were focused on the model.

As a matter of fact, adult scientists use model aircraft to learn about the performance of full-sized aircraft. They build carefully scaled replicas and test these models in wind tunnels. This is a much more economical process than to build a full-sized airplane and then to test *it* in a wind tunnel (a mammoth wind tunnel is a fabulously expensive piece of equipment). This type of argument by analogy has proved quite successful and is used all the time by aircraft engineers.

I do want to emphasize that the aircraft engineers do not trust the method entirely, that they carefully test the full-sized aircraft as well as the model. In other words, it does not follow that one can *automatically* obtain useful information about the original phenomena from the study of a model. Whether a model will be useful or not will have to be learned from experience, by comparing the performances of the original phenomenon and the replica.

The model represents a process of abstraction. The real aircraft has many properties or attributes such as shape, weight, and so on. Only a few of these properties are duplicated in the model. The wind tunnel model, for example, duplicates only the shape. However, the aerodynamic performance depends largely on this one characteristic; the other properties are more or less irrelevant.

This is an example of an effective process of abstraction. It allows us to focus our attention on a much simpler phenomenon without much loss from the fact that many details have been neglected.

This particular type of abstraction, the construction of a physical model, is used in various branches of science, engineering, and industry. Models are used to design ocean liners, bridges, water supply systems, and all sorts of products from automobiles to stage scenery. Not all models involve a change in size. In aircraft construction, for example, a full-sized model of a part of a plane is sometimes constructed out of wood in order to insure that an absent-minded designer does not put components in places which cannot be reached for repairs. In this situation the relevant factor is size, and the mock-up (as it is commonly called) eliminates other factors such as weight, function, and so on.

Abstract Models

In the scientific world physical models are occasionally used for instructional purposes. In a planetarium you will generally find a model— little spheres which revolve on wire arms around a big sphere—which presents a picture of the astronomer's conception of the solar system. This sort of model is often used to demonstrate a phenomenon such as an eclipse. A rather similar physical model is sometimes employed to explain the atom to the general public. The solar model and the atom model illustrate one striking and sometimes confusing characteristic of models; two very diverse phenomena can sometimes be represented by similar models.

The solar model which you can see in a planetarium has had a very interesting history. Nowadays we think of the sun as a giant globe with a large family of little spheres circling around it. We locate ourselves on the third little sphere (counting out from the sun), and this notion does not cause us any mental anguish. In earlier days the picture was quite different and the earth was regarded as the center of the system. Of course if we go back still further there are all sorts of fabulous models which involve giants, turtles, and sea serpents. The history of astronomy is the story of the evolution of a model.

Did you notice that in describing the solar model I was actually taking a further step in abstraction? I was going from a physical model to a *verbal* model. The little balls were replaced by their symbols, the words "little balls."

All of us are accustomed to using verbal models in our thinking processes and we do it intuitively. Verbal models have played an important role in science, especially in the preliminary exploration of a topic and presentation of results. Verbal models are subject to a variety of difficulties, some of which I have discussed earlier, and most scientific fields have advanced (or are trying to advance) to the next stage—symbolic models of a mathematical nature. Astronomy was one of the first subjects to make this transition to the symbolic model. It should be noted that *until* this stage was reached there was really no reason to prefer a model with the sun as a center to a model with the earth as a center.

Symbolic Models

In a symbolic model the balls and wire arms of the physical model of the solar system are replaced by mathematical concepts. Geometrical points are substituted for the balls. The next problem is to replace the wire arms which hold the balls in place. Now the wire arms have fixed lengths, and these lengths can be stated numerically. If all of the little balls revolve in the same plane, only one additional number is needed to locate the geometrical point. This number would be the angle between the wire arm and a stationary arm which would serve as a reference point.

Hence two numbers—the radius (length of arm) and an angle—will fix the location of the geometrical point just as effectively as the wire arm fixes the location of the little sphere in the physical model. Actually the astronomer's model is much more complicated than the symbolic model which I have described, but the general principle of construction is the same.

Now suppose that the astronomer wants to use his model to predict eclipses. He will have to take observations to obtain specific numbers to use for the radius and angle. These empirically determined quantities are substituted in the mathematical model and, after various manipulations, the astronomer announces: "There will be an eclipse of the moon visible in the northeastern part of North America on such-and-such a date and at so-and-so time."

It is at this point that a comparison of alternative models can be made. If the predictions are borne out, the successful model can be used for future predictions. If, on the other hand, the eclipse does not occur at the specified time, the scientist must begin looking for another model.

The Ptolemaic astronomers set up a mathematical model of the solar system with the earth as a center. They first considered that the other astronomical bodies moved in circles. When this picture did not lead to adequate predictions the Ptolemaic astronomers decided the paths of the heavenly bodies were epicycles. If you would like to visualize an epicycle, imagine two gears, one large and standing still and the other small and rolling around the rim of the large one. An epicycle is the path of a tooth of the small gear.

This complication led to a little improvement in prediction, but the forecasts were still quite unsatisfactory so the model was complicated still further. This time the astronomers postulated that the paths of the heavenly bodies were epicycles *on* epicycles, literally a "gears within gears" situation.

If you think that this is getting too complicated consider the sad plight of the astronomers. *They* had to make the calculations which go along with this model of the solar system. Nonetheless it was many years before the simpler model with the sun at the center of the solar system was widely accepted.

There is a moral in this epicycle story. Scientists occasionally become attached to a model even though it does not give adequate prediction. They try to use the model by cutting off a piece here or adding a piece there. This patchwork can go on for many years, and the resulting crazy quilt may prevent the development of new and more efficient models. After all, when it takes a scientist ten years to master a complex model, he has a vested interest in it, and he sometimes is hostile to labor-saving devices which may deprive him of his job. "Epicyclitis" is a symptom of senility in a scientific field.

Mathematical Models

It might be puzzling to understand why the astronomers should go from a nice simple physical model with little spheres on wire arms to a symbolic model with all sorts of queer mathematical signs when, if sufficient care were taken in the construction of the physical model, it would be possible to use it directly in order to predict eclipses. The astronomer's choice is a matter of taste. From the astronomer's point of view it is the mathematical model which is the *simple* one and the physical model with balls and wire which is complex. Since the physical model is made out of metal it not only has attributes which are intended to simulate the solar system, but it also has a lot of attributes which depend on the materials used in its construction and the way in which it is made. Thus the wire arms can be geared to rotate at an appropriate speed but the mounting and drive arrangements of the model are attributes of the model and *not* attributes of the solar system which it is supposed to represent.

Even though great care is lavished on the construction of the physical model the predictions which would come out of it would depend on friction, vibration, and other characteristics of the *model*. Hence the prediction would be rendered inaccurate by the entrance of attributes other than the ones which were deliberately built into the model to simulate the solar system.

In a *mathematical* model, on the other hand, the material of the model itself—in this case the symbolic language—does not ordinarily contribute such extraneous and undesirable attributes. If we want friction in the mathematical model we can put it in symbolically, but otherwise this friction will not appear in the model and hence cannot disturb our predictions. In the physical model the process of abstraction tends to introduce new and irrelevant details, while in the mathematical model the process of abstraction does not.

In this sense, therefore, a mathematical model is simple whereas a physical model is complex. It may strike you as curious that I should say that Einstein is working with an extremely simple model in his theory of relativity, while a schoolboy is working with an extremely complex model when he builds an airplane. If you think it over carefully, however, you may see the justice of the statement.

Now and then a mathematical model gets beyond the resources of the mathematicians who construct it, so a physical model is substituted to obtain an answer. This is done in the Monte Carlo method, a device for solving mathematical problems by having one of the giant brain computers play gambling games with itself. However, such devices are used for computational convenience rather than conceptual simplicity.

The construction of symbolic models is an important part of the job of the scientist, and the great advances in science are those in which a useful new model is introduced. In physics the powerful model devised by Isaac Newton is one landmark, the relativity model of Einstein is another, and the quantum models are a third landmark. In chemistry the gas laws, the mass action laws, and the periodic table are all the end results of successful models of atomic and molecular processes. In biology the evolutionary model of Charles Darwin (a verbal model) has been developed into a mathematical model by R. A. Fisher and Sewell Wright. Another important biological model is the one which describes genetic inheritance. In medicine the models are mainly verbal, but they are of great importance. Harvey's model of the circulatory system, and the various models of the reaction of the human body to invading organisms have influenced the development of the modern treatment of diseases.

Effective verbal models which describe the transmission of disease have been useful in the eradication of many of the epidemic diseases which used to terrorize humanity. Efforts are currently in progress to translate these verbal models into mathematical ones (epidemic theory), but the earlier models have been so successful that a modern investigator is often hard put to find enough data to test his new mathematical models!

Currently, there is research under way which is attempting to devise mathematical models for sociological phenomena, such as the growth of cities, and for psychological phenomena. Norbert Wiener in *Cybernetics*[1] deals with a mathematical model associated with the operation of the human brain.

One of the key steps in the progress of a field of knowledge toward scientific maturity is the fabrication of models which enable successful prediction in that field. A tremendous amount of imagination and insight is needed for the creation of new models, but they are only half of the story. The mere creation of models is not enough; the models must survive exacting tests, they must meet the pragmatic criterion, they must work.

This brings us back to data. The test of the model involves data from the real world. Without adequate data the construction of models is a mathematical pastime. Purely speculative mathematical models may be as useless as purely speculative verbal models. For example, I might construct a very fancy mathematical model to describe the mechanism of transmission of some virus disease. No good diagnostic test may be known for the disease, and consequently the available data may be quite unreliable. If a doctor comes along with a quick, cheap, and effective skin test for this disease, it may then be possible to get adequate data to test my fancy model. Until this happens my model is just another mathematical game. After the development of the skin test, the model may turn out to be useful in the understanding and control of the disease or, as is more likely, it may turn out to be a complete waste of time.

Progress in science is based on this constant interplay between model and data. Sometimes there is a tremendous amount of observational data available but no satisfactory model, so that little progress is made. This was the situation in astronomy before the heliocentric model and it also has occurred repeatedly in the biological sciences. At other times there are elaborate models but little adequate data. Something resembling this situation occurred in economics where an elaborate mathematical theory was developed which did rather poorly when tested with actual data.

Occasionally a scientist not only works out the model but also obtains the data. Darwin and Galileo accomplished this feat. More often one man, such as Brahe, gathers good data and another man, such as Kepler, supplies the model. When this division of labor occurs it is rather pointless to say that the model-maker is a greater scientist than the data-grubber, for the advance depends on teamwork.

Advantages

Why should a model be used? The real answer to this question is that this procedure has been followed in the development of the most

[1] N. Wiener, *Cybernetics* (New York: John Wiley & Sons, Inc., 1948).

successful predicting systems so far produced, the predicting systems used in science. It is simply a matter of going along with a winner.

Some of the advantages of model-making might, however, deserve a separate statement. A big advantage of a model is that it provides a frame of reference for consideration of the problem. This is often an advantage even if the preliminary model does not lead to successful prediction. The model may suggest informational gaps which are not immediately apparent and consequently may suggest fruitful lines for action. When the model is tested the character of the failure may sometimes provide a clue to the deficiencies of the model. Some of the greatest scientific advances have been produced by *failure* of a model! Einstein's work was the outgrowth of the Michelson-Morley experiment in which the aether model led to unsuccessful prediction.

Another advantage of model-making is that it brings into the open the problem of abstraction. The real world is a very complex environment indeed. An ordinary apple, for example, has a great many properties—size, shape, color, chemical composition, taste, weight, ad infinitum. In making a decision about the apple, such as whether to eat it or not, only a few of these characteristics are considered. Some degree of abstraction is necessary for decision.

The model-maker must, therefore, decide which real world attributes will be incorporated in the model. He may decide that the size of the apple rather than shape is important to decision. He may, if he is setting up an inspection plan, concentrate on the number of worm holes. If he is interested in the velocity of a falling apple, on the other hand, he may include only the weight of the apple in his model.

By making this process of abstraction deliberate, the use of a model may bring such questions to light. Moreover, it may suggest preliminary experiments to determine which characteristics are relevant to the particular decision problem under consideration.

Once the problem is expressed in symbolic language there is the advantage of the manipulative facility of that language. The symbolic language also offers advantages in communication. It allows a concise statement of the problem which can be published. Moreover, it is more easily integrated with the other scientific work which is also in symbolic language.

Another advantage of mathematical models is that they often provide the *cheapest* way to accomplish prediction. Sometimes it is possible to reach the same results by the sheer mass of data—by a "brute force" attack on the problem—but the mathematical route is generally more economical.

One reason for this is that a newly-minted Ph.D. in mathematics can be hired (alas) for a salary which could not entice a good plumber. A Ph.D., a pencil, and some paper may be all the equipment necessary to handle the symbolic manipulations of the model. Only a very small proportion of the millions currently spent for research goes into model-making. Even when the scientists are well paid, most of the money goes into the process of collecting data.

Disadvantages

The use of models also has some drawbacks. The model is subject to the usual dangers inherent in abstraction. A mathematically feasible model may require gross oversimplifications. There is no guarantee that an investment of time and effort in constructing the model will pay dividends in the form of satisfactory prediction. No process, however, can provide such a guarantee.

The symbolic language is also subject to limitations. It may be beyond the ability of a mathematician to manipulate the symbolic language so as to obtain useful results. In such cases it may be more efficient to use direct methods. In gambling-game problems, such as the game of solitaire, it may be easier to play a large number of solitaire games and determine the probabilities by the Direct System than to embark on a mathematical analysis of the probabilities.

There is another very grave danger in the use of models. After a scientist plays for a long time with a given model he may become attached to it, just as a child may become, in the course of time, very attached to a doll (which is also a model). A child may become so devoted to the doll that she insists that her doll is a real baby, and some scientists become so devoted to their model (especially if it is a brain child) that they will insist that this model *is* the real world.

The same sort of thing happens with verbal models, as the semanticists point out, when a word and its counterpart in the real world are regarded as the same thing. This identification in the world of words has led to unhappy results which are reflected in the real world. The behavior of individuals who are unable to distinguish between words and the real world may become so bizarre as to lead to the classification "insane."

Now things are not this bad at the scientific level largely because of the self-corrective features of the sequential process of model-making which provide a periodic return to the real world after each excursion into the symbolic world. The test of the model acknowledges, as it were, the supremacy of the real world. If the model fails to predict what will happen in the real world, it is the model that must give way. This is the standard of scientific sanity.

When this standard is not admitted, a conflict between a model's predictions and happenings in the real world will sometimes lead instead to the rejection of the real world. This course is the prelude to disaster. To guard against such disasters it is well to remember the following rule for working with models: A model is neither true nor false.

The standard for comparing models is utility, i.e., successful prediction. The evaluation of a model is therefore dependent on the situation in which it is to be used; it is not *intrinsic* (i.e., dependent only on the model itself). If this point is understood several apparent paradoxes in science disappear.

One such paradox is the simultaneous use of two contradictory models. An example of this paradox occurs in the field of physics in which a *wave* and a *photon model* for light are both accepted. Wave theories are used when *they* provide successful prediction, and in other situations the photon theory is employed. Hence the paradox arises only if the models are identified with the real world.

Another paradox is the occurrence of scientific revolutions which (unlike political revolutions) do not interrupt the orderly development of the area. If models are not identified with the real world, the revolution is merely the substitution of a refined model for a cruder earlier model. Most of the time the older theory continues to be useful in the original applications; it is only in extended applications that the newer theory gives better prediction. The older theory is often a special case of the new theory. This explains why, despite the revolutionary work of Einstein, the older Newtonian physics is still used. In designing a dam or bridge, for example, both models would lead to essentially the same predictions (or in other words, the predictions are indistinguishable at the practical level).

One class of scientific workers does not worry about the testing of its models. They are the mathematicians. Their only interest (as long as they are functioning as mathematicians) lies in symbolic derivations from the models. Their business is to provide models in which the symbolic implications are worked out—anyone who wants to use the model for real world predictions will have to test it first. Nevertheless, the mathematicians serve a useful purpose in society (though a pure mathematician would strenuously deny it) by providing the scientists with ready-worked models. Often the models created by mathematicians are not used for years, or even centuries, but the literature of mathematics is a sort of Sears-Roebuck catalogue of models which may be consulted whenever a special type of model is needed. Unfortunately it takes some mathematical sophistication in order to use this catalogue.

As long as the model is completely divorced from the real world the criterion of utility cannot be used. Instead the mathematicians employ an *intrinsic* standard, *consistency*. Various attempts have been made, all unsuccessful, to extend this standard to the real world. The only result which these attempts have accomplished is to confuse matters and cause an identification of models and the real world.

Role of the Model

The disadvantages inherent in the use of models can be avoided to a large extent by a judicious balancing of the two processes, model-making and data collection. The relationship between these two aspects of Scientific Method deserves careful consideration; it provides one of the main keys to scientific success, and it also involves several notions which can be carried over into our thinking about everyday problems. The relationship can be represented diagrammatically by Figure 1.

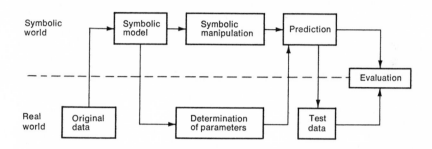

Figure 1

The model itself should be regarded as arbitrary; it represents an act of creation like a painting or a symphony. The model can be anything its creator desires it to be. In practice, of course, it is generally stimulated (and therefore affected) by data from the real world (which is labeled "Original data" in Figure 1). Artistic creations also use sensory data. Even in abstract canvases there is some influence from the original data (sensory experience). If the modern artist paints the portrait of a woman, it may not look like a human being to me. But presumably the dabs of paint have some relationship to the woman, though it may require an expert to understand this relationship. Similarly, a physicist's mathematical model of the atom may be far removed from any material substance; again only an expert can appreciate it.

In many cases the symbolic representation used in the model is chosen because it was successfully used in previous models, because it seems plausible to the creator, or because it is convenient. However, some very useful models are based on assumptions which are not evident from common sense or—as in the quantum model—are actually repugnant to common sense.

I would not consider it very plausible to be seated at a desk in Los Angeles and then suddenly to find myself at a desk in Baltimore. It is even less sensible for this jump to have been accomplished in no time at all and without passing through any intermediate point in the process. Yet electrons jump around in this remarkable manner in the quantum theories of physics. Models which embody this curious behavior lead to successful prediction.

Scientists are generally pictured as coldly logical creatures with no disposition to embark on wild flights of fancy. But the geniuses of science have at least as much imagination as any other creative artist. In some respects the symbolic language of science allows greater freedom for expression than the printed word, musical notation, or oil paint.

There is one very important respect in which the scientist differs from the artist, however. The model itself may be arbitrary, but once it is constructed it must meet exacting and carefully specified tests before it is acclaimed as a masterpiece. In the artistic world the criteria for judging the finished product are vague and unsystematic.

There is a second respect in which science and art differ. In art the portrait is the end of the job; in science it is just the beginning. Once the model has been created there are two lines of development—one in the symbolic world and the other in the real world.

In the symbolic world the implications of the model are pursued by manipulations of the symbolic language. If I am interested in the behavior of a pendulum I can set up a mathematical model in which the bob of the pendulum is replaced by a geometrical point. The cord or arm of the pendulum is replaced by a symbol, L, which can be interpreted as the length of the cord. The Newtonian laws may be applied to this model and, by manipulations of the symbolic language, I may derive as a consequence of my model a relatively simple relation between the period (the length of time it takes to complete a full swing) and the length, L. All of this takes place in the symbolic language.

In the real world the numerical value for the length must be obtained. This quantity, L, is often called a "parameter." The word "parameter" is merely mathematical jargon for a symbolic quantity, such as L, which may be associated with some measurable quantity in the real world. The process of measuring the length of the cord would therefore be called the "determination of the parameter." In most problems there will be more than one parameter involved.

The two paths from the model now join again when the numerical value from the real world is substituted in the formula (derived by symbolic manipulation) in order to obtain the period. The period is found, mathematically, to be proportional to the square root of the length, L. If my pendulum is 4 feet long it is easy to calculate that the period will be about 2.2 seconds. This statement is made as a prediction.

In order to test this prediction it is necessary to return once again to the real world. I set up my pendulum and time the swings. I find that the period as determined experimentally is about 2.2 seconds. Perhaps I go ahead and try a whole series of different lengths and the agreement between prediction and experiment seems to be good.

As a consequence of this agreement, I am encouraged to use my mathematical model for prediction purposes and also in the design of clocks or other equipment which utilizes a simple pendulum.

The reader may find it worth while to consider another example, such as the astronomical model of the solar system, and trace through the steps in Figure 1 in order to clarify his own ideas on the role of the model.

One striking characteristic of the relationship between the model and the data is the periodic return to the real world which is indicated in Figure 1. It should be noted that the original data used in the construction of the model may be quite useless for the determination of parameters or testing the model. Hence the return to the real world may not mean merely the collection of additional data, but it may require collection of data of a completely different *type* from the original data.

Now a reader who has forgotten his elementary physics may have wondered why I did not include the weight of the bob as well as the length of the cord in the model of the pendulum. An interesting feature of the mathematical model of the pendulum is that if this additional factor, weight, is included in the symbolic structure, it will cancel out in the manipulations. In other words, the model implies that the period of the pendulum does not depend on the weight of the bob, i.e., the weight is irrelevant in this particular problem. The same thing happens if other factors, such as the way in which the pendulum is set into motion, are included in the model. Thus the symbolic model has served the useful purpose of focusing our attention on the length of the cord. It has therefore suggested an efficient way of experimenting on the pendulum; the *model* has told us what *data* need to be collected.

The little story about the pendulum had a happy ending, for the model was satisfactory. However, few scientists are so fortunate or clever as to devise a useful model on the first attempt. If prediction from the first model turns out very badly the scientist will have to start over again. The way in which the predictions break down sometimes provides valuable information which can be used to construct a second model.

The role of the model as given by Figure 1 is therefore only a part of a larger sequential process. This sequential role is indicated by Figure 2.

The evolution of a successful model generally follows the above pattern. The first shots are often very wide of the mark, but by gradual stages the scientist zeros in on his target. There is really no end to the sequence. Even after a model has years of successful usage (i.e., Newtonian models in physics), a situation may come along which will not be adequately predicted by the model. A new model must then be developed.

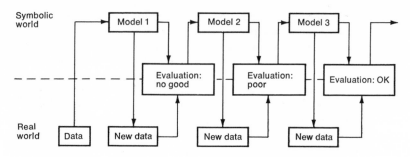

Figure 2

Some readers may find this viewpoint rather unpleasant because they would like this sequence to stop somewhere (i.e., at the truth). Nowhere in the scientific world has this stopping place been attained, although now and then the models have survived for many years. The attitude that the truth had been attained was often a barrier to progress.

A Model for Data

The mathematical model for the solar system or for a pendulum can be used for prediction and then tested against actual data. In this test it is not expected that the data and prediction will agree *exactly*. In the pendulum example the predicted period of a 4-foot pendulum is 2.2 seconds. If a 4-foot pendulum is constructed and the period is measured with a stopwatch or other timing device, the periods so measured will be about 2.2 seconds, but there may be some departure from this figure.

Note that these departures of the data from the predicted value have received no allowance in the mathematical model for the pendulum. In order to *evaluate* the model, however, this behavior of the data must be taken into consideration. This may be done intuitively by an argument such as "the departures from the predicted value are very small and quite negligible for practical purposes." A more sophisticated approach is to set up a second model, a model to deal with the measurement data.

Such a model would be a *statistical* model; it would characterize the measurement process itself in mathematical terms. One parameter of this model might be interpreted as the *precision* or repeatability of the method of measurement and this might be estimated from new data collected for this purpose. Many scientific measurements are given in the following form: 2.22 ± 0.10 seconds. The number after the plus-and-minus sign relates to the precision of the measurement. Thus 2.22 might be the average period calculated from a series of measurements on the period of the pendulum. The 0.10 second might indicate that the average is only reliable to $\frac{1}{10}$ of a second. We would not be very surprised, therefore, if we had gotten 2.32 or 2.12 seconds as our average period. Consequently, there is no reason to feel that the data contradict our predicted value of 2.2 seconds. If, on the other hand, we had found the average period to be 3.22 ± 0.10 seconds, we would feel that something was wrong either with the model or with the data.

When we set about constructing a mathematical model which will describe data we immediately are confronted with the problem of including, in the mathematical formulation, the well-known inadequacies of data. Thus the inadequacies of the measuring instrument must appear in the model: it must include such things as sensory lapses of the human measuring instrument; various errors introduced by the inanimate instruments as microscopes, telescopes, or clocks; and, in biological work, where an animal is used in the measurement process, all sorts of additional sources of variation due to the animal.

Then there will be incompleteness of the data due to the various steps in abstraction. Some of the data may be irrelevant; some of the relevant factors may have been neglected. Also, only part of the available data may have been collected and only part of this data actually used. In short, any real data will be inadequate and incomplete, and these deficiencies must be included in the model.

It would be hopeless to try to catalogue all the things which might go sour in the process of collecting and utilizing the data, to analyze all of the factors which might operate to influence the experimental results. About all that is possible is to consider broad categories of deficiencies and to include these broad categories in the model.

Now how can these inadequacies, and the resulting uncertainties, be handled mathematically? As you might suspect, this is accomplished by the introduction of the concept of probability into the model. In fact, the notion of probability can be regarded as the distinguishing feature which sets statistical models apart from other mathematical models.

Statistical Models

The role of a statistical model is in many respects quite similar to that of any other mathematical model. The diagrammatic representation is indicated in Figure 3.

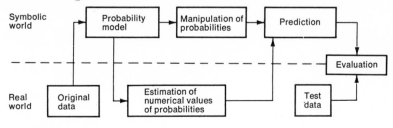

Figure 3

The gambling game models which were introduced earlier are instances of statistical models. Occasionally a simple model of this type can be applied to situations in everyday experience. Suppose that I am interested in the proportion of male babies in 10,000 records of live births. There are two outcomes possible when a baby is born (just as in a coin flip)—the baby can be a boy or a girl. I might therefore think of sex determination as analogous to the process of flipping a coin.

One distinction between the coin toss and sex determination is that while the mechanism for determining heads and tails on a coin is fairly well understood, the corresponding mechanism for fixing the sex of a baby is not well understood. Consequently it would be specious to argue that each sex was equally likely. There is, in fact, a large amount of data to show that this is not the case. Hence if a symbol, p, is used in the mathematical model to indicate the probability that a baby will be male, it may not be assumed that $p = \frac{1}{2}$.

Consequently, one of the things that will have to be done in order to use the model is to obtain data which will enable us to estimate the value of this parameter, p. Perhaps a number such as $p = 0.52$ will be determined from this excursion into the real world.

A second chain of reasoning stays in the symbolic world. Taking the probability as p that a live baby will be a boy, we must answer the question: What will happen in 10,000 births? I will not burden you with the manipulations of probabilities required to answer this question. The mathematics involved in calculating the probabilities for each of the 10,001 possible outcomes becomes too tedious, even for a statistician, and in practice a mathematical approximation which yields useful results with little effort is employed.

With the aid of this device, and substituting the value $p = 0.52$, we can obtain a prediction of the following form: The probability that there will be between 5100 and 5300 male births in the sample of 10,000 is equal to about 0.95. In other words, if I am convinced that the model is a good one and that my value of $p = 0.52$ is also reliable, I would be very confident that the actual data should show between 5100 and 5300 live male births.

This particular model has taken into consideration only one source of variability in the data on live birth—the variation due to sampling. Now in practice there are a number of other inadequacies of the data which might very well cause trouble. The reporting procedures may introduce difficulties. In a well-run department of vital statistics in the Western World the tabulation of births may be done rather carefully. On the other hand, if my 10,000 live births were reported by tribal chieftains in a colonial administrative district there might well be a tendency to forget female children.

The problem of *evaluation* of the statistical model is a tricky one. If I found 4957 boys in the sample of 10,000, I could not say that this result was *impossible* insofar as my model was concerned. The model itself allows a very small chance of this sort of sample.

To a large extent the users of nonstatistical mathematical models can dodge the problem of evaluation by making the evaluation intuitive and simply stating that the agreement of prediction and data is either satisfactory or unsatisfactory. In statistical models one must come to grips with the problem. . . . A major part of a statistician's job lies in the no-man's-land between the symbolic world and the real world, and in particular he must evaluate the predictions of models relative to actual data.

Summary

The key role played by models in scientific thinking is illustrated by several examples. The notion of a model for data is introduced and leads to the concept of a statistical model. The advantages and disadvantages of models are considered. Special stress is laid on the distinction between models of the real world and the real world itself.

Exercises

1. Are all symbolic models mathematical? Are all mathematical models symbolic? Can a physical model be an abstraction?

2. Determine an economic model of man. What human characteristics are omitted? What effect do these omissions have on predictions made using the model?

3. Bross suggests that one advantage of a model is that once a problem has been translated into a symbolic language the manipulative facility of that language becomes available for the model builder's use. What about the cost of acquiring skill with the manipulations, and the reduction in the number of people who share a capacity to deal with the translated problem? Discuss.

4. In Bross's terms, compare and contrast the Westley-MacLean model and the March and Simon model.

Introduction to "The Image"

Kenneth Boulding

The image, as Boulding sees it in the following selection, is a model—one of the ways available to us for conceptualizing the world. Although it does not take the form of some of the other models presented in this section, the image can profitably be compared and contrasted with them. Boulding maintains that the way people behave depends on the image or images they have. The corollary to this is that if we change someone's images, we will change his behavior. Therefore, this essay is particularly pertinent for those concerned with shaping the responses of receivers.

As I sit at my desk, I know where I am. I see before me a window; beyond that some trees; beyond that the red roofs of the campus of Stanford University; beyond them the trees and the roof tops which mark the town of Palo Alto; beyond them the bare golden hills of the Hamilton Range. I know, however, more than I see. Behind me, although I am not looking in that direction, I know there is a window, and beyond that the little campus of the Center for the Advanced Study in the Behavioral Sciences; beyond that the Coast Range; beyond that the Pacific Ocean. Looking ahead of me again, I know that beyond the mountains that close my present horizon, there is a broad valley; beyond that a still higher range of mountains; beyond that other mountains, range upon range, until we come to the Rockies; beyond that the Great Plains and the Mississippi; beyond that the Alleghenies; beyond that the eastern seaboard; beyond that the Atlantic Ocean; beyond that is Europe; beyond that is Asia. I know, furthermore, that if I go far enough I will come back to where I am now. In other words, I have a picture of the earth as round. I visualize it as a globe. I am a little hazy on some of the details. I am not quite sure, for instance, whether Tanganyika is north or south of Nyasaland. I probably could not draw a very good map of Indonesia, but I have a fair idea where everything is located on the face of this globe. Looking further, I visualize the globe as a small speck circling around a bright star which is the sun, in the company of many other similar specks, the planets. Looking still further, I see our star the sun as a member of millions upon millions of others in the Galaxy. Looking still further, I visualize the Galaxy as one of millions upon millions of others in the universe.

I am not only located in space, I am located in time. I know that I came to California about a year ago, and I am leaving it in about three weeks. I know that I have lived in a number of different places at different times. I know that about ten years ago a great war came to an end, that about forty years ago another great war came to an end. Certain dates are meaningful: 1776, 1620, 1066. I have a picture in my mind of the formation of the earth, of the long history of geological time, of the brief history of man. The great civilizations pass before my mental screen. Many of the images are vague, but Greece follows Crete, Rome follows Assyria.

I am not only located in space and time, I am located in a field of personal relations. I not only know where and when I am, I know to some extent who I am. I am a professor at a great state university. This means that in September I shall go into a classroom and expect to find some students in it and begin to talk to them, and nobody will be surprised. I expect, what is perhaps even more agreeable, that regular salary checks will arrive from the university. I expect that when I open my mouth on certain occasions people will listen. I know, furthermore, that I am a husband and a father, that there are people who will respond to me affectionately and to whom I will respond in like manner. I know, also, that I have friends, that there are houses here, there, and everywhere into which I may go and I will be welcomed and recognized and received as a guest. I belong to many societies. There are places into which I go, and it will be recognized that I am expected to behave in a certain manner. I may sit down to worship, I may make a speech, I may listen to a concert, I may do all sorts of things.

I am not only located in space and in time and in personal relationships, I am also located in the world of nature, in a world of how things operate. I know that when I get into my car there are some things I must do to start it; some things I must do to back out of the parking lot; some things I must do to drive home. I know that if I jump off a high place I will probably hurt myself. I know that there are some things that would probably not be good for me to eat or to drink. I know certain precautions that are advisable to take to maintain good health. I know that if I lean too far backward in my chair as I sit here at my desk, I will probably fall over. I live, in other words, in a world of reasonably stable relationships, a world of "ifs" and "thens," of "if I do this, then that will happen."

Finally, I am located in the midst of a world of subtle intimations and emotions. I am sometimes elated, sometimes a little depressed, sometimes happy, sometimes sad, sometimes inspired, sometimes pedantic. I am open to subtle intimations of a presence beyond the world of space and time and sense.

What I have been talking about is knowledge. Knowledge, perhaps, is not a good word for this. Perhaps one would rather say my *Image* of the world. Knowledge has an implication of validity, of truth. What I am talking about is what I believe to be true: my subjective knowledge. It is this Image that largely governs my behavior. In about an hour I shall rise, leave my office, go to a car, drive down to my home, play with the children, have supper, perhaps read a book, go to bed. I can predict this behavior with a fair degree of accuracy because of the knowledge which I have: the knowledge that I have a home not far away, to which I am accustomed to go. The prediction, of course, may not be fulfilled. There may be an earthquake, I may have an accident with the car on the way home, I may get home to find that my family has been suddenly called away. A hundred and one things may happen. As each event occurs, however, it alters my knowledge structure or my image. And as it alters my image, I behave accordingly. *The first proposition of this work, therefore, is that behavior depends on the image.*

What, however, determines the image? This is the central question of this work. It is not a question which can be answered by it. Nevertheless, such answers as I shall give will be quite fundamental to the understanding of how both life and society really operate. One thing is clear. The image is built up as a result of all past experience of the possessor of the image. Part of the image is the history of the image itself. At one stage the image, I suppose, consists of little else than an undifferentiated blur and movement. From the moment of birth if not before, there is a constant stream of messages entering the organism from the senses. At first, these may merely be undifferentiated lights and noises. As the child grows, however, they gradually become distinguished into people and objects. He begins to perceive himself as an object in the midst of a world of objects. The conscious image has begun. In infancy the world is a house and, perhaps, a few streets or a park. As the child grows his image of the world expands. He sees himself in a town, a country, on a planet. He finds himself in an increasingly complex web of personal relationships. Every time a message reaches him his image is likely to be changed in some degree by it, and as his image is changed his behavior patterns will be changed likewise.

We must distinguish carefully between the image and the messages that reach it. The messages consist of *information* in the sense that they are structured experiences. *The meaning of a message is the change which it produces in the image.*

When a message hits an image one of three things can happen. In the first place, the image may remain unaffected. If we think of the image as a rather loose structure, something like a molecule, we may imagine that the message is going straight through without hitting it. The great majority of messages is of this kind. I am receiving messages all the time, for instance, from my eyes and my ears as I sit at my desk, but these messages are ignored by me. There is, for instance, a noise of carpenters working. I know, however, that a building is being built nearby and the fact that I now hear this noise does not add to this image. Indeed, I do not hear the noise at all if I am not listening for it, as I have become so accustomed to it. If the noise stops, however, I notice it. This information changes my image of the universe. I realize that it is now five o'clock, and it is time for me to go home. The message has called my attention, as it were, to my position in time, and I have re-evaluated this position. This is the second possible effect or impact of a message on an image. It may change the image in some rather regular and well-defined way that might be described as simple addition. Suppose, for instance, to revert to an earlier illustration, I look at an atlas and find out exactly the relation of Nyasaland to Tanganyika. I will have added to my knowledge, or my image; I will not, however, have very fundamentally revised it. I still picture the world much as I had pictured it before. Something that was a little vague before is now clearer.

There is, however, a third type of change of the image which might be described as a revolutionary change. Sometimes a message hits some sort of nucleus or supporting structure in the image, and the whole thing changes in a quite radical way. A spectacular instance of such a change is conversion. A man, for instance, may think himself a pretty good fellow and then may hear a preacher who convinces him that, in fact, his life is worthless and shallow, as he is at present living it. The words of the preacher cause a radical reformulation of the man's image of himself in the world, and his behavior changes accordingly. The psychologist may say, of course, that these changes are smaller than they appear, that there is a great mass of the unconscious which does not change, and that the relatively small change in behavior which so often follows intellectual conversion is a testimony to this fact. Nevertheless, the phenomenon of reorganization of the image is an important one, and it occurs to all of us and in ways that are much less spectacular than conversion.

The sudden and dramatic nature of these reorganizations is perhaps a result of the fact that our image is in itself resistant to change. When it receives messages which conflict with it, its first impulse is to reject them as in some sense untrue. Suppose, for instance, that somebody tells us something which is inconsistent with our picture of a certain person. Our first impulse is to reject the proffered information as false. As we continue to receive messages which contradict our image, however, we begin to have doubts, and then one day we receive a message which overthrows our previous image and we revise it completely. The person, for instance, whom we saw as a trusted friend is now seen to be a hypocrite and a deceiver.

Occasionally, things that we see, or read, or hear, revise our conceptions of space and time, or of relationships. I have recently read, for instance, Vasiliev's *History of the Byzantine Empire*. As a result of reading this book I have considerably revised my image of at least a thousand years of history. I had not given the matter a great deal of thought before, but I suppose if I had been questioned on my view of the period, I would have said that Rome fell in the fifth century and that it was succeeded by a little-known empire centering in Constantinople and a confused medley of tribes, invasions, and successor states. I now see that Rome did not fall, that in a sense it merely faded away, that the history of the Roman Empire and of Byzantium is continuous, and that from the time of its greatest extent the Roman Empire lost one piece after another until only Constantinople was left; and then in 1453 that went. There are books, some of them rather bad books, after which the world is never quite the same again. Veblen, for instance, was not, I think, a great social scientist, and yet he invented an undying phrase: "conspicuous consumption." After reading Veblen, one can never quite see a university campus or an elaborate house in just the same light as before. In a similar vein, David Riesman's division of humanity into inner-directed and other-directed people is no doubt open to serious criticism by the methodologists. Nevertheless, after reading Riesman one has a rather new view of the universe and one looks in one's friends and acquaintances for signs of inner-direction or other-direction.

One should perhaps add a fourth possible impact of the messages on the image. The image has a certain dimension, or quality, of certainty or uncertainty, probability or improbability, clarity or vagueness. Our image of the world is not uniformly certain, uniformly probable, or uniformly clear. Messages, therefore, may have the effect not only of adding to or of reorganizing the image. They may also have the effect of clarifying it, that is, of making something which previously was regarded as less certain more certain, or something which was previously seen in a vague way, clearer.

Messages may also have the contrary effect. They may introduce doubt or uncertainty into the image. For instance, the noise of carpenters has just stopped, but my watch tells me it is about four-thirty. This has thrown a certain amount of confusion into my mental image. I was under the impression that the carpenters stopped work at five o'clock. Here is a message which contradicts that impression. What am I to believe? Unfortunately, there are two possible ways of integrating the message into my image. I can believe that I was mistaken in thinking that the carpenters left work at five o'clock and that in fact their day ends at four-thirty. Or, I can believe that my watch is wrong. Either of these two modifications of my image gives meaning to the message. I shall not know for certain which is the right one, however, until I have an opportunity of comparing my watch with a timepiece or with some other source of time which I regard as being more reliable.

The impact of messages on the certainty of the image is of great importance in the interpretation of human behavior. Images of the future must be held with a degree of uncertainty, and as time passes and as the images become closer to the present, the messages that we receive inevitably modify them, both as to content and as to certainty.

The subjective knowledge structure or image of any individual or organization consists not only of images of "fact" but also images of "value." We shall subject the concept of a "fact" to severe scrutiny in the course of the discussion. In the meantime, however, it is clear that there is a certain difference between the image which I have of physical objects in space and time and the valuations which I put on these objects or on the events which concern them. It is clear that there is a certain difference between, shall we say, my image of Stanford University existing at a certain point in space and time, and my image of the value of Stanford University. If I say "Stanford University is in California," this is rather different from the statement "Stanford University is a good university, or is a better university than X, or a worse university than Y." The latter statements concern my image of values, and although I shall argue that the process by which we obtain an image of values is not very different from the process whereby we obtain an image of fact, there is clearly a certain difference between them.

The image of value is concerned with the *rating* of the various parts of our image of the world, according to some scale of betterness or worseness. We, all of us, possess one or more of these scales. It is what the economists call a welfare function. It does not extend over the whole universe. We do not now, for instance, generally regard Jupiter as a better planet than Saturn. Over that part of the universe which is closest to ourselves, however, we all erect these scales of valuation. Moreover, we change these scales of valuation in response to messages received much as we change our image of the world around us. It is almost certain that most people possess not merely one scale of valuation but many scales for different purposes. For instance, we may say A is better than B for me but worse for the country, or it is better for the country but worse for the world at large. The notion of a hierarchy of scales is very important in determining the effect of messages on the scales themselves.

One of the most important propositions of this theory is that the value scales of any individual or organization are perhaps the most important elements determining the effect of the messages he receives on his image of the world. If a message is perceived that is neither good nor bad it may have little or no effect on the image. If it is perceived as bad or hostile to the image which is held, there will be resistance to accepting it. This resistance is not usually infinite. An often repeated message or a message which comes with unusual force or authority is able to penetrate the resistance and will be able to alter the image. A devout Moslem, for instance, whose whole life has been built around the observance of the precepts of the Koran will resist vigorously any message which tends to throw doubt on the authority of his sacred work. The resistance may take the form of simply ignoring the message, or it may take the form of emotive response: anger, hostility, indignation. In the same way, a "devout" psychologist will resist strongly any evidence presented in favor of extrasensory perception, because to accept it would overthrow his whole image of the universe. If the resistances are very strong, it may take very strong, or often repeated messages to penetrate them, and when they are penetrated, the effect is a realignment or reorganization of the whole knowledge structure.

On the other hand, messages which are favorable to the existing image of the world are received easily and even though they may make minor modifications of the knowledge structure, there will not be any fundamental reorganization. Such messages either will make no impact on the knowledge structure or their impact will be one of rather simple addition or accretion. Such messages may also have the effect of increasing the stability, that is to say, the resistance to unfavorable messages, which the knowledge structure or image possesses.

The stability or resistance to change of a knowledge structure also depends on its internal consistency and arrangement. There seems to be some kind of principle of minimization of internal strain at work which makes some images stable and others unstable for purely internal reasons. In the same way, some crystals or molecules are more stable than others because of the minimization of internal strain. It must be emphasized that it is not merely logical consistency which gives rise to internal cohesiveness of a knowledge structure, although this is an important element. There are important qualities of a nonlogical nature which also give rise to stability. The structure may, for instance, have certain aesthetic relationships among the parts. It may represent or justify a way of life or have certain consequences which are highly regarded in the value system, and so on. Even in mathematics, which is of all knowledge structures the one whose internal consistency is most due to logic, is not devoid of these nonlogical elements. In the acceptance of mathematical arguments by mathematicians there are important criteria of elegance, beauty, and simplicity which contribute toward the stability of these structures.

Even at the level of simple or supposedly simple sense perception we are increasingly discovering that the message which comes through the senses is itself mediated through a value system. We do not perceive our sense data raw; they are mediated through a highly learned process of interpretation and acceptance. When an object apparently increases in size on the retina of the eye, we interpret this not as an increase in size but as movement. Indeed, we only get along in the world because we consistently and persistently disbelieve the plain evidence of our senses. The stick in water is not bent; the movie is not a succession of still pictures; and so on.

What this means is that for any individual organism or organization, there are no such things as "facts." There are only messages filtered through a changeable value system. This statement may sound rather startling. It is inherent, however, in the view which I have been propounding. This does not mean, however, that the image of the world possessed by an individual is a purely private matter or that all knowledge is simply subjective knowledge, in the sense in which I have used the word. Part of our image of the world is the belief that this image is shared by other people like ourselves who also are part of our image of the world. In common daily intercourse we all behave as if we possess roughly the same image of the world. If a group of people are in a room together, their behavior clearly shows that they all think they are in the same room. It is this shared image which is "public" knowledge as opposed to "private" knowledge. It follows, however, from the argument above that if a group of people are to share the same image of the world, or to put it more exactly, if the various images of the world which they have are to be roughly identical, and if this group of people are exposed to much the same set of messages in building up images of the world, the value systems of all individuals must be approximately the same.

The problem is made still more complicated by the fact that a group of individuals does not merely share messages which come to them from "nature." They also initiate and receive messages themselves. This is the characteristic which distinguishes man from the lower organisms—the art of conversation or discourse. The human organism is capable not only of having an image of the world, but of talking about it. This is the extraordinary gift of language. A group of dogs in a pack pursuing a stray cat clearly share an image of the world in the sense that each is aware to some degree of the situation which they are all in, and is likewise aware of his neighbors. When the chase is over, however, they do not, as far as we know, sit around and talk about it and say, "Wasn't that a fine chase?" or, "Isn't it too bad the cat got away?" or even, "Next time you ought to go that way and I'll go this way and we can corner it." It is discourse or conversation which makes the human image public in a way that the image of no lower animal can possibly be. The term, "universe of discourse" has been used to describe the growth and development of common images in conversation and linguistic intercourse. There are, of course, many such universes of discourse, and although it is a little awkward to speak of many universes, the term is well enough accepted so that we may let it stay.

Where there is no universe of discourse, where the image possessed by the organism is purely private and cannot be communicated to anyone else, we say that the person is mad (to use a somewhat old-fashioned term). It must not be forgotten, however, that the discourse must be received as well as given, and that whether it is received or not depends upon the value system of the recipient. This means that insanity is defined differently from one culture to another because of these differences in value systems and that the schizophrenic of one culture may well be the shaman or the prophet of another.

Up to now I have sidestepped and I will continue to sidestep the great philosophical arguments of epistemology. I have talked about the image. I have maintained that images can be public as well as private, but I have not discussed the question as to whether images are *true* and how we know whether they are true. Most epistemological systems seek some philosopher's stone by which statements may be tested in order to determine their "truth," that is, their correspondence to outside reality. I do not claim to have any such philosopher's stone, not even the touchstone of science. I have, of course, a great respect for science and scientific method —for careful observation, for planned experience, for the testing of hypotheses and for as much objectivity as semirational beings like ourselves can hope to achieve. In my theoretical system, however, the scientific method merely stands as one among many of the methods whereby images change and develop. The development of images is part of the culture or the subculture in which they are developed, and it depends upon all the elements of that culture or subculture. Science is a subculture among subcultures. It can claim to be useful. It may claim rather more dubiously to be good. It cannot claim to give validity.

In summation, then, my theory might well be called an organic theory of knowledge. Its most fundamental proposition is that knowledge is what somebody or something knows, and that without a knower, knowledge is an absurdity. Moreover, I argue that the growth of knowledge is the growth of an "organic" structure. I am not suggesting here that knowledge is simply an arrangement of neuronal circuits or brain cells, or something of that kind. On the question of the relation between the physical and chemical structure of an organism and its knowledge structure, I am quite prepared to be agnostic. It is, of course, an article of faith among physical scientists that there must be somewhere a one-to-one correspondence between the structures of the physical body and the structures of knowledge. Up to now, there is nothing like empirical proof or even very good evidence for this hypothesis. Indeed, what we know about the brain suggests that it is an extraordinarily unspecialized and, in a sense, unstructured object; and that if there is a physical and chemical structure corresponding to the knowledge structure, it must be of a kind which at present we do not understand. It may be, indeed, that the correspondence between physical structure and mental structure is something that we will never be able to determine because of a sort of "Heisenberg principle" in the investigation of these matters. If the act of observation destroys the thing observed, it is clear that there is a fundamental obstacle to the growth of knowledge in that direction.

All these considerations, however, are not fundamental to my position. We do not have to conceive of the knowledge structure as a physico-chemical structure in order to use it in our theoretical construct. It can be inferred from the behavior of the organism just as we constantly infer the images of the world which are possessed by those around us from the messages which they transmit to us. When I say that knowledge is an organic structure, I mean that it follows principles of growth and development similar to those with which we are familiar in complex organizations and organisms. In every organism or organization there are both internal and external factors affecting growth. Growth takes place through a kind of metabolism. Even in the case of knowledge structures, we have a certain intake and output of messages. In the knowledge structure, however, there are important violations of the laws of conservation. The accumulation of knowledge is not merely the difference between messages taken in and messages given out. It is not like a reservoir; it is rather an organization which grows through an active internal organizing principle much as the gene is a principle or entity organizing the growth of bodily structures. The gene, even in the physico-chemical sense may be thought of as an inward teacher imposing its own form and "will" on the less formed matter around it. In the growth of images, also, we may suppose similar models. Knowledge grows also because of inward teachers as well as outward messages. As every good teacher knows, the business of teaching is not that of penetrating the student's defenses with the violence or loudness of the teacher's messages. It is, rather, that of co-operating with the student's own inward teacher whereby the student's image may grow in conformity with that of his outward teacher. The existence of public knowledge depends, therefore, on certain basic similarities among men. It is literally because we are of one "blood," that is, genetic constitution, that we are able to communicate with each other. We cannot talk to the ants or bees; we cannot hold conversations with them, although in a very real sense they communicate to us. It is the purpose of this work, therefore, to discuss the growth of images, both private and public, in individuals, in organizations, in society at large, and even with some trepidation, among the lower forms of life. Only thus can we develop a really adequate theory of behavior.

Exercises

1. Try to produce a written message similar to the first five paragraphs of Boulding's essay. What are the differences between your message and his? How do you account for those differences?

2. What would you say would be the difference between "image change" and "learning?" What objections do you think a psychologist would raise to your discussion of this difference?

3. Boulding says that "for any individual organism or organization, there are no such things as 'facts.'" Find someone who disagrees. Account for the disagreement. Do *you* agree or disagree? Why?

4. From what you have read about the image and about the author's ideas, what sort of classroom situation do you think you would find if you were one of Professor Boulding's students?

Perception, Communication, and Educational Research: A Transactional View

Hans Toch
Malcolm S. MacLean, Jr.

Toch and MacLean summarize much of what is said and argued about perception. The transactional view is much like the "systems" view. That is, the system of human interactions (or transactions) operates to make alterations in our environment in a systematic fashion. "Systematic" does not imply certainty or causality. Things in perception, as everywhere, are probable rather than certain.

The transactional approach to perception has relatively limited aspirations. It does not pretend to offer a systematic set of principles concerning the mechanics of the perceptual process. Instead, it supplies a point of

Reprinted by permission from *AV Communication Review,* Vol. 10, No. 5, September–October, 1962, pp. 55–77.

regard or emphasis or perspective—or, if you please, a *bias*. This transactional bias has been described as (among other things) neo-Gestalt, neo-behaviorist, radical empiricist and common sense. None of these labels can be totally rejected, but reservations may be entered to all of them.

Common Sense and Perception

Of most interest is common sense: Perception viewed through the eyes of common sense is clearly a passive affair. The eye is the equivalent of a motion picture camera, and hearing functions in the fashion of a tape recorder. The chemical senses act in the manner of variegated litmus paper; the mechanical senses register physical weights and measures. In other words, perception unassumingly transcribes on the slate of our awareness whatever the world presents to us. It dispassionately and uncritically records the gamut of bewildering impressions which reach us—mostly from without, but sometimes from within. This information, having been duly recorded, is then sorted, edited, and evaluated subsequently and—very importantly—elsewhere.

In due fairness, one must add that common sense, when pressed, may admit that there is probably more to the story. The senses, for example, don't appear to receive impressions at random: the eyes must be directed at some portion of the world, and the glass of wine must be sipped before anything of consequence is perceived in either case. Moreover, there is obviously some measure of control over the quality of the product: the languid gaze, the shameless stare, and the vacant look don't transmit comparable data. Sophisticated common sense also discovers that there is some question as to whether we always perceive equally well. Assuming, for example, that the cochlea responds with the same precision when a person sits in a concert hall or in his living room immersed in his newspaper, everyone knows that auditory awareness clearly differs in these situations.

These and other observations of perception in action may suggest to common sense that the process is not altogether passive nor invariant. Perception seems to provide, within limits, the type of information the perceiver needs. Perception, in other words, is invoked, suppressed, and modified in the context of what the rest of the person is about. In order to be instrumental in this fashion, perception must be flexible and active. The vocabulary is full of words which imply recognition of this truism. The eye, for example, does not merely mirror or transmit; it scans, peeks, watches, stares, scrutinizes, and inspects. Such terms reflect a recognition of directionality, selection, or variability in perception.

Transactional Departure
from Common Sense

At this point, however, common sense assumes that it is the "user" of the perceptual process who is active, while perception itself is simply being manipulated. In other words, the perceptual apparatus is seen as subject to the same type of manipulation as the motion picture camera which may be switched on and off, variously aimed, and possibly even changed to different speeds at the whim of its owner and the flick of a switch. These manipulations, of course, would be viewed as extrinsic to the process of receiving and recording information. The transactional view does not accept this argument. It regards perception as continuously and inextricably enmeshed in the enterprise of living. Do we ever encounter perception as a "pure" process? Or, for that matter, can we conceive of a person behaving without perceiving? Is not behavior both an outcome of past perceptions and a starting point for future perceptions? And is not the "user" of perception himself a perceptual result? This conclusion would clearly follow from the fact that every human being is a product—a constantly changing product—of the situations through which he moves. Each encounter with life leaves its chink in the armor or its depression in the hide; the person who arises in the morning is never the same one who returns to his pillow that evening. His successor may be broadened, chastised, wiser, or warier; his jaw may be more set or his brow more furrowed—more likely, he may see things a little differently or feel somewhat different. Whatever the change, it represents a deposit of perceptions and will, in turn, affect future perceptions.

Perception, then—in transactional parlance—is so wedded to the rest of the human enterprise that it has no meaning outside this context. If common sense finds this conception hard to deal with, the next step may prove even harder to take. Because unlike common sense, which assumes that a person perceives the world, the transactional view denies the independent existence of both the perceiver and his world. The term "transaction" was first used by Dewey and Bentley to distinguish this new view of epistemology from the common sense "interaction" conception. Dewey and Bentley summarize their transactional approach to perception by saying, "Observation of this general (transactional) type sees man-in-action not as something radically set over against an environing world, nor yet as merely action 'in' a world, but as action *of* and *by* the world in which the man belongs as an integral constituent (7:228)." Ittelson and Cantril illustrate the meaning of this statement by considering the case of a baseball batter:

> It is immediately apparent that the baseball batter does not exist independent of the pitcher. We cannot have a batter without a pitcher. It is true that someone can throw a ball up in the air and hit it

with a bat, but his relationship to the batter in the baseball game is very slight. Similarly, there is no pitcher without a batter. The pitcher in the bull-pen is by no means the same as the pitcher in the game. But providing a pitcher for a batter is still not enough for us to be able to define and study our batter. The batter we are interested in does not exist outside of a baseball game, so that in order to study him completely we need not only pitcher, but catcher, fielders, teammates, officials, fans, and the rules of the game. Our batter, as we see him in this complex transaction, simply does not exist anywhere else independent of the transaction. The batter is what he is because of the baseball game in which he participates and, in turn, the baseball game itself is what it is because of the batter. Each one owes its existence to the fact of active participation with and through the other. If we change either one, we change the other (15:3–4).

Another baseball analogy bearing on the meaning of the perceptual transaction is cited by Cantril, who quotes the following story about three umpires swapping views as to their professional function:

> The first umpire said, 'Some's balls and some's strikes and I calls 'em as they is.' The second umpire said, 'Some's balls and some's strikes and I calls 'em as I sees 'em.' While the third umpire said, 'Some's balls and some's strikes but they ain't nothin' till I calls 'em (4:126).'

This story nicely illustrates the basic characteristic of the transactional view of perception, which may be summarized as follows: Each percept, from the simplest to the most complex, is the product of a creative act. The raw material for this creation is lost to us since in the very act of creating, we modify it. We can never encounter a stimulus before some meaning has been assigned to it by some perceiver. Moreover, the perceiver himself becomes available to us only when he has entered into his task and has been modified in the process.

Both of these statements hold true because meanings are given to things in terms of all prior experience the person has accumulated. Therefore, each perception is the beneficiary of all previous perceptions; in turn, each new perception leaves its mark on the common pool. A percept is thus a link between the past which gives it its meaning and the future which it helps to interpret.

Neo-behaviorist View

Perception, in other words, is a form of learning. This view makes it possible to speak of the transactional position as a neo-behaviorist approach. And transactionalism clearly approximates behaviorism not only in its emphasis on learning, but also in its conception of how learning takes place. According to behavioristic learning theory, learning is stimulated and strengthened by rewards (reinforcing situations) and inhibited by punishments or disappointments. The transactional conception is analogous. Each experience or perception helps to provide us with unconscious expectations or assumptions about reality. We expect the world to behave in accord with these assumptions. Like the data supplied in a racing form about the performance of horses under particular conditions, the accumulation of our past experiences provides the basis for bets as to success or failure of our intended enterprises. These bets are repeated or discontinued depending on whether they pay off or fail to pay off.

Just as a horse which has a long record of "wins" becomes a favorite and is assigned a high probability of success, certain interpretations come to be endowed with considerable confidence because of their repeated accuracy in the past. I have no hesitation in sitting down on what appears to me to be a chair, and I point my pencil at the paper in front of me with little doubt about the physical outcome. In other situations, however, past experience has not been as fully rewarding, and interpretations became long shots. The trustworthiness of friends, the reliability of colleagues, and the receptivity of students are not necessarily as punctually encountered as the seats of chairs. And even relatively simple perceptual dimensions such as size or distance may be incorrectly deduced—as has been the sad experience of many motorists. As a rule, however, perception results in confirmation, in the sense that our assumptions lead to successful conduct, thereby reinforcing our images of reality and our confidence in them.

Gestaltist View

The scheme we have just outlined differs from the thinking of students of learning only in its emphasis on personal experience, which behaviorism has traditionally refused to discuss. In turn, Gestalt psychologists, who share the transactionalist bias favoring perceptual experiences as the basis of human conduct, reject the premise that such experiences are essentially learned. According to Gestalt thinking, the essential qualities of experience are, rather, built into the process of perception. The following statement by Wolfgang Köhler illustrates the Gestaltist rejection of the assumption that perceived meanings are acquired through past experience:

> When I see a green object, I can immediately tell the name of the color. I also know that green is used as a signal on streets and as a symbol of hope. But from this I do not conclude that the color green as such can be derived from such knowledge. Rather, I know that, as an independently existent sensory fact, it has acquired secondary meanings, and I am quite willing to recognize the advantages which these acquired meanings have in practical life. In exactly the same fashion, Gestalt Psychology holds, sensory units have acquired names, have become richly symbolic, and are now known to have certain practical uses, while nevertheless they have existed as units before any

of these further facts were added. Gestalt Psychology claims that it is precisely the original segregation of circumscribed wholes which makes it possible for the sensory world to appear so utterly imbued with meaning to the adult; for, in its gradual entrance into the sensory field, meaning follows the lines drawn by natural organization; it usually enters into segregated wholes (20:139).

Besides the difference, apparent in this quote, between the Gestalt emphasis on innate perceptual qualities as against the transactional stress on learning, there is another divergence in emphasis between these two views of perception. This difference rests in the fact that perception, in transactional parlance, is *functional,* in the sense that it exists to enable the perceiver to carry out his purposes, whereas Gestalt thinking sometimes assumes that man strives for veridicality or accuracy for its own sake.

There is, however, an even greater difference between the transactional premise that perception derives its meaning from the human enterprise and the contention of some people that needs and fears can shape perceptual products. Unlike these New Look theorists, the advocates of the transactional view do *not* assume that we tend to see steaks when hungry, or that we have difficulty in hearing threatening language. In fact, the transactional assumption would be that it is never in the long-run interest of people to see what they want to see or to fail to perceive what doesn't meet their fancy, just as the deer is not aided by failing to notice the jumping lion. The greatest survival value lies in accurate perception. The purpose of perception is to help us cope with the world by assigning meanings to it which can stand the test of subsequent experiences.

Perception and Communication

The above exposition of what—essentially—the transactional view is and is not, makes possible a few statements about perception which might have special bearing on non-verbal communication. Sample experiments illustrating some of these statements may help clarify them:

Shared Experiences Result in Perceptual Communalities

There are many types of experience which people have in common, almost by virtue of their human condition. These range from the elements of geometry to their intimate exposures to other human beings which create the beginning of social awareness. Common human experiences create similarities in perception and make possible easy communication. Universally shared meanings, in fact, are the *simplest* means of communication because they require little translation from one person's frame of reference into another. When *A* offers *B* a chair, when *B* smiles at *C*, or when *C* makes love to *D*, communication problems are minimized.

Probably the most famous of the "Ames Demonstrations" (so-called because they were originated by Adelbert Ames, Jr.) is the "Rotating Trapezoidal Window" Demonstration. This device helps to show the perceptual role of assumptions which have their origin in relatively universal human experiences. The demonstration consists of a trapezoidally-shaped window which can be slowly rotated, and which is invariably perceived as a rectangle (in perspective) oscillating from side to side. If a rod is placed in the window, it will appear to fold around it or to cut through it while the window is in motion. A box attached to one corner of the apparatus seems to take to flight. Why do those illusions occur? Ames himself offers this explanation:

> In his past experience the observer, in carrying out his purposes, has on innumerable occasions had to take into account and act with respect to rectangular forms, e.g., going through doors, locating windows, etc. On almost all such occasions, except in the rare case when his line of sight was normal to the door or window, the image of the rectangular configuration formed on his retina was trapezoidal. He learned to interpret the particularly characterized retinal images that exist when he looks at doors, windows, etc., as rectangular forms. Moreover, he learned to interpret the particular degree of trapezoidal distortion of his retinal images in terms of the positioning of the rectangular form to his particular viewing point (2:14).

These assumptions about rectangularity are in most situations not apparent because they lead to accurate perceptions, so that the perceiver can argue, "I see *X* (rectangular) because it *is* *X* (rectangular)." The "trapezoidal window" reveals assumptions because it is deliberately designed to be misleading.

**Differences in
Experience Cause
Perceptual Divergence**

The "trapezoidal window" depends for its effect on universal human experiences with rectangular objects in perspective. But are experiences such as these really equally shared by every human being? In the case of rectangularity, for instance, some people may be more intensively exposed to rectangular objects than others. Zulu members of the Bantu culture in South Africa stand out as having relatively little experience with man-made rectangles.

> Huts are invariably round (rondavels) or else beehive shaped, whereas in other Bantu tribes they are sometimes square or rectangular. Round

huts arranged in a circular form with round stockades to fence in animals, constitute a typical African homestead (kraal). Fields follow the irregular contours of the rolling land, and never seem to be laid out in the neat rectangular plots so characteristic of western culture. The typical Zulu hut has no windows, and no word for such an aperture exists. In the more primitive beehive grass huts, doors are merely round entrance holes; in the round mud huts, doors are amorphous, seldom if ever neatly rectangular. Cooking pots are round or gourd-shaped . . . (1:106).

When tested with the "trapezoidal window," in a study by Allport and Pettigrew, non-westernized Zulus tended to perceive the illusion less frequently—under sub-optimal conditions—than did westernized persons who have more intensive experience with rectangularity (1). One can infer from this fact that differences in experience, even in cumulative experience that is common to people, can create subtle differences in the way the world is perceived.

Perceptual Differences Can Be Readily Produced

Social psychologists are frequently concerned with attitudes, values, and habits that are prevalent among groups of people and are transmitted from generation to generation. Less obviously, ways of perceiving also come to be acquired and transmitted collectively. Two experiments, both involving a relatively new research technique, may serve to illustrate this fact:

In 1955, a psychologist named Engel published a set of observations involving subjects who had been exposed to two different pictures—one to the left eye and the other to the right (9). One effect he discussed is that of perceptual dominance by more familiar pictures when they are paired with less familiar pictures. "A 'right side up' face, for instance, tends to perceptually prevail over the same face 'upside down.' "

This observation has given rise to a number of experiments, one of which included matched Mexican and American observers. These persons were exposed to several sets of pictures, in each of which a typically American scene (such as a baseball game) was paired with a typically Mexican view (like a bullfight). The investigator, Bagby, concludes:

> Ss report scenes of their own culture as predominant in binocular rivalry over scenes from another culture. The national cultural differences appear critical in affecting perceptual predominance in the majority of the stereogram slide pairs . . . Differences in ways of perceiving come about as a consequence of differences in past experiences and purposes. These in turn emerge from influences in the

home, in the school, and in the various groups with which an individual identifies. Thus, under conditions of perceptual conflict as found in the binocular rivalry situation, those impingements possessing the more immediate first-person meaning would be expected to predominate in visual awareness (3:334).

This statement, of course, need not be confined to past experiences associated with different cultures. Subgroups in the same culture also frequently become differentially indoctrinated, and such differences in indoctrination should leave their mark on perception.

To test for this possibility, terminal candidates in a Midwestern police training program were presented with a set of slides, each of which featured a violent scene for one eye, and a similar but non-violent picture for the other. Beginning students in the training program and comparable liberal arts students served as control groups. The persons trained in police work saw a considerably larger number of "violent" pictures in this situation. The investigators comment:

> Assuming that extremely violent scenes are comparatively unfamiliar, we would thus expect violence to be relatively infrequently perceived in true binocular rivalry. We would predict the type of result we obtained from our Control Groups. We could assume that law enforcement training *supplements* this experiential deficit in the area of violence and crime. Unusual experiences, after all, become 'familiar' in the course of *any* specialization. The funeral director or the medical intern, for instance, may learn to accept corpses as part and parcel of everyday experience. The dedicated nudist may acquire a special conception of familiar attire. The air pilot may come to find nothing unusual about glancing down out of a window at a bank of clouds. In the same fashion, law enforcement training can produce a revision of unconscious expectations of violence and crime. This does not mean that the law enforcer necessarily comes to exaggerate the prevalence of violence. It means that the law enforcer may come to accept crime *as a familiar personal experience,* one which he himself is not surprised to encounter. The acceptance of crime as a familiar experience in turn increases *the ability or readiness to perceive violence where clues to it are potentially available* (29:392).

Subtle perceptual differences of this sort, although universally present, only manifest themselves for our inspection under special conditions such as binocular rivalry. At other times, we may deal with people under the assumption that their perceptions coincide with ours, although in fact differences in past experience have produced fundamental divergences in outlook.

The same point holds true over time, since research shows that subtle *changes* in perception continuously take place without our being aware of them. To illustrate: Two photographs, each of a different face, were mounted in a stereoscopic device. When the observer first looked into the stereoscope, he was presented with just one of the faces with normal illumination. Then the illumination was cut. Next, he was given the first face normally lit, with the second face under very low illumination. The procedure was repeated with a slight increase in light on the second face, and so on until the subject was observing both faces each with the same normal light. At each step he was asked whether any change had taken place in what he saw. Most said they saw no change! But the second phase of the experiment was even more startling. In the same way, by small steps, the light on the first photograph was reduced to zero. At this point, the observer was looking at the second face, quite different from the first. He continued to claim that no change had taken place, that he was still looking at the same face. Engel reports that observers were much perplexed when they were again presented with the original face (8).

Any Given Event Is Differently Perceived By Different People

The more complex a perceptual situation becomes, the greater the tendency for variations in perception to occur. Whereas a chair, for instance, provides a minimum of opportunity for differences in perception —at least, for members of our Western culture—any standard *social* situation constitutes a veritable perceptual cafeteria. This is the case not only because complexity multiplies the opportunity for the perceiver to assign meanings—for instance, one can choose to attend to one of many aspects of a complex situation in preference to others—but also because complexity usually evokes a wide gamut of personal experiences and needs which enter into the assignment of meaning.

Hastorf and Cantril illustrate this process in their study of the infamous football game between Dartmouth and Princeton which took place on November 23, 1951. The events which occurred in this game are conservatively catalogued as follows:

> A few minutes after the opening kick-off, it became apparent that the game was going to be a rough one. The referees were kept busy blowing their whistles and penalizing both sides. In the second quarter, Princeton's star left the game with a broken nose. In the third quarter, a Dartmouth player was taken off the field with a broken leg. Tempers flared both during and after the game. The official statistics of the game, which Princeton won, showed that Dartmouth was penalized 70 yards, Princeton 25, not counting more than a few plays in which both sides were penalized (13:129).

The sequel of these events was a prolonged and intense exchange of recriminations between players, students, coaches, administrative officials, student publications, alumni and partisans of the two universities, each of whom claimed to have sustained the brunt of the injuries.

Hastorf and Cantril submitted a questionnaire concerning the game to both Princeton and Dartmouth students and alumni, the results of which confirmed the divergent position of the two sides relating to the game. A film of the game also was shown to some 100 students; it yielded widely discrepant reports of the number of infractions committed by each side and the seriousness of these infractions. The Princeton students, for instance, "saw" the Dartmouth team make more than twice the number of infractions "seen" by Dartmouth students in watching the same film. They also "saw" two "flagrant" to each "mild" infraction for the Dartmouth team, and one "flagrant" to three "mild" offenses for their own team, a ratio considerably dissimilar to that of ratings by Dartmouth students. Hastorf and Cantril conclude:

> . . . the 'same' sensory impingements emanating from the football field, transmitted through the visual mechanism to the brain, obviously gave rise to different experiences in different people. The significances assumed by different happenings for different people depend in large part on the purposes people bring to the occasion and the assumptions they have of the purposes and probable behavior of other people involved (13:132). . . .
>
> It is inaccurate and misleading to say that different people have different 'attitudes' concerning the same 'thing.' For the 'thing' simply is *not* the same for different people whether the 'thing' is a football game, a presidential candidate, Communism, or spinach. We do not simply 'react to' a happening or to some impingement from the environment in a determined way (except in behavior that has become reflexive or habitual). We behave according to what we bring to the occasion, and what each of us brings to the occasion is more or less unique (13:133).

**All Aspects of a
Percept Are Related to
Each Other**

A fundamental discovery of Gestalt psychology was that the basic unit of perception is the organized configuration which the perceiver perceives. Perceptual objects, in other words, function as indivisible units. This statement extends beyond the geometric or formal properties of stimuli. Thus, the perceived motion of the Ames "trapezoidal window" results from its perception as a rectangle in perspective: Object-identification and movement-direction are dependent on each other.

Hastorf has shown that the perceived size of a white square can range widely, depending on whether it is identified as an envelope or a calling card (12). This perceived size, in turn, can determine the apparent distance of the figure from the observer.

Less obviously, positive or negative feelings can also determine perceived size and distance. Thus, G. H. Smith set out to determine whether "faces regarded as friendly or pleasant" would be seen as "larger than those regarded as unfriendly or unpleasant in order to appear opposite the same target post (27:47)." His findings confirmed these expectations. He concludes:

> Ss responded to the meaning which faces elicited in this situation; and . . . this meaning emerged out of the assumptions, attitudes, expectations, purposes, and special sensitizations which Ss had acquired through experience. . . . The fact that 'pleasant' or 'liked' faces were made larger (closer) than others indicates that attributed meaning, rather than size of retinal image alone, determined the responses. . . . perception of a human face literally changed before the eyes of the Ss as a function of alterations in beliefs, assumptions, etc. (27:60–61).

Another set of experiments showing a relationship between affective significance and the perceptions of physical properties was provided by the "honi phenomenon" (30). This effect was first observed in an Ames Demonstration known as the "monocular distorted room," which is a geometrically distorted structure that looks square when viewed with one eye. Since the room appears to be normal (although it is in fact distorted), any face viewed through a window of the room becomes expanded or contracted. The "honi phenomenon" was born one day when this customary illusion did not materialize. The face which refused to change belonged to a New York attorney, and the viewer was his devoted wife. Subsequent investigation showed that it is not uncommon for newlyweds to perceive their marital partners as relatively unchanged when optical distortions have in fact taken place. Similar phenomena can occur involving other kinds of affects (as with amputees and authority figures). The lesson to be drawn from such instances is that the apparent physical properties of a percept cannot be divorced from its other connotations.

Perception and Educational Research

Working Assumptions

What difference might the viewpoint expounded above make in the ways we think about and treat audiovisual communication and learning resources development? How would it affect our research into problems in these areas? Before trying to answer these questions, we might follow the tradition of restating our teaching points. We will present these views so as to have at hand some statements we can readily refer to.

Here we go:

There is no behavior without perception.

Behavior is both an outcome of past perceptions and a starting point for future perceptions.

Every human being is a constantly changing product of the situations through which he moves.

The perceiver and his world do not exist independently.

Each percept is the product of a creative act.

We never find a stimulus with unassigned meaning.

Meanings are given to things by the perceiver in terms of all prior experience he has accumulated.

A percept is a link between the past which gives it its meaning and the future which it helps to interpret.

Each experience or perception helps to provide us with expectations or assumptions about "reality." We expect the world to behave in accord with these assumptions.

We make bets on the outcomes of our behavior and continue or modify these bets according to our assessment of the payoff.

How assured we are in our bets depends on the amount and consistency of past relevant experience.

We are often surer in our assumptions about simple physical things than we are about complex social relationships.

Perceptual experiences are personal and individual, and they are learned.

Perception is functional. It exists to enable the perceiver to carry out his purposes. It helps him to cope with the world by assigning meanings to it which can stand the test of subsequent experiences.

Though no two persons can have exactly the same meanings for things-observed, common experiences tend to produce shared meanings which make communication possible.

Most failures in communication are due to mistaken assumptions about correspondence of meanings.

Systematic differences in experiences arising from cultural and sub-cultural differences create reliable differences in perception.

Those things that have been tied in most closely and most often with past personal experience predominate perceptually over the unusual or the unfamiliar.

The more complex a situation-observed, the more we are likely to differ in our situation perceptions. We will likely attend to somewhat different aspects and draw on much wider ranges of personal experience.

The thing-observed can never be exactly the *same* thing for two different people or for the "same" person at two different times (since he cannot be the same person).

Apparent physical properties of a percept (size of retinal image, for example) cannot be divorced from its other connotations.

There are other pertinent transactional views. Let's look at them:

Impingements on the senses are not uniquely determined. Many different distorted rooms, for example, can look to an observer like the same "normal" room.

There is no revealed reality.

The object is not necessarily less an abstraction than the word which refers to it.

Since two people cannot be in the same place at the same time, they must see at least slightly different environments.

Experience is cumulative and compounding in its effects on our perceptions.

Though we work with subjective, functional probabilities, in acting we must deal with them as absolutes. In order to make decisions from one moment to the next, we act as though our assumed world is the real world.

We tend to hold on to assumptions which were reliable in the past even when we are experiencing situations in which they no longer appear reliable (18).

We remember past events as directly as we perceive present events. A poor memory is similar to unreliable perception (26).

There can be no such thing as pure objectivity in terms of the meanings most people seem to assign to this concept.

The only world we know is determined by our assumptions.

Science is an activity designed by man to increase the reliability and verifiability of his assumptive world.

Behaviors are present events converging pasts into futures (5:26).

We can change the behavior of others only to the extent that we can help to produce situations and experiences which lead them to modify relevant assumptions.

If common assumptions are not available, the only possibility of coming to perceptual agreement lies in making them available through common experience (17:288).

Some people get pretty angry when presented such statements.

"Nonsense!" they say. "Just a bagful of mystical philosophy. There are real things. We can see them and touch them and we can measure them. The aim of science is to reveal to us what they really are and how they really behave. Don't tell *us* that ours is a world of assumptions."

At least part of the resistance to transactional thinking stems from the implications it holds for many of our professional vested interests.

Implications

What are some of the implications of transactional viewpoints?

They seem to say about any field: One of the most vital continuing activities we can perform is to examine our assumptions about what we are doing, our values, our beliefs, what we "know" about the world. This examination may be especially required where things don't seem to be working as well as we would like. But there is a danger here. Especially in education and communication we may be blithely assuming that things are working well while events are leading us toward crisis. A change in viewpoint, a tentative revision of assumptions might allow us to see the makings of crises we had been blind to before. Many of us go along talking chiefly with people who believe and think pretty much as we do. We have roughly similar philosophies of education, audiovisual communication, civil liberties, male-female relationships or what-have-you. We all "know" what is true and right and good, we know what works and how and why . . . we think. Then, whammo! We get mixed up with people from other cultures or other specialties. . . .

You are a researcher, a teacher, an audiovisual specialist, a you-name-it. Suppose, one of these fine days, even though you feel quite well, the best medical specialists tell you that you have at most six weeks still to live. What would you do?

Perhaps you have already had some experience which led you to reexamine seriously your values, your purposes in life. Most people apparently put off or avoid entirely such considerations of their own value systems. They get caught up in the busyness of their work and play and continue along, sometimes with even rather severe discontent. Questioning the adequacy of one's own values seems to be one of the hardest of human tasks.

Toch and Cantril conducted a simple demonstration-experiment in which experimental subjects were given a contrived letter (28). This letter from "Steve" merely asked the subject to put himself in the shoes of a man with only six weeks to live and to write notes on what he would do. Control subjects were given a crossword puzzle to solve. Most of the experimental subjects found even this minor excursion into personal values a tough but rewarding experience. Those subjects who worked individually on the problem found it more fun than did those who did so in groups.

Transactional viewpoints suggest that both our research and our educational efforts might much more than they do presently take into account our own purposes and assumptions and those of our students. They suggest, too, that our modern, rapidly developing world requires more contemplation of our own and others' values and greater readiness to modify our assumptions creatively.

Kelley has indicated some implications of transactional views for education (16). Much of our school work, he says, seems to be based on the assumption that we adults know things as they really are. Thus, we can show the child the correct or true version of life. We act as though there are bodies of knowledge somehow distinct from observers. We seem to assume that if you tell the child he will know.

Though we give frequent lip service to the fact that all humans are different, our educational efforts often assume that they are highly similar in the ways that they learn and the kinds of things they grasp as meaningful and salient.

Some of the new developments in self-instruction may be very helpful here—especially those that take into account some of those assumptions which seem to be relatively common in the culture where they are used. In addition, they must allow some flexibility in starting from somewhat different assumptions.

The Educational Transaction

Knowledge is what we know after we have learned and not some object outside of us. Kelley suggests the following procedures and ways of looking at education:

1. Let us find out what our learner is like. What are his values, purposes, beliefs, assumptions, *etc.?*
2. As teachers, let us consider ourselves as persons who facilitate growth. What experiences can we lead our learners through to help them test and modify their assumptions about the world?
3. Let us give our learners plenty of opportunity and freedom for honest creative expression. Let us not assume that the "reality" we know is necessarily better and more workable than the "reality" they know.
4. If we seriously put into question our assumptions concerning the efficacy of the lecture, we may wind up severely modifying this approach or getting rid of lectures altogether.
5. Let us remember that a learner can put meaning into reading matter—or for that matter films or slides or self-instruction programs—only when he has something in experience and purpose to put into them.
6. Let's get rid of the artificial separation of process and subject matter, the how and the what of learning experience.
7. One is always learning. We teachers can simply help to determine rate, direction, and quality by the variety and richness of experiences we lead our students into.

The Audiovisual Transaction

In the first issue of *AV Communication Review,* Norberg suggested some implications of transactional research for audiovisual education (24). If we can say, Norberg writes, that we learn from a "look" at something only when this "look" stands in a series of experiences linked together in a course of purposeful action, then our production, utilization, and research should reflect this.

We might, for example, more often present things in slides or films from various points of view, perhaps starting with those points of view most likely to relate to viewers' previous personal experience.

Since words and memories, as well as present physical objects or pictures or sounds, all play a part in our perceptual experience, and since this experience always involves an abstracting process, we may be kidding ourselves when we consider the "thing" or the picture to be more concrete than the word or the memory. Norberg writes:

> We cannot say what an individual will learn from any discrete visual presentation, as such, and aside from a context of other experiences, in time. Learning results from a *series* of purposeful acts carried out with continuity of purpose and direction. All action is not overt or 'physical,' but to maintain and carry forward a line of purposeful action, in time, requires adequate conditions of sensory contact with the environment. We learn *from* visual presentations in so far as they make it possible, or easier, for us to carry out our purposes. As we learn *from* perceptions, and *to* new ways of perceiving things, our 'assumptive form' world changes and this involves the most complex organizations of our behavior including social attitudes and conceptions.
>
> We cannot learn without acting. We cannot act without perceiving (24:28).

A . . . research-educational project developed by Elizabeth Drews and her colleagues presents some interesting applications of transactionalism. Dr. Drews for a number of years has been working with and studying gifted children. She noticed that many such children seemed seriously limited by their values and assumptions in their own creative expression and in accepting creativity by others. For example, some children believe that most adults who are highly creative in their work are also emotionally sick. They tend to reject other children around them who express odd or unusual ideas.

. . . Drews and her team produced a series of films showing highly creative adults at work, at play, talking with their families, *etc.* They also prepared a catalog of biographies, essays, novels, and magazine articles. These are all being used in experimental "careers" courses at the ninth-grade level along with such things as class discussions, the writing of essays and diaries, and the preparation of scrapbooks.

The major purpose of this course is to modify some of those assumptions about the future adult world which might seriously restrict students in their educational and career choices. Some children seem to think that there is only one occupational niche into which they will be able to fit. Some girls practically exclude certain professions (that of judge, for example) from their thinking about careers because they are "men's work." (Half of the films present personalized biographies of professional women, including a woman judge.) In the same way, Negro children may have a potentially self-fulfilling prophecy about the kinds of careers open to them (14). A child may feel, even in the ninth grade, that he ought to make a career choice now and stick to it. The whole project has been set up to discover what kinds of assumptions the children are making and to move them purposefully through a set of related experiences designed to help modify assumptions which are likely to be debilitating.

The experimental courses will be compared with "typical" traditional careers courses taught by the same teachers. The careers courses common to many high schools simply present lectures and outside readings about different jobs and have the students write a research report on one occupation of their choice. The experimental course is expected to:

> reduce unfavorable stereotypes of artists and scientists
> increase awareness of the existence of successfully creative adults
> increase acceptance of creative qualities and potential in self and in others
> increase the number and variety of careers perceived by students as open and rewarding to them
> strengthen the value of intellectual creativity as a purpose in life
> develop a more open and flexible process view of career choice
> perceive work on the job and other aspects of life more as an integrated whole
> engage voluntarily in more independent, creative projects
> talk more with peers about goals and careers and creative values.

Our assumptions about how the Drews course may modify students' assumptions about adult life remain to be tested. We feel, however, that the focus on evaluation of assumptions and on their modification is likely to prove a great deal more enlightening and useful than that on gains in factual information.

Multiple Transactions

Gerbner describes well how points of view, contexts, and assumptions become complex in mass media communication (11). We frequently observe somebody else's observation of somebody else's observation, etc., and then we tell somebody about it from our own point of view. Writes Gerbner:

> The analysis of communications is, therefore, compounded observation: In looking at a picture, for example, we do not merely observe a 'thing'; we observe an observation.
> What's in a picture? A 'thing' viewed from a 'built-in' point of view, in a certain context, and probably on the basis of some implicit assumptions about the nature of the object or event portrayed. For

example, the angle of the camera and the position of the lights used to take a photograph (and used to convey, implicitly, a point of view) are just as much objective elements of the picture as is the 'thing' portrayed. If we are unaware of the fact that we are observing the picture *through the eye of a camera* (or of an artist), we have lost some of our own power of observation; we fall in, unwittingly, with a 'given' point of view (11:271–2).

In a study of group photographs of the kind commonly seen in newspapers, Oshiki found (25) that camera viewpoint, lighting, and the arrangement of persons mattered much less in people's "like-dislike" ratings of the pictures than did smiles resulting from the photographer's simple instruction: "Smile, please!" Koch-Weser got similar results in a study of "ideal self-identification" with persons portrayed in advertising photographs (19). In Q sorts, most subjects ranked pictures of people smiling, especially "happy" family groups, considerably higher than those of "serious" people. Some recent work by Randall Harrison using cartoon faces indicates that when a smiling mouth is accompanied by eyebrows in a modified *V*, quite a different result obtains. People usually assume that a "normal" smile means that the person portrayed is happy and friendly, while they interpret the smile with the *V* eyebrows as meaning that the person is fiendish or happy with evil intentions. The latter expression is typical of the Charles Addams cartoons.

Transactional views and experimentation seem to support the widely held assumption that visuals which present things simply and relevantly (to the purposes and experiences of both teacher and learner) and with functional viewpoints and contexts, will best facilitate meaningful perception and learning. In diverse studies and teaching programs, it has been found that the learning of materials defined by instructors as irrelevant to their purposes can take place at the expense of materials defined as relevant (6 and 21).

Some other assumptions commonly held by audiovisual specialists may not be so well supported. For example, most such specialists argue that teachers, if they are to have their students obtain full value from a film, say, must introduce it before the showing and encourage discussion of it afterward. There is some evidence that students do indeed learn more "facts" from a film when this is done. But there is also some evidence which should lead to at least a more sophisticated view of what we may be doing when we introduce a film. Several transactional demonstration-experiments using the distorted rooms have indicated that verbal explanations of the distortion have tended to *inhibit* rather than facilitate re-interpretation of the forms perceived (18). It may well be that the subjects who were given the verbal explanation would be better able to repeat this back in a verbal test of "facts." But the finding is that they could less readily shift to a functionally more adequate perception of the distorted rooms. Too much attention to the map may keep one from learning the territory.[1]

The Learning Resources Transaction

Another area which we believe may be suffering from traditional assumptions rigidly held is that of learning resources development. Most educators who discuss this subject seem to be picturing learning resources merely as a kind of bolstered audiovisual center-library-computer combination in the context of the school-as-is, but with more than the usual number of students around. We suggest that if our educational administrators can break away no further than this from traditional assumptions, we face extravagant waste of time and money. Here, intensive creative effort and bold, dramatic experimentation might really pay off (22). We need to examine our instrumental and ultimate values. We need to examine the assumptions underlying present and proposed techniques. Why do students have to come to a university, for example, rather than the university coming to them?

The Research Transaction

Transactional views imply a great deal of research, but research well integrated with action, research with purpose. They raise doubts about some of our traditional ways of viewing science. Take "validity," for example. Many textbooks define this term as "the degree to which our instruments measure what we say they measure." The transactionalist is not alone in considering this a ridiculous, non-functional kind of statement since it assumes an objective reality "out there" isolated from the observer and his measures. Rather, we think in terms of the predictive reliability of our assumptions. Meaning is not in events or words nor is it in people, somehow isolated from events. Beauty, say, is not in the sunset but it may very well be in the sunset-observed. "Science is an activity designed by man to increase the reliability and verifiability of his assumptive world (5:9)." Man, the scientist, or just plain man is in a continuing process something like the following:

1. He senses inadequacies in certain of his assumptions. They don't seem to hold as well as they did in the past. This is problem awareness.

---

[1] A similar finding was obtained by the Norwegian psychologist R. Rommetveit in experiments involving concept formation by children. "Verbalized" concepts, according to Rommetveit, can inhibit the perception of relevant dimensions of problems. (R. Rommetveit's paper delivered at 1961 Meetings of Michigan Psychology Association, Detroit.)

2. He tries to locate those aspects of phenomena *except for* which the functional activities in question would not exist.
3. He chooses those aspects he feels are most crucial.
4. He works out some methods for changing those aspects and experimenting with the changes.
5. He modifies his assumptions on the basis of empirical evidence.

Notice that values are implied at each step. The notion that science is value-free—that is, purely objective—is a strange one, indeed.

Since the assumptive worlds of ourselves and the people we study are so complex, good research requires a great deal of speculation about research problems. We must explore different ways of viewing them and speculate about different potential outcomes for various alternative actions. Many experiments suffer from insensitivity to many of the crucial circumstances operating in the situations they investigate. In purifying and controlling, the experimenter may squeeze so much of the life blood out of the situation that the results provide us little help in dealing with our real-life worlds (23).

These are reasons why the present writers prefer, in research on complex problems, some of the more open-ended, comprehensive methods such as focused interviewing, inventories of relevant past experience, theme analysis, group interviews, Q methodology, field studies, and the like. Not that we would discard the controlled experiment. Not at all. Confirmation or disconfirmation of assumptions requires such research. But we wish to jump into the strictures of controlled experimentation only when we feel reasonably sure that we can take into account those aspects of the phenomena under study which are likely to be functionally crucial.

Summary

We have not presented a transactional theory, since, so far as we know, there is no one such theory to present. Instead, we have outlined some transactional viewpoints which we consider potentially useful in audiovisual communication, learning resources development, and research in these areas. We have suggested some implications and advantages of transactional assumptions.

References

1. Allport, G. W., and Pettigrew, T. F. "Cultural Influence on the Perception of Movement: the Trapezoidal Illusion among Zulus," *Journal of Abnormal and Social Psychology* 55:104–13; 1957.
2. Ames, A., Jr. "Visual Perception and the Rotating Trapezoidal Window." *Psychological Monographs* 65:1–31; 1951.

Conceptual Frames

3. Bagby, J. W. "A Cross-cultural Study of Perceptual Predominance in Binocular Rivalry." *Journal of Abnormal and Social Psychology* 54:331–34; 1957.

4. Cantril, H. "Perception and Interpersonal Relations." *American Journal of Psychiatry* 114:119–26; 1957.

5. Cantril, H., Ames, A., Hastorf, A. H., and Ittelson, W. H. "Psychology and Scientific Research." *Explorations in Transactional Psychology,* edited by F. P. Kilpatrick. New York: New York University, 1961, p. 6–35.

6. Deutschmann, P. J., Barrow, L. C., Jr., and McMillan, A. "The Efficiency of Different Modes of Communication." *AV Communication Review* 10:3: 176–78; May–June 1962.

7. Dewey, J., and Bentley, A. F. *Knowing and the Known.* Boston: Beacon Press, 1949.

8. Engel, E. "Binocular Methods in Psychological Research." *Explorations in Transactional Psychology,* edited by F. P. Kilpatrick. New York University Press, 1961, p. 290–305.

9. Engel, E. "The Role of Content in Binocular Resolution." *American Journal of Psychology* 69:87–91; 1956.

10. Finn, J. D. "Some Notes for an Essay on Griswold and Reading." *AV Communication Review* 7:111–21; 1959.

11. Gerbner, G. "Education and the Challenge of Mass Culture." *AV Communication Review* 7:264–78; 1959.

12. Hastorf, A. H. "The Influence of Suggestion on the Relationship Between Stimulus Size and Perceived Distance." *Journal of Psychology* 29:195–217; 1950.

13. Hastorf, A. H., and Cantril, H. "They Saw A Game: A Case Study." *Journal of Abnormal and Social Psychology* 49:129–34; 1954.

14. Hayakawa, S. I. "How to Be Sane Though Negro." *Contact 1.* Sausalito, California: Angel Island Publications, 1958, p. 5–20.

15. Ittelson, W. H., and Cantril, H. *Perception: A Transactional Approach.* New York: Doubleday and Company, 1954.

16. Kelley, E. C. "Education is Communication." *Etc.* 12:248–56; 1955.

17. Kilpatrick, F. P. "Assumptions and Perception: Three Experiments." *Explorations in Transactional Psychology,* edited by F. P. Kilpatrick. New York: New York University Press, 1961, p. 257–89.

18. Kilpatrick, F. P. "Perception Theory and General Semantics." *Etc.* 12:257–64; 1955.

19. Koch-Weser, Elke. "A Q-Study in Role Identification Using a Sample of Advertising Photographs." Master's Thesis. Michigan State University, 1961.

20. Köhler, W. *Gestalt Psychology.* New York: Liveright Publishing Corporation, 1947.

21. Kumata, H. "Teaching Advertising by Television—Study II." Mimeo. East Lansing: Communications Research Center, Michigan State University, 1958.
22. Kumata, H., and MacLean, M. S., Jr. "Education and the Problems of the New Media in the United States of America." *The Year Book of Education.* Tarrytown-on-Hudson, New York: World Book Company, 1960.
23. MacLean, M. S., Jr. "Critical Analysis of 12 Recent Title VII Research Reports." *Research Abstracts and Analytical Review,* Installment 4, p. A102–14. (*AV Communication Review,* Vol. 10, No. 3; May–June 1962.)
24. Norberg, K. "Perception Research and Audio-Visual Education." *AV Communication Review* 1:18–29; 1953.
25. Oshiki, K. "Effects of Smiles, Subject Arrangement, and Lighting on Reader Satisfaction from Pictures of Groups of People." Master's Thesis. University of Wisconsin, 1956.
26. Piatt, D. A. "The Import of the Word 'Transaction' in Dewey's Philosophy." *Etc.* 12:299–308; 1955.
27. Smith, G. H. "Size-distance Judgments of Human Faces." *Journal of Genetic Psychology* 49:45–64; 1953.
28. Toch, H., and Cantril, H. "The Learning of Values: An Experimental Inquiry." *Explorations in Transactional Psychology,* edited by F. P. Kilpatrick. New York: New York University Press, 1961, p. 321–31.
29. Toch, H., and Schulte, R. "Readiness to Perceive Violence as a Result of Police Training." *British Journal of Psychology* 52:389–93; 1961.
30. Wittreich, W. J., Grace, M., and Radcliffe, K. B., Jr. "Three Experiments in Selective Perceptual Distortion." *Explorations in Transactional Psychology,* edited by F. P. Kilpatrick. New York: New York University Press, 1961, p. 188–202.

Exercises

1. What do *you* perceive? What do you see that others overlook? Why do fishermen "see" ponds and streams others overlook? Why does the football coach "see" more in a football game than a layman? Why is it difficult for many people in the United States to become enthusiastic about soccer?

2. What are the implications of transactional psychology for education? For advertising? For world affairs?

A Conceptual Model for Communications Research

Bruce H. Westley
Malcolm S. MacLean, Jr.

A paradox confronts the student who examines conceptual models of human behavior. The more sensible and valid the model is, the more dangerous it is; the easier it is to forget that it is only a model and not the real world. As Bross pointed out in his selection, a model does not "operate." It only suggests ways to analyze the operation of things.

The Westley-MacLean model is a good one. It includes most of the relevant factors across levels of analysis. In fact, one of its major virtues as a model is that it does seem to handle more than one level. It can be applied at the personality or intrapersonal level, as well as at the two-person and the mass-communication levels. The model becomes even more useful when viewed as another description of March and Simon's "uncertainty absorption." In the final and most complex version of the model, the function labeled "C" is very much the function of an uncertainty absorber. As March and Simon will point out, function "C" is one of the most important in our time because of the number of organizations with which we must deal and within which we must operate.

Communications research and theory have blossomed from a variety of disciplinary sources in recent years. People probing the communications area have here focused on theoretical issues and there on "practical" concerns. Thus, one finds today a jungle of unrelated concepts and systems of concepts on the one hand and a mass of undigested, often sterile empirical data on the other.

From Bruce H. Westley and Malcolm S. MacLean, Jr., "A Conceptual Model for Communications Research," *Journalism Quarterly* (Winter 1957), pp. 31–38. Reprinted by permission of *Journalism Quarterly*. This article is drawn from two published earlier by these authors and has been revised. See Bruce H. Westley and Malcolm S. MacLean, Jr., "A Conceptual Model for Communications Research," *Audio-Visual Communications Review*, Vol. 3 (Winter 1955), pp. 3–12; MacLean and Westley, "Research on 'Fortuitous' Communication: A Review," same journal, Vol. 3 (Spring 1955), pp. 119–137.

In this paper, we are trying to develop a single communications model which may help to order existing findings. It also may provide a system of concepts which will evoke new and interrelated research directions, compose old theoretical and disciplinary differences, and in general bring some order out of a chaotic situation. Clearly, we do not propose here a full-blown theory of mass communications, but rather a paradigm or model as a preliminary orientation to a theoretical system.

Can a simple, parsimonious model be built capable of drawing together many of the existing approaches to mass communications without serious loss in utility?

From Face-to-Face to Mass

First, let us look at a simple act of communication. Person A transmits something about an object X to person B. Newcomb[1] has found this simple model of interpersonal communications useful in the study of roles and norms. He says that, when A communicates to B about X (other things being equal), systematic changes in the condition of the system can be predicted. For example, if B likes A (or, at least, does not dislike him), B's perception of X will be more similar to A's after than before the communicative act.

This model frees one from the limitations of either the personality or social systems as such. Can it serve as a guide to both face-to-face and mass

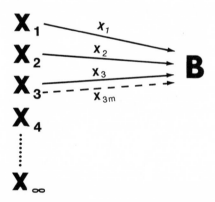

Figure 1. Objects of orientation (X_1 . . . X_∞) in the sensory field of the receiver (B) are transmitted directly to him in abstracted form (X_1 . . . X_3) after a process of selection from among all Xs, such selection being based at least in part on the needs and problems of B. Some or all are transmitted in more than one sense (X_{3m}, for example).

[1] See Theodore M. Newcomb, "An Approach to the Study of Communicative Acts," *Psychological Review*, Vol. 60 (November 1953), pp. 393–404.

communications? Need the extension from the simple communicative act to the mass communicative act destroy its system character?

Two basic distinctions between face-to-face and mass communications are suggested: Face-to-face communication involves more sense modalities. It also provides immediate "feedback"—that is, information from B back to A about the changed condition of B. In other words, more senses (and kinds of stimuli) can come into play in the person-person act than in any other situation. Thus, B has a "cross-modality" check. He can clear impressions he gets through one sense with those he gets through another. And A has the advantage of learning B's response almost immediately— for instance, "message received."

Mass communications, then, differ from face-to-face communications to the extent that (a) the number of modalities tends to be minimized and (b) "orientative" feedback is minimized or delayed.

Now for a look at X, which may be taken as an "object of orientation." From the standpoint of B, the world consists of a confusion of Xs. And these Xs may include As. B has within his sensory field an infinity of potential Xs. He has learned that in order to maximize satisfactions and solve security problems he must orient toward Xs selectively. But the mature B, Newcomb emphasizes, does not orient toward X alone, but tends, in the presence of an A, to orient simultaneously toward both A and X. This means that he comes to orient toward an X not alone on the basis of its intrinsic capacity to provide satisfactions and help solve problems but also with respect to the relationship between A and X. This also means that A and X relate systematically to B.

Let us assume that an X is any object (or event) that has character-

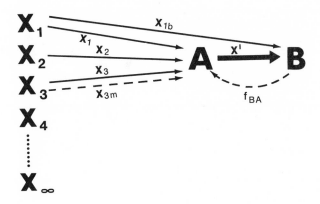

Figure 2. The same Xs are selected and abstracted by communicator (A) and transmitted as a message (X') to B, who may or may not have part or all of the Xs in his own sensory field (X_{1b}). Either purposively or non-purposively B transmits feedback (f_{BA}) to A.

istics capable of being transmitted in some abstracted form.[2] Let us assume further that a system[3] has a need for transmissible messages as a means of orienting itself in its environment and as a means of securing problem solutions and need satisfactions. The significant thing is that Xs have stimulus characteristics that can be responded to in the absence of an A.

For instance, B looks out his window and sees flames in the house of his neighbor. This event as surely transmits information to him as would the shouts of his neighbor *about* the fire.

With respect to the As and Xs in his own immediate sensory field, B is capable of receiving and acting upon information thus transmitted to him and must do so if he is to maintain an adequate orientation to his immediate environment. But what of As and Xs relevant to such orientation but lying outside his immediate reach? If these are to impinge on him, there is need for another role, which we will call C.

C is conceived of as one who can (a) select the abstractions of object X appropriate to B's need satisfactions or problem solutions, (b) transform them into some form of symbol containing meanings shared[4] with B, and finally (c) transmit such symbols by means of some channel or medium to B.

The added element C will be recognized as the "gatekeeper" of Lewin[5] as adapted to mass communications by White.[6] It is also recognizable as the "encoder" suggested by Bush[7] as an adaptation of the encoding process in information theory.

---

[2] It need hardly be said that what is transmitted is not the event but an abstraction from it converted in some way to transmissible form. We are indebted to the semanticists for their emphasis on this point, particularly Wendell Johnson. See especially his "The Communication Process and General Semantic Principles," in Lyman Bryson (ed.), *The Communication of Ideas* (New York: Harper & Bros., 1948).

[3] We here choose the general term "system" because we mean that the B, or "behavioral system" in this paradigm, sometimes called the "receiver," may be an individual (personality system) or a group, large or small (social system). The assumption is that any system in this sense is motivated to seek information about its surroundings.

[4] We are once again indebted to Newcomb for his emphasis on the *shared* symbol system. It is an advantage of a paradigm based on his *ABX* system that this concept is derivable from the system itself without additional assumptions: communication about an X leads to shared perceptions of it and attaches shared meanings to it.

[5] Kurt Lewin, "Psychological Ecology," in Dorwin Cartwright (ed.), *Field Theory in Social Science* (New York: Harper & Bros., 1951).

[6] David M. White, "The 'Gate-keeper': A Study in the Selection of News," *Journalism Quarterly*, Vol. 27 (Fall 1950), pp. 283–290.

[7] Chilton R. Bush, *The Art of News Communication* (New York: Appleton-Century-Crofts, Inc., © 1954), pp. 1–3.

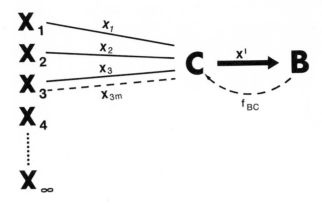

Figure 3. What Xs B receives may be owing to selected abstractions transmitted by a non-purposive encoder (C), acting for B and thus extending B's environment. C's selections are necessarily based in part on feedback (f_{BC}) from B.

It may be asked why C would choose Xs "appropriate" to the requirements of B. The answer would appear to be that the C role can survive only to the extent that this is true. For B is still a selector among the offerings of various Cs and this means that Cs are in effect competitors for the attention of Bs (and for that matter competitors with As and Xs in B's immediate field). Cs therefore survive as Cs to the extent that they satisfy needs for Bs. And Bs, on the basis of the most obvious propositions of learning theory, will tend to return to those Cs which have provided past need satisfactions and problem solutions.

C, then, is capable of serving as an agent for B in selecting and transmitting information about an X (or an A-X relationship[8]). He does so by means of symbols expressing shared meanings about Xs through channels that provide connection between X and B. And he does so in circumstances where such a connection is otherwise impossible for B. Thus B has a basis for increasing his security in the larger environment and for gaining increased need satisfactions. In other words, *the effect of the addition of the C role is to provide B with a more extended environment.*

For Newcomb, A and B can only be persons. While we have tended to imply persons in these roles, it should now be made clear that we do not intend to confine the model to the level of the individual personality. The role of B, for instance, may be that of a person, or a primary group, or a total social system.

---

[8] Following Newcomb, *op. cit.*, we treat an "opinion statement" as an A-X relationship on the assumption that the A and the X are systematically related: the opinion attains full meaning only in the light of who expresses it and the image of the speaker is influenced by the nature of the opinion.

In stating that any "system" has need for transmissible messages as a means of orienting itself in its environment, it is meant that this statement be applied to a person, a primary group, or even a social system. Any of these levels can be plugged into the role of B. At the personality level, B

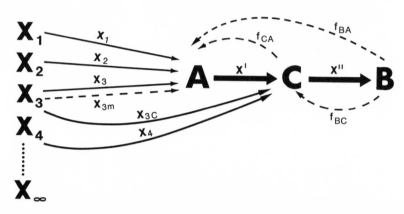

Figure 4. The messages C transmits to B (X″) represent his selections from both messages to him from A's (X′) and C's selections and abstractions from Xs in his own sensory field (X₃c, X₄), which may or may not be Xs in A's field. Feedback not only moves from B to A (f_BA) and from B to C (f_BC) but also from C to A (f_CA). Clearly, in the mass communication situation, a large number of Cs receive from a very large number of As and transmit to a vastly larger number of Bs, who simultaneously receive from other Cs.

can be the housewife, too busy to rush around the neighborhood in order to observe the details of her surroundings; in such a case the C function can be attributed to the neighborhood gossip, who observes, selects, encodes, and transmits a limited portion of all possible messages supplying the information needs of B. At something like the primary group level, one can think of the relatively isolated frontier colony, which posted sentinels as Cs to observe and report the condition of the environment by means of a special code such as a rifle shot and greeted eagerly another kind of C, the information-bearing circuit rider. At the social system level, a national state requires and maintains an elaborate network of Cs performing such special information functions as that of the diplomatic service.

It might even be possible that the model holds for even "lower" levels than that of the personality. For instance, at the physiological level, it would appear that homeostasis[9] requires some sort of "transmission" of "information" with respect to states of parts of the body.

[9] See W. B. Cannon, *The Wisdom of the Body* (New York: W. W. Norton & Co., Inc., 1932).

Conceptual Frames

Not only is the model highly general with respect to levels, it is highly general with respect to kinds of messages. Messages can be seen as either *purposive* or *non-purposive*.[10] Other models have tended to obscure one or the other.

"Purposive" or "Non-Purposive"?

A purposive message is one A originates for the purpose of modifying B's perception of an X. A non-purposive message is one which is transmitted to B directly or by means of a C and in the absence of any communicator's intent to influence him. The absence of a communicator's intent to influence B transforms his act into an X. When a person says something he hopes will reach another person's ears, he is an A; but if he says it without such intent and it nevertheless is transmitted to B, his act must be conceived of as an X, the selection and transmission having been performed by a C. The reasons we consider this distinction to be crucial for mass communications theory will be discussed below.

Messages are transmitted in codes (symbol systems). But this model is by no means limited to the most obvious ones—linguistic systems. In fact, as Newcomb has already emphasized, the crucial characteristic is the shared meanings associated with symbols. Such symbols can take virtually any form, so long as and to the extent that there exist shared meanings and that they are transmissible. Such shared meanings surrounding symbols can be either *affective* or *cognitive*. Language has both affective and cognitive elements. Poetry, for instance, emphasizes the former. This emphasis is, of course, characteristic of all the arts. For instance, modern artist A in communicating with a series of Bs casts his message in a symbol system which is shared, even though with only a few of them; those Bs who share it or part of it will attain satisfaction from the communication of an affective state; those who cannot decode the message but attempt to do so will

---

[10] The original articles referred to "purposive" and "fortuitous" messages (and feedback). Perhaps the latter term was unfortunate, for it appears to have been generally misunderstood. Of course we do not mean to say "chance" messages, for messages are *selected* (by As, Bs, and Cs) on the basis of their utility in providing need satisfactions and problem solutions. It is the occurrence of the events (Xs) that is "fortuitous." We also wish to emphasize that it is in the "role prescriptions," not in the actual performance, that the distinction is made between the purposive or "advocacy" characteristic of the A role and the non-purposive or "gate-keeper" characteristic of the C role. A reporter may consciously or unconsciously be an advocate in his gate-keeper job; we treat this situation as a discrepancy between his "role prescriptions" and his actual "role behaviors," and treat the size of this discrepancy as an empirical question. For a helpful discussion of these terms, see Theodore M. Newcomb, *Social Psychology* (New York: Holt, Rinehart and Winston, Inc.), especially Chapter 8, "Social Norms and Common Attitudes," pp. 264–297.

probably be frustrated in the attempt and express hostility toward the message,[11] or the communicator, or conceivably even the gatekeeper.

The example above leads into further illustration of how the model deals with "special publics." These are illustrated by the immense segment of the media consisting of trade publications, scholarly journals, hobby and craft media, house organs, and the like. These are often defined out of the area of mass communications, usually on the grounds of audience size; and this in spite of the fact that some of these special interest publications attain circulations in the millions. The fact would seem to be that these media shade off from the specificity of the *Turkey Grower's Gazette* to the generality of *Holiday*, suggesting that decisions as to what is "mass" and what is not mass must necessarily be arbitrary.

The present model requires no such distinction. Our *B*s vary in the degree to which they share common problems. Common problems imply the necessity of attaining communication with common *X*s. Media serving to bring such *X*s to such *B*s arise out of the perceptions by *C*s of the existence of just such a need. Special symbol systems are developed to maximize transmission.

It will be noted that we have consistently referred to both "need satisfactions" and "problem solutions." These concepts relate directly to the "immediate" and "delayed" rewards of Schramm[12] which seem to us to be provocative and potentially fruitful. Building on the two-factor learning theory of Mowrer,[13] Schramm proposed a "reader reward" basis for characterizing the content of news stories. The correspondence is, of course, between his "immediate reward" and our "need satisfactions" and between his "delayed reward" and our "problem solutions."

Feedback

Another concept crucial to the model is that of "feedback." In the first place it should be clear from the foregoing that it is feedback that assures the system character of the *ABX* (or *ABCX*) relationship. If *A* is to utilize his experience in influencing *B*, he must have information about any changes in the condition of *B* attributable to his communications. *C*

[11] This statement is of course not derivable from the paradigm (and the reader is reminded that this is a paradigm and not a full-blown theory). But because the *B* system is *seeking* problem solutions and need satisfactions there are grounds in the literature of psychology for assuming that when his search is frustrated, aggressive behavior may follow. See Neal E. Miller, *et al.*, "The Frustration-Aggression Hypothesis," *Psychological Review,* Vol. 48 (1941), pp. 337–342.

[12] Wilbur Schramm, "The Nature of News," *Journalism Quarterly,* Vol. 26 (September 1949), pp. 259–269.

[13] O. H. Mowrer, *Learning Theory and Personality Dynamics* (New York: The Ronald Press Co., 1950), pp. 222–317.

is equally concerned with effects on B if he is to make realistic adjustments in his role as B's "agent." Such As as advertisers facilitate feedback by means of elaborate market research; public relations men obtain feedback by means of public-opinion polls and other devices for determining the effects of their messages. Such Cs as newspaper publishers sponsor readership surveys and, more recently, reader motivation studies to estimate and predict reader response. Radio's concern with "fan mail" and popularity ratings is well known.

Although feedback originates with B under most circumstances, it need not be assumed that B is necessarily trying to communicate back to C or A. When he does try to do so, we may think of this as *purposive* feedback. This is the case when an angry reader writes a letter "straightening out" the editor on some favorite issue. But there are also many ways B can feed back without intending to. These we will call *non-purposive* feedback. When a television fan decides to try a well-advertised detergent, his purchase becomes part of the data of a market survey, even though he may not have intended to let the sponsor know he had won a convert.

Other Models

In the final analysis the worth of such a model as this lies in its heuristic value. In view of the fact that several other models already exist in this field, it is reasonable to ask why another is necessary. A brief look at some others may be in order.[14]

Perhaps the most pervasive of existing "models" is that of Lasswell: "*Who* says *what* through *what channels* to *whom* with *what effect*."[15] The difficulty here is that the model seems to demand the presence of a communicator—the *who*—and to imply that his communication is a purposive one. It is no accident that our model has included the non-purposive case, transmitting Xs to Bs by the way of Cs in the total absence of As. The fortuitous origination of a great deal of the news material transmitted in all media seems to demand a place in the model. There is also an unidirectional implication in the Lasswellian formulation that ignores feedback phenomena.

[14] Several other general models or partial theories of the total mass communication process have appeared recently. They include Franklin Fearing, "Toward a Psychology of Human Communication," *Journal of Personality*, Vol. 22 (September 1953), pp. 71–88; Wilbur Schramm, "How Communication Works," in Schramm (ed.), *The Process and Effects of Mass Communications* (Urbana: University of Illinois Press, 1954); and George Gerbner, "Toward a General Model of Communication," *Audio-Visual Communication Review*, Vol. 4 (Summer 1956), pp. 171–199.

[15] Harold D. Lasswell, "The Structure and Function of Communication in Society," in Bryson, *op. cit.*, pp. 37–51.

The information theory-cybernetics paradigm[16] has excited some interesting theoretical contributions[17] but would appear to have certain drawbacks. It, too, appears to require the presence of a communicator, although not necessarily a purposive one. In addition it poses all the problems of a "borrowed" model. Taylor's use of the redundancy concept[18] would appear to be an example of an exact mapping from mass communications phenomena to an element in the model. But such precise correspondences appear to be rare, and mappings become contrived and tenuous. The model strains common knowledge, for instance, in assuming perfect correspondence of symbol systems encoded and decoded.[19]

Summary

A conceptual model of the total communication process has been presented in the belief that such a model will prove useful in ordering existing data in mass communications research, point to areas of strength and weakness in our knowledge, and stimulate further efforts. The model is intended to be sufficiently general to treat all kinds of human communication from two-person face-to-face interaction to international and intercultural communications. It assumes that a minimum number of roles and processes are needed in any general theory of communications and attempts to isolate and tentatively define them. It must not be viewed as a theory but as a preliminary step to the construction of a general theory.

The principal elements in the model are these:

[16] See Claude E. Shannon and Warren Weaver, *The Mathematical Theory of Communication* (Urbana: University of Illinois Press, 1949).

[17] See especially Bush, *op. cit.*, and Wilbur Schramm, "Information Theory and Mass Communication," *Journalism Quarterly*, Vol. 32 (Spring 1955), pp. 131–146.

[18] Wilson L. Taylor, " 'Cloze Procedure': A New Tool for Measuring Readability," *Journalism Quarterly*, Vol. 30 (Fall 1953), pp. 415–433.

[19] In information theory, the "ensembles" for purposes of encoding and decoding are equivalent. There is no provision for decoding errors as such; only "noise" in the channel can produce encoder-decoder disagreement. Noise is defined as random events. Various writers, including Bush, *op. cit.*, have suggested distinguishing "channel noise" from "semantic noise," the latter being defined more or less as decoding errors attributable to ensemble differences at the encoding and decoding stages. The distinction is important, of course, but this would appear to be a case of bending the model to satisfy common sense. It is not easy to see how the mathematical relations in information theory could survive the incorporation of this new concept; such noise must surely be systematic and not random, for instance. For a more technical treatment of essentially the same point, see Lee J. Cronbach, "On the Non-Rational Application of Information Measures in Psychology," in Henry Quastler (ed.), *Information Theory in Psychology: Problems and Methods*, pp. 14–25.

As (Advocacy roles). This is what is usually meant by "the communicator"—a personality or social system engaged in selecting and transmitting messages *purposively*.

Bs (Behavioral system roles). This is what is usually meant by "the receiver," "the public," etc.—a personality or social system requiring and using communications about the condition of its environment for the satisfaction of its needs and solution of its problems.

Cs (Channel roles). Often confounded with *As, Cs* serve as the agents of *Bs* in selecting and transmitting non-purposively the information *Bs* require, especially when the information is beyond the immediate reach of *B*.

X. The totality of objects and events "out there." X^1 is these objects and events as abstracted into transmissible form: "messages" about *Xs* and *A-X* relationships (such as "opinions").

Channels. The means by which *Xs* are moved by way of *As* and/or *Cs* to *Bs*. Channels include "gates" manned by *Cs* who in various ways alter messages.

Encoding. The process by which *As* and *Cs* transform *Xs* into X^1s. *Decoding* is the process by which *Bs* interiorize messages.

Feedback. The means by which *As* and *Cs* obtain information about the effects of messages on Bs.

Exercises

1. In terms of the distinctions made between face-to-face and mass communication, what is the difference between performing a play and reading a play aloud with others? What is the difference between attending a board meeting and reading silently to yourself the policy directive produced there?

2. Consider the effect upon this essay if all B's assume all C's to be liars. Discuss. What is the effect if only some B's assume all C's to be liars?

3. Who decides when feedback is non-purposive? According to what criteria might this decision be made?

Communication

James G. March
Herbert A. Simon

In this selection the term "programmed" refers to activities that have been foreseen and for which routines have been planned. These may be communication activities. "Nonprogrammed" means activities that are either unforeseen or not repetitive and for which, therefore, no routines have been planned. March and Simon also describe communication within organizations in terms of "coordination by plan" and "coordination by feedback."

In discussing inspection activities and intraorganizational dependence, March and Simon use the term "efficiency of communication." One of the ideas to which they refer is that a great deal of information can be transmitted if the users of the communication system agree upon some code. Time and energy can be saved in transmission if one element of the code can stand for a series of facts about the operation of the organization. But remember that these savings must always be balanced against the cost of coding and decoding the message.

This selection has been included for its discussion of "uncertainty absorption." Someone who tells you about an event reduces your uncertainty about what actually happened. He acts as the uncertainty absorber to the extent that you, the hearer, think him credible. However, even trained observers make mistakes, so you should be wary of assuming that, after hearing someone's account, you know exactly what happened.

March and Simon's discussion hinges upon their notion of how the organization is affected by its model of reality. If the organization permits itself to complicate its perception of reality without limit, it is overwhelmed by the complex environment and is less capable of dealing with it. In other words, there are definite limits on the number of factors an organization can keep track of, let alone try to control. Again, think how impossible an executive's job would become if every single datum that might be relevant to his decisions were placed upon his desk. The executive must hire people to reduce the amount of data he personally handles. As this amount is reduced, the executive becomes further removed from the complexity of the organization's operations. His uncertainty about what to do is reduced, too. Therefore, those who sift and condense data are uncertainty absorbers, at least potentially. Whether they can function efficiently depends upon the degree to which the executive places confidence in them. Or, in terms used by Hovland, Janis, and Kelley elsewhere in this book, the sifters and condensers can function as uncertainty absorbers to the extent that they are perceived as credible by those who make decisions based upon the data they forward.

We may classify the occasions for communication as follows:

1. Communication for nonprogrammed activity. This is a catchall category that will need further analysis later.
2. Communication to initiate and establish programs, including day-to-day adjustment or "coordination" of programs.
3. Communication to provide data for application of strategies (i.e., required for the execution of programs).
4. Communication to evoke programs (i.e., communications that serve as "stimuli").
5. Communication to provide information on the results of activities.

The distinction between the first two categories and the last three is the familiar distinction between communication relating to procedural matters and communication relating to substantive content.

Empirical evidence for the distinction among the last three categories was obtained from a study of the use of accounting data by operating departments in manufacturing concerns. It was found that accounting information was used at various executive levels to answer three different kinds of questions: (a) Problem-solving questions: Which course of action is better? This corresponds to our category 3. (b) Attention-directing questions: What problems shall I look into? This corresponds to category 4. (c) Score-card questions: How well am I (or is he) doing? This corresponds to category 5. Some of the accounting information was also used in connection with less programmed activity. We will consider this point below.

Communication and Coordination

The capacity of an organization to maintain a complex, highly interdependent pattern of activity is limited in part by its capacity to handle the communication required for coordination. The greater the *efficiency of communication* within the organization, the greater the tolerance for interdependence. The problem has both quantitative and qualitative aspects.

As we noted earlier, it is possible under some conditions to reduce the volume of communication required from day to day by substituting coordination by plan for coordination by feedback. By virtue of this substitution, organizations can tolerate very complex interrelations among their component parts in the performance of repetitive activities. The coordination of parts is incorporated in the program when it is established, and the need for continuing communication is correspondingly reduced.

From James G. March and Herbert A. Simon, *Organizations* (New York: John Wiley & Sons, Inc., 1958), pp. 161–169. Reprinted by permission of John Wiley & Sons, Inc.

Each specific situation, as it arises, is largely covered by the standard operating procedure.

A different method for increasing the organization's tolerance for interdependence is to increase the efficiency of communication by making it possible to communicate large amounts of information with relatively few symbols. An obvious example is the blueprint, which provides a common plan stated in extreme detail. The blueprint employs a carefully defined, highly developed "language" or set of symbolic and verbal conventions. Because of this standardized language, it can convey large quantities of information. The same attention to standardization of language is seen in accounting systems and other reporting systems that employ numerical data.

Accounting definitions and blueprint conventions are examples of a still more general phenomenon: technical languages, whose symbols have definite and common meanings to the members of an organization. Prominent in these technical languages are categories for classifying situations and events.

The role of unambiguous technical terms in permitting coordination by feedback is shown by the Christie-Luce-Macy experiments with "noisy marbles" in the Bavelas network. Participants in the experiment were given some colored marbles, and they were required to discover what color was held by all of them. Control groups were given marbles that had solid colors like "red," "yellow," etc. Experimental groups were given streaked marbles whose colorings did not correspond in any simple way to color designations in common language. Comparison of the performance of the control with the experimental groups showed (a) that the latter were much hindered by the lack of adequate technical vocabulary, and (b) that their performance became comparable to that of the control groups only when they succeeded in inventing such a vocabulary and securing its acceptance throughout the group.

Classification schemes are of particular significance for the program-evoking aspects of communication. When an event occurs that calls for some kind of organization response, the question is asked, in one form or other: "What *kind* of event is this?" The organization has available a repertory of programs, so that once the event has been classified the appropriate program can be executed without further ado. We can make this process more specific with a pair of examples.

The oil gauge on the dashboard of an automobile is an example of the use of classification in program-evoking. For most drivers, the oil pressure is either "all right" or "low." In the first case, no action is taken; in the second case a remedial program is initiated (e.g., taking the automobile to a repair shop). Some auto manufacturers have substituted a red light, which turns on when the oil pressure is not in the proper range, for the traditional gauge. This example also illustrates how substituting standards of satisfactory performance for criteria of optimization simplifies communication.

Similarly, inspection activities often involve dichotomous decisions. In these cases, the choice is not usually between evoking a program or not evoking one (action or inaction), but between different programs. Thus, if the item being inspected meets the standards, one program is evoked (it is passed on for further processing); if it fails to meet standards, another program is evoked (scrapping, or reworking, as the case may be).

One reason that classifying is so economical of communication is that most of the coordination can be preprogrammed; the organization has a repertory of responses to stimuli, and it only needs to know what kind of stimulus it is confronted with in order to execute an elaborate program. On the other hand, if the communication system could handle a more complete description of the program-evoking event, and if the action part of the organization had the capacity to develop programs on the spot to meet present needs, no doubt one could conceive tailor-made programs that would be more accurately adapted to each separate situation than are the preprogrammed responses.

Here again the normative or adaptive problem of organization design is one of balance. If its model of reality is not to be so complex as to paralyze it, the organization must develop radical simplifications of its responses. One such simplification is to have (a) a repertory of standard responses, (b) a classification of program-evoking situations, (c) a set of rules to determine what is the appropriate response for each class of situations. The balance of economies and efficiencies here is exactly the same as it is in all cases of standardization. Note that what we have described in an organizational framework is quite comparable to discrimination learning in individuals. In the individual case, as in the organizational, there is a close relationship between the categories used in the cognitive code and the operational decision rules.

In our culture, language is well developed for describing and communicating about concrete objects. The blueprint has already been mentioned as an important technical device for this purpose. Language is also very effective in communicating about things that can be classified and named, even if they are intangible. Thus, when there are standard repertories of programs, it is easy to refer to them.

On the other hand, it is extremely difficult to communicate about intangible objects and nonstandardized objects. Hence, the heaviest burdens are placed on the communications system by the less structured aspects of the organization's tasks, particularly by activity directed toward the explanation of problems that are not yet well defined. We shall see in the next chapter that this difference in communication difficulty has important implications for the organization of nonprogrammed activities.

Where the available means of communication are primitive—relative to the communication needs—so will be the system of coordination. There will tend to be less self-containment of organizational units and a greater reliance on coordination through communication the greater the efficiency of communication. This relation may sometimes be obscured by the fact that pressure toward coordination (e.g., under conditions of rapid change) may compel attempts at feedback coordination even though available communication is inefficient. It should also be noted that self-containment decreases and interdependencies increase the likelihood of developing an efficient communication code.

The Absorption of Uncertainty

The use of classification schemes in communication has further consequences, some of which go back to our earlier discussion of perception and identification. The technical vocabulary and classification schemes in an organization provide a set of concepts that can be used in analyzing and in communicating about its problems. Anything that is easily described and discussed in terms of these concepts can be communicated readily in the organization; anything that does not fit the system of concepts is communicated only with difficulty. Hence, the world tends to be perceived by the organization members in terms of the particular concepts that are reflected in the organization's vocabulary. The particular categories and schemes of classification it employs are reified, and become, for members of the organization, attributes of the world rather than mere conventions.

The reification of the organization's conceptual scheme is particularly noticeable in *uncertainty absorption*. Uncertainty absorption takes place when inferences are drawn from a body of evidence and the inferences, instead of the evidence itself, are then communicated. The successive editing steps that transform data obtained from a set of questionnaires into printed statistical tables provide a simple example of uncertainty absorption.

Through the process of uncertainty absorption, the recipient of a communication is severely limited in his ability to judge its correctness. Although there may be various tests of apparent validity, internal consistency, and consistency with other communications, the recipient must, by and large, repose his confidence in the editing process that has taken place, and, if he accepts the communication at all, accept it pretty much as it stands. To the extent that he can interpret it, his interpretation must be based primarily on his confidence in the source and his knowledge of the biases to which the source is subject, rather than on a direct examination of the evidence.

By virtue of specialization, most information enters an organization at highly specific points. Direct perception of production processes is limited largely to employees in a particular operation on the production floor. Direct perception of customer attitudes is limited largely to salesmen. Direct evidence of the performance of personnel is restricted largely to immediate supervisors, colleagues, and subordinates.

In all of these cases, the person who summarizes and assesses his own direct perceptions and transmits them to the rest of the organization becomes an important source of informational premises for organizational action. The "facts" he communicates can be disbelieved, but they can only rarely be checked. Hence, by the very nature and limits of the communication system, a great deal of discretion and influence is exercised by those persons who are in direct contact with some part of the "reality" that is of concern to the organization. Both the amount and the *locus of uncertainty absorption* affect the *influence structure of the organization*.

Because of this, uncertainty absorption is frequently used, consciously and unconsciously, as a technique for acquiring and exercising power. In a culture where direct contradiction of assertions of fact is not approved, an individual who is willing to make assertions, particularly about matters that do not contradict the direct perceptions of others, can frequently get these assertions accepted as premises of decision.

We can cite a number of more or less "obvious" variables that affect the absorption of uncertainty. The more complex the data that are perceived and the less adequate the organization's language, the closer to the source of the information will the uncertainty absorption take place, and the greater will be the amount of summarizing at each step of transmission. The locus of absorption will tend to be a function of such variables as: (*a*) the needs of the recipient for raw as against summarized information (depending upon the kinds of data used in selecting the appropriate program), (*b*) the need for correction of biases in the transmitter, (*c*) the distribution of technical competence for interpreting and summarizing raw data, and (*d*) the need for comparing data from two or more sources in order to interpret it.

The way in which uncertainty is absorbed has important consequences for coordination among organizational units. In business organizations, expected sales are relevant to decisions in many parts of the organization: purchasing decisions, production decisions, investment decisions, and many others. But if each organizational unit were permitted to make its own forecast of sales, there might be a wide range of such estimates with consequent inconsistencies among the decisions made by different departments—the purchasing department, for example, buying raw materials that the production department does not expect to process. It may be important in cases of this kind to make an *official* forecast and to use this official forecast as the basis for action throughout the organization.

Where it is important that all parts of an organization act on the same premises, and where different individuals may draw different conclusions from the raw evidence, a formal uncertainty absorption point will be established, and the inferences drawn at that point will have official status in the organization as "legitimate" estimates. The greater the need for coordination in the organization, the greater the *use of legitimized "facts."*

The Communication
Network

Associated with each program is a set of information flows that communicate the stimuli and data required to evoke and execute the program. Generally this communication traverses definite channels, either by formal plan or by the gradual development of informal programs. Information and stimuli move from sources to points of decision; instructions move from points of decision to points of action; information of results moves from points of action to points of decision and control.

Rational organization design would call for the arrangement of these channels so as to minimize the communication burden. But insofar as the points of origin of information and the points of action are determined in advance, the only mobile element is the point of decision. Whatever may be the position in the organization holding the formal authority to legitimize the decision, to a considerable extent the effective discretion is exercised at the points of uncertainty absorption.

In large organizations, specialization of communication functions will be reflected in the division of work itself. Among the specialized communication units we find are (*a*) units specializing in the actual physical transmission of communications: a telephone and teletype unit, messenger group, or the like; (*b*) units specializing in recording and report preparation: bookkeeping and other record-keeping units; (*c*) units specializing in the acquisition of raw information, usually referred to as intelligence units, sometimes as research units; (*d*) units specializing in the provision of technical premises for decision: research units, technical specialists; (*e*) units specializing in the interpretation of policy and organizational goals, a function usually not much separated from the main stem of the hierarchy; and (*f*) units specializing in the retention of information: files, archives units.

In part, communication channels are deliberately and consciously planned in the course of programming. In part, they develop through usage. We will make two hypotheses about such development. First, the greater the communication efficiency of the channel, the greater the *communication channel usage.* The possession by two persons, or two organization units, of a common, efficient language facilitates communication. Thus, links between members of a common profession tend to be used in the communication system. Similarly, other determinants of language compatibility—ethnic background, education, age, experience—will affect what channels are used in the organization.

Second, channel usage tends to be self-reinforcing. When a channel is frequently used for one purpose, its use for other unrelated purposes is encouraged. In particular, formal hierarchical channels tend to become general-purpose channels to be used whenever no special-purpose channel or informal channel exists or is known to the communicator. The self-reinforcing character of channel usage is particularly strong if it brings individuals into face-to-face contact. In this case (the Homans hypothesis) informal communication, much of it social in character, develops side-by-side with task-oriented formal communication, and the use of the channel for either kind of communication tends to reinforce its use for the other.

In part, the communication network is planned; in part, it grows up in response to the need for specific kinds of communication; in part, it develops in response to the social functions of communication. At any given stage in its development, its gradual change is much influenced by the pattern that has already become established. Hence, although the structure of the network will be considerably influenced by the structure of the organization's task, it will not be completely determined by the latter.

Once a pattern of communication channels has become established, this pattern will have an important influence on decision-making processes, and particularly upon nonprogrammed activity. We may anticipate some of the analysis of the next chapter by indicating briefly the nature of this influence.

The existing pattern of communication will determine the relative frequency with which particular members of the organization will encounter particular stimuli, or kinds of stimuli, in their search processes. For example, a research and development unit that has frequent communication with sales engineers and infrequent communication with persons engaged in fundamental research will live in a different environment of new product ideas than a research and development unit that has the opposite communication pattern.

The communication pattern will determine how frequently and forcefully particular consequences of action are brought to the attention of the actor. The degree of specialization, for example, between design engineers, on the one hand, and installation and service engineers, on the other, will have an important influence on the amount of awareness of the former as to the effectiveness of their designs.

From our previous propositions concerning time pressure effects, we would predict that the pattern of communication would have a greater influence on nonprogrammed activities carried out with deadlines and under time pressure than upon activities that involve relatively slow and deliberate processes of decision. For, given sufficient time, if particular information is available anywhere in an organization, its relevance to any particular decision is likely to be noticed. Where decisions are made relatively rapidly, however, only the information that is locally available is likely to be brought to bear. We see here another reason why specialization (in this case specialization with respect to possession of information) is tolerated to a greater degree under "steady-state" conditions than when the organization is adapting to a rapidly changing environment.

Exercises

1. As an operator of an automobile, which would you prefer, an oil gauge that shows pounds of pressure or an on-off red light? Under what circumstances is it disadvantageous to have the pressure gauge? Under what circumstances is it disadvantageous to have the red light?

2. Imagine that you are writing something for senior high school students that would help them understand the ideas and relationships March and Simon refer to as "uncertainty absorption." Then analyze the dimensions in which you would be a success and those in which you would be a failure as an uncertainty absorber.

3. In discussing patterning of communication channels, March and Simon talk about two patterns of communication into which a research and development team might fall. Which of these two patterns would you prefer? Why? What is the best justification you can think of for the *other* pattern?

Communication: The Flow of Information

Daniel Katz
Robert L. Kahn

This chapter from Katz and Kahn provides a good summary and expansion of some of the concepts discussed at other places in the present book. For example, the discussion of upward, downward, and lateral communication can be compared with the Lloyd and Warfel essay on the languages of business. The section on the coding process can be related to the March and Simon chapter on organizations. The section on communication networks is interesting to discuss in terms of the Westley-MacLean model.

We feel that this selection should provide the opportunity for drawing together many of the notions found in other selections. The discussion of research in terms of informational sub-systems has ap-applicability to government, business, and education.

The world we live in is basically a world of people. Most of our actions toward others and their actions toward us are communicative acts in whole or in part, whether or not they reach verbal expression. This is as true of behavior in organizations as in other contexts. We have said . . . that human organizations are informational as well as energic systems, and that every organization must take in and utilize information. The intake and distribution of information are also energic processes, of course; acts of sending and receiving information demand energy for their accomplishment. Their energic demands, however, are negligible in comparison with their significance and implications as symbolic acts—as acts of communication and control.

When one walks from a factory to the adjoining head-house or office, the contrast is conspicuous. One goes from noise to quiet, from heavy electrical cables and steam pipes to slim telephone lines, from a machine-dominated to a people-dominated environment. One goes, in short, from a sector of the organization in which energic exchange is primary and information exchange secondary, to a sector where the priorities are reversed. The closer one gets to the organizational center of control and decision-making, the more pronounced is the emphasis on information exchange.

In this sense, communication—the exchange of information and the transmission of meaning—is the very essence of a social system or an organization. The input of physical energy is dependent upon information about it, and the input of human energy is made possible through communicative acts. Similarly the transformation of energy (the accomplishment of work) depends upon communication between people in each organizational subsystem and upon communication between subsystems. The product exported carries meaning as it meets needs and wants, and its use is further influenced by the advertising or public relations material about it. The amount of support which an organization receives from its social environment is also affected by the information which elite groups and wider publics have acquired about its goals, activities, and accomplishments.

Communication is thus a social process of the broadest relevance in the functioning of any group, organization, or society. It is possible to subsume under it such forms of social interaction as the exertion of influence, cooperation, social contagion or imitation, and leadership. We shall consider communication in this broad sense, with emphasis upon the structural aspects of the information process in organizations, but with attention also to the motivational basis for transmitting and receiving messages.

It is a common assumption that many of our problems, individual and social, are the result of inadequate and faulty communication. As Newcomb (1947) points out, autistic hostility decreases communication and in turn decreased communication enhances autistic hostility. If we can only increase the flow of information, we are told, we can solve these problems. This assumption is found in our doctrine of universal education. It is fundamental in most campaigns of public relations and public enlightenment. Our democratic institutions, with their concern for freedom of speech and assembly, their rejection of censorship, and their acceptance of the principle of equal time for the arguments of opposing political parties, have extended the notion of competition in the market place to a free market for ideas. Truth will prevail if there is ready access to all the relevant information.

The glorification of a full and free information flow is a healthy step forward in intraorganizational problems as well as in the relations of an organization to the larger social system. It is, however, a gross oversimplification. Communication may reveal problems as well as eliminate them. A conflict in values, for example, may go unnoticed until communication is attempted. Communication may also have the effect, intended or unintended, of obscuring and confusing existing problems. The vogue enjoyed by the word *image* in recent years reflects in part an unattractive preoccupation with communication as a means of changing the perception of things without the expense and inconvenience of changing the things themselves. The television commercials, with their incessant and spurious assertion of new products and properties, are the worst of numberless examples. In short, the advocacy of communication needs to be qualified with respect to the kind of information relevant to the solution of given problems and with respect to the nature of the communication process between individuals, between groups, and between subsystems.

Communication needs to be seen not as a process occurring between any sender of messages and any potential recipient, but in relation to the social system in which it occurs and the particular function it performs in that system. General principles of communication as a social-psychological process are fine; they set the limits within which we must operate. But they need to be supplemented by an analysis of the social system, so that they can be applied correctly to given situations.

The discovery of the crucial role of communication led to an enthusiastic advocacy of increased information as the solution to many organizational problems. More and better communication (especially, more) was the slogan. Information to rank-and-file employees about company goals and policies was the doctrine; the means too often were stylized programs and house organs homogenized by the Flesch formula for basic English. Communication up the line to give top echelons a more accurate picture of the lower levels was a complementary emphasis.

Social Systems as Restricted Communication Networks

Though there were and are good outcomes of this simplistic approach, there are also weak, negligible, and negative outcomes. The blanket emphasis upon more communication fails to take into account the functioning of an organization as a social system and the specific needs of the subsystems.

In the first place, as Thelen (1960) points out, an organized state of affairs, a social system, implies the restriction of communication among its members. If we take an unorganized group, say 60 people milling around at random in a large room, the number of potential channels of communication is $n(n-1)/2$ or 1770. If, however, they are organized into a network of twelve combinations of five such that each person on a five-man team has one clearly defined role and is interdependent with four other people, the number of channels within the work group is reduced to *ten* in a completely interdependent condition or to *four* in a serial dependent position.

Without going into such complexities as task-relevant communication, the major point is clear. To move from an unorganized state to an organized state requires the introduction of constraints and restrictions to reduce diffuse and random communication to channels appropriate for the accomplishment of organizational objectives. It may require also the introduction of incentives to use those channels and use them appropriately, rather than leave them silent or use them for organizationally irrelevant purposes. Organizational development sometimes demands the creation of new communication channels. The very nature of a social system, however, implies a selectivity of channels and communicative acts—a mandate to avoid some and to utilize others.

In terms of information theory, unrestricted communication produces noise in the system. Without patterning, without pauses, without precision, there is sound but there is no music. Without structure, without spacing, without specifications, there is a Babel of tongues but there is no meaning.

The same basic problem of selectivity in communications can be considered in terms of Ashby's (1952) conceptual model. Thelen summarizes the Ashby contribution in these terms.[1]

> *Any living system* is an infinitely complex association of subsystems. The complex suprasystem has all the properties of a subsystem plus communication across the boundaries of subsystems. Ashby's brilliant treatment (1952) shows that stability of the suprasystem would take infinitely long to achieve *if* there were "full and rich communication" among the subsystems (because in effect all the variables of all the subsystems would have to be satisfied at once—a most unlikely event). If communication among the subsystems is restricted or if they are temporarily isolated, then each subsystem achieves its own stability with minimum interference by the changing environment of other systems seeking *their* stability. With restricted communication, success can accumulate (from successive trials, for example), whereas in the single suprasystem, success is all-or-none. . . . Thus the way an overall system moves toward its equilibrium depends very much on the functional connectedness of its parts. Adaptation of the whole system makes use of two conditions: enough connectedness that operation of one subsystem can activate another so that the contributions of all can contribute to the whole; and enough separation of subsystems that some specialization of function is possible and such that "equilibrium" can be approached in the system as a whole. But no complex suprasystem would ever have equilibrium in all its subsystems at the same time. Each subsystem has the "power of veto" over equilibria in other subsystems, and under a variety of conditions one subsystem can dominate another.

Our loosely organized political system reflects the system requirements of restriction of full and free communication. Chaos in national decision-making is avoided by the device of the two-party system. Instead of representing in clear fashion in Congress all the factional groups and subsystems within the nation, we go through a quadrennial process of successive agreements within the major parties, culminating in the nomination of a presidential candidate by each of them. This is in effect a restriction and channeling of the communication process. Once candidates are selected, the factional groups within each party tend to unite behind one ticket, and the amount of communication to the candidates is restricted. The rank-and-file voter neither communicates up the line nor receives much in the way of communication down the line except for the projected image of the candidate and the general image of the party.

In fact, the average voter is woefully ignorant of the stand of his party on most political issues. On sixteen major issues of the 1956 presidential election, the proportion of people who had an opinion, knew what

[1] Mimeographed paper, 1960.

the government was doing, and saw some differences between the parties never exceeded 36 per cent and for some issues was as low as 18 per cent (Campbell, Converse, Miller, and Stokes, 1960). This is one price we pay for the organizational restrictions of a two-party system and the communication distance between the voters and political leaders. Nevertheless, the two-party system has the advantage of overall political stability and facilitation of national decision-making. If all interested groups and ideological factions had their own parties and their own representatives in Congress, we would have more complete communication between the people and their elected leaders but we would have terrific problems of attaining system stability. We would have many possibilities of veto by coalition of minority groups, of legislative stalemates, and of national indecision. Some European countries with multiple-party systems, with more communication, and perhaps better-informed electorates have had such problems.

The Coding Process

Individuals, groups, and organizations share a general characteristic which must be recognized as a major determinant of communication: the coding process. Any system which is the recipient of information, whether it be an individual or an organization, has a characteristic coding process, a limited set of coding categories to which it assimilates the information received. The nature of the system imposes omission, selection, refinement, elaboration, distortion, and transformation upon the incoming communications. Just as the human eye selects and transforms light waves to which it is attuned to give perceptions of color and objects, so too does any system convert stimulation according to its own properties. It has been demonstrated that human beings bring with them into most situations sets of categories for judging the facts before them. Walter Lippmann (1922) called attention to the coding process years ago in the following famous passages. Even then he was merely putting into dramatic form what had been recognized by the ancient philosophers.

> For the most part we do not first see, and then define, we define first and then see. In the great blooming, buzzing confusion of the outer world, we pick out what our culture has already defined for us, and we tend to perceive that which we have picked out in the form stereotyped for us by our culture. (p. 31)
> What matters is the character of the stereotypes and the gullibility with which we employ them. And these in the end depend upon those inclusive patterns which constitute our philosophy of life. If in that philosophy we assume that the world is codified according to a code we possess, we are likely to make our reports of what is going on describe a world run by our code. (p. 90)

Most of us would deal with affairs through a rather haphazard and shifting assortment of stereotypes, if a comparatively few men in each generation were not constantly engaged in arranging, standardizing, and improving them into logical systems, known as the Laws of Political Economy, the Principles of Politics, and the like. (pp. 104–105)

Organizations, too, have their own coding systems which determine the amount and type of information they receive from the external world and the transformation of it according to their own systemic properties. The most general limitation is that the position people occupy in organizational space will determine their perception and interpretation of incoming information and their search for additional information. In other words, the structure and functions of a given subsystem will be reflected in the frame of reference and way of thinking of the role incumbents of that sector of organizational space. The different functions and dynamics of the production structure, the maintenance system, and the adaptive system . . . imply that each of these subsystems will respond to the same intelligence input in different ways and that each will seek out particular information to meet its needs.

All members of an organization are affected by the fact that they occupy a common organizational space in contrast to those who are not members. By passing the boundary and becoming a functioning member of the organization, the person takes on some of the coding system of the organization since he accepts some of its norms and values, absorbs some of its subculture, and develops shared expectations and values with other members. The boundary condition is thus responsible for the dilemma that the person within the system cannot perceive things and communicate about them in the same way that an outsider would. If a person is within a system, he sees its operations differently than if he were on the outside looking in. It is extremely difficult to occupy different positions in social space without a resulting differential perception. Where boundary conditions are fluid and organizational members are very loosely confined within the system (as with people sent abroad to live among foreign nationals for some governmental agency) there will be limited tours of duty, alternation between foreign and domestic service, and careful debriefing sessions to insure that life outside the physical boundaries of the country has not imparted too much of the point of view of the outsider.

The Problem of Translation across Subsystem Boundaries

Within an organization there are problems of clear communication across subsystems. The messages emanating in one part of the organization need translation if they are to be fully effective in other parts. In an earlier

Conceptual Frames

chapter, reference was made to Parsons' (1960) specific application of this principle to the chain of command. Instead of a unitary chain from the top to the bottom of an organization, Parsons pointed out that there are significant breaks between the institutional and managerial levels and again between the managerial and technical levels. Communications, then, must be transmitted in general enough terms to permit modification within each of these levels. The same type of translation problem occurs between any pair of substructures having their own functions and their own coding schema. Without adequate translation across subsystem boundaries, communications can add to the noise in the system.

Information Overload

Causes of Overload

To view social systems as restricted networks of communication, and as networks which treat communication very selectively even in accepted channels, implies the possibility of information overload—of communication input greater than the organization or certain of its components can handle. In Chapter 7 we called attention to the need for coordination of the many specialized activities in a complex organization, and to the consequent combining of numerous subsystem roles in single offices. The person holding such an office, as a member of multiple subsystems, receives information input from all of them. Incumbents of roles at major intersecting cycles of organizations are often so deluged by the requests reaching them that they respond only to two types of messages—telegrams and long-distance telephone calls. Programmed handling of some types of input with little intervention on the part of the officer reduces his overload so long as the programmed solutions are not outmoded by environmental changes and new inputs of information.

In physical networks the limitations of the communication system with respect to overloading and underloading are readily recognized by the concept of channel capacity. Social systems also exist in a space-time manifold and are also subject to limitations of their communication capacity. The coordination of many cycles of interrelated behavior is necessarily geared to a time schedule. Any given act must be stipulated not only with respect to its adjacencies to other acts in space, but also with respect to its duration and its precedence, simultaneity, or succession to other acts. Temporal planning in the interests of efficiency allows little or no free time in the organization for handling unanticipated information. The receipt, assessment, and transformation of information is geared into the productive process and follows a corresponding time schedule. Even if some decision makers are freed from direct production responsibilities, they still must make their decisions within a limited time period.

Coordination of activity according to a time schedule, however, encounters the difficulty that social organizations do not exist in a constant social environment. Their potential sources of supply may diminish and require additional search or may change in character and require additional selective processes. The markets for their products may grow or decline. To maintain the same proportion of the market may require increased effort. The organizational structure, however, is geared to certain assumed constancies of production input, throughput, and output. Fluctuations overload the system at some point. Decreased input and volume of work, it is true, will create conditions of underload for some units in the organization. For the upper echelons, however, the decline in inputs means more information-seeking both within and without the organization. New inputs have to be found or cuts have to be made in the organizational structure.

Change is not limited to the production system and its adjuncts of procurement and disposal. The maintenance inputs of people to man the organization and to assume its many roles are necessary to keep the system viable. Here again inputs are not a constant. The labor market fluctuates and personnel attrition takes place at differential rates. Moreover, the values and requirements of personnel change with changes in the culture and subcultures in which they live. Any departure from an assumed normal level of operation creates problems of overload for certain echelons within the system. A threatened strike may mean that more demands are made on the production manager and his lieutenants so that they must attend both to production and maintenance problems. An actual strike may give this same group a holiday but may overload top management with other problems.

In summary, since organizational activity must be geared to certain constancies in a time schedule, changed inputs create a condition of overload in one or more of the organizational subsystems.

Inconstancies in the environment of organizations are basically manmade and are largely a consequence of our organized search for knowledge and our technological exploitation of this knowledge. We have developed sources of new input which provide a constantly changing environment for social systems. In Miller's terms (1960), information input overload is a product of the technology and science of our times. Every year over 1,200,000 articles appear in 60,000 books and 100,000 research reports. Scientific and technical publications have doubled in size in the United States approximately every twenty years since 1800.

Miller's Analysis of
Reactions to Overload

The responses to information input overload have been classified by Miller (1960) into the following seven categories: (1) omission, failing to process some of the information; (2) error, processing information incorrectly; (3) queuing, delaying during periods of peak load in the hope of catching up during lulls; (4) filtering, neglecting to process certain types of information, according to some scheme of priorities; (5) approximation, or cutting categories of discrimination (a blanket and nonprecise way of responding); (6) employing multiple channels, using parallel channels, as in decentralization; and (7) escaping from the task.

The Miller classification of responses to overload is useful but it treats all seven types of responses as mechanisms of adjustment. In applying this classification to social organizations, however, there are definite advantages in distinguishing between adaptive and maladaptive mechanisms for the functioning of the system. The use of one or more of these types of response will have consequences for organizational functioning and may result in changes in function and structure.

In differentiating between adaptive and maladaptive ways of responding we shall follow the distinction, commonly employed in individual psychology, between coping and defensive mechanisms. Coping or adaptive mechanisms are concerned with solving the problems which the individual encounters. Defensive mechanisms protect the individual from breakdown but do not solve the problem. Denial, for example, is the defense mechanism by which the individual closes his eyes to the objective facts but in so doing protects himself from intolerable anxiety. In similar fashion, the failure to process information may keep a social system from total breakdown, but it is still not the optimal way to handle the problem of overload. Keeping the system functioning even at a low level of efficiency may be considered an adjustive outcome, as Miller does, but there is still the need to examine both the dysfunctional and the coping aspects of the process. Even a "successful" coping response can be evaluated in terms of the duration of the solution, the amount of organizational space to which the solution applies, and the cost to the organization of arriving at and implementing the solution. The shorter the duration, the more limited the area of application, and the greater the cost to the organization, the more dysfunctional do we consider the response.

Both omission and error are dysfunctional types of response to overload. Omission by definition denies information to the organization, and it characteristically does so on an irrational basis. Specifically, omission or failure to process information tends to be selective in terms of the ease with which input can be assimilated, rather than in terms of its importance for the organization. Failure to process critical inputs can magnify the problems with which the organization is sooner or later forced to deal. The grievance case which is not processed because of its ambiguities may be taken to court, and the precedent established there may permit thousands of workers to file suit. Such an actual instance in a large railroad company cost the company millions of dollars because of the failure to process the difficult case early in the game.

Error is also maladaptive by definition, and more or less costly to the organization. The cost often may be minimal, but devices are necessary to check against errors of potential seriousness. One common source of serious error in processing information is the tendency to reverse the meaning of the message. Under certain circumstances, it is easy to omit the *not* in a communication or to add it when it should not be there, and so change the meaning completely. One mechanism in thought association is constrast; we group together concepts at either end of a continuum, like sink or swim, failure or success. This conceptual affinity of opposites results in disastrous errors of the reversal type.

Queuing or delaying the processing of information can be either dysfunctional or adaptive. If the queuing is invoked merely to serve the ease of operation of the individual receiver, it is likely to be dysfunctional. But if it is utilized under circumstances of real overload and with equally realistic anticipation of a future lull, it can be adaptive.

Similarly, filtering or the selective receiving of information can be adaptive if it is set by priorities assigned by the organization and based upon an assessment of organizational needs. But without thoughtfully established guidelines, filtering is likely to be maladaptive. People are likely to process the familiar elements in a message, which they readily understand and which do not constitute major problems for them. Under time pressures the parts of the communication difficult to decode are neglected for the more easily assimilated parts, even though the former may be more critical for the organization. In general, approximation or cutting of categories under conditions of overload would be dysfunctional. There are situations, however, in which the exchange of quality for quantity is justifiable and realistic. Escape from the task is by definition dysfunctional.

Finally, the use of multiple channels is in many instances highly adaptive in terms of organizational efficiency and effectiveness. Its inclusion in Miller's list suggests that he is in fact using two different criteria in talking about response to overload. On the one hand, he is referring to the inability of a given system with given capacities to handle overload (as when a nerve fibre cannot respond to continuous input in excess of its frequency rate, i.e., during its refractory period), and on the other hand, he is including system mechanisms which have been developed for handling overload and now are system structures in themselves.

Decentralization, which Miller cites as an example of multiple channels, is not so much the spontaneous dividing up of messages among parallel channels at times of overflow as it is the deliberate restructuring of an organization to handle overload. In the same manner, queuing and filtering can become institutionalized as devices for handling overload. In chain department stores, the priority drilled into clerks is to take the customers' money and make change first, and then meet other demands of the task. To the extent that these institutionalized devices handle the problem, we no longer should speak of information overload save as a causal condition of changes in organizational structures.

A very different approach to problems of overload is to reverse the usual stance of seeking new mechanisms for handling overload and to seek instead ways of reducing the input. This is, of course, extremely difficult with respect to the external environment. Most organizations cannot control the environmental demands which are made upon them, except by eliminating some function of their own. To take an obvious but unlikely example, an automobile dealer might solve his agency's traffic and parking problems by eliminating certain of its repair and service functions, but this would be an expensive and risk-laden approach to the problem of overload. *Within* organizations, however, the planned reduction of input is a more promising possibility.

Part of the overload within organizations is created by the various subsystems and the various hierarchical levels inundating one another with information. The premise, as already noted, is the more communication between levels and units the better. What is often needed, however, is a method for cutting down on the output of information and of restricting its flow. Some organizations restrict interoffice memoranda to a single page. The accessibility of all members of the organization to messages at any time during the working day is a technological triumph which has its drawbacks. Research, writing, the pondering of executive decisions, and other phases of creative work require uninterrupted blocks of time. The organization needs to put as much effort into protecting these activities from interruption as it does in facilitating communication where it is functionally required.

Though external demands usually cannot be curtailed at their source, organizations can be more protective of the many roles which their members assume within the interlocking structures of our bureaucratic society. Since universities are now concerned with research as well as teaching, with community and national service as well as maintaining ties with alumni, staff members of universities are subject to an increasing variety of demands as they take on new roles. The same process occurs in other growing organizations.

In his study of a university library, Meier (1961) analyzed the changes which occurred as a result of the increasing demand for books. He noted, among other processes: (1) the setting of priorities, such as giving precedence to the request of a faculty member over that of an undergraduate; (2) destruction of lowest priorities as the queue builds in size (wastebasket policy for communications), the library no longer attempting to preserve everything printed; (3) establishing active files, first the reserve desk and then the closed reserve; (4) creating branch facilities or decentralization; (5) encouraging middlemen or utilizing extraorganizational channels such as publicizing availability of paperback editions in nearby bookstores; (6) creating a mobile personnel reserve, i.e., training people in a variety of skills so that they can be shifted about as the pressures demand; and (7) reducing standards of performance to give legitimacy to actual lowering of performance and thus maintaining morale. Meier (1961) generalizes further about the organizational effects of overload as follows:

> The structural effects of being tested up to or even beyond the long run capacity for completing transactions can be expressed in various forms. *Spatially,* the institution becomes decentralized, functionally differentiated in its various branches and *outliers,* develops a complex boundary for the receipt of messages, and evolves a strong headquarters unit. *Economically,* it accumulates deferred maintenance and generally transforms capital assets into a network of interdependencies with individuals and other institutions whose resources can be drawn upon in an emergency. *Status* within the institution depends much more upon functional effectiveness than upon official rank. As a *decision system* it is more complex and adaptive, having developed many alternative sets of rules during the test which can be reapplied as soon as the need arises. The *value* structure is permanently changed because operating at capacity has revealed the importance of conserving resources which were not otherwise scarce. Considered as a *network* of positions and relations, the institution develops a greater variety of relations, adds more positions, and greatly increases the centrality of some positions. Overload causes the destruction of relations more rapidly than they can be rebuilt through experience and instruction (internal communications). (pp. 55–56)

Direction of Communication Flow and Characteristics of Communication Circuits

We shall discuss communication processes within organizations both with respect to the direction of the flow of information (who communicates to whom) and with respect to the structure of the communication network and the content of the messages carried (how and what is being communicated). The direction of the information flow can follow the authority pattern of the hierarchical positions (*downward communication*); can move among peers at the same organizational level (*horizontal communication*); or can ascend the hierarchical ladder (*upward communication*).

The major characteristics of communication networks which we shall consider are (1) the size of the loop, the amount of organizational

Conceptual Frames

space covered by given types of information, (2) the nature of the circuit, whether a simple repetitive pattern or a chain modification type, (3) the open or closed character of the circuit, (4) the efficiency of the circuit for its task, and (5) the fit between the circuit and the systemic function it serves.

1. *Size of loop.* Communication circuits may embrace the entire system, may be restricted to a major subsystem, or may involve only a small unit within a subsystem. Some communication loops may be confined to officer personnel or even to top level echelons. A common organizational problem is the discrepancy between the size of given information loops as perceived by the ranking authorities and the size of the circuit which actually is found. Leaders characteristically overestimate the number of persons reached by their intended communications. Also, the larger the loop, the greater will be the problems of communication, particularly where the penetration of subsystem boundaries is involved.

2. *Repetition versus modification in the circuit.* A large information loop may reach many members of the system through a repetitive pattern of transmitters. For example, a directive may go down the line and be echoed at each level to the one below it. A different pattern of transmission is often used whereby a chain of command will pass along messages with appropriate translation at each level in the system. The same amount of organizational space is involved in both patterns, so that the size of the loop is the same, but the second pattern calls for some modification of the message. The first pattern has the advantages of simplicity and uniformity. Everyone is exposed to identical information. What is announced publicly topside is the same as what people hear from their own superior. Nonetheless, the simplicity of this system may be advantageous only for simple problems. For complex matters a directive repeated in uniform fashion is not necessarily uniform in its meaning across subsystems. It may need translation in different units to be effective.

3. *Feedback or closure character.* Though the flow of a communication pattern may have a dominant organizational direction (down the line, for example) there is a circular character to communicative acts. There is a reaction to the transmission which can furnish feedback to the transmitter, though it may only be the acknowledgement of the receipt of the message.

Closure of a set of communicative acts can vary from immediate fixed response of acknowledgement and acceptance of the initial message to reports of its inadequacy and attempts to alter its character. In the latter case, though the communication cycle has been completed through feedback about the faulty character of the original communication, the communication process is immediately reactivated. In a larger sense, closure has not been achieved for the organization by the first set of communicative acts. Thus, while almost all processes of communication are cyclical, with a return to the original transmitter, we can characterize some communication circuits as having more of a closed character for systemic functioning than others.

A closed communication loop would be one in which the cycle of transmission acts is not open to change once it has been initiated. In other words, no new information and no radical modifications in the process are provided for by the structural procedures. If the communication process is one of issuing directives and responding to the signal of mission accomplished, we have a closed circuit. The directive cannot be substantially modified. Rigid codes block out sources of information either by definition or practice. There is just no provision for admitting new information at various points in the transmission chain.

4. *The efficiency of communication nets.* A related but somewhat different aspect of communication systems is the efficiency, which can be measured in terms of the number of communication links in a given network. In the beginning of our discussion of communication we pointed out that restriction in the communication process was part of the essential nature of social organizations. Experimental work has generally supported the hypothesis that the smaller the number of communication links in a group, the greater the efficiency of the group in task performance (Dubin, 1959). There are more links, for example, in the all-channel pattern than in the circle pattern, and more links in the circle than in the wheel pattern (see Figure 1).

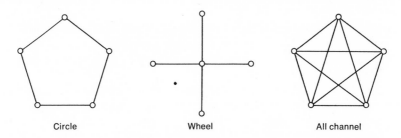

Circle   Wheel   All channel

Figure 1. Types of communication network

Using a sentence construction task, Heise and Miller (1951) found that a two-link system was more efficient than various three-link systems, as measured by the number of words spoken and the time taken to complete the task.

In an extension of Leavitt's earlier work (1951), Guetzkow and Simon (1955) used five-man groups in which the task was to discover which one of six symbols was held in common by all group members. The subjects were seated around a circular table, separated by five vertical partitions. They did not talk to one another, but communicated by passing messages through interconnecting slots. Each person was given a card with five symbols. The missing symbol was different for each subject. The experimenters employed three different networks of communication to which 56 groups were randomly assigned. In the circle net (see Figure 1) subjects could pass their messages to either or both of two neighbors. In the wheel net there is a key man to whom all four colleagues can communicate. In the all-channel pattern everyone can communicate with everyone else. Since messages must flow to some decision center for action and must flow back to the senders to inform them of the decision, the wheel provides a two-level hierarchy and the circle and all-channel nets a three-level hierarchy. In the circle, for example, two neighbors can send information to their opposite neighbors, who in turn relay this information with their own to the fifth member. He can then send the solution back to his group, but three levels are involved in the process.

Leavitt (1951) had found the two-level hierarchy of the wheel to be the most efficient for task accomplishment. Guetzkow and Simon, however, reasoned that this superiority might well be due to the time it took a group to discover and use the optimal organizational pattern for its specific type of net, rather than to the patterns of the networks themselves. For example, a group assigned to the circle might spend considerable time in a more complex interaction than the optimal pattern described above. Hence the experimenters provided a two-minute period between task trials for the groups to discover the best organizational pattern for their situation by allowing them to write messages to each other. The results confirmed the prediction of the experimenters. When groups in the all-channel or circle nets discovered the optimal organizational pattern, they were just as efficient as the wheel groups.

The advantages, then, for the system employing fewer links was not in the efficiency of the simpler network per se, but in the fact that it required little trial and error by the group to use it effectively. Moreover, since the networks with more links allow the possibility for insufficient usage, there is some advantage to ruling out this possibility by means of more restrictive patterns.

These experiments were concerned with task-oriented communications and should not be generalized to socio-emotional or supportive types of communication. In subsequent experiments Guetzkow and Dill (1957) found that groups seemed to prefer a minimum linkage system. Seventeen out of twenty groups which had started with a pattern permitting ten links had, by the end of twenty trials, cut this to four links. Pressures were generated within the groups themselves to move toward the simpler communication networks. The groups that did not follow this pattern, moreover, were less efficient in task accomplishment.

5. *The fit between the communication circuit and systemic functioning.* A circuit may be too large, involving irrelevant people, or too small, omitting key informants. One factor in information overload is the creation of many large communication loops so that people receive frequent messages which have little if anything to do with carrying out their organizational roles. Role incumbents are called upon to decide what is functional and what is nonfunctional in the information they receive. Though they may make wise decisions, the time of decision-making is taken from their own basic tasks.

A common dysfunctional arrangement in organizations is to have communication loops of disproportionate sizes with respect to message-sending and message-receiving. Top echelons issue directives for the whole organization, yet achieve closure from the acquiescence of their immediate subordinates. In other words, the loop involves all levels of the organization on the sending side but only the top two echelons on the receiving side.

Another lack of fit between the communication circuit and the functional needs of the system occurs when closed circuits are used for purposes other than the carrying out of directives in an emergency setting. With complex problems, where time is not highly critical, a communication loop which permits the introduction of new information at various points in the circuit can be highly adaptive. Yet the logic of the closed circuit is carried over into the inappropriate areas of information search. The questions for which information is sought are so formulated by some executives that they predetermine the answers to be supplied. The communication process returns upon itself. For example, a department head concerned about a recent productivity decline calls in his division heads; he wants the problem explored, but it has been his experience, he informs them, that the lax practices of certain types of supervisors are the key factor in this sort of situation. His division heads report back after their exploration that he was indeed right, and they have taken the necessary steps to handle the problem. An open search for the causes of the productivity decline might have furnished a different answer.

Communication down the Line

Communications from superior to subordinate are basically of five types:

1. Specific task directives: *job instructions.*
2. Information designed to produce understanding of the task and its relation to other organizational tasks: *job rationale.*
3. Information about organizational *procedures and practices.*
4. *Feedback* to the subordinate about his performance.

5. Information of an ideological character to inculcate a sense of mission: *indoctrination of goals*.

The first type of communication is generally given priority in industrial and military organizations and in hospitals. Instructions about the job are worked out with a great deal of specificity and are communicated to the role incumbent through direct orders from his superior, training sessions, training manuals, and written directives. The objective is to insure the reliable performance of every role incumbent in every position in the organization.

Less attention is given to the second type of information, designed to provide the worker with a full understanding of his job and of how it is geared to related jobs in the same subsystem. Many·employees know what they·are to do, but not why they are doing it, nor how the patterned activities in which they are involved accomplish a given objective. "Theirs not to reason why" is often the implicit, if not explicit, assumption of managerial philosophy. It is often assumed that an emphasis upon information about full job understanding will conflict with strict allegiance to specific task instructions. If the worker thinks he knows why he is to do a certain thing, he may attempt to do it in other than the specified fashion and the organizational leaders may not want to tolerate the variability of behavior this introduces into the system.

Information about organizational procedures completes the description of the role requirements of the organizational member. In addition to instructions about his job, he is also informed about his other obligations and privileges as a member of the system, e.g., about vacations, sick leave, rewards, and sanctions.

Feedback to the individual about how well he is doing in his job is often neglected or poorly handled, even in organizations in which the managerial philosophy calls for such evaluation. Where emphasis is placed upon compliance to specific task directives, it is logical to expect that such compliance will be recognized and deviation penalized. This is necessary to insure that the system is working, and it is a matter of some motivational importance for the individual performer. The frequent complaint, however, by the individual is that he does not know where he stands with his superiors. Often an employee is identified as a major problem for an organization so late in the game that his poor performance or weak citizenship seems beyond remedy ... even transfer or discharge is difficult. There is belated recognition that there should have been an earlier review with him of his performance. Yet systematic procedures for rating and review of the work of employees by their superiors have not proved a panacea.

The reasons are not hard to find. The whole process of critical review is resented both by subordinate and superior as partaking of surveillance. The democratic values of the culture have permeated organizational members so that the superior sees himself as a leader of men, and not as a spy and disciplinarian. The subordinate, in wanting to know how well he is doing, really wants to have his merits recognized and to know how to develop his own talents more fully.

Another major reason for the unpopularity of supervisory appraisal is that many employees have little individual discretion in task accomplishment and little opportunity to excel. Both the company norms and the informal standards of the group set a uniform rate of accomplishment. The performance of workers is often so system-determined that there is little to be gained from evaluating workers as autonomous individuals. The occasional deviant does constitute a problem for the organization, particularly when his deviance is not formally recognized until it is too late. Nevertheless, such slips are probably less costly to the organization than a thorough surveillance system in which the individual does get early and systematic feedback on his performance.

The fifth type of downward-directed information has as its objective the inculcation of organizational goals, either for the total system or a major subsystem. An important function of an organizational leader is to conceptualize the mission of his enterprise in an attractive and novel form. This can be done with particular effectiveness in organizations which are conspicuous for their contribution to societal welfare or for the hazardous character of their activities. For example, a police commissioner may describe the role of his police force as the work of professional officers engaged in a constructive program of community improvement.

Though organizational leaders are quick to recognize the importance of involving their followers in system goals, they are slow to utilize the most natural devices available to them in the form of job rationale. The second type of information in our listing, the understanding of one's role and how it relates to other roles, is a good bridge to involvement in organizational goals. If the psychiatric nurse in a hospital knows why she is to follow certain procedures with a patient and how this relates to the total therapy program for him, it is much easier for her to develop an ideological commitment to the hospital. This is one reason why some hospitals have developed the concept of the therapy team, which permits the doctor, nurse, and attendant to discuss the treatment program for given patients. On the other hand, if the role incumbent receives information about job specifics without job understanding, it is difficult for him to see how his role is related to the organizational objective and hence difficult for him to identify with the organizational mission.

Withholding information on the rationale of the job not only is prejudicial to ideological commitment of the member, but it also means that the organization must bear down heavily on the first type of informaton—specific instructions about the job. If a man does not understand fully why he should do a thing or how his job relates to the tasks of his fellow workers, then there must be sufficient redundancy in his task instructions so that he behaves automatically and reliably in role performance. This type of problem was dramatically illustrated in the conflict about the information to be given to astronauts about their task in orbit. Some officials were in favor of reducing the astronaut's behavior to that of a robot; others wanted to utilize his intelligence by having him act on his understanding of the total situation. The result was a compromise.

The advantages of giving fuller information on job understanding are thus twofold: if a man knows the reasons for his assignment, this will often insure his carrying out the job more effectively; and if he has an understanding of what his job is about in relation to his subsystem, he is more likely to identify with organizational goals.

Size of the loop and downward communication. The size of the communication loop is an interesting variable in processing information down the line, and has implications for organizational morale and effectiveness. In general the rank-and-file member gets his task instructions from those immediately above him. The loop covers very little of the organizational structure. Upper echelons neither know what the specific task directives are, nor would acquiring such knowledge be an appropriate way for them to spend time and energy. In industry the methods department may have worked out the standard procedures for a job, but these are transmitted to the employee by his immediate boss. On the other hand, communications about the goals of the organization in theory cover a loop as large as the organization itself. The rank-and-file member, however, may in practice be minimally touched by this loop. His degree of effective inclusion within it depends primarily upon how he is tied into the organization. If he is tied in on the basis of being paid for a routine performance, information about the goals and policies of the larger structure will be of no interest to him.

The size of the loop is also important in terms of the understanding of the message. Communications from the top addressed to all organizational members are often too general in character and too remote from the limited daily experiences of the individual to convey their intended meaning. To be effective, messages about organizational policy need to be translated at critical levels as they move down the line, i.e., translated into the specific meanings they have for given sectors of the structure. Katz and Lazarsfeld (1955) demonstrated a two-step process in the flow of communication in a community in which opinion leaders affected by the mass media in turn influenced the rank and file. Within organizations, however, not enough attention has been given to this problem of translation. Communications down the line must be converted to the coding systems of the substructures if they are to register and have impact.

A partial substitute for translation is the ability of some organizational leaders to develop confidence and liking for themselves as personalities among the rank and file. Their position on a policy issue will be accepted not because it is understood, but because people trust them and love them. This is more characteristic of political leadership than leadership in nonpolitical organizations.

The translation problem is related to the fit between the communication cycle and the functional requirements of the organization. The information loop about how a job is to be done should have the immediate supervisor as the key communicant. This does not necessarily mean that a worker should get all his job directives from a single boss, but it does mean that additional bosses should be introduced only if they have an expertness about a clearly demarcated function. The research worker, in addition to listening to his project director, can also listen with profit to the sampling and statistical expert. Where the functional lines are fuzzy, the rule of a single boss has much to be said for it.

Transmitting information down the line may partake of a closed-circuit character if there is little opportunity for clarification of directives from above. Two things occur when directives remain limited and unclear because people down the line have no way of getting a fuller explanation. People will give minimal compliance so as to be apparently observing the letter of the law, or they will test out in actual behavior their own ideas of what can be done. If there is inadequate feedback up the line, this behavioral testing out can produce real deviations in organizational practice. Such deviations can run from constructive actions in support of organizational objectives to actions crippling and destructive to the organization.

Horizontal Communications

Organizations face one of their most difficult problems in procedures and practices concerned with lateral communication, i.e., communication between people at the same hierarchical level. The machine model would be highly restrictive of lateral communication. A role incumbent would receive almost all his instructions from the man above him, and would deal with his associates only for task coordination specified by rules. Though such a plan neglects the need for socio-emotional support among peers, it is still true that unrestricted communication of a horizontal character can detract from maximum efficiency. What are the conditions under which lateral communication is desirable?

We shall start with the proposition that some types of lateral communication are critical for effective system functioning. Many tasks cannot be so completely specified as to rule out coordination between peers in the work process. The teamwork by which a varsity team beats an alumni group of greater prowess has many parallels in other organizations. (In fact, there is something to be said for not mechanizing coordination devices for a group task unless the whole process can be mechanized.)

Communication among peers, in addition to providing task coordination, also furnishes emotional and social support to the individual. The mutual understanding of colleagues is one reason for the power of the peer group. Experimental findings are clear and convincing about the importance of socio-emotional support for people in both unorganized and organized groups. Psychological forces always push people toward communication with peers; people in the same boat share the same problems. *Hence, if there are no problems of task coordination left to a group of peers, the content of their communication can take forms which are irrelevant to or destructive of organizational functioning.* Informal student groups sometimes devote their team efforts to pranks and stunts or even to harassing the administration and faculty.

The size of the communication circuit and its appropriateness to the function of the subsystem are important considerations for horizontal communication. By and large the nature and extent of exchanges among people at the same level should be related to the objectives of the various subsystems in which they are involved, with primary focus on their own major task. Thus there are real disadvantages in lateral communication that cuts across functional lines and that nevertheless attempts to be highly specific. For example, if divisions with differentiated functions are part of a department, the communication between peers in different divisions should be on departmental problems and not on divisional matters. Peer communication on divisional matters can better be conducted within divisional boundaries.

Horizontal communication implies a closed circuit in that it satisfies people's needs to know from their own kind without taking into account other levels in the organization. In hierarchical structures it can mean that people overvalue peer communication with a neglect of those below them. Cabots talk only to Cabots, and vice-presidents only to vice-presidents. It is interesting to observe how often organizational leaders, when going outside their own structures for information, will seek their own status level, i.e., their counterparts in other organizations. Sometimes, however, the really critical information is at levels below them.

It is important to look at lateral communication in terms of the control function in organizations. Horizontal communication, if in operation at various levels in an organization, is a real check on the power of the top leaders. The more authoritarian and hierarchical the system, the more information is a secret property of select groups, and the more it can be utilized to control and punish people at lower levels. In such a system there is little horizontal communication across levels of equal rank. The department chief knows about his ten division heads and their respective divisions, but each one of them knows only about himself and his own division. Hence the department chief is in a powerful position to manipulate them as he will.

The simple paradigm of vertical funneling up the line with no horizontal flow of information is a fundamental basis of social control in most social systems. As systems move toward greater authoritarian structure, they exert more and more control over any flow of horizontal information. This is done by abolishing institutional forms of free communication among equals and by instilling suspicion of informers, so that people will be restricted in their communication even to friends. Without such communication there can be a great deal of unrest without organized revolt. People cannot organize cooperative efforts when they cannot communicate with one another.

Totalitarian regimes have shown ingenuity in their use of techniques to restrict and direct the flow of information. By blocking out the channels of horizontal communication and other sources of information, they have made their people dependent solely upon communication from above. This channeling works to strengthen the hierarchical structure, but in modern society it is impossible to maintain such tight control of the communication processes over time.

Communication Upward

Communication up the line takes many forms. It can be reduced, however, to what the person says (1) about himself, his performance, and his problems, (2) about others and their problems, (3) about organizational practices and policies, and (4) about what needs to be done and how it can be done. Thus the subordinate can report to his boss about what he has done, what those under him have done, what his peers have done, what he thinks needs to be done, his problems and the problems of his unit, and about matters of organizational practice and policy. He can seek clarification about general goals and specific directives. He may under certain circumstances bypass his own superior and report directly to a higher level. Or he can utilize the suggestion system of the company (an approved institutional method of bypassing). Grievance procedures represent another institutional pattern of getting problems referred to a higher level. In addition, systematic feedback and research may develop as formal processes in the system. They constitute such an important form of communication about organizational functioning that they will be considered in a separate section of this chapter.

The basic problem in upward communication is the nature of the hierarchical administrative structure. The first role requirement of people in executive and supervisory positions is to direct, coordinate, and control the people below them. They themselves are less in the habit of listening to their subordinates than in telling them. The subordinates also fall into this role pattern and expect to listen to their bosses rather than be listened to. Moreover, information fed up the line is often utilized for control purposes. Hence there are great constraints on free upward communication. The boss is not likely to be given information by his subordinates which will lead to decisions affecting them adversely. It is not only that they tell the boss what he wants to hear, but what they want him to know. People do want to get certain information up the line, but generally they are afraid of presenting it to the most relevant person or in the most objective form. Full and objective reporting might be penalized by the supervisor or regarded as espionage by peers. To these difficulties must be added the fact that full and objective reporting is difficult, regardless of the organizational situation; no individual is an objective observer of his own performance and problems.

For all these reasons the upward flow of communication in organizations is not noted for spontaneous and full expression, despite attempts to institutionalize the process of feedback up the line. Suggestions for improvement of work procedures and company practices are also limited in quantity and quality in most organizations. The more top-heavy the organizational structure and the more control is exercised through pressure and sanctions, the less adequate will be the flow of information up the line. It is not a matter of changing the communication habits of individuals, but of changing the organizational conditions responsible for them.

The typical upward communication loop is small and terminates with the immediate supervisor. He may transmit some of the information to his own superior, but generally in a modified form. The open-door policy of some high-level officers extends the theoretical size of the circuit to include all levels below them. It generally contributes more to the self-image of the officer as an understanding, democratic person, however, than to adequacy of information exchange. The closed nature of the upward circuits has already been indicated and resides both in restricted communication passed upward and in the limited codes of the recipients.

Obstacles to vertical communication occur in both industrial organizations and democratic structures. Labor unions, in which the membership possesses the formal power to elect officers and command referenda on basic issues, manifest striking gaps in understanding between top echelons and local leaders closer to the rank and file. In the fall of 1964 officials of the United Auto Workers concluded negotiations for a contract with General Motors and were ready to announce the outcome as a main accomplishment, only to have the pact rejected by their local unions. The top leaders were apparently not in effective communication with lower levels of leadership and the rank and file.

The Longshoremen's Union came to terms with shipping companies in January 1965 in a contract which the top union people regarded as favorable. It was promptly rejected by the membership. The officials responded with all sorts of measures to reach their men by way of the mass media and by a broadside of letters. In other words, the information channels between leaders and membership were closed over before and during the contract negotiations and the public demonstration of this phenomenon led to desperate efforts on the part of officials to restore communication. It is typical that the attempted solution was not only delayed, but took the form of communication *downward*.

Asymmetry of Communication Needs and Communication Flow

There are no studies of the distinctive types of communication which characteristically flow horizontally, upward, or downward in organizations, although such research is much needed. The information requirements of superior and subordinate are not symmetrical. What the superior wants to know is often not what the subordinate wants to tell him; what the subordinate wants to know is not necessarily the message the superior wants to send. The greater the conflict between the communication needs of these two hierarchically situated senders and recipients of information, the more likely is an increase in lateral communication. Among peers there will be greater complementarity of information needs. Where a foreman finds little reception from his superior, he will readily turn to fellow foremen to talk about his problems. Horizontal exchange can be an escape valve for frustration in communicating upward and downward; and sometimes it can operate to accomplish some of the essential business of the organization.

Another type of communication flow, thus far not considered, is criss-crossing, in which a subordinate in one unit talks to the boss of another unit or vice-versa. Again, this process is furthered by blockages in communication up and down the line. A department head perceived as a sympathetic person may be sought out by people in other departments as an audience for their problems because they feel they cannot talk to their own department head.

Information and Research Structures

Organizations cannot rely on communication processes which develop naturally both for internal coordination and feedback from the external world. Hence formal structures are devised to protect against the idiosyncratic perceptions and systematic biases of people in different subsystems, as well as to increase the total amount of relevant information. These structures make explicit the search process, the coding categories to be employed, and the procedures for processing and interpreting information according to these categories. Three types of informational procedures can be distinguished: (1) direct operational feedback, (2) operational research, and (3) systemic research. Operational feedback is basically a process of immediate routine control; systemic research, to use the distinctions employed by Rubenstein and Haberstroh (1960), is a process of delayed evaluation. Operational research is a mixture of these two processes.

Operational Feedback

Operational feedback is systematic information-getting which is closely tied to the ongoing functions of the organization and is sometimes an integral part of those functions. For example, the number of units turned out by any division of an organization and the number of units marketed are necessary items of record-keeping for everyday operations. . . . the regulatory mechanisms which distinguish organizations from primitive groups . . . are based upon built-in intelligence circuits which are parts of the operating mechanism itself or are close adjuncts to the mechanism. Information provided in this fashion can be readily systematized so that its reporting follows standard rules and includes detailed specifications about elements of time and quality. It is readily converted into terms of cost accounting and can be compared in many respects with similar figures of competing companies. In most organizations direct operational feedback is available for the performance of the total organization and for its major subsystems. It is frequently not informative about the performance of work groups or of individuals, and it does not deal with the effectiveness of social-psychological practices of the organization in carrying out its mission, e.g., the value of given types of leadership procedures, of morale-building practices, or of training programs.

The major function of operational feedback is to provide routine control over operations. It is thus similar to the negative feedback of the servo-mechanism which keeps the subsystem on course. This type of control information involves relatively short loops in the communication system. Information is generated by the operating unit involved and the backflow of information is directly to that unit. It follows that this type of operational feedback is a continuous rather than a delayed process. It is a form of routine control which permits decisions without lengthy consideration of a variety of inputs. The latter process involves a delayed evaluation (Rubenstein and Haberstroh, 1960).

Direct operational feedback is limited to reporting of current operations. It is not concerned with an assessment of trends in the external environment nor with a detailed analysis of the functioning of subsystems or the total system. It is less a search for new information than a utilization of existing operational records. For this utilization, little additional organizational structure is required beyond existing managerial, production, and maintenance structure. A small unit is sometimes attached to the managerial structure to study the company records in relation to the records of competitors, but for the most part we are dealing with information-processing that is built into the ongoing operations.

The major limitations of this type of intelligence have already been noted: its coding categories are restricted to existing practices, and hence can report how well they may be working but not the reasons for their success or failure. The impact of environmental change may be felt by the organization, but the nature of such change is not revealed by direct operational feedback. The basic determinants of organizational functioning are hardly touched by the knowledge such feedback supplies. Nevertheless, this is still the basic institutional form of information upon which many organizations rely. They will supplement it in various ways; i.e., through the insight, observations, and wisdom of men in leadership positions; through the use of consultants; or even through an occasional special investigation or research project.

Though these supplementary means of intelligence gathering may prove of great value in critical situations, they do not provide an organization with a reliable means for getting adequate information about its prospects for survival and effectiveness in a changing world. So long as the coding categories and information processing are confined to the regulatory mechanisms of ongoing operations, there is a closed circuit informational system—a circuit, moreover, whose circular enclosure covers a small area of the relevant universe.

Operational Research

Organizations in a changing world develop adaptive structures, and within these structures may be housed departments of research and development. The most common type of intelligence activity which takes on an institutionalized form is operational research. It actively institutes search for new information and it seeks explanations as well as descriptions, but its focus is upon two targets: the improvement of specific products, and the improvement of methods for turning them out. It is technologically oriented, and its achievements are depth, not breadth. Operational research examines various problems in the production system and supplies information on the basis of which efficiencies can be effected. It supplements the inadequate descriptive function of operational feedback and logically derives from this more central organizational process.

The great limitation of operational research is that it deals so sparingly with the problems of the managerial structure, the maintenance structure, and the institutional relations with the larger environment.

Since these structures are based upon human interaction rather than upon the technological transformation of materials, they are not seen as affecting productivity in a measurable way. When operational research ventures into the field of human relationships, it deals more with ecological patternings and with personnel measures than with the social structure of the organization. It is concerned with the improvement of technical operations and not with the relations of the organization to the external social world.

The coding categories of operational research provide a circuit of information which has no ready way of dealing with intelligence of a nontechnological type; for example, the causes of such events as workers threatening to strike, the legislature in the state increasing its taxes on local business, consumers boycotting a certain type of product, the production department at loggerheads with the sales department, or the personnel department having problems with the line production people about personnel procedures. In other words, the information loops of operational research, though larger than those of operational feedback, do not embrace the organization as it functions in its environment. Though there is more evaluation than in immediate routine control, the questions raised and the answers sought by such research are largely in terms of control.

Systemic Research

Organizations can and do extend their information resources by moving towards systemic research. Systemic research, like operational research, seeks new information, but its target is the functioning of the total system in relation to its changing environment. The objectives of systemic research include study of environmental trends, long-term organizational functioning, the nature of organizational structure, the interrelationship of the subsystems within the total system, and the impact of the organization on its environment. Where operational research concentrates upon improving technical aspects of production, systemic research explores the organizational changes which technical improvement would produce, including both the intended and the usually unanticipated consequences of the technical change. Operational research would be governed by the *satisficing* principle, to use the terminology of March and Simon (1958), whereas systemic research would be governed by an optimizing principle. This distinction refers to the difference between finding some minimally acceptable answer and seeking for an optimal answer.

Stated in these sweeping terms, systemic research seems Utopian in organizations with limited financial resources and with limited, fallible human beings to initiate and carry out such research. The concept, however, is critical and of great practical importance. In some organizations the thinking of top leaders is systemic; they utilize whatever intelligence is available about the present and future relationship of their system to its environment, and they initate research to guide them on central problems. For example, some oil companies with foreign holdings and foreign markets have economists and political experts on their staffs to study the development of the European common market, social forces in the developing African nations, and similar problems. The approach here is systemic even though the program of research to support it is tiny in relation to the firm's needs and resources. Another device of systemic research is the occasional study by a concern of its institutional relations with society, e.g., the corporate image held by various sectors of the public or the public response to corporate bigness. Sometimes the organization may ask its own research unit to ascertain how a training program for supervisors is affecting the whole organization.

Various compromises are attempted by organizational leaders to provide some degree of systemic intelligence without an adequate allocation of resources and manpower to this function. Research units are set up to bring together and analyze data already available from other sources, such as governmental agencies, other companies, and university institutes. Outside consultants are hired not only for expert opinion, but for their knowledge of what is happening in the research world. These compromises may be of considerable value in giving top leadership guidance in their decision-making. The greatest weakness in using them is the reliance upon data gathered in another context and sometimes for a different purpose. The specific determinants of the organization's own problems may be slighted, and the existing data may not dig deep enough into causes.

Disaster may lead to a specific investigation of a systemic type. After the collaboration of some American soldiers in the Korean War, the Army instituted an investigation, not only of the incidence of various kinds of behavior in captivity, but also of the causes of collaboration and the capacity to resist brainwashing. The President's code for captured soldiers was the outcome of this investigation, but the procedural lesson of the intelligence failure was not learned in that no steps were taken to provide the armed services with continuing research on the relation of its members to their mission.

Organizations will also attempt the compromise of using market research in place of more systematic investigation of the relationship of the organization to its environment. Though market research is concerned with consumer demand, which is an important aspect of system survival, its characteristic frame of reference comes from operational feedback. The search for new data will not go much beyond the sales figures of the organization. Additional surveys may pick up consumers' reactions to a form of packaging or the more obvious properties of the product. Thorough studies of the basic psychology of the consumer, with adequate samples, field experiments, and continuing panels, are the exception rather than the rule.

Motivation research had its brief period of popularity because it was supposedly a cheap short cut to people's motives as buyers and consumers. What was subsumed under motivational research, however, was essentially idea research in which a few individuals' reactions were interpreted according to various theories of personality. Motivational research helped copy writers who had run out of ideas, but it was not research in the scientific sense of the term. The Ford Motor Company lost heavily in attempting to produce and market a new model, the Edsel, in part because it was not willing to do genuine research on the marketing side and accepted the ersatz of motivational research. In summary, market research is much more of a control process than an evaluation process.

Systemic research then is limited by three factors. The first is the amount of resources available to an organization to carry on a continuing research operation concerned with systemic variables. The second factor is the conception of management held by the top leaders of an organization. If they do not think in system terms, or if they think in system terms only when confronted with disaster, then the coding of whatever systemic information is available will be fragmentary and inadequate. . . . The third factor which encourages or limits systemic research is the jolting of the organization as it pursues its course in the environment. A series of reverses in which successive *satisficing* moves have been only temporarily ameliorative may lead to a more *optimizing* search.

The Organizational Locus of Informational Subsystems

Informational processes can have their primary locus at any level in the organization or in any one of its substructures. Operational feedback is received first by the appropriate operating unit and then filtered up the line as overall summaries of operations at each level to the managerial level just above. Thus the head of each production unit knows the number of pieces turned out by his unit at the end of a given time period. The superintendent of production has summary figures for all the units reporting to him, and he again makes a summary for the echelons above him.

Since this kind of feedback is tied closely to actual operations, little distortion is possible over time, though some filtering may result in an oversimplified picture at top levels. The units with poor records may not be pinpointed in average figures covering all units. Interpretations of these figures may be supplied by the heads of units or divisions, but such interpretations tend to be coded by their transmitters as favorable to their own way of operating. If the forge shop is below expectations in productivity for any given month, the head of the forge shop will furnish reasons which do not suggest poor management on his part. He may assert that the materials were not up to par or absenteeism due to illness was great. But the major distortion is probably not the defensive explanation; it is the selective bias of each unit head, who will utilize as his basis of judgment the specific frame of reference of the operations in which he is daily involved.

Operational research is generally geared into some part of the production system. Its reports, however, can go beyond the production system to top management. Since the changes its information may suggest for organizational functioning require some degree of acceptance by the production structure, there is some advantage to tying operational research closely to the operations under investigation. A common procedure is to have the group conducting the operational research report to one level higher than the specific operation being researched. This helps to protect its results from being ignored.

Information, however, that has direct relevance for system functioning, as in all cases of systemic research, should be reported to top management. This is even true of market research, which is often placed very low in the sales structure. The locus of market research thus does not provide the organization with information about the success of its product. Rather, it supplies the sales department with ideas for promotional campaigns. What may be necessary for organizational success is an actual change in product. This cannot be achieved through a research unit serving the sales department, since the function of the sales department is to sell what is being produced, and not to tell the production people what to produce. The information of the market research unit follows the general principle of being coded by the sales department as sales information, and it fails to be coded with its proper implications for the production structure.

Another common failing is to assign to a given substructure whose primary function is noninformational the secondary mission of providing information about the relations of the organization with the external world. The primary task determines the types of information which will be received and its mode of processing. For example, the State Department has traditionally utilized its diplomatic personnel abroad to report on the political, economic, social, and psychological conditions of the foreign country. In their primary roles as diplomats, State Department personnel move in very limited circles; they meet primarily with their counterparts in the diplomatic corps of that nation. They are not necessarily expert in the subject about which information is sought; they seldom have training or knowledge of research procedures; and their major motivation is to carry out their function in the implementation of State Department policy. It is no wonder then that we have been consistently misinformed about the structures of foreign countries and the prevailing currents within them. Reliance upon the impressions of exclusively upper-class informants, refugees from disaffected elements, and émigrés from dispossessed groups has aggravated the problem. A reverse situation occurred in the Cuban fiasco in which the Central Intelligence Agency, supposedly an information structure, became absorbed in overthrowing the Castro regime rather than in obtaining accurate information about it. In both cases, however, we are dealing with closed intelligence circuits which are not open to relevant information.

Two points are involved in the above examples. One concerns the necessity of a system of information with its own staff to carry on its own function and develop its own norms, standards, and expertness. The other concerns the place in the system to which intelligence should be reported.

The first problem has so far been presented as if there were only one answer. When information concerning the system as a whole and its relations to its environment is involved, there are genuine advantages in a subsystem which has this information-gathering as its major responsibility. This can mean that specialized expertness is made possible, that the coding limitations of an irrelevant function are obviated, and that standards of accurate prediction and valid assessment develop as in a scientific research organization.

These advantages do not inevitably follow. The major values of the system still operate to affect the subsystem; directives of top management control the freedom of the subsystem and may indicate receptivity to only certain types of information. Cigarette manufacturers, for example, could set up a research agency reporting to top management with the task of investigating the relationship of cigarette smoking to lung cancer, heart disease, and related health problems. They could hire competent researchers (though perhaps not top scientists) with an adequate budget to pursue a research program. It is not likely, however, that the researchers would furnish top management unambiguous reports on the injurious effects of the use of tobacco and recommendations that the company change its goals and turn to the use of nicotine as a poison against insects or some such alternative.

To avoid the corruption of information by the system of which it is a part, it is necessary to guarantee to the researcher within an organization some of the same freedoms he would enjoy in a university setting. Some of the big electric and utility companies have actually done this in the natural sciences, and the resulting discoveries have more than justified the policy. With the exception of one or two token units, no industrial concern has ever done this in the social sciences even though it is in this area that management needs information most desperately. One type of freedom absolutely essential for such research is that the directives of top management do not pose specific questions they want answered. General problem areas can be indicated, but once the lines of inquiry are restricted in particularistic fashion, we are back to a closed system of intelligence. Answers are easily predetermined by the questions asked, especially when these questions originate at the top of a power structure. This applies both to an intelligence system which is conducting basic research and to one which is gathering information at a more descriptive level. A narrow definition of the mission of an information-gathering agency means that the answers it furnishes will also be extremely limited and frequently erroneous.

Another means by which an organization can avoid corrupting or being corrupted by its own information service is the astute use of multiple channels as check procedures. Multiple channels, if based upon the same sources of information, can merely duplicate error. But they can be set up so as to utilize various sources of information and process it in similar enough fashion to produce a consistent or inconsistent picture for decision makers.

The problem of the latitude to be permitted to an intelligence operation is an extremely difficult one for top management. On the one hand, the organization needs useful information, and if it gives researchers a completely free hand, the relevance of their findings for organizational functioning is not insured. To this rational consideration is added the irrational fear of the incomprehensible techniques and language of a suspect group of "longhairs." On the other hand, there is not much advantage to management in setting up an intelligence agency if it merely reflects management's coding processes.

The critical question is whether the task of the intelligence or research unit is system research or operational research. If the former is the case, then management has to be able to tolerate the differences in values, methods, and approach of specialists in information-gathering. In fact, these differences are among the major reasons for hiring specialists. Some restriction on their activities can nevertheless be imposed in terms of the general objectives assigned to them. And even if no specific and immediate answers are demanded, over time the information agency must provide some useful information to the organization or forfeit its right to organizational support. An important factor working toward organizational control of information specialists (and often working too well) is the natural tendency for specialists to take on the coloration of the system and behave too much as conforming members rather than as objective outsiders.

Outside research agencies are occasionally called in to provide the types of information which organizational leaders think cannot be readily supplied by their own personnel. The more research-oriented outside agencies will seek to obtain a broader definition of the problem than management generally presents. In other words, the tendency of organizational leaders is to narrow the problem to the visible and troublesome symptoms, whereas adequate intelligence about it has to probe into the causes. The process of redefining the problem for management is often easier for the outside group than for the captive agency.

The question of the optimal place for reporting the results of systemic research becomes complicated in large organizations. Though top echelons should be the recipients of information about the functioning of the total system, it is difficult for them to find the time to take adequate note of it, let alone absorb it and give it some weight in their decisions. Hence there is generally more relevant information in an organization than its top leaders utilize. Several changes are necessary in organizational structure to achieve reform in this respect. One is the elevation of the head of the information agency in status, so that he not only reports to top levels but also can command a hearing when he and his aides believe they have some vital intelligence. The second is the perfecting of translation mechanisms, so that critical pieces of information can be transmitted up the line in the information agency itself and finally to the top echelons of the organization. A third is the restructuring of the top jobs to reduce the component of routine administration; this will not guarantee the acquisition and use of systemic information, but it will have a powerful facilitating effect.

Summary

Human organizations are informational as well as energic systems, and both the exchange of energy and the exchange of information must be considered in order to understand the functioning of organizations. Information exchange is itself energic, of course, but its energic aspects are of minor significance compared to its symbolic aspects. In other words, information transmission is significant for what it implies, triggers, or controls. In general, the closer one gets to the center of organizational control and decision-making, the greater is the emphasis on information exchange and transmittal.

The importance of information processes to organizational functioning does not imply, however, a simple relationship between amount of communication and organizational effectiveness. The advocacy of communication as a desideratum of organization needs to be qualified with respect to the kind of information required for the solution of given problems, and with respect to the nature of the communication process between individuals, groups, and subsystems of organization. Indeed, social systems can be defined as *restricted* communication networks; unrestricted communication implies noise and inefficiency.

Every organization thus must solve the problem of what pattern of communication shall be instituted, what information shall be directed to what offices. One issue in establishing such a pattern is information overload. There are limits to the amount of communication which can be received, coded, and effectively handled by any individual. The tendency to overload certain executive offices with communications is strong, and the responses of individuals to information overload are often maladaptive. Miller has identified seven categories of response to information overload, each of which can be assessed in terms of its adaptive or maladaptive implications for the individual and the organization. These categories include omission, error, queuing, filtering, approximation, multiple channels, and escape.

Five dimensions are proposed for characterizing communications circuits in organizations:

(a) The size of the loop; that is, the amount of organizational space encompassed by the communication circuit;
(b) The nature of the circuit;
(c) The openness of the circuit; that is, the extent to which messages can be modified once the communication process has been initiated;
(d) The efficiency of the circuit for task completion; that is, the speed and accuracy with which the circuit permits the completion of specified tasks; and
(e) The goodness of fit between the circuit and its systemic function.

Further distinctions are made between communications in a hierarchical organization directed upward, those directed downward, and those directed horizontally. Each of these directions implies characteristic content in message.

The chapter concludes with a discussion of formal communication devices, such as operational feedback, operations research, and systemic research. The hypothesis is offered that communication and information subsystems are often located disadvantageously in organizations, both in terms of accessibility to top leaders and in terms of contamination of the information-getting process.

References

Ashby, W. R., *Design for a Brain*. New York: Wiley, 1952.
Campbell, A., P. E. Converse, W. E. Miller, and D. E. Stokes, *The American Voter*. New York: Wiley, 1960.
Dubin, R., Stability of human organization. In M. Haire (ed.), *Modern Organization Theory*. New York: Wiley, 1959, pp. 218–253.
Guetzkow, H., and H. A. Simon, "The impact of certain communication nets upon organization and performance in task-oriented groups," *Management Science*, 1 (1955), 233–250.
Guetzkow, H., and W. R. Dill, "Factors in the organizational development of task-oriented groups," *Sociometry*, 20 (1957), 175–204.
Heise, G. A., and G. A. Miller, "Problem solving by small groups using various communication nets," *Journal of Abnormal and Social Psychology*, 46 (1951), 327–335.

Katz, E., and P. Lazarsfeld, *Personal Influence: The Part Played by People in the Flow of Mass Communication*. New York: Free Press, 1955.

Leavitt, H. J., "Some effects of certain communication patterns on group performance," *Journal of Abnormal and Social Psychology*, 46 (1951), 38–50.

Lippmann, W., *Public Opinion*. New York: Harcourt, Brace, 1922.

March, J. G., and H. A. Simon, *Organizations*. New York: Wiley, 1958.

Meier, R. L., *Social Change in Communication Oriented Institutions*. Ann Arbor: Mental Health Research Institute, University of Michigan, 1961.

Miller, J. G., "Information input, overload, and psychopathology," *American Journal of Psychiatry*, 116 (1960), 695–704.

Newcomb, T. M., "Autistic hostility and social reality," *Human Relations*, 1 (1947), 69–86.

Parsons, T., *Structure and Process in Modern Societies*. New York: Free Press, 1960.

Thelen, H. A., "Exploration of a growth model for psychic, biological, and social systems," mimeographed paper, 1960.

Exercises

1. What are the implications of increased communication? Is "more" communication "good"? What are the advantages and disadvantages?

2. Discuss the coding systems of organizations. How do these relate to the notions of transactional psychology as discussed by Toch and MacLean?

3. Can you find examples of information overload? Do individuals become overloaded with information, or does the concept apply only to organizations?

4. How can you differentiate between effective communication and efficient communication?

Section Two

Persuasion

Man deals with his environment by adjusting to it and by trying to make it adjust to him. This is true of the physical world (think of the furnace-thermostat combination), and it is certainly true of the social world. Indeed, the social world is the product of the attempts men have made to deal with one another. Men not only adjust but also try to change those about them so that their own efforts at adjustment will be more satisfactory. To adjust successfully, men must predict the results of their efforts to bring about changes (as discussed in the general introduction).

There are several ways of looking at what is going on when one man sets about persuading another to change. The conceptual models described and discussed in Section One are useful, but in Section Two the reader will find selections that deal more directly with the communication situation as one in which persuasion is always taking place. This section, then, perhaps more than any other, is concerned with the major theme of this book.

The selections are arranged from general to specific. Goffman's presentation, like Boulding's in Section One, is perhaps the most general and stimulating. But Section Two goes a step further than Section One by reporting a study of human behavior in persuasive situations done under controlled conditions (the Asch study).

Introduction to "The Presentation of Self in Everyday Life"

Erving Goffman

The more skillful a communicator is at persuading, the wider the range of responses he can evoke. But no matter how skillful he may become, there will always be limits on what responses can be evoked in a given situation. If the communicator finds that the preferred response cannot be elicited, then he must direct his efforts toward redefining the situation into one in which his goal is possible. He then tries to alter probabilities so that the satisfactory response becomes the most probable one.

The Goffman selection is mainly concerned with the definition of situations. One of Goffman's main points is that situations are defined by the roles people adopt to deal with them. Further, the author suggests that a major cause of failure to persuade may be that the communicator has brought to a new situation a role that, while appropriate to a former situation, no longer makes possible the responses he would like from others.

When an individual enters the presence of others, they commonly seek to acquire information about him or to bring into play information about him already possessed. They will be interested in his general socioeconomic status, his conception of self, his attitude toward them, his competence, his trustworthiness, etc. Although some of this information seems to be sought almost as an end in itself, there are usually quite practical reasons for acquiring it. Information about the individual helps to define the situation, enabling others to know in advance what he will expect of them and what they may expect of him. Informed in these ways, the others will know how best to act in order to call forth a desired response from him.

For those present, many sources of information become accessible and many carriers (or "sign-vehicles") become available for conveying this information. If unacquainted with the individual, observers can glean clues from his conduct and appearance which allow them to apply their previous experience with individuals roughly similar to the one before them or, more important, to apply untested stereotypes to him. They can also assume from past experience that only individuals of a particular kind are likely to be found in a given social setting. They can rely on what the individual says about himself or on documentary evidence he provides as to who and what he is. If they know, or know of, the individual by virtue of experience prior to the interaction, they can rely on assumptions as to the persistence and generality of psychological traits as a means of predicting his present and future behavior.

However, during the period in which the individual is in the immediate presence of the others, few events may occur which directly provide the others with the conclusive information they will need if they are to direct wisely their own activity. Many crucial facts lie beyond the time and place of interaction or lie concealed within it. For example, the "true" or "real" attitudes, beliefs, and emotions of the individual can be ascertained only indirectly, through his avowals or through what appears to be involuntary expressive behavior. Similarly, if the individual offers the others a product or service, they will often find that during the interaction there will be no time and place immediately available for eating the pudding that the proof can be found in. They will be forced to accept some events as conventional or natural signs of something not directly available to the senses. In Ichheiser's terms,[1] the individual will have to act so that he intentionally or unintentionally *expresses* himself, and the others will in turn have to be *impressed* in some way by him.

The expressiveness of the individual (and therefore his capacity to give impressions) appears to involve two radically different kinds of sign activity: the expression that he *gives,* and the expression that he *gives off.* The first involves verbal symbols or their substitutes which he uses admittedly and solely to convey the information that he and the others are known to attach to these symbols. This is communication in the traditional and narrow sense. The second involves a wide range of action that others can treat as symptomatic of the actor, the expectation being that the action was performed for reasons other than the information conveyed in this way. As we shall have to see, this distinction has an only initial validity. The individual does of course intentionally convey misinformation by means of both of these types of communication, the first involving deceit, the second feigning.

Taking communication in both its narrow and broad sense, one finds that when the individual is in the immediate presence of others, his activity will have a promissory character. The others are likely to find that they must accept the individual on faith, offering him a just return while he is present before them in exchange for something whose true value will not

<hr>

[1] Gustav Ichheiser, "Misunderstandings in Human Relations," Supplement to *The American Journal of Sociology,* Vol. 55 (September 1949), pp. 6–7.

be established until after he has left their presence. (Of course, the others also live by inference in their dealings with the physical world, but it is only in the world of social interaction that the objects about which they make inferences will purposely facilitate and hinder this inferential process.) The security that they justifiably feel in making inferences about the individual will vary, of course, depending on such factors as the amount of information they already possess about him, but no amount of such past evidence can entirely obviate the necessity of acting on the basis of inferences. As William I. Thomas suggested:

> It is also highly important for us to realize that we do not as a matter of fact lead our lives, make our decisions, and reach our goals in everyday life either statistically or scientifically. We live by inference. I am, let us say, your guest. You do not know, you cannot determine scientifically, that I will not steal your money or your spoons. But inferentially I will not, and inferentially you have me as a guest.[2]

Let us now turn from the others to the point of view of the individual who presents himself before them. He may wish them to think highly of him, or to think that he thinks highly of them, or to perceive how in fact he feels toward them, or to obtain no clear-cut impression; he may wish to ensure sufficient harmony so that the interaction can be sustained, or to defraud, get rid of, confuse, mislead, antagonize, or insult them. Regardless of the particular objective which the individual has in mind and of his motive for having this objective, it will be in his interests to control the conduct of the others, especially their responsive treatment of him.[3] This control is achieved largely by influencing the definition of the situation which the others come to formulate, and he can influence this definition by expressing himself in such a way as to give them the kind of impression that will lead them to act voluntarily in accordance with his own plan. Thus, when an individual appears in the presence of others, there will usually be some reason for him to mobilize his activity so that it will convey an impression to others which it is in his interests to convey. Since a girl's dormitory mates will glean evidence of her popularity from the calls she receives on the phone, we can suspect that some girls will arrange for calls to be made, and Willard Waller's finding can be anticipated:

[2] Quoted in E. H. Volkart (ed.), *Social Behavior and Personality*, Contributions of W. I. Thomas to Theory and Social Research (New York: Social Science Research Council, 1951), p. 5.

[3] Here I owe much to an unpublished paper by Tom Burns of the University of Edinburgh. He presents the argument that in all interaction a basic underlying theme is the desire of each participant to guide and control the responses made by the others present. A similar argument has been advanced by Jay Haley in a recent unpublished paper, but in regard to a special kind of control, that having to do with defining the nature of the relationship of those involved in the interaction.

It has been reported by many observers that a girl who is called to the telephone in the dormitories will often allow herself to be called several times, in order to give all the other girls ample opportunity to hear her paged.[4]

Of the two kinds of communication—expressions given and expressions given off—this report will be primarily concerned with the latter, with the more theatrical and contextual kind, the non-verbal, presumably unintentional kind, whether this communication be purposely engineered or not. As an example of what we must try to examine, I would like to cite at length a novelistic incident in which Preedy, a vacationing Englishman, makes his first appearance on the beach of his summer hotel in Spain:

> But in any case he took care to avoid catching anyone's eye. First of all, he had to make it clear to those potential companions of his holiday that they were of no concern to him whatsoever. He stared through them, round them, over them—eyes lost in space. The beach might have been empty. If by chance a ball was thrown his way, he looked surprised; then let a smile of amusement lighten his face (Kindly Preedy), looked round dazed to see that there *were* people on the beach, tossed it back with a smile to himself and not a smile *at* the people, and then resumed carelessly his nonchalant survey of space.
>
> But it was time to institute a little parade, the parade of the Ideal Preedy. By devious handlings he gave any who wanted to look a chance to see the title of his book—a Spanish translation of Homer, classic thus, but not daring, cosmopolitan too—and then gathered together his beach-wrap and bag into a neat sand-resistant pile (Methodical and Sensible Preedy), rose slowly to stretch at ease his huge frame (Big-Cat Preedy), and tossed aside his sandals (Carefree Preedy, after all).
>
> The marriage of Preedy and the sea! There were alternative rituals. The first involved the stroll that turns into a run and a dive straight into the water, thereafter smoothing into a strong splashless crawl towards the horizon. But of course not really to the horizon. Quite suddenly he would turn on to his back and thrash great white splashes with his legs, somehow thus showing that he could have swum further had he wanted to, and then would stand up a quarter out of water for all to see who it was.
>
> The alternative course was simpler, it avoided the cold-water shock and it avoided the risk of appearing too high-spirited. The point was to appear to be so used to the sea, the Mediterranean, and this particular beach, that one might as well be in the sea as out of it. It involved a slow stroll down and into the edge of the water—not even

[4] Willard Waller, "The Rating and Dating Complex," *American Sociological Review*, Vol. 2, p. 730.

noticing his toes were wet, land and water all the same to *him!*—with his eyes up at the sky gravely surveying portents, invisible to others, of the weather (Local Fisherman Preedy).[5]

The novelist means us to see that Preedy is improperly concerned with the extensive impressions he feels his sheer bodily action is giving off to those around him. We can malign Preedy further by assuming that he has acted merely in order to give a particular impression, that this is a false impression, and that the others present receive either no impression at all, or, worse still, the impression that Preedy is affectedly trying to cause them to receive this particular impression. But the important point for us here is that the kind of impression Preedy thinks he is making is in fact the kind of impression that others correctly and incorrectly glean from someone in their midst.

I have said that when an individual appears before others his actions will influence the definition of the situation which they come to have. Sometimes the individual will act in a thoroughly calculating manner, expressing himself in a given way solely in order to give the kind of impression to others that is likely to evoke from them a specific response he is concerned to obtain. Sometimes the individual will be calculating in his activity but be relatively unaware that this is the case. Sometimes he will intentionally and consciously express himself in a particular way, but chiefly because the tradition of his group or social status require this kind of expression and not because of any particular response (other than vague acceptance or approval) that is likely to be evoked from those impressed by the expression. Sometimes the traditions of an individual's role will lead him to give a well-designed impression of a particular kind and yet he may be neither consciously nor unconsciously disposed to create such an impression. The others, in their turn, may be suitably impressed by the individual's efforts to convey something, or may misunderstand the situation and come to conclusions that are warranted neither by the individual's intent nor by the facts. In any case, in so far as the others act *as if* the individual had conveyed a particular impression, we may take a functional or pragmatic view and say that the individual has "effectively" projected a given definition of the situation and "effectively" fostered the understanding that a given state of affairs obtains.

There is one aspect of the others' response that bears special comment here. Knowing that the individual is likely to present himself in a light that is favorable to him, the others may divide what they witness into two parts; a part that is relatively easy for the individual to manipulate at will, being chiefly his verbal assertions, and a part in regard to which he seems to have little concern or control, being chiefly derived from the expressions

[5] William Sansom, *A Contest of Ladies* (London: Hogarth, 1956), pp. 230–232.

he gives off. The others may then use what are considered to be the ungovernable aspects of his expressive behavior as a check upon the validity of what is conveyed by the governable aspects. In this a fundamental asymmetry is demonstrated in the communication process, the individual presumably being aware of only one stream of his communication, the witnesses of this stream and one other. For example, in Shetland Isle one crofter's wife, in serving native dishes to a visitor from the mainland of Britain, would listen with a polite smile to his polite claims of liking what he was eating; at the same time she would take note of the rapidity with which the visitor lifted his fork or spoon to his mouth, the eagerness with which he passed food into his mouth, and the gusto expressed in chewing the food, using these signs as a check on the stated feelings of the eater. The same woman, in order to discover what one acquaintance (A) "actually" thought of another acquaintance (B), would wait until B was in the presence of A but engaged in conversation with still another person (C). She would then covertly examine the facial expressions of A as he regarded B in conversation with C. Not being in conversation with B, and not being directly observed by him, A would sometimes relax usual constraints and tactful deceptions, and freely express what he was "actually" feeling about B. This Shetlander, in short, would observe the unobserved observer.

Now given the fact that others are likely to check up on the more controllable aspects of behavior by means of the less controllable, one can expect that sometimes the individual will try to exploit this very possibility, guiding the impression he makes through behavior felt to be reliably informing.[6] For example, in gaining admission to a tight social circle, the participant observer may not only wear an accepting look while listening to an informant, but may also be careful to wear the same look when observing the informant talking to others; observers of the observer will then not as easily discover where he actually stands. A specific illustration may be cited from Shetland Isle. When a neighbor dropped in to have a cup of tea, he would ordinarily wear at least a hint of an expectant warm smile as he passed through the door into the cottage. Since lack of physical obstructions outside the cottage and lack of light within it usually made it possible to observe the visitor unobserved as he approached the house, islanders sometimes took pleasure in watching the visitor drop whatever expression he was manifesting and replace it with a sociable one just before reaching the door. However, some visitors, in appreciating that this examination was occurring, would blindly adopt a social face a long distance from the house, thus ensuring the projection of a constant image.

---

[6] The widely read and rather sound writings of Stephen Potter are concerned in part with signs that can be engineered to give a shrewd observer the apparently incidental cues he needs to discover concealed virtues the gamesman does not in fact possess.

This kind of control upon the part of the individual reinstates the symmetry of the communication process, and sets the stage for a kind of information game—a potentially infinite cycle of concealment, discovery, false revelation, and rediscovery. It should be added that since the others are likely to be relatively unsuspicious of the presumably unguided aspect of the individual's conduct, he can gain much by controlling it. The others of course may sense that the individual is manipulating the presumably spontaneous aspects of his behavior, and seek in this very act of manipulation some shading of conduct that the individual has not managed to control. This again provides a check upon the individual's behavior, this time his presumably uncalculated behavior, thus re-establishing the asymmetry of the communication process. Here I would like only to add the suggestion that the arts of piercing an individual's effort at calculated unintentionality seem better developed than our capacity to manipulate our own behavior, so that regardless of how many steps have occurred in the information game, the witness is likely to have the advantage over the actor, and the initial asymmetry of the communication process is likely to be retained.

When we allow that the individual projects a definition of the situation when he appears before others, we must also see that the others, however passive their role may seem to be, will themselves effectively project a definition of the situation by virtue of their response to the individual and by virtue of any lines of action they initiate to him. Ordinarily the definitions of the situation projected by the several different participants are sufficiently attuned to one another so that open contradiction will not occur. I do not mean that there will be the kind of consensus that arises when each individual present candidly expresses what he really feels and honestly agrees with the expressed feelings of the others present. This kind of harmony is an optimistic ideal and in any case not necessary for the smooth working of society. Rather, each participant is expected to suppress his immediate heartfelt feelings, conveying a view of the situation which he feels the others will be able to find at least temporarily acceptable. The maintenance of this surface of agreement, this veneer of consensus, is facilitated by each participant concealing his own wants behind statements which assert values to which everyone present feels obliged to give lip service. Further, there is usually a kind of division of definitional labor. Each participant is allowed to establish the tentative official ruling regarding matters which are vital to him but not immediately important to others, e.g., the rationalizations and justifications by which he accounts for his past activity. In exchange for this courtesy he remains silent or noncommittal on matters important to others but not immediately important to him. We have then a kind of interactional *modus vivendi*. Together the participants contribute to a single over-all definition of the situation which involves not so much a real agreement as to what exists but rather a real agreement as to whose claims concerning what issues will be temporarily honored. Real agreement will also exist concerning the desirability of avoiding an open conflict of definitions of the situation.[7] I will refer to this level of agreement as a "working consensus." It is to be understood that the working consensus established in one interaction setting will be quite different in content from the working consensus established in a different type of setting. Thus, between two friends at lunch, a reciprocal show of affection, respect, and concern for the other is maintained. In service occupations, on the other hand, the specialist often maintains an image of disinterested involvement in the problem of the client, while the client responds with a show of respect for the competence and integrity of the specialist. Regardless of such differences in content, however, the general form of these working arrangements is the same.

In noting the tendency for a participant to accept the definitional claims made by the others present, we can appreciate the crucial importance of the information that the individual *initially* possesses or acquires concerning his fellow participants, for it is on the basis of this initial information that the individual starts to define the situation and starts to build up lines of responsive action. The individual's initial projection commits him to what he is proposing to be and requires him to drop all pretenses of being other things. As the interaction among the participants progresses, additions and modifications in this initial informational state will of course occur, but it is essential that these later developments be related without contradiction to, and even built up from, the initial positions taken by the several participants. It would seem that an individual can more easily make a choice as to what line of treatment to demand from and extend to the others present at the beginning of an encounter than he can alter the line of treatment that is being pursued once the interaction is underway.

In everyday life, of course, there is a clear understanding that first impressions are important. Thus, the work adjustment of those in service occupations will often hinge upon a capacity to seize and hold the initiative in the service relation, a capacity that will require subtle aggressiveness on the part of the server when he is of lower socio-economic status than his client. W. F. Whyte suggests the waitress as an example:

[7] An interaction can be purposely set up as a time and place for voicing differences in opinion, but in such cases participants must be careful to agree, not to disagree, on the proper tone of voice, vocabulary, and degree of seriousness in which all arguments are to be phrased, and upon the mutual respect which disagreeing participants must carefully continue to express toward one another. This debaters' or academic definition of the situation may also be invoked suddenly and judiciously as a way of translating a serious conflict of views into one that can be handled within a framework acceptable to all present.

The first point that stands out is that the waitress who bears up under pressure does not simply respond to her customers. She acts with some skill to control their behavior. The first question to ask when we look at the customer relationship is, "Does the waitress get the jump on the customer, or does the customer get the jump on the waitress?" The skilled waitress realizes the crucial nature of this question. . . .

The skilled waitress tackles the customer with confidence and without hesitation. For example, she may find that a new customer has seated himself before she could clear off the dirty dishes and change the cloth. He is now leaning on the table studying the menu. She greets him, says, "May I change the cover, please?" and, without waiting for an answer, takes his menu away from him so that he moves back from the table, and she goes about her work. The relationship is handled politely but firmly, and there is never any question as to who is in charge.[8]

When the interaction that is initiated by "first impressions" is itself merely the initial interaction in an extended series of interactions involving the same participants, we speak of "getting off on the right foot" and feel that it is crucial that we do so. Thus, one learns that some teachers take the following view:

> You can't ever let them get the upper hand on you or you're through. So I start out tough. The first day I get a new class in, I let them know who's boss . . . You've got to start off tough, then you can ease up as you go along. If you start out easy-going, when you try to get tough, they'll just look at you and laugh.[9]

Similarly, attendants in mental institutions may feel that if the new patient is sharply put in his place the first day on the ward and made to see who is boss, much future difficulty will be prevented.[10]

Given the fact that the individual effectively projects a definition of the situation when he enters the presence of others, we can assume that events may occur within the interaction which contradict, discredit, or otherwise throw doubt upon this projection. When these disruptive events occur, the interaction itself may come to a confused and embarrassed halt. Some of the assumptions upon which the responses of the participants had been predicated become untenable, and the participants find themselves

---

[8] W. F. Whyte (ed.), "When Workers and Customers Meet," Chapter VII, *Industry and Society* (New York: McGraw-Hill Book Co., Inc., 1946), pp. 132–133.

[9] Teacher interview quoted by Howard S. Becker, "Social Class Variations in the Teacher-Pupil Relationship," *Journal of Educational Sociology*, Vol. 25, p. 459.

[10] Harold Taxel, "Authority Structure in a Mental Hospital Ward" (unpublished Master's thesis, Department of Sociology, University of Chicago, 1953).

lodged in an interaction for which the situation has been wrongly defined and is now no longer defined. At such moments the individual whose presentation has been discredited may feel ashamed while the others present may feel hostile, and all the participants may come to feel ill at ease, nonplussed, out of countenance, embarrassed, experiencing the kind of anomy that is generated when the minute social system of face-to-face interaction breaks down.

In stressing the fact that the initial definition of the situation projected by an individual tends to provide a plan for the co-operative activity that follows—in stressing this action point of view—we must not overlook the crucial fact that any projected definition of the situation also has a distinctive moral character. It is this moral character of projections that will chiefly concern us in this report. Society is organized on the principle that any individual who possesses certain social characteristics has a moral right to expect that others will value and treat him in an appropriate way. Connected with this principle is a second, namely that an individual who implicitly or explicitly signifies that he has certain social characteristics ought in fact to be what he claims he is. In consequence, when an individual projects a definition of the situation and thereby makes an implicit or explicit claim to be a person of a particular kind, he automatically exerts a moral demand upon the others, obliging them to value and treat him in the manner that persons of his kind have a right to expect. He also implicitly forgoes all claims to be things he does not appear to be[11] and hence forgoes the treatment that would be appropriate for such individuals. The others find, then, that the individual has informed them as to what is and as to what they *ought* to see as the "is."

One cannot judge the importance of definitional disruptions by the frequency with which they occur, for apparently they would occur more frequently were not constant precautions taken. We find that preventive practices are constantly employed to avoid these embarrassments and that corrective practices are constantly employed to compensate for discrediting occurrences that have not been successfully avoided. When the individual employs these strategies and tactics to protect his own projections, we may refer to them as "defensive practices"; when a participant employs them to save the definition of the situation projected by another, we speak of "protective practices" or "tact." Together, defensive and protective practices comprise the techniques employed to safeguard the impression fostered by an individual during his presence before others. It should be added that while we may be ready to see that no fostered impression would survive if

---

[11] This role of the witness in limiting what it is the individual can be has been stressed by Existentialists, who see it as a basic threat to individual freedom. See Jean-Paul Sartre, *Being and Nothingness,* trans. by Hazel E. Barnes (New York: Philosophical Library, 1956), p. 365 ff.

defensive practices were not employed, we are less ready perhaps to see that few impressions could survive if those who received the impression did not exert tact in their reception of it.

In addition to the fact that precautions are taken to prevent disruption of projected definitions, we may also note that an intense interest in these disruptions comes to play a significant role in the social life of the group. Practical jokes and social games are played in which embarrassments which are to be taken unseriously are purposely engineered.[12] Fantasies are created in which devastating exposures occur. Anecdotes from the past—real, embroidered, or fictitious—are told and retold, detailing disruptions which occurred, almost occurred, or occurred and were admirably resolved. There seems to be no grouping which does not have a ready supply of these games, reveries, and cautionary tales, to be used as a source of humor, a catharsis for anxieties, and a sanction for inducing individuals to be modest in their claims and reasonable in their projected expectations. The individual may tell himself through dreams of getting into impossible positions. Families tell of the time a guest got his dates mixed and arrived when neither the house nor anyone in it was ready for him. Journalists tell of times when an all-too-meaningful misprint occurred, and the paper's assumption of objectivity or decorum was humorously discredited. Public servants tell of times a client ridiculously misunderstood form instructions, giving answers which implied an unanticipated and bizarre definition of the situation.[13] Seamen, whose home away from home is rigorously he-man, tell stories of coming back home and inadvertently asking mother to "pass the _____ing butter."[14] Diplomats tell of the time a near-sighted queen asked a republican ambassador about the health of his king.[15]

To summarize, then, I assume that when an individual appears before others he will have many motives for trying to control the impression they receive of the situation. This report is concerned with some of the common techniques that persons employ to sustain such impressions and with some of the common contingencies associated with the employment of these techniques. The specific content of any activity presented by the individual participant, or the role it plays in the interdependent activities of an on-going social system, will not be at issue; I shall be concerned only with the participant's dramaturgical problems of presenting

[12] Erving Goffman, "Communication Conduct in an Island Community" (Unpublished Ph.D. dissertation, Department of Sociology, University of Chicago, 1953), pp. 319–327.

[13] Peter Blau, *Dynamics of Bureaucracy* (Chicago: University of Chicago Press, 1955), pp. 127–129.

[14] Walter M. Beattie, Jr., "The Merchant Seaman" (unpublished M.A. Report, Department of Sociology, University of Chicago, 1950), p. 35.

[15] Sir Frederick Ponsonby, *Recollections of Three Reigns* (New York: E. P. Dutton & Co., Inc., 1952), p. 46.

the activity before others. The issues dealt with by stagecraft and stage management are sometimes trivial but they are quite general; they seem to occur everywhere in social life, providing a clear-cut dimension for formal sociological analysis.

It will be convenient to end this introduction with some definitions that are implied in what has gone before and required for what is to follow. For the purpose of this report, interaction (that is, face-to-face interaction) may be roughly defined as the reciprocal influence of individuals upon one another's actions when in one another's immediate physical presence. *An* interaction may be defined as all the interaction which occurs throughout any one occasion when a given set of individuals are in one another's continuous presence; the term "an encounter" would do as well. A "performance" may be defined as all the activity of a given participant on a given occasion which serves to influence in any way any of the other participants. Taking a particular participant and his performance as a basic point of reference, we may refer to those who contribute the other performances as the audience, observers, or co-participants. The pre-established pattern of action which is unfolded during a performance and which may be presented or played through on other occasions may be called a "part" or "routine."[16] These situational terms can easily be related to conventional structural ones. When an individual or performer plays the same part to the same audience on different occasions, a social relationship is likely to arise. Defining social role as the enactment of rights and duties attached to a given status, we can say that a social role will involve one or more parts and that each of these different parts may be presented by the performer on a series of occasions to the same kinds of audience or to an audience of the same persons.

Exercises

1. Compare Goffman's distinction between "deceit" and "feigning" with the Westley-MacLean distinction between "purposive" and "non-purposive."

2. Goffman quotes William I. Thomas on decisions, statistics, and science. How would that quotation compare and contrast with the assertion that follows it?

[16] For comments on the importance of distinguishing between a routine of interaction and any particular instance when this routine is played through, see John von Neumann and Oskar Morgenstern, *The Theory of Games and Economic Behaviour* (2nd ed.; Princeton, N.J.: Princeton University Press, 1947), p. 49.

3. Find an analogy of the behavior of the Shetland Islanders in your daily behaviors and those of the people among whom you live.

4. An interesting suggestion is that among the more sophisticated communicators are the operators of confidence swindles. Discuss this idea. (A book that discusses the operation of confidence games in this light is *The Big Con* by David W. Maurer.)

Persuasion and Interpersonal Relations

James H. Campbell
Hal W. Hepler

Here we try to suggest some additional notions about the influence that interpersonal relationships have upon the effectiveness of persuasive messages. In one sense, this selection is an extension of the Goffman article. In another sense, it deals with the ways in which we detect inconsistencies in our beliefs, which is the topic of the Preston article. Certainly from this discussion it is possible to derive some ways to build your credibility. It would be interesting to consider how some of the models we present here might be operating in the experimental situation to be reported in the Asch article at the end of this section.

Let's begin by setting up a communication situation that is as elementary as we can imagine. Suppose that you are a jet pilot forced to parachute from your aircraft over central Australia. You descend safely and disentangle yourself from your parachute. You look up and see loping toward you across the plain an Australian aborigine. He is naked except for a spear. He approaches you and stops about twenty feet away.

The situation is now fairly clear. You must communicate with this man, and you must be able to understand and deal with his efforts to communicate with you. You must make some effort to shape his behavior so that it will be of some benefit to you, and you must endeavor to present yourself to him in such a way that he will be favorably impressed by your actions. You, of course, do not know his language, and he does not know yours. His culture is as foreign to you as yours is to him. The need to communicate with him is urgent and the penalty for failing to communicate may lead him merely to trot off and forget about you, or it may lead him to use his spear if he perceives you as some sort of threat.[1]

The situation then stands with the aviator hoping that he can elicit a favorable reaction from the aborigine and with the aborigine hoping that he can elicit a favorable reaction from the aviator. Where can they start? The aborigine has never seen an aviator. The aviator has never seen an aborigine. They have no language in common. They have no cultural elements in common. What, then, *do* they hold in common? Their humanness. They both must eat and drink and rest and be protected in some way from the elements.

If we focus our attention upon the aviator, we can perhaps decide upon some actions that he might wish to avoid and some actions that might have a fairly good probability of eliciting a positive reaction. For example, it would probably be unwise for the aviator to stride toward the native and abruptly thrust forth his hand in the typically American gesture of greeting. It is entirely possible that the native, not having any experience with hand-shaking as a code, might interpret this as an unfriendly and threatening act and use his spear. The aviator might, however, rub his stomach and make small groaning sounds, and this might remind the native that this strange creature from the skies was a man much like himself in *some* ways and capable of being hungry.

We are dealing here with the relationships that exist between two men in a situation foreign in many ways to both. This communication situation is much like those that all of us face. In some ways it is more difficult than most of our communicative situations and in other ways it is far easier.

We can use a pair of circles as a model for this situation. Let each circle represent a man, and let the amount of overlap of the circles represent the knowledge, information, facts, language skills, etc. that the two men hold in common. In the present situation we could draw two circles that just barely touch each other. This will indicate that the two men have in common only very few elements, the most basic being their membership in the same species.

Very few of us will ever have so little in common with the person with whom we must communicate. Most people we communicate with share with us a common language and culture. However, overlap varies greatly. Total overlap never occurs, but what would be the situation with

[1] There was an incident paralleling this hypothetical one some years ago involving missionaries and Indians in South America. The missionaries evidently misevaluated the effects of their communicative efforts and were killed by the Indians. Most of our day-to-day communication, happily, does not involve such directly unpleasant and final results!

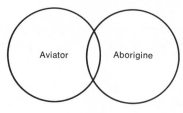

Figure 1

the most complete overlap? It probably comes closest to occurring in the case of identical twins reared together in a *similar* environment. Identical twins often are able to anticipate each other's words and emotions, but not always. Even here the two organisms are not identical in every respect. Environments *can* be similar, but they cannot be *identical* for any two humans—not even twins.

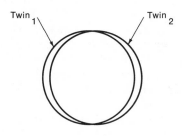

Figure 2

What happens when the amount of overlap between two people is not as complete as for identical twins and not as incomplete as for the aviator and the aborigine? We make predictions (judgments, guesses, or estimates) about the effect our behavior will have upon the behavior of other people. Those who consistently make accurate predictions are often called "effective communicators" or "good salesmen" or "good teachers" or something equally complimentary.

We generalize from our interpersonal relationships to classes of such relationships. That is, we decide how valuable, to us, some given message is on the basis of our experience with other messages from similar sources in the past.

Is it possible to conceive of a message that has no source? Even government documents, we know, were composed by some one individual somewhere. They were then, probably, revised by many. But one man was the source; two people cannot manipulate a typewriter simultaneously. The point is that our response to the message depends upon many things, and one of the more important of these is the credibility that this source has for this particular message.

Persuasion

Credibility is a curious thing. It does not rest wholly upon either emotion or logic. A source may be credible for us because he is our friend or relative. Or he may be credible because he is neither. Much depends upon our own personalities. But most important is the way our personality interacts with that of the other person (or persons) in a communication situation. (Consider the types of reaction the subjects made in Asch's study included in this section.)

There are a lot of different ways of looking at a communication situation. One way can be called *an analytic model of the interaction process*. Let us suppose that two men come into each other's presence for the first time. Let's call them Bob and Bill. As they enter each other's presence, they have notions about what they themselves are like; they think of themselves as having certain vices and virtues. These self-evaluations are unevenly accurate from person to person, but we have all made these evaluations and are making more all the time.

Within a very few seconds of their first contact, Bob and Bill have formed some more or less durable impression of each other. That is, they each have added to their notions of themselves a set of notions about the other. Where Bob had a notion of what he himself was like before (a Bob's Bob), he now has also a Bob's Bill. He now has made some more or less reliable decisions about the character and personality of the other person in this communication situation. Bill, of course, has done the same.

Another quick mutual evaluation is the one about what the other fellow thinks of *him*. Bob becomes concerned about what Bill thinks Bob is like. But can Bob know what Bill thinks? No. Bob can only update his previous estimate of the character and personality of Bill. Bob probably says something like this to himself: "Given that I believe Bill to have X characteristics and that I think myself to be of Y personality, then what will someone like Bill think of someone like me?" Remember that the best way to know how someone thinks of you is to interact with him and observe what he does, and what you do, when you are in each other's company. As we all do before we have had enough time together to be very certain of our evaluations, Bob is making predictions based on his past experience. But that is not all his predictions are based upon. He also has the evidence of his present encounter, and this form of evidence grows in importance as it increases in quantity.

Figure 3 illustrates three categories of evidence stemming from the encounter. Descriptive labels that might be attached to each of these categories are: gross acts, linguistic acts, and minimal cues.

You can hardly miss noticing gross acts in human behavior. They are things like a punch in the nose; or the fact that Mr. Z always moves out of a group that you join; or the friendship of someone who walks beside you as you move among groups at a large party. These things are all gross, grand, large-scale acts. However, they can be misleading. They can be shammed. They are sometimes used to announce a dramatic shift in the nature of a relationship.

Figure 3. The square boxes are ideas that Bob and Bill carry with them all the time. The balloon shapes indicate ideas formed as a direct result of the interaction. Keep in mind that the notions in the balloons are also based on the past experiences of Bob and Bill.

Minimal cues are at the opposite pole in terms of ease of detection. These are often indetectable unless there has already been considerable contact and interaction between the people involved. The study of the small acts that reveal internal states is called kinesics by Ray Birdwhistell.[2] His attempt to categorize posture and facial expressions, among other things, is the beginning of the work that will hopefully lead to some system for increasing the accuracy of predictions about attitudes of others toward ourselves and what we say.

We all know the stereotyped facial expressions used by actors and comedians to convey attitudes or emotional states. But we seldom mistake the comedians' version for the actors' version. And we do not often mistake the actors' version for the real thing. (Remember that the "real thing" may be a carefully contrived demonstration designed to cause us to think what someone else wants us to think.) The way in which the individual uses these expressions and gestures and the way in which he personally modifies them and makes them his own tells us a good deal about him and helps us predict his future responses.

[2] Ray L. Birdwhistell, *Introduction to Kinesics: An Annotation System for Analysis of Body Motion and Gesture* (Washington, D.C.: Foreign Service Institute, Department of State, 1952).

Last, but certainly far from least, let's take a look at linguistic acts. There are several levels on which these may be approached. First of all, what sort of subject does the other fellow choose to bring up and pursue in your presence? Americans seem to be willing to discuss baseball with anyone. They will not talk about their moral values at all except under certain very special circumstances and only with certain very special people.

Secondly, given some particular topic, how does a person talk? Is he condescending and impatient as a listener, and dogmatic as a speaker? If so, then you certainly can conclude that he thinks little of your understanding of the subject, and perhaps of any subject. One of the better clues we have to the attitude of a speaker is the intonation patterns he imposes on sentences or utterances. For instance, how many ways can you think of to say "fine"? It is possible to say "fine" so that it sounds as though you mean anything *but* fine. You can say "fine" in such a way that the listener still cannot decide what your attitude is toward some particular object, event, or person. Modifications of meaning are, of course, also present in even the most complex messages, as well as in this short one-word utterance.

Now that the categories of evidence are somewhat more fully explained, let's go back to Bob and Bill and see what they have been up to since we left them. Isn't it quite likely that each will now have begun to wonder what the other fellow thinks he has decided about him? That is, Bob, in addition to having a Bob's Bob, a Bob's Bill, and a Bob's Bill's Bob, may have generated a Bob's Bill's Bob's Bill.

We are approaching the limit, schematically, of this model. If we wish to pursue it further, we will need some pseudomathematical symbols to prevent the tongue twisting into which the Bob and Bill labels quickly lead us. Certain it is that, so far, this analysis is unrealistic because it is so very incomplete. In human encounters, many more evaluations are made than the few we have suggested here.

Not only are the numbers of evaluations greater than we have suggested in the two-person situation, but consider the complexities introduced when a third person, John, is added. John now needs to make estimates of what Bob thinks Bill has decided about John. And John must remember that the Bob whose decisions about Bill's decisions about John are important to John is a Bob who exists only within John's head; it is the Bob whose characteristics are assigned by John to Bob on the basis of estimates and inferences. Further, John must remember that Bob knows that these estimates and inferences are being made and that therefore Bob may have taken steps to hide his true attitudes and thereby cause John to think Bob has none. Or Bob may want John to think Bob's attitudes are the exact opposite of the ones which Bob does, in fact, hold.

Finally, these face-to-face personal encounters are the basis for the ways in which we interpret messages that are not delivered face to face.

We recall, when interpreting a written message, the intonation patterns we have heard this particular writer use, the facial expressions we have seen associated with those intonation patterns, and the body posture customary to the individual, as well as a great many other factors. On the basis of these memories we infer the mannerisms that the source might have exhibited if he had delivered the message in person; from these inferences we make predictions about the meaning of the message. That is, we *interpret* the message. If we have no personal knowledge of the source of a written message, then we interpret the message on other bases. We can consider the magazine, journal, or paper in which it appears. We can note the style in which it is written. We can even apply a sort of "stereotype" notion about the source which we have to use when we have no other kinds of information. (These ideas are discussed in the Hovland, Janis, and Kelley essay in this section.)

The next big question becomes: "What factors contribute to the views that we hold of ourselves and of others?" This is, obviously, a question that cannot be dealt with in a short essay, but some lines of thought may be indicated. It seems clear that most of our values, beliefs, and attitudes are derived from the groups that we come into contact with and that we belong to. Some of these groups we have no choice about joining and others we do. We have no choice about the family that we are born into, or about the cultural or ethnic groups of which we are a part. As children, we have almost nothing to say about the schools and other groups of which we are a part, or about the town we live in or the church we attend. As we grow older we have, in theory at least, some choice about the groups that we join voluntarily. You appear to be free to become a member of Alpha Beta Gamma or of the Loyal and Intense Order of the Aardvark. But even here the pressures that have moulded you throughout your life will bear heavily upon your decisions. All of the groups with which you have associated will contribute to the expectations you will have of other humans, and will contribute to the roles you will play in your life.

What do we mean by expectations or mutual expectations? These mutual expectations consist of the modes of behavior that we expect from those that we come to associate with and know. For example, if we know that Egbert Kranz is, among other things, a citizen of the United States, Caucasian, Protestant, and a native of a city of 2,300 people in the Middle Western state of Iowa we can roughly predict his behavior. But we may be completely mistaken.

A concept that parallels the notion of mutual expectations is one termed "role" or "role behavior." We daily play a number of roles that are largely determined by the groups of which we are and have been members. If you are a college student, you can play a number of roles if you wish. You may play the role of "campus intellectual" and cultivate the groups that further this image. You may frequent certain places, carry certain books, and enroll in the classes that will further the role that you have chosen to play. If the role of "intellectual" does not appeal to you, there are countless other roles and combinations of roles that you may assume or attempt to assume. You may decide to play the role of "campus politician," "campus playboy," or "campus athlete." Each of these roles will require that you behave in certain fairly well prescribed manners. (Goffman describes this behavior elsewhere in this section.)

An objection that is often raised to the concept of role playing is: "I'm not going to play *any* role. I'm just going to be myself." This implies two things. One is that role playing is somehow bad or dishonest. The other implication is that we can avoid role playing. This essay maintains that we all play roles to a greater or lesser extent and those who play roles consciously will be more effective in shaping the behavior of others than will those not conscious of their image or of the influence it has on others.

What are other ways of shaping behavior? What can we do to influence the behavior of the people with whom we interact? Answers to these questions are numerous and some have been suggested in this and other essays in this volume.

It seems clear that much of our behavior is to some extent under the control of others. If we can consider that many of our actions are randomly emitted, then it seems reasonable that we will tend to continue to do those things that get approval from our contemporaries and associates. In this sense, then, we can say that our role behavior is determined, to an extent, by the reactions of those with whom we associate.

In summary, we have made the following points:

1. All communicative activity is directed to changing behavior.

2. The amount of *knowledge* held in common by two interacting communicators will determine in large part the manner in which they will interact.

3. There are many levels of interaction.

4. Much of our interaction will depend on the mutual expectations that assist us in determining the roles played by the communicators.

5. The effective communicator/persuader will be conscious of the part played by expectations and roles and will be aware of what he is doing when he communicates.

6. Our roles, and the roles we expect others to take, are determined by the groups to which we belong and by the behavior of others toward us in interaction.

Exercises

1. What change in your behavior do you think will occur if you deliberately attempt to consider more variables in communication situations in which you find yourself?

2. Is the purpose of an educational institution to increase or to decrease the amount of overlap between pairs of people who pass through it? No matter which way you answer, discuss the effects of such a purpose upon other social and commercial institutions in terms of the impact people so educated will have upon communication within those institutions.

3. Consider the statement: If we were all *exactly* alike we would need no channels of communication. If that statement is true, what does it imply about contemporary man?

Inconsistency: A Persuasive Device

Ivan Preston

" Homeostasis " describes the state of an organism that is in equilibrium or in balance with its environment. People are interested in preserving the status quo; they want to remain in balance, and they will attempt to restore equilibrium if something should disturb it. The persuader can use this human characteristic as a lever.

In this essay, Preston outlines theories dealing with homeostasis and examines them under the headings of "consistency" and "inconsistency." He then explains how you can use consistency-inconsistency to increase the probability of eliciting the desired response from the receivers of your messages.

This essay is valuable because it shows a way in which you are being persuaded each day and outlines how to use the same method to persuade others. This essay should be compared with the others in this section. The theory and practice advanced here have relevance to the discussion of credibility by Hovland, Janis, and Kelley, the discussion of group pressures by Asch, the discussion of the presentation of self by Goffman, and the Campbell-Hepler essay on interpersonal relations. In each of these essays we see evidence of people changing their behavior to restore consistency.

"Consistency theory" is a comprehensive label for the work of several writers who have sought to describe and explain men's attempts to maintain consistency in their thoughts and actions. Perhaps it should be called inconsistency theory, because it is inconsistency (the theorists say) which prompts people to act and which produces some of the most interesting results of the communication process. Make a man consistent, the argument goes, and he will do nothing to change the situation. Make him inconsistent, and he will begin acting; he will work to alter the situation until consistency is regained. Then he will rest once more.

A furnace and thermostat have two states, "on" and "off." When external conditions throw them on, they set to work to restore the off state. They operate in the interests of the status quo, we could say. Their entire operation is aimed at staying off. But there is more to it than that, because the furnace never goes from off to on and back again to off without generating an important result, warmth, which was not present originally. The original off condition has not been restored precisely, but only approximately; an additional characteristic has been added.

So it is with inconsistency. A man who sees inconsistencies in his beliefs will strive to change these conditions and thus return to his original and preferred state of consistency. But he, too, usually will not return toward the status quo without altering it in certain ways. As the furnace produced new warmth, the individual may produce new beliefs and feelings about things, and these may orient him toward actions quite different from those he carried out before. In the hands of the persuader, the creation of inconsistency may be used, then, as a device for obtaining behaviors that the persuadees originally had not considered performing.

Consistency is something that people attribute to sets of beliefs. Suppose one belief implies that something (let's call it "X") is true. If a second belief also implies that X is true, then the two beliefs are consistent. But if the second belief implies that X is false, then the two beliefs are inconsistent because they suggest that X is both true and false. When this happens, we almost always try to do something about it. If we don't alter it, then we cannot act in the proper way toward X. We are uncomfortable in such a situation. Accordingly, we consider the set of beliefs and look for a solution. We might get rid of one belief and let the remaining one stand alone. We might change one belief to make it consistent with the other. We might change both beliefs to reach consistency. We might add new beliefs that somehow manage to eliminate the inconsistency or else reduce it to a tolerable amount.

Suppose that I want to buy either a Chevrolet or a Ford. Imagine that two things matter to me about these cars. The Chevrolet, let's say, looks more attractive. The Ford, let's say, is less expensive to run. The facts

This is an original essay prepared for the first edition of this book. All rights reserved. Permission to reprint must be obtained from the author and the publisher. Dr. Preston is Associate Professor of Journalism at The University of Wisconsin.

are equally important to me, and they are inconsistent because one implies "buy this car" and the other implies "buy the other car." As long as this inconsistency exists I cannot act meaningfully, and thus I have good reason for wanting to change my set of beliefs somehow. The stronger the inconsistency, the more I will want to reduce it.

Consistency, on the other hand, does not produce the desire for change. If I feel that one car is both more attractive and more economical, then the set of beliefs is quite acceptable and there is no reason to desire their change.

The theory of consistency and its relation to behavior is the product of several writers who have used different terms to describe concepts that are largely similar. Leon Festinger (*A Theory of Cognitive Dissonance*; Evanston, Ill.: Row, Peterson & Co., 1957) uses the terms "consonance" (consistency) and "dissonance" (inconsistency) to describe the relationship between two elements of belief. Charles E. Osgood and Percy H. Tannenbaum ("The Principle of Congruity in the Prediction of Attitude Change," *Psychological Review*, Vol. 62, 1955, pp. 42–55) use the terms "congruity" and "incongruity" to discuss the relationships among three elements of belief; these elements include an individual's attitude toward some topic (person, place, thing, concept, subject matter, etc.), his attitude toward a second person who expresses an attitude toward the topic, and the attitude that that second person expresses. These three elements may fit "congruently" or "incongruently." For example, "incongruity" exists for the individual when he likes the topic and he likes the second person, but the second person dislikes the topic. Suppose, for example, that I like a book, but an expert whom I respect dislikes the book. The three beliefs are not "congruent" (consistent), and I desire to change them.

Fritz Heider (*The Psychology of Interpersonal Relations*; New York: John Wiley & Sons, Inc., 1958) uses the terms "balance" (consistency) and "imbalance" (inconsistency) to describe similar sets of three beliefs. Another writer, Theodore Newcomb ("An Approach to the Study of Communicative Acts," *Psychological Review*, Vol. 60, 1953, pp. 393–404), speaks of "symmetry" (consistency) and "asymmetry" (inconsistency) of beliefs.

These writers present a variety of materials, and their discussions differ (and perhaps conflict) in some respects. Our purpose here is served by emphasizing the similarities of their presentations, and we have attempted to carry this out by introducing "consistency" and "inconsistency" as generic terms under which we may state the germinal ideas common to all of the writers.[1]

[1] Our generic terms are based largely upon Festinger's specification of "consonance" and "dissonance" as types of relationships between two entities. Our terms are broader, however, since they imply a reference to the work of several writers collectively rather than to the work of Festinger alone.

In all of its forms, consistency theory offers suggestions to those who wish to exercise control over others' behavior. Men act on the basis of their beliefs. Change their beliefs and you will change their actions. Give them inconsistency and you will change their beliefs. Let's look, then, at some kinds of inconsistencies that men typically have.

A common type of inconsistency occurs when an association is established between two beliefs that did not seem previously to be related. Suppose I know a college student and believe that he is a good one. Suppose, too, that I read an examination paper and decide that it is a bad one. The bad exam, I will say to myself, has undoubtedly been written by a bad student. Good students, after all, do good work; otherwise they would not be good students. It is the nature of the accomplishment, good or bad, which determines the evaluation of the student, good or bad.

What can I conclude, then, when I subsequently learn that it was indeed the "good" student who has written the "bad" exam? Circumstances seem to have played a trick on me. Completely against my desires, I find that I have accepted beliefs that the student is both good and not good, and that the exam is both bad and not bad. The student must have been bad, by implication, because he wrote a bad exam. The exam must have been good, by implication, because it was written by a good student. Any single belief of the set seems justified. But the entire set, as a whole, is completely unthinkable. There is nothing to do but reject something. I can retain the belief that the student is good; then I must change my belief that the exam was bad. I can retain the belief about the exam but change the other. Perhaps I can re-evaluate the student as one who is usually good but sometimes bad, thus enabling myself to accommodate the belief about the exam yet retain the belief about the student in a form not too different from the original. Perhaps I can re-interpret the importance to me of all this, deciding that the situation is really so insignificant that it doesn't matter. There are many things that I can do, and undoubtedly I will do one of them.

Though circumstances such as these often occur through the workings of impartial forces, the purveyor of influence knows that they can be produced through deliberate actions also. The advertiser, for example, knows that many of the people who are not now buying his product admire a certain famous baseball star. He knows that if I like the baseball player and believe that the player likes (uses, buys) the product, or is identified with it in some way, then I can have a consistent set of beliefs about the product only if I like it myself. For many people, the connection between an admired public figure and an advertised product, by means of a testimonial, undoubtedly produces inconsistency. Among the persons so affected, there are apparently many who reduce the inconsistency by deciding to favor or otherwise identify with the product. This effect happens often enough, in advertisers' opinions, to make the testimonial a popular device. It does not happen invariably, though, because the reader or listener reserves the choice of restoring consistency through some method not desired by the advertiser. Some uncooperative readers might decide that they no longer care for the admired personality, while others might decide to reject the belief that this person actually should be identified with the product as claimed in the ad.

Testimonials, thus, may be less than perfectly efficient in capitalizing on the inconsistency they produce. It is inefficient to produce inconsistency in people and then have many of them eliminate it by retaining their old beliefs and reject those you are trying to establish. But if the advertiser or other persuader could eliminate the chance of reducing inconsistency through alternate means, then all of the persuadees' changes of beliefs will be exactly those that the persuader wants. If the reader continues to like the baseball star, and accepts the assertion that the baseball star prefers the advertised product, then the reader will be strongly influenced to like the product. But how can this control of alternatives be established?

In a free society there will always be severe limits on what a persuader can do along these lines, but he can at any rate consider the possibilities. Many persuaders in our society are given free rein in channeling the reduction of the inconsistency they produce. Among them, for example, are public school teachers. Teachers are not often thought of as persuaders or manipulators, but this is only because they are fully and completely licensed by their society to act as such. This semantic trick has enabled us to think of certain people (i.e., those who carry out persuasion under full sanction of the entire adult population) as being educators rather than persuaders. Nonetheless, the elementary teacher produces considerable inconsistency in the child who insists that two and two make five. And the teacher sees that the inconsistency gets reduced by rejecting *this* belief, not by retaining it and rejecting another. This she does by making it clear to the student that his rejection of "two plus two make four" will not result in restoring consistency but will result in even stronger inconsistency due to the existence of other beliefs that he has. The teacher, indeed, is a far better persuader than the advertiser, because she has better control over the process of creating and reducing inconsistency.

Anybody can produce inconsistency simply by asserting something that the listener thinks is not true. But only the person who exercises some influence over the listener's decisions can hope to produce changes in beliefs by this frontal assault method. The teacher exercises control because she has, with society's help, first established in the student's mind the belief that "What teacher says is right." Then the student is confronted with the belief that "Teacher says 'Two and two make four' is right." If the student has previously adopted the belief that "Two and two make five," he now experiences inconsistency and the need to make a change somewhere in this set of three beliefs. One of the beliefs, "Teacher says

'Two and two make four' is right," can hardly be rejected by the student unless he is willing to entertain doubts about his capacity for receiving and interpreting light and sound waves. The other two beliefs are more susceptible to rejection simply because the student desires to reject them, and the fight is now on to see which one wins.

The defeated belief will generally be the one held with less intensity and/or confidence. The weaker the belief, the less likely its rejection will uproot the believer, and thus the more readily it may be overthrown. In elementary school, "What teacher says is right" will generally be believed with utmost intensity.

The teacher, in other words, has been granted the attribute of "source credibility" (the title of another selection in this book). To achieve this is the principal goal of the serious persuader, and the toughest problem facing most of them is that they have to earn their credibility entirely through their own actions rather than see it decreed by legislation and upheld by social fiat. The teacher may exercise persuasion through the direct establishment of "What teacher says is right" as a rule of society for students (subject to alteration in individual cases, of course).

But most persuaders do not have this advantage over their persuadees. A corporation executive, for example, must earn his source credibility with the board of directors by performing acceptable work. A public official must earn his credibility with the electorate through appropriate achievement. If they succeed, they are in a position to produce inconsistency and exercise control over its reduction. If they do not succeed, then they cannot have this control. A non-credible source who says you ought to do something you don't want to do, will only succeed in convincing you that you were right in not wanting to do it. He will produce inconsistency only for himself, not for others.

Many persuaders fail to achieve credibility when they might reasonably have succeeded. Certain persuaders, however, are confronted with a "built-in" hindrance to credibility which may make even the most skillful efforts fruitless. Advertisers, for example, must face the fact that anyone who looks at an advertisement knows immediately that the source of this message wants him to do something that he will not necessarily want to do. Advertisers, in other words, can never be highly credible sources because they are working within a framework that announces loudly and clearly that their credibility deserves to be questioned. Under conditions like these, the persuader still has the option of striving for high credibility, but he may prefer to try another means to produce and control inconsistency.

There are two alternate means. Both involve setting up a key belief which the persuadee accepts as true, and then showing him that such belief stands in inconsistent relationship with the belief to be changed.

The first way to set up an inconsistency-producing belief is to call forth a belief that the listener already possesses somewhere in the depths of his mind. Perhaps he has completely forgotten it. Perhaps he recalls it at certain times, but never considers it in connection with the topic of persuasion. The task of the persuader, then, is to make the persuadee recall the belief and recognize that it is salient to (i.e., has something to do with) the topic. A potentially inconsistent set of beliefs will never be recognized as such unless all the beliefs are consciously considered at one time. Making the key belief salient to the others will produce inconsistency and lead subsequently to change.

For example, a newspaper whose readers are largely businessmen may want to increase its readership among this group. The belief to be changed is "I don't need a subscription to this newspaper." The newspaper officials feel that the content of the paper is valuable to businessmen; it gives them information that helps them do a better job. If they do a better job, they will be promoted. Therefore, liking the newspaper is consistent with liking promotions. All this is obvious enough, the newspapermen feel, once it is stated. But that's the problem: the reader may not think about his long-held belief "I would like to be promoted" at the moment when he is evaluating the newspaper. What needs to be done, then, is to make the belief salient at the right time by using the argument that "You want to be promoted, and one of the ways to get promoted is to read and use the information available in our paper." Thereupon the persuadee will be confronted with the inconsistency of his set of beliefs and will change them. He is free, of course, to change whichever belief he chooses, and the newspaper's success will depend upon its ability to establish beliefs that resist rejection.

The other way to set up the key belief is to establish something that the persuadee has never previously considered at all. This often will be brand new information, such as the fact (alleged by some) that tobacco has a significant relationship to lung cancer. (This piece of news is one of the biggest producers of inconsistency in America today.) To cite other examples, one has only to look through advertisements for the word "new." Knowledge is constantly changing, and each day brings new facts that contradict old ones. Again, the persuader's success will depend upon his use of beliefs that the persuadee is willing to accept over the opposition of longer-established beliefs.

To sum up these few ideas, the persuader needs first of all to produce inconsistency in the mind of the persuadee. This he can easily do, but the deed is trivial if another condition is not also met. In addition, then, the persuader must attempt to channel the reduction of inconsistency so that the desired results are produced. The most efficient channeling can be obtained by the persuader who can force the persuadee to accept him as a credible source under penalty of punishment to be meted out by the society. When this is impossible, the next most efficient channeling can be had by obtaining the persuadee's voluntary willingness to attribute source credibility to the persuader. If this cannot be accomplished, then the persuader must find some other belief that, if accepted, will make the belief that he wants to change seem inconsistent. Established beliefs that can be made salient are one source to turn to, and another source is information that the persuadee has never previously considered.

In this brief treatment of consistency theory we have regarded the human being's susceptibility to inconsistency as being something like a natural resource, a source of energy available to persuaders in the same way that the water power of a descending stream is available to the factories on its banks. We have not discussed whether the unlimited tapping of this particular resource is a good or bad thing for mankind. Certainly the things we have baldly suggested as possible are not always desirable. One who is tempted to regard these potentialities with annoyance, however, should remember that humans are fated to suffer inconsistency in order to undergo the changes that constitute progress or improvement in their lives. Though the uses of inconsistency may include the most repugnant types of manipulation of human beings, it is also true that the accomplishments that we value most highly cannot occur apart from this phenomenon. The question of value is a matter of how, not whether, man's vulnerability to inconsistency should be capitalized upon by his fellow man.

Exercises

1. Preston discusses one reason an advertiser may use a testimonial from a baseball star. Pursue the analysis further, considering the differential effect of various types of celebrities. For example, why have you seen no great scholars appearing in advertisements to offer testimonials for shaving cream?

2. Under what conditions might an educator want his credibility to be questioned? Why?

3. Compare Preston's essay with Asch's research findings. Where are they consistent and where are they inconsistent?

Credibility of the Communicator

Carl I. Hovland
Irving L. Janis
Harold H. Kelley

Whether or not we do as another asks, or suggests, depends in part on what this selection calls "credibility." But how do we go about assigning credibility levels to the people who attempt to persuade us? One way to gain or lose confidence in the messages of a source is to check our ability to predict his behavior. If, in the past, we have been able to predict with some accuracy what he would do, we come to trust him because we feel that he will not surprise us. That is, his credibility is increased. If the source seldom does as we predict, his credibility is decreased.

There are other ways to assess the credibility of the source. For instance, if he includes verifiable material in his message, we can check it for truth. If our check confirms the source's claims, we raise our estimate of his credibility. Again, we are more likely to rate a source as highly credible if he can successfuly link his message with the messages of a source whose credibility is already high with us.

In this selection, Hovland, Janis, and Kelley are primarily interested in what effect the receiver's rating of source credibility has upon the persuasive efforts of the source.

The effectiveness of a communication is commonly assumed to depend to a considerable extent upon who delivers it. Governmental agencies take great pains to have their statements presented to Congress by the most acceptable advocates. Backyard gossips liberally sprinkle the names of respectable sources throughout their rumors. The debater, the author of scientific articles, and the news columnist all bolster their contentions with quotations from figures with prestige.

Approval of a statement by highly respected persons or organizations may have much the same positive effect as if they originate it. The organizer of a publicity campaign acquires a list of important persons who, by allowing their names to be displayed on the letterheads of the campaign

From Carl I. Hovland, Irving L. Janis, and Harold H. Kelley, *Communication and Persuasion: Psychological Studies of Opinion Change* (New Haven, Conn.: Yale University Press, 1953), pp. 19–48. Reprinted as edited by permission of Yale University Press.

literature, tacitly approve the campaign's objectives. The impact of a message probably depends also upon the particular publication or channel through which it is transmitted. The credibility of an advertisement seems to be related to some extent to the reputation of the particular magazine in which it appears.

The examples above suggest the importance of persons, groups, or media which can be subsumed under the general category of "sources." Differences in effectiveness may sometimes depend upon whether the source is perceived as a speaker who originates the message, an endorser who is cited in the message, or the channel through which the message is transmitted. However, the same basic factors and principles probably underlie the operation of each of the many types of sources, so an analysis of the psychological processes mediating the reactions to one kind of source may be expected to be applicable to other types. In this chapter we shall deal primarily with situations in which the effects are attributable to a single clear-cut source, which is usually an individual speaker who communicates directly to the audience and gives his own views on an issue. We shall refer to this kind of source as a "communicator."

In terms of the analysis of opinion change . . . , a communicator can affect the change process in a variety of ways. For example, if he is a striking personality and an effective speaker who holds the attention of an audience, he can increase the likelihood of attentive consideration of the new opinion. If he is personally admired or a member of a high status group, his words may raise the incentive value of the advocated opinion by suggesting that approval, from himself or from the group, will follow its adoption. When acceptance is sought by using arguments in support of the advocated view, the perceived expertness and trustworthiness of the communicator may determine the credence given them.

We shall assume that these various effects of the communicator are mediated by attitudes toward him which are held by members of the audience. Any of a number of different attitudes may underlie the influence exerted by a given communicator. Some may have to do with feelings of affection and admiration and stem in part from desires to be like him. Others may involve awe and fear of the communicator, based on perceptions of his power to reward or punish according to one's adherence to his recommendations or demands. Still other important attitudes are those of trust and confidence. These are related to perceptions of the communicator's credibility, including beliefs about his knowledge, intelligence, and sincerity.

These and other attitudes which affect communicator influence are learned by each individual in a variety of influence situations. Through his experiences of accepting and rejecting social influences, the individual acquires expectations about the validity of various sources of information and learns that following the suggestions of certain persons is highly rewarding whereas accepting what certain others recommend is less so. The products of this learning, which constitute a complex set of attitudes toward various persons as sources of influence, generalize to a wide variety of other persons, groups, and agencies and thereby affect the individual's reactions to communications which he perceives to emanate from them.

If the conditions of learning these attitudes are variable (as they almost inevitably are), the communicator characteristics relevant to the amount of influence exerted cannot be expected to fall into neat categories; they are probably specific as to time and cultural setting. For example, the specific attributes of persons who are viewed as powerful or credible can be expected to differ from culture to culture. There is also likely to be some degree of variability within a given culture, particularly as different subject matters are considered. However certain kinds of attitudes, such as those related to affection, the communicator's power, and his credibility, are probably important in all societies. Moreover, the general principles concerning the antecedents and consequences of such attitudes may be expected to have a high degree of generality, at least within our own culture.

The limited area chosen for investigation in our research program concerns the factors related to *credibility* of the source. Analysis of this area in the present chapter will focus on two problems. How do differences in the credibility of the communicator affect (1) the way in which the content and presentation are perceived and evaluated? (2) the degree to which attitudes and beliefs are modified? In analyzing the findings bearing on these questions, we shall briefly consider possible psychological processes underlying the observed effects and the changes that occur with the passage of time.

Background

An individual's tendency to accept a conclusion advocated by a given communicator will depend in part upon how well informed and intelligent he believes the communicator to be. However, a recipient may believe that a communicator is capable of transmitting valid statements, but still be inclined to reject the communication if he suspects the communicator is motivated to make nonvalid assertions. It seems necessary, therefore, to make a distinction between (1) the extent to which a communicator is perceived to be a source of valid assertions (his "expertness") and (2) the degree of confidence in the communicator's intent to communicate the assertions he considers most valid (his "trustworthiness"). In any given case, the weight given a communicator's assertions by his audience will depend upon both of these factors, and this resultant value can be referred to as the "credibility" of the communicator. In this section we shall review some of the background material bearing upon the two components of credibility: expertness and trustworthiness.

A variety of characteristics of the communicator may evoke attitudes related to expertness. For example, the age of a communicator may sometimes be regarded as an indication of the extent of his experience. A position of leadership in a group may be taken as an indication of ability to predict social reactions. In certain matters persons similar to the recipient of influence may be considered more expert than persons different from him. An individual is likely to feel that persons with status, values, interests, and needs similar to his own see things as he does and judge them from the same point of view. Because of this, their assertions about matters of which the individual is ignorant but where he feels the viewpoint makes a difference (e.g., about the satisfaction of a given job or the attractiveness of some personality) will tend to carry special credibility. Hence the research on the factors of age, leadership, and similarity of social background may involve the expertness factor to some extent.[1]*

Few systematic investigations have been made of the effects of variations in expertness on opinion change, but suggestive results come from a number of studies. Typical findings are those of Bowden, Caldwell, and West, concerning attitudes toward various solutions of the economic problem of an appropriate monetary standard for the United States. Using subjects from a broad age range, they determined the amount of agreement with statements when attributed to men in different professions (e.g., lawyers, engineers, educators). The statements were approved most frequently when attributed to educators and businessmen, and least frequently when attributed to ministers. A study by Kulp provides evidence that for graduate students in education the social and political opinions of professional educators and social scientists are somewhat more influential than the opinions of lay citizens. While other factors may have been involved, it seems likely that the results of these studies are partly attributable to differences in perceived expertness of the various sources.

With respect to the second component of credibility, there have been numerous speculations about the characteristics of communicators which evoke attitudes of trust or distrust and about the consequences of these attitudes for acceptance of communications. One of the most general hypotheses is that when a person is perceived as having a definite *intention* to persuade others, the likelihood is increased that he will be perceived as having something to gain and, hence, as less worthy of trust. As Lazarsfeld, Berelson, and Gaudet have pointed out, casual and nonpurposive

---

* At various points in the text additional comments about pertinent research evidence or elaborations of theoretical points are necessary. In order to avoid interrupting the main presentation, this additional material is covered separately in a series of Notes, referred to by superscripts in the text and presented at the end. . . .

conversations probably derive part of their effectiveness from the fact that the recipient of a remark does not have the critical and defensive mental set that he typically carries into situations where he knows others are out to influence him. Remarks such as those overheard in subways and other crowded public places would be especially effective in this respect because under such circumstances it is quite apparent that the speaker has no intention to persuade the bystanders. This phenomenon seems to be exploited in some of the techniques currently used in commercial advertising.

A specific set of cues as to the motives or intentions of the communicator has to do with symbols of his social role. Persons in some occupations and offices (e.g., radio announcers, publicity agents, salesmen) are known to be under special pressures to communicate certain things and not others. For other roles, for example that of the newspaper reporter, the pressures may be perceived to operate in the direction of giving all the facts as accurately as he can ascertain them. That publicity men assume greater credibility will be accorded news stories as compared with advertisements is manifested by their repeated attempts to obtain publicity for their clients in the news columns.

Suggestive evidence on the importance of the communicator's being considered sincere rather than "just another salesman" is provided by Merton's analysis of Kate Smith's war bond selling campaign during which she broadcast continuously for eighteen hours. It appears that one of the main reasons for her phenomenal success was the high degree of sincerity attributed to her by the audience: ". . . *she really means* anything she ever says." Even though she appeared frequently on commercially sponsored programs and engaged in much the same promotional activities as other radio stars, the public felt that in carrying out the bond drive she was interested only in the national welfare and did not care about the personal publicity she would obtain. One of the most interesting suggestions of Merton's analysis is that the marathon effort itself may have contributed to her reputation as a sincere, unselfish person. Even among the persons who regularly listened to her programs (as well as among nonlisteners), more of those who heard the marathon were convinced of her selflessness in promoting the bonds than of those who failed to hear it. "Above all," Merton says, "*the presumed stress and strain of the eighteen-hour series of broadcasts served to validate Smith's sincerity.*"

The possible effects on opinion change of attitudes of trust or distrust toward communicators are suggested by some correlational data from Hovland, Lumsdaine, and Sheffield. The basic data involve audience reactions to the War Department's orientation films. The pertinent attitudes were not specifically directed toward the communicator but consisted rather of general judgments as to the purposes for which the film was being presented. After viewing "The Battle of Britain" the soldiers were asked this open-ended question: "What did you think was the reason for showing this movie to you and the other men?" On the basis of their answers, the men were classified as to whether they considered the film's purpose to be "propagandistic" (in the sense of having a manipulative intent) or "informational." A comparison of the two groups in terms of the opinion changes produced by the film revealed it to be less effective with men who judged its intent to be manipulative than with men considering it informational. This correlation may merely indicate a general attitude toward the content of the film which is reflected in both opinion change and judgments of the film. But another possible interpretation is that there exists a tendency to reject communications which are perceived as being manipulative in intent.

The material just considered suggests that attitudes related to the expertness and trustworthiness of a communicator may affect his influence. Evidence from systematic research can contribute much to determining the conditions under which this phenomenon occurs and, in addition, can answer questions as to the specific processes involved. In the next section we shall consider the available evidence from the point of view of the two following problems:

First, do variations in the characteristics of a communicator with respect to expertness and trustworthiness affect recipients' evaluations of his presentation and of the arguments and appeals he uses? This problem becomes particularly important when a communication is constructed so as to derive much of its effectiveness from persuasive arguments and motivating appeals. Sometimes a communication presents only a conclusion, without supporting argumentation, and its acceptance appears to be increased merely by attributing it to a prestigeful or respected source. A large proportion of past experimental investigations of communicator effects—the studies of "prestige suggestion"—have concentrated upon this particular phenomenon. Presumably, the observed effects are mediated by an increased incentive value of the recommended opinion brought about through implicit promises of approval from the communicator or the group he represents, or through implicit assurances, by virtue of the authoritativeness of the source, that the opinion has adequate justification in fact and logic. But when a communication includes explicit supporting evidence and arguments, the question arises as to whether they are judged to be any more relevant, sound, or logical when presented by a highly credible source than by a less credible one. In brief, to what extent is the effectiveness of the supporting argumentation dependent upon attitudes toward the communicator?

Second, how do variations in the communicator characteristics related to expertness and trustworthiness affect the amount of opinion change produced by a communication? This, of course, is the crucial problem for persuasive communications. It is necessary to investigate opinion change independently of the kinds of changes specified above. As we shall see, the characteristics of the communicator may affect evaluations of the presentation without necessarily affecting the degree to which the conclusion is accepted.

Research Evidence

As noted earlier, it has been suggested that perceptions of the communicator's intentions to persuade his audience may affect judgments of his credibility. A study by Ewing deals with a special aspect of this problem—the degree of agreement between a communicator's announced intentions and the audience's initial bias. The results suggest that this variable affects the amount of opinion change produced and that this effect may be mediated by different evaluations of the presentation. Two groups of subjects were given the same communication which, as compared with the subjects' initial opinions, was unfavorable toward Henry Ford. In the introduction and throughout his presentation the propagandist made explicit statements about his intention: in one group he claimed that his purpose was to make people feel more favorable toward Ford and in the other group to make them feel less favorable.

The results on opinion change show that more change in the direction of the communication was produced in the first group where the intent of the propagandist was represented as being in agreement with the subjects' initial bias.

In general, Ewing's results support the hypothesis that when a communication comes from an unknown or ambiguous source, acceptance will be increased if, at the beginning, the communicator explicitly claims that his own position is in accord with that held by the audience. His results suggest that this effect occurs even when the communication advocates a view directly opposed to the audience's initial opinions. This outcome would not be expected, of course, when the content of the communication obviously and repeatedly belies the communicator's statement of his intent.

Ewing presents further analysis of his data which suggests that this result may be influenced by how favorably the recipients react to the communication in terms of its bias, logic, etc. Apparently these evaluations depend not only upon the content but upon the amount of conflict between the initial bias of the recipient and the avowed intention of the communicator. If a communicator presents material in support of a conclusion somewhat different from his avowed position, this may sometimes be taken to indicate great objectivity in his thinking and form the basis for confidence in his arguments.

An experimental variation in source credibility through the use of communicators differing in trustworthiness was produced in the study by

Hovland and Weiss of retention effects. The general procedure consisted of presenting an identical communication to two groups, in one case from a source of high credibility and in the other from one of low credibility. Opinion questionnaires were administered before, immediately after, and a month after the communication. Four different topics were selected, each presented to some subjects by a source of high credibility and to other subjects by one of low credibility. Affirmative and negative versions of each topic were employed.

Each of the subjects (college students in an advanced undergraduate course) received a booklet containing one article on each of the four topics with the name of the source given at the end of each article.

The four topics and the sources used in the experiment were as follows:

	High Credibility Source	*Low Credibility Source*
A. *Antihistamine Drugs:* Should the antihistamine drugs continue to be sold without a doctor's prescription?	*New England Journal of Biology and Medicine*	Magazine A (A mass circulation monthly pictorial magazine)
B. *Atomic Submarines:* Can a practicable atomic-powered submarine be built at the present time?	Robert J. Oppenheimer	*Pravda*
C. *The Steel Shortage:* Is the steel industry to blame for the current shortage of steel?	*Bulletin of National Resources Planning Board*	Writer A (An antilabor, anti-New Deal, "rightist" newspaper columnist)
D. *The Future of Movie Theaters:* As a result of TV, will there be a decrease in the number of movie theaters in operation by 1955?	*Fortune* magazine	Writer B (A woman movie-gossip columnist)

A questionnaire administered before the communication obtained judgments from the subjects as to the trustworthiness of a long list of sources, including the specific ones used. An analysis of these judgments revealed very definitely that the sources used with the communications differed greatly in their credibility. The four high credibility sources were judged to be trustworthy by 81 to 95 per cent of the subjects; the low credibility sources were judged trustworthy by 1 to 21 per cent.

Evaluations of Presentation. The differences in initial attitudes toward the sources definitely affected audience evaluations of the presentation, which were obtained immediately after exposure to the communication. Even though the communications being judged were identical as to content, the presentations were considered to be "less fair" and the conclusions to be "less justified" when the source was of low rather than of high credibility. Although responses to these questions may have involved reactions to the entire communication situation rather than just evaluations of the arguments and conclusions per se, they do indicate that judgments of content characteristics, such as how well the facts in a given communication justify the conclusion, are significantly affected by variations in the source.

Opinion Change. Opinion change in the direction advocated by the communication occurred significantly more often when it originated from a high credibility source than when from a low one. The expected difference is obtained on three of the four topics, the exception being the one having to do with the future of movie theaters.

When data were obtained on opinion changes shown four weeks after having read the articles, the differential effectiveness of sources with high and low credibility had disappeared; there were no significant differences between them. This resulted from decreased acceptance of the point of view advocated by the high credibility sources and increased acceptance of the position of the low credibility sources. The former result could be attributed to forgetting of the content, decreased awareness of the communicator's credibility, or both. The increase in opinion change shown by the low credibility group, however, suggests that the negative effects of the "untrustworthy" source wore off and permitted the arguments presented in the communication to produce a delayed positive effect. According to this explanation, the effect of the source is maximal at the time of the communication but decreases with the passage of time more rapidly than the effects of the content. This is one of the mechanisms that can account for an increased adherence to the communicator's conclusion after a lapse of time.

This explanation suggests that in the present experiment there was relatively independent retention of the source and content, with the sustained effects apparently determined primarily by retention of the content. The phenomenon would be expected to occur when the communication contains not only the source's opinion but supporting evidence and arguments. This expectation is based upon the assumption that these supporting aspects of the communication can be evaluated on their own merits and without regard to the source. They will not initially evoke evaluative responses involving the source to the degree that the purely "opinion" aspects of the message will. Subsequently they will more frequently occur without accompanying responses which label the source and bring it to mind.

Under other conditions, however, one may expect the source and the content to be closely associated in memory. For example, when the communication presents a message that only one or a few persons could have originated, retention of the content will tend to be accompanied by retention of the source. If a person hears a radio talk by a cabinet member about policy decisions made in the President's Cabinet, he is likely to recall the source when he recalls the assertion. On the other hand, if the assertion could have emanated from a variety of sources, retention of the two will tend to be independent.

The preceding hypotheses may be specific cases of a more general proposition: the stronger the perceptual response to the source during initial exposure to the communication, the more likely it is that the source will be evoked when, on subsequent occasions, any aspect of the communication situation is present. Strong responses to a communicator would presumably occur when the communication situation highlights his uniqueness as a source or when the situation forces the audience to consider his characteristics in evaluating the assertion. Other factors may operate in the same manner; e.g., when the communicator's manner of speaking elicits a strong emotional response to him, the audience will be especially likely to remember who presented the message. A systematic exploration of these factors awaits further investigation. . . .

In summary, the research evidence indicates that the reactions to a communication are significantly affected by cues as to the communicator's intentions, expertness, and trustworthiness. The very same presentation tends to be judged more favorably when made by a communicator of high credibility than by one of low credibility. Furthermore, in the case of two of the three studies on credibility, the immediate acceptance of the recommended opinion was greater when presented by a highly credible communicator.

From the results, it is not possible to disentangle the effects of the two main components of credibility—trustworthiness and expertness—but it appears that both are important variables. In the Hovland and Mandell study where the suspect source differed from the nonsuspect one primarily in characteristics relevant to trustworthiness (motives, intentions), a marked effect occurred on judgments of the fairness of the presentation, but there was little effect on amount of opinion change. The small effect on opinions may be attributable to a special combination of factors such that the content of the speech and the qualifications of the speaker were more important than his personal motives. On the other hand, in the Kelman and Hovland investigation, it appears that variations in attitudes related to fairness and trustworthiness were responsible for the sizable differences in amount of opinion change.

It may be noted in passing that even with untrustworthy sources the over-all effect was usually in the direction favored by the communication.

The negative communicator tended merely to produce *less* positive change than the positive source. Presumably, the arguments contained in the communications produced large enough positive effects to counteract negative effects due to the communicator. Negative or boomerang effects might be expected where no arguments are contained in a communication delivered by a negative source or when the audience members anticipate that his conclusions will consistently be in opposition to their best interests.

Bases of Differential Effects

The fact that identical communications are evaluated differently by subjects exposed to sources of different credibility is subject to several interpretations. Judgments about content and style are often merely specific symptoms of general approach or avoidance reactions to the entire communication situation. On the basis of psychological studies of the manner in which expectations influence perceptions and of the phenomenon of "halo effect" in judgmental behavior, these broad effects of different labeling of the communicator come as no surprise. They do, however, raise some question as to the processes which mediate or make possible the differential opinion changes. For example, do persons initially negative toward the source listen less closely to the communication? Or do they, perhaps, distort the meaning of what is said, and hence judge it to have been less well presented? The more general problem here is essentially this: At what point in the process of attending to, perceiving, interpreting, learning, and believing the content of the communication do attitudes toward the source have their effect?

In accounting for the different amounts of opinion change produced by communicators of high versus low credibility, one obvious possibility would be that people tend not to expose themselves to communications from sources toward whom they have negative attitudes. However, the present experiments all involve captive audiences, typically college classes, whose members could hardly avoid being exposed to the communication. Under these conditions there remain two different explanations for the lesser effectiveness of unfavorable (e.g., low credibility) communicators in bringing about opinion change:

1. Because of their unfavorable attitudes, members of the audience do not pay close attention to the content and/or do not attempt to comprehend the exact meaning of what is said. The former could result from thinking about the communicator, while the latter might result from "reading into" the content various implications that correspond to the assumed intent of the communicator. As a result, they *learn* the material less well than when it is presented by a favorable source and, failing to learn it, are unable to adhere to the recommended conclusions.

2. Because of their unfavorable attitudes, members of the audience are not motivated to *accept* or believe what the communicator says and recommends.

With respect to choosing between these two explanations, the foregoing studies present recall data which indicate the extent to which the materials presented by the various communicators were learned. In the study of high versus low credibility sources, on a variety of topics, Hovland and Weiss found no significant difference in the number of fact quiz items answered correctly immediately after the communication. In the study of suspect versus nonsuspect sources, Hovland and Mandell administered a fact quiz on the economics of devaluation immediately after the communication. There was no difference between the two source versions in the number of items answered correctly.

In the Kelman and Hovland study, recall for items on the communication was determined at the delayed after-test. Here again there was no significant difference between the positive and negative sources. An interesting incidental finding was that recall was significantly better when the communication was given by the neutral source than by either the positive or negative source. The authors suggest that affective responses may adversely influence the amount of material learned and recalled, and that both the positive and negative communicators were responded to with greater affect than the neutral one. An emotional reaction to the communicator may focus attention upon him to the detriment of attending to his conclusions and learning his arguments.[2] This result indicates, as we would expect, that there are some instances in which the communicator affects the degree to which the content is acquired.

In summary, the present studies of various sources in general reveal little difference between the most and least credible sources in the degree to which the content of their communications is *learned*. In most instances, the differences were certainly not large enough to account for the differential opinion changes produced by high and low credibility communicators. Thus, persons exposed to a low credibility communicator evidently learned as much of what was said as did persons exposed to a high credibility source, but the former accepted the recommendations much less than did the latter. These findings, together with those from Weiss's investigation, indicate that some recipients learned what was said without believing the communicator or modifying their attitudes accordingly. Change of opinion obviously requires not only learning what the new point of view is but also becoming motivated to accept it.

In some instances where there is strong resistance to the content and an opportunity to avoid exposure to it, the recipient may, of course, neither learn the content nor accept it. Not only were the captive audiences of the present experiments in classroom situations where they are generally set to pay close attention, but the communications were generally highly structured and permitted relatively little misinterpretation. Although under these conditions subjects apparently are motivated to learn and remember most of the assertions in the communications, there are large differences among experimental treatments in the degree to which the arguments are accepted and incorporated as changes in opinions. This strongly suggests that a critical aspect of opinion change is the degree to which recipients become motivated to accept the assertions contained in the communication. The evidence is quite clear that acceptance or rejection depends in part upon attitudinal reactions toward the source of the communication.

Why is acceptance likely to be heightened by increasing the credibility of the communicator? Our principle assumption is that the individual is motivated to accept conclusions and recommendations which he anticipates will be substantiated by further experiences or will lead to reward, social approval, and avoidance of punishment. These anticipations are increased when a recommendation is presented by a person who is believed to be informed, insightful, and willing to express his true beliefs and knowledge, and are decreased when cues of low credibility are present. Thus the motives of the audience to accept recommendations are higher the more credible the person making them. It should also be noted that the strength of these motives probably depends upon the situation in which the recipient of the communication finds himself and upon his corresponding dependence upon others for information and advice. The motivation to seek and accept advice from credible sources seems to be increased considerably when the person is in a situation which requires finer discriminations than he is capable of or which demands specialized information not at his disposal.

Are the Effects of High Credibility Sources Enduring?

We have noted that in terms of immediate opinion change high credibility sources tend to be somewhat more effective than low credibility sources. However, delayed after-tests in the experiments by Hovland and Weiss and Kelman and Hovland indicated that this differential effectiveness had disappeared after an interval of about three weeks. These results are summarized in Figure 1. In both studies there was a highly significant difference between high and low communicators on the immediate after-test, but in both instances this difference had virtually disappeared several weeks later.

These results raise important questions about the long-term significance of the credibility of the communicator. Unfortunately, little other evidence is available on the degree to which communicator effects are sustained.[3] The main implication of the present results is that the credibility of the communicator may, under certain circumstances mentioned earlier, be important only with respect to the amount of *immediate* opinion change produced. Under circumstances where there is a very close association between the source and content of a communication, however, the effect of the communicator may be more enduring. The immediate effects reported here may have considerable practical significance if the purpose of the communication is to elicit some type of immediate action and if subsequent behavior is of little concern. Furthermore, if the immediate action involves some type of formal or informal commitment, lasting effects may be obtained.

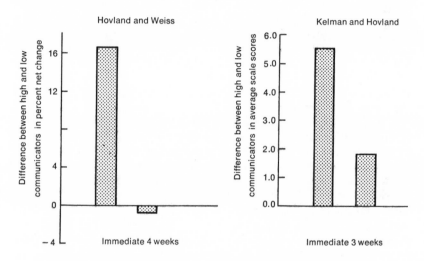

Figure 1. Differential effectiveness, immediate and delayed, of high versus low credibility communicators

The problems posed by the retention data must be considered in relation to other factors affecting retention. . . .

Implications for Further Research

The findings in the preceding section indicated that the delivery of a communication by a communicator of high credibility increases the amount of opinion change measured immediately after exposure, and that a communicator of low credibility may bring about a decrease in opinion change. What are the limiting conditions under which such effects are obtained?

Let us begin with cases of the type where the source has been found to *augment* acceptance. Typically a source of high credibility delivers a communication containing arguments and assertions which, because of their lack of compellingness, their inadequate substantiation, or incompatibility with pre-existing opinions, the recipient has little tendency to accept. There are certain variations from this situation in which it is fairly obvious that the credibility of the source will have little or no effect on opinion change. For example, if the message is fully accepted on its own merits, the highly credible source can have no added effect on acceptance; if the credibility of the source is negligible (e.g., the source is trustworthy but completely uninformed), the message may be accepted to no greater degree than if it were reacted to in terms of its intrinsic qualities. In general, it appears that source credibility has maximal effects on acceptance when the source and content are such that there would be considerable discrepancy between the attitudinal responses to each of them alone—in this particular case, when the communicator would produce a considerable tendency to accept whatever he says and the communication, in and of itself, would produce little or no tendency toward acceptance.

There are important variations of the typical case which would seem on theoretical grounds to represent limiting conditions for the generalization that positive communicators increase acceptance for their messages. The first to be considered consists of a highly reliable communicator giving a communication which, on its own merits, would be strongly rejected.

With respect to this first situation, the following hypothesis is suggested: Under conditions where positive attitudes toward the source are very strong (e.g., he is considered as highly credible) and where the tendency to reject the conclusions and arguments in the communication is very strong, *there is a tendency to dissociate the source and the content.* We may also speculate as to the various forms this dissociation may take. At the time of exposure, it may consist either in denying the source's responsibility for the communication or in reinterpreting the content and conclusion of the message. In effect, the individual can conclude either that "someone else gave this communication" or that "this communicator meant something else when he gave it." Dissociation may also occur in the form of not recalling who said what, as is suggested by the retention data described in the preceding section. In any event, the importance of dissociation for the effectiveness of persuasive communications is that it reduces or eliminates the direct influence of the source on acceptance of the content. To the extent that the recipient is able to dissociate source and message, *the acceptance of the message will be independent of the source.*

Phenomena which appear to be related to these dissociation effects have been noted in the literature and in the present research. In several reports, it appears that where a communication was highly incompatible with the audience's preconception of the alleged source, denial was made that the suggested source was really responsible for the assertion. For example, Lewis had college students judge political slogans as to their social significance, compellingness to action, intelligence of their authors, etc. Subsequently, some of the subjects (those who were in sympathy with the Communist party) were given evaluations of the slogans allegedly made by Earl Browder, at that time leader of the party in the United States. The purpose was to see whether this communication, which was in considerable disagreement with the subjects' previous judgments, would affect their evaluations of the slogans. Several of the subjects suspected a hoax and refused to believe that the evaluations had been made by Browder. Another subject suggested that Browder had been misquoted by newspapermen. A similar phenomenon was observed in Birch's study. Another phenomenon of this type consists in attributing special motives to the communicator or assuming that his delivery of the communication can be discounted because of unusual circumstances. This defines the communication as a special act not to be taken at face value. For instance, confronted with contradictory evaluations supposedly coming from Franklin Roosevelt, one of Lewis' subjects, who respected Roosevelt, stated: "Roosevelt's ranking seems to me to be slightly off. Perhaps it was before he became social-conscious." Other subjects felt Roosevelt was trying to be objective or was deliberately using special criteria in making his judgments. Asch provides other examples in which an incongruity between source and content is resolved by making highly specific interpretations of the source's motives for communication.

The reinterpretation of the message is related to a phenomenon which has been emphasized by Asch. It has frequently been assumed, at least implicitly, that communication-induced changes in opinion indicate re-evaluation of the same objects or statements judged initially. Asch has challenged this assumption and argued strongly that these processes involve *"a change in the object of judgment, rather than in the judgment of the object."* The example most often cited to illustrate change in the object of judgment appears in Asch's study of college students' judgments of professions as influenced by evaluations allegedly made by 500 other students. When told that the other students had judged the profession of politics highest with respect to intelligence, social usefulness, etc., the subjects markedly raised their valuation of politicians. In subsequent interviews they reported having shifted their conception of politics from that of local ward politics to that of national politics and statesmanship. Thus, they apparently reinterpreted what it was that the 500 students were evaluating. Similar examples found in studies by Lewis and Luchins also indicate that the type of change emphasized by Asch may occur at least under some conditions.

Credibility of the Communicator

The effects noted by these investigators suggest what happens when subjects dissociate the original source and content: they are likely to deny that the source actually was responsible for the communication or to reinterpret the "real" meaning they believe the message to have. For example, if the message given by a highly respected source is repugnant to the audience's values, the source may be thought to be someone else capable of originating such ideas, or the message will be interpreted so as to be congruent with the actual respected source. These specific tendencies, as well as some of the other effects discussed here, can be derived from Heider's logical analysis of "attitudes and cognitive organization." He suggests that we tend to maintain the same attitude toward persons as toward their possessions and actions. As applied to the problem of source credibility, the implications would be as follows: When we attribute high credibility to a person but dislike what he communicates, our attitudes related to him are in an "unbalanced" state. This tends to be resolved in any of three ways: (1) change in attitudes toward the communication (which would include either accepting it or reinterpreting it), (2) change in attitudes toward the communicator, and (3) change in perception of the communicator's role in originating the communication. These changes tend to be of such a nature as to restore a state of balance or congruence among the various attitudes related to the communicator and his actions.

Dissociation of source and content may also occur following exposure to the communication and may take the form of forgetting that the particular communicator gave the specific content. Some of the results on retention from the experiment by Hovland and Weiss bear on this hypothesis. High credibility sources initially produced greater acceptance of the conclusion than low credibility ones. With the passage of time, this difference disappeared. However, the subjects were able, when asked, to recall both the original source and content. The authors suggest that with the passage of time there is a decrease in tendency to "associate spontaneously" the content with the source. Some results from Kelman and Hovland on reinstatement of source, suggest that subjects can be made to re-establish the association of source and content, with a resulting reappearance of the original differences in the degree to which the communications of high and low credibility sources are accepted. The results are generally consistent with the hypotheses that dissociation between source and content can occur following the communication and that to the degree that dissociation does occur the effect of the source on acceptance is attenuated.

We have already speculated as to the conditions under which dissociation through time of source and content are likely to occur. The central hypothesis is that dissociation will occur to a lesser degree the more vivid and intimate the relation between source and content at the time of the initial exposure. A vivid and intimate relation would occur, for example, if a particular source is one of the few persons who could possess the "inside" information contained in the communication or if, in evaluating new or unexpected information of great importance, the recipient must rely heavily on evaluations of the source.

Several hypotheses may also be mentioned which specify the conditions under which denial of the source's responsibility for the message or reinterpretation of the content will occur. One would expect a greater tendency for denial of the source to occur the more ambiguous the evidence is as to his responsibility. The evidence will be most clear-cut when the source appears personally and presents the communication directly. It will be more ambiguous when the speech is recorded, printed, or filmed, and even more so when the source is quoted by someone else. We may also hypothesize that reinterpretation of the content will occur more frequently when there is some ambiguity as to the question raised and the conclusion suggested in the communication. This would be true for complicated issues which have many sides and where the conclusion is qualified in several ways.

When source and content are such that they tend to elicit radically different reactions from the audience, a problem arises as to whether a contrast effect occurs. Consider, for example, a communicator who is viewed as highly expert and of whom stimulating and insightful ideas are expected. If he makes a banal or trivial statement, he may seriously violate the audience's high expectations. If a listener cannot readily dissociate him from the statement (via the processes described above) the statement may seem much less acceptable than if it had been presented by a source for whom expectations were not so high. This raises the possibility of a special situation in which there is an inverse relation between credibility of source and acceptance of his conclusions.

Interesting problems also arise when highly objectionable content is presented by communicators of only moderate credibility. For example, let us consider the instance where the content is unsubstantiated and runs counter to the audience's loyalties. In this case the recipient is likely to remain uninfluenced by the content and, instead, change his evaluation of the communicator. In other words, attitudes toward a communicator are not maintained without reference to what he says and does. In this regard, Duncker and Asch have pointed out that the prestige of a source is too often viewed as something that can be "tacked on" to any assertion and that is equally effective no matter what is being said. The hypothesis which requires investigation is that under these conditions, where the assertion is repulsive to the audience and the source is only mildly respected, there is a tendency to change one's attitude toward the communicator in the direction of attributing less credibility to him or otherwise becoming more negative toward him. This result is more probable the less positive are the initial attitudes toward him. (It may be noted that this type of change is one of those suggested by Heider's analysis mentioned above.)

Examples of changes in attitudes toward the communicator as a result of objectionable content are infrequent in the literature. In two studies involving length judgments, some of the subjects began to doubt the source's eyesight after hearing assertions greatly at variance with reality. In another case, initially negative attitudes toward the source seem to have been strengthened by the "absurdity" of the assertion. The paucity of examples of this type can be attributed to the fact that most investigators in this field have been primarily interested in changing attitudes on the issues discussed in the communication. As a result, the typical investigation has used highly prestigeful sources toward whom initial attitudes are fairly strong and stable, and has not included measures of attitudes toward the communicators, so that even if changes in these attitudes occurred, they would not have been detected.

The preceding discussion has been limited to situations where the credibility of the source might be expected to heighten acceptance. What of situations where material is presented by low credibility sources? Dissociation effects and changes in attitudes toward the communicator might also be expected to occur here. For example, if arguments are presented by a communicator whose motives are open to suspicion, acceptance would ordinarily be lowered; but if the arguments are well substantiated and very impressive, the content may be dissociated from the source in the manner described above. If the initial negative attitudes toward the source are not very strong, they may be improved by the favorable presentation. This does not mean that the positive and negative communicators act upon the process of opinion change in exactly the same way. For example, inattentiveness will be more marked with communicators of low credibility, so that even though their message might be quite convincing it may never receive an adequate hearing. The positive communicator who gives an unacceptable message will probably have the audience's attention, at least during the initial part of his presentation. However, certain generalizations about dissociation phenomena and changes in attitudes toward communicators probably apply to both positive and negative, high and low credibility communicators.

The foregoing analysis suggests some of the possible limiting conditions under which the relationship between source credibility and acceptance may be eliminated or greatly attenuated. It also indicates some of the effects other than variations in acceptance (e.g., dissociation of source and content, change in attitude toward source) which can arise out of situations where, for example, unacceptable content is presented by a positive source. In order to understand these various effects and the conditions under which they occur, one is led to a fact which is obvious but has rarely been incorporated into investigations of communicator effects: Attitudes toward the communicator and the cues which elicit them operate in interaction with many other factors of the communication situation. These other factors include such variables as initial attitudes toward the content, cues as to the source's responsibility for the content, the congruence between what is said and prior knowledge about the source's position on the issue, the complexity of the question raised in the communication, the ambiguity of the proposed answer, and the vividness of the source.

Another broad set of factors includes the characteristics of the situation in which the communication occurs. While the individual has attitudes of reliance and trust toward various kinds of communicators, the extent to which these attitudes are evoked at any given time depends to some degree upon the kind of situation in which he finds himself. For example, in a situation where he is confronted with a problem whose solution he believes requires highly technical information, an individual will be especially susceptible to influence from persons who are perceived to be experts. In like manner, when involved in a conflict with a socially disapproved impulse, an individual may seek reassuring advice from older persons who resemble his parents and are in positions of authority with respect to dominant moral values. When the problem is one of gaining social acceptance, the most effective communicators probably will be those group leaders and officials viewed as most able to predict majority reactions. In these and other ways the nature of the problem situation which exists at the time of receiving a communication will affect a person's responsiveness to specific kinds of communicators.[4] We should also note the possible influence of attitudes toward the communicator which are unrelated to credibility, such as affection, admiration, awe, and fear. The existence of these attitudes may make changes in attitudes toward the source less probable. For example, a person may less readily deny the expertness of a communicator for whom he has great affection, even though that communicator transmits objectionable material.

All of these various factors in the communication situation interact with attitudes toward the communicator's credibility and determine the degree to which the fact of the source's being reliable will heighten acceptance or whether the other outcomes we have suggested will occur. Unfortunately, evidence bearing on the kinds of hypotheses considered here is almost nonexistent. What is needed is investigations using modern experimental designs which will permit systematic analysis of the interaction among these variables. As theory in this area develops, we can expect additional hypotheses as to the limiting conditions for the differential effects on opinion change of various types of sources. Some of these will undoubtedly shed further light upon the persistence of source effects. The evaluation of such hypotheses through the use of experimental procedures promises to be a very fruitful area for future research.

Notes

1. That older persons tend to be more influential than younger ones is suggested by a variety of investigations. Some of the relevant findings come from research aimed at identifying the persons within a community from whom advice is sought. Such characteristics as education, income, and participation in local organizations do not differentiate those frequently sought for advice and those little sought. However, there is some tendency for persons to seek advice from those somewhat older than themselves.

Several studies involve simultaneous variations in the ages of recipients and communicator. Duncker found young children more likely to be influenced by the food preference of an older child than vice versa. Berenda found a similar relation in a length-judging situation where a single child was exposed to the unanimous and wrong answers of eight classmates. The younger children were influenced more than the older ones. However, her evidence on age is complicated by changes in the social relationships with increased age and by age differences in ability to make the necessary judgments in the absence of social influence. Both Duncker and Berenda find that adults had surprisingly little influence in these situations. We take this to indicate the operation of other important factors which are unrelated or inversely related to the age difference between influencer and recipient (e.g., desire to retain the approval of other members of one's peer group, similarity of influencer to recipient in status and interests). Age appears as an important variable in a number of other studies of influence but usually as a characteristic of the recipients rather than of the communicator.

As a special case of the expertness factor, leaders of groups might be expected to be more influential in matters pertaining to the group norms than rank-and-file members. Recent research by Chowdhry and Newcomb indicates that leaders are superior to other group members in their ability to estimate the consensus of opinion within the group on matters related to the common interests and goals. (That this is not true for all intragroup issues is indicated by Hites and Campbell who find no superiority for leaders.) Such superiority could form the basis for acquiring confidence in leaders' assertions about how various events will be received by the members or about future decisions of the group. Relatively little existing evidence is directly pertinent to this generalization. Other studies demonstrate the influence of opinions attributed to national leaders and the heads of churches and political parties, but it is likely that subjects in these studies possess not only attitudes of trust toward these persons but attitudes of affection and respect.

In their analysis of the special properties of direct face-to-face influence, Lazarsfeld, Berelson, and Gaudet suggest that one of the advantages of personal contacts may be that the individual tends to encounter persons similar to himself. Redl discusses the importance of similarity as a factor in the infectious spread of influence among the members of a face-to-face group, a phenomenon frequently observed among delinquent adolescents and referred to as "behavioral contagion." When several persons are in similar conflicts between their "undesirable" impulses and internalized social prohibitions, the act of one of them, whether it be in the direction of expressing the impulses or in reaffirming conformity to the prohibitions, serves to evoke the same act in the others. In short, the conflict resolution found by one person is imitated by others who have similar conflicts. This is, perhaps, a specific instance of the more general tendency when confronted with a problem to imitate the solutions found by others in the same dilemma. Perhaps the term "expert" should be broadened to include persons who have found adequate solutions to the problem an individual faces, even though in other respects they may be no more experienced than he and may be very much like him. This may account for some of the instances noted by Duncker and Berenda where peers or slightly older children were found to be more influential than adults. . . .

2. Kelman's and Hovland's explanation of their result is reminiscent of earlier discussions of the importance in prestige suggestion of an emotional relation between the influencer and influencee. Murphy, Murphy, and Newcomb refer to contradictory ideas and habits which ordinarily inhibit the individual's conformity to verbal suggestions. They go on to say: "The fixation of attention upon the experimenter whom one respects (or perhaps sometimes fears) seems sufficient to block these ordinarily available counter-suggestions." A major difference lies in the fact that whereas these authors use emotional constriction of attention as an explanation of heightened susceptibility to influence, Kelman and Hovland suggest that it may interfere with learning what the communicator says. It seems probable that an emotional reaction to the communicator may have a double-barreled effect. On the one hand, it may have a facilitating effect where it serves to focus attention on what he says and to exclude irrelevant influences in the environment. On the other hand, when the focusing is upon the communicator per se—upon his person, dress, style of speaking, mannerisms, and so on—an emotional reaction may interfere with the acquisition of his content and hence with his effectiveness as a communicator.

3. Results from Kulp are often cited as indicating the persistence of the effects of prestigeful sources over a considerable period (eight weeks). Unfortunately the absence of a control group at the time of the delayed after-tests leaves some uncertainty as to whether the results do indicate genuine retention of the original effects. Assuming they do, a possible explanation for the greater permanency of prestige effects in Kulp's study is his method of introducing prestige. Subjects were asked to indicate their agreement or disagreement with opinion items, using test blanks that were already marked with responses attributed to certain prestige groups. This procedure may create a condition where the "source" becomes closely associated with the test items themselves, so that on subsequent occasions they "reinstate" the prestigeful source. Note should also be taken of another important difference between Kulp's procedure and that generally used in the present studies on source credibility: the latter not merely involve the "conclusion" or opinion of the source but also include arguments and evidence in support of the conclusion. This type of supporting content may be retained in a different manner than conclusions alone; for example, arguments and evidence may be dissociated from the source more readily.

4. The problem situation confronting a person can affect his reactions to communicators in various ways. As indicated earlier, the individual's responses

to various communicators depend, at least in part, on the degree to which he generalizes from earlier experiences in which he has acquired expectations about the expertness, trustworthiness, and so forth of certain sources. The effects of the communication situation upon reactions to various sources may be examined in terms of how it influences this process of generalization.

In learning studies on stimulus generalization, it has been shown that the learned response to a given stimulus is elicited by other similar cues, but that it tends to appear less frequently and less strongly the more different from the original stimulus are the others. To describe these results, a gradient of generalization may be drawn. The solid line in Figure 2 suggests how such a generalization gradient might apply in the case of communicator expertness. On the ordinate is represented the strength of tendency to accept communications given by any specific source and on the abscissa are the cues as to the various sources' expertness. At the left end of the abscissa would be a source identical with or very similar to one whom the person had learned to regard as extremely expert. Moving to the right, one would encounter sources presenting cues increasingly different from those associated with high expertness and, as indicated by the gradient, there would be a decreasing tendency to accept the sources' recommendations.

Any factor which affects the shape or height of this generalization curve will affect the person's responsiveness to various communicators. We shall consider here only the manner in which the communication situation can produce such effects by changing the individual's *motivation*. Animal experiments have shown that increasing the level of drive produces a general elevation of the gen-

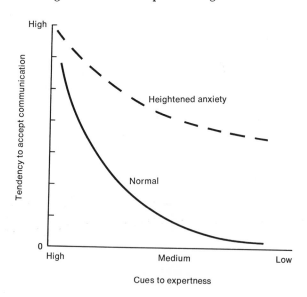

Figure 2. Hypothetical generalization gradients for communicator expertness (modeled after Rosenbaum's empirical curves for manual habits)

eralization curve. An experiment with humans by Rosenbaum suggests that heightened anxiety elevates the gradient and also flattens it out. The dotted line in Figure 2 shows how this effect of anxiety might appear in the case of communicator expertness. From a comparison of the two curves in Figure 2, it would be expected that if the person is in a situation which raises his anxiety level his responses to various communicators will be affected in three ways: (1) The tendencies to accept communications from sources differing in expertness will be more nearly equal; in other words, the person will appear to discriminate less sharply between sources of different degrees of expertness. (2) The tendency to accept communications will be heightened for all sources normally having an effect, this being most marked for those at the low end of the scale. (3) Certain sources at the low end who normally elicit no acceptance whatever will tend, under heightened anxiety conditions, to exert some influence.

These three effects require systematic investigation. For the present, we may note that the literature on social influence contains certain hypotheses and evidence which are consistent with the assumption that such effects can be produced by situational factors. One such hypothesis is that times of stress and uncertainty are especially propitious for the spread of rumors and acceptance of new leaders. One of the possible factors contributing to this phenomenon may be the tendency, under conditions of high anxiety, to accept recommendations from persons who normally would produce little or no acceptance. A related hypothesis concerns the "problematic" nature of the situation confronting the individual at the time of receiving a communication. If faced with an important problem which is quite difficult to solve, the individual's anxiety level is likely to be heightened. As a consequence, he might be less sensitive to differences among sources of advice with respect to their credibility. In a difficult situation, any person's advice may be welcomed: there is less tendency to question whether the garage man is a master mechanic or whether the doctor is a qualified specialist.

Other hypotheses have to do with the amount of evidence or support a person can muster for a given belief or judgment. An individual generally desires to feel that his judgments are "correct" or valid. This feeling is usually derived from checking his judgments against evidence obtained directly from the physical world or against other persons' opinions. In circumstances where these kinds of evidence are absent, the individual becomes highly motivated to obtain some sort of validation for his beliefs. Accordingly, we might expect him to make less fine discriminations among persons with respect to their credibility and to be responsive to the opinions of persons who had previously carried little weight with him. This effect of heightened motivation on the generalization gradients may account in part for the heightened susceptibility to social influence observed in situations where the stimulus situation is quite ambiguous or unstructured or where social support for initial opinions is lacking.

Exercises

1. What is the difference between "prestige" and "status"? Why do the authors use the former rather than the latter in their first paragraph?

2. Some suggest that the word "informed" should be added to "expertness" and "trustworthiness." Why do they think that? What are some counter arguments?

3. Does the study by Ewing support the contention that honesty is the best policy? Does it support P. T. Barnum's remark that there is a sucker born every minute? Why or why not?

4. Outline the steps you take to build your credibility with your instructors.

Effects of Group Pressure upon the Modification and Distortion of Judgments

S. E. Asch

Can someone be persuaded to vouch for something that is against the evidence of his senses? This question lies at the root of many persuasive efforts in the mass media and also in a substantial portion of the interpersonal, face-to-face situations we encounter every day. Asch's study takes up this question experimentally. Some of Asch's subjects verbally agreed with group opinions that contradicted the evidence of their senses. But some of these same subjects, according to their subsequent statements, would not have made overt responses other than verbal—that is, they would not have *acted* just because they agreed with group sentiments. It is important, then, to make an estimate of the man you are trying to persuade, if you want him to do more than just agree verbally.

We shall here describe in summary form the conception and first findings of a program of investigation into the conditions of independence and submission to group pressure.[1]

Our immediate object was to study the social and personal conditions that induce individuals to resist or to yield to group pressures when the latter are perceived to be *contrary to fact*. The issues which this problem raises are of obvious consequence for society; it can be of decisive importance whether or not a group will, under certain conditions, submit to existing pressures. Equally direct are the consequences for individuals and our understanding of them, since it is a decisive fact about a person whether he possesses the freedom to act independently, or whether he characteristically submits to group pressures.

The problem under investigation requires the direct observation of certain basic processes in the interaction between individuals, and between individuals and groups. To clarify these seems necessary if we are to make fundamental advances in the understanding of the formation and reorganization of attitudes, of the functioning of public opinion, and of the operation of propaganda. Today we do not possess an adequate theory of these central psycho-social processes. Empirical investigation has been predominantly controlled by general propositions concerning group influence which have as a rule been assumed but not tested. With few exceptions investigation has relied upon descriptive formulations concerning the operation of suggestion and prestige, the inadequacy of which is becoming increasingly obvious, and upon schematic applications of stimulus-response theory.

Basic to the current approach has been the axiom that group pressures characteristically induce psychological changes *arbitrarily*, in far-reaching disregard of the material properties of the given conditions. This mode of thinking has almost exclusively stressed the slavish submission of individuals to group forces, has neglected to inquire into their possibilities for independence and for productive relations with the human environment, and has virtually denied the capacity of men under certain conditions to rise above group passion and prejudice. It was our aim to contribute to a clarification of these questions, important both for theory and for their human implications, by means of direct observation of the effects of groups upon the decisions and evaluations of individuals.

Reprinted by permission from *Readings in Social Psychology*, pp. 174–183, edited by Eleanor E. Maccoby, Theodore M. Newcomb, and E. L. Hartley, New York, © 1958, Holt, Rinehart and Winston, Inc. Prepared by the author from data previously reported in: S. E. Asch, "Effects of Group Pressure upon the Modification and Distortion of Judgments," in Harold Guetzkow (ed.), *Groups, Leadership and Men* (Pittsburgh: Carnegie Press, 1951).

[1] The earlier experiments out of which the present work developed and the theoretical issues which prompted it are discussed in S. E. Asch, *Social Psychology* (Englewood Cliffs, N.J.: Prentice-Hall, Inc., 1952), Chapter 16.

The Experiment and
First Results

To this end we developed an experimental technique which has served as the basis for the present series of studies. We employed the procedure of placing an individual in a relation of radical conflict with all the other members of a group, of measuring its effect upon him in quantitative terms, and of describing its psychological consequences. A group of eight individuals was instructed to judge a series of simple, clearly structured perceptual relations—to match the length of a given line with one of three unequal lines. Each member of the group announced his judgments publicly. In the midst of this monotonous "test" one individual found himself suddenly contradicted by the entire group, and this contradiction was repeated again and again in the course of the experiment. The group in question had, with the exception of one member, previously met with the experimenter and received instructions to respond at certain points with wrong—and unanimous—judgments. The errors of the majority were large (ranging between ½" and 1¾") and of an order not encountered under control conditions. The outstanding person—the critical subject—whom we had placed in the position of a *minority of one* in the midst of a *unanimous majority*—was the object of investigation. He faced, possibly for the first time in his life, a situation in which a group unanimously contradicted the evidence of his senses.

This procedure was the starting point of the investigation and the point of departure for the study of further problems. Its main features were the following: (1) The critical subject was submitted to two contradictory and irreconcilable forces—the evidence of his own experience of a clearly perceived relation, and the unanimous evidence of a group of equals. (2) Both forces were part of the immediate situation; the majority was concretely present, surrounding the subject physically. (3) The critical subject, who was requested together with all others to state his judgments publicly, was obliged to declare himself and to take a definite stand *vis-à-vis* the group. (4) The situation possessed a self-contained character. The critical subject could not avoid or evade the dilemma by reference to conditions external to the experimental situation. (It may be mentioned at this point that the forces generated by the given conditions acted so quickly upon the critical subjects that instances of suspicion were infrequent.)

The technique employed permitted a simple quantitative measure of the "majority effect" in terms of the frequency of errors in the direction of the distorted estimates of the majority. At the same time we were concerned to obtain evidence of the ways in which the subjects perceived the group, to establish whether they became doubtful, whether they were tempted to join the majority. Most important, it was our object to establish the grounds of the subject's independence or yielding—whether, for example, the yielding subject was aware of the effect of the majority upon him, whether he abandoned his judgment deliberately or compulsively. To this end we constructed a comprehensive set of questions which served as the basis of an individual interview immediately following the experimental period. Toward the conclusion of the interview each subject was

Table 1. Lengths of standard and comparison lines

Trial	Length of Standard Line (in Inches)	Comparison Lines (in Inches)			Correct Response	Group Response	Majority Error (in Inches)
		1	2	3			
1	10	8¾	10	8	2	2	—
2	2	2	1	1½	1	1	—
3	3	3¾	4¼	3	3	1 *	+¾
4	5	5	4	6½	1	2 *	−1.0
5	4	3	5	4	3	3	—
6	3	3¾	4¼	3	3	2 *	+1¼
7	8	6¼	8	6¾	2	3 *	−1¼
8	5	5	4	6½	1	3 *	+1½
9	8	6¼	8	6¾	2	1 *	−1¾
10	10	8¾	10	8	2	2	—
11	2	2	1	1½	1	1	—
12	3	3¾	4¼	3	3	1 *	+¾
13	5	5	4	6½	1	2 *	−1.0
14	4	3	5	4	3	3	—
15	3	3¾	4¼	3	3	2 *	+1¼
16	8	6¼	8	6¾	2	3 *	−1¼
17	5	5	4	6½	1	3 *	+1½
18	8	6¼	8	6¾	2	1 *	−1¾

* Starred figures designate the erroneous estimates by the majority.

informed fully of the purpose of the experiment, of his role and of that of the majority. The reactions to the disclosure of the purpose of the experiment became in fact an integral part of the procedure. The information derived from the interview became an indispensable source of evidence and insight into the psychological structure of the experimental situation, and in particular, of the nature of the individual differences. It should be added that it is not justified or advisable to allow the subject to leave without giving him a full explanation of the experimental conditions. The experimenter has a responsibility to the subject to clarify his doubts and to state the reasons for placing him in the experimental situation. When this is done most subjects react with interest, and some express gratification at having lived through a striking situation which has some bearing on them personally and on wider human issues.

Both the members of the majority and the critical subjects were male college students. We shall report the results for a total of fifty critical subjects in this experiment. In Table 1 we summarize the successive comparison trials and the majority estimates. The reader will note that on certain trials the majority responded correctly; these were the "neutral" trials. There were twelve critical trials on which the majority responded incorrectly.

The quantitative results are clear and unambiguous.

1. There was a marked movement toward the majority. One third of all the estimates in the critical group were errors identical with or in the direction of the distorted estimates of the majority. The significance of this finding becomes clear in the light of the virtual absence of errors in the control group, the members of which recorded their estimates in writing. The relevant data of the critical and control groups are summarized in Table 2.

Table 2. Distribution of errors in experimental and control groups

Number of Critical Errors	Critical Group* (N = 50) F	Control Group (N = 37) F
0	13	35
1	4	1
2	5	1
3	6	
4	3	
5	4	
6	1	
7	2	
8	5	
9	3	
10	3	
11	1	
12	0	
Total	50	37
Mean	3.84	0.08

* All errors in the critical group were in the direction of the majority estimates.

2. At the same time the effect of the majority was far from complete. The preponderance of estimates in the critical group (68 percent) was correct despite the pressure of the majority.

3. We found evidence of extreme individual differences. There were in the critical group subjects who remained independent without exception, and there were those who went nearly all the time with the majority. (The maximum possible number of errors was 12, while the actual range of errors was 0–11.) One fourth of the critical subjects was completely independent; at the other extreme, one third of the group displaced the estimates toward the majority in one half or more of the trials.

The differences between the critical subjects in their reactions to the given conditions were equally striking. There were subjects who remained completely confident throughout. At the other extreme were those who became disoriented, doubt-ridden, and experienced a powerful impulse not to appear different from the majority.

For purposes of illustration we include a brief description of one independent and one yielding subject.

Independent. After a few trials he appeared puzzled, hesitant. He announced all disagreeing answers in the form of "Three, sir; two, sir"; not so with the unanimous answers on the neutral trials. At Trial 4 he answered immediately after the first member of the group, shook his head, blinked, and whispered to his neighbor: "Can't help it, that's one." His later answers came in a whispered voice, accompanied by a deprecating smile. At one point he grinned embarrassedly, and whispered explosively to his neighbor: "I always disagree—darn it!" During the questioning, this subject's constant refrain was: "I called them as I saw them, sir." He insisted that his estimates were right without, however, committing himself as to whether the others were wrong, remarking that "that's the way I see them and that's the way they see them." If he had to make a practical decision under similar circumstances, he declared, "I would follow my own view, though part of my reason would tell me that I might be wrong." Immediately following the experiment the majority engaged this subject in a brief discussion. When they pressed him to say whether the entire group was wrong and he alone right, he turned upon them defiantly, exclaiming: "You're *probably* right, but you *may* be wrong!" To the disclosure of the experiment this subject reacted with the statement that he felt "exultant and relieved," adding, "I do not deny that at times I had the feeling: 'to heck with it, I'll go along with the rest.'"

Yielding. This subject went with the majority in 11 out of 12 trials. He appeared nervous and somewhat confused, but he did not attempt to evade discussion; on the contrary, he was helpful and tried to answer to the best of his ability. He opened the discussion with the statement: "If I'd been first I probably would have responded differently"; this was his way of stating that he had adopted the majority estimates. The primary factor in his case was loss of confidence. He perceived the majority as a decided group, acting without hesitation: "If they had been doubtful I probably would have changed, but they answered with such confidence." Certain of his errors, he explained, were due to the doubtful nature of the comparisons; in such instances he went with the majority. When the object of the experiment was explained, the subject volunteered: "I suspected about the middle—but tried to push it out of my mind." It is of interest that his suspicion did not restore his confidence or diminish the power of the majority. Equally striking is his report that he assumed the experiment to involve an "illusion" to which the others, but not he, were subject. This assumption too did not help to free him; on the contrary, he acted as if his divergence from the majority was a sign of defect. The principal impression this subject produced was of one so caught up by immediate difficulties that he lost clear reasons for his actions, and could make no reasonable decisions.

A First Analysis of Individual Differences

On the basis of the interview data described earlier, we undertook to differentiate and describe the major forms of reaction to the experimental situation, which we shall now briefly summarize.

Among the *independent* subjects we distinguished the following main categories:

1. Independence based on *confidence* in one's perception and experience. The most striking characteristic of these subjects is the vigor with which they withstand the group opposition. Though they are sensitive to the group, and experience the conflict, they show a resilience in coping with it, which is expressed in their continuing reliance on their perception and the effectiveness with which they shake off the oppressive group opposition.
2. Quite different are those subjects who are independent and *withdrawn*. These do not react in a spontaneously emotional way, but rather on the basis of explicit principles concerning the necessity of being an individual.
3. A third group of independent subjects manifest considerable tension and doubt, but adhere to their judgment on the basis of a felt necessity to deal adequately with the task.

The following were the main categories of reaction among the *yielding* subjects, or those who went with the majority during one half or more of the trials.

1. *Distortion of perception* under the stress of group pressure. In this category belong a very few subjects who yield completely, but are not aware that their estimates have been displaced or distorted by

the majority. These subjects report that they came to perceive the majority estimates as correct.

2. *Distortion of judgment.* Most submitting subjects belong to this category. The factor of greatest importance in this group is a decision the subjects reach that their perceptions are inaccurate, and that those of the majority are correct. These subjects suffer from primary doubt and lack of confidence; on this basis they feel a strong tendency to join the majority.

3. *Distortion of action.* The subjects in this group do not suffer a modification of perception nor do they conclude that they are wrong. They yield because of an overmastering need not to appear different from or inferior to others, because of an inability to tolerate the appearance of defectiveness in the eyes of the group. These subjects suppress their observations and voice the majority position with awareness of what they are doing.

The results are sufficient to establish that independence and yielding are not psychologically homogeneous, that submission to group pressure and freedom from pressure can be the result of different psychological conditions. It should also be noted that the categories described above, being based exclusively on the subjects' reactions to the experimental conditions, are descriptive, not presuming to explain why a given individual responded in one way rather than another. The further exploration of the basis for the individual differences is a separate task.

Experimental Variations

The results described are clearly a joint function of two broadly different sets of conditions. They are determined first by the specific external conditions, by the particular character of the relation between social evidence and one's own experience. Second, the presence of pronounced individual differences points to the important role of personal factors, or factors connected with the individual's character structure. We reasoned that there are group conditions which would produce independence in all subjects, and that there probably are group conditions which would induce intensified yielding in many, though not in all. Secondly, we deemed it reasonable to assume that behavior under the experimental social pressure is significantly related to certain characteristics of the individual. The present account will be limited to the effect of the surrounding conditions upon independence and submission. To this end we followed the procedure of experimental variation, systematically altering the quality of social evidence by means of systematic variation of the group conditions and of the task.

Evidence obtained from the basic experiment suggested that the condition of being exposed *alone* to the opposition of a "compact majority" may have played a decisive role in determining the course and strength of the effects observed. Accordingly we undertook to investigate in a series of successive variations the effects of *nonunanimous* majorities. The technical problem of altering the uniformity of a majority is, in terms of our procedure, relatively simple. In most instances we merely directed one or more members of the instructed group to deviate from the majority in prescribed ways. It is obvious that we cannot hope to compare the performance of the same individual in two situations on the assumption that they remain independent of one another; at best we can investigate the effect of an earlier upon a later experimental condition. The comparison of different experimental situations therefore requires the use of different but comparable groups of critical subjects. This is the procedure we have followed. In the variations to be described we have maintained the conditions of the basic experiment (e.g., the sex of the subjects, the size of the majority, the content of the task, and so on) save for the specific factor that was varied. The following were some of the variations studied:

1. *The presence of a "true partner."* (*a*) In the midst of the majority were *two* naïve, critical subjects. The subjects were separated spatially, being seated in the fourth and eighth positions, respectively. Each therefore heard his judgments confirmed by one other person (provided the other person remained independent), one prior to, the other after announcing his own judgment. In addition, each experienced a break in the unanimity of the majority. There were six pairs of critical subjects. (*b*) In a further variation the "partner" to the critical subject was a member of the group who had been instructed to respond correctly throughout. This procedure permits the exact control of the partner's responses. The partner was always seated in the fourth position; he therefore announced his estimates in each case before the critical subject.

The results clearly demonstrate that a disturbance of the unanimity of the majority markedly increased the independence of the critical subjects. The frequency of promajority errors dropped to 10.4 percent of the total number of estimates in variation (*a*), and to 5.5 percent in variation (*b*). These results are to be compared with the frequency of yielding to the unanimous majorities in the basic experiment, which was 32 percent of the total number of estimates. It is clear that the presence in the field of *one other* individual who responded correctly was sufficient to deplete the power of the majority, and in some cases to destroy it. This finding is all the more striking in the light of other variations which demonstrate the effect of even small minorities provided they are unanimous. Indeed, we have been able to show that a unanimous majority of 3 is, under the given conditions, far more effective than a majority of 8 containing 1 dissenter. That critical subjects will under these conditions free themselves of a majority of 7 and join forces with one other person in the minority is, we believe, a result significant for theory. It points to a fundamental psychological difference between the condition of being alone and having a minimum of human support. It further demonstrates that the effects obtained are not the result of a summation of influences proceeding from each member of the group; it is necessary to conceive the results as being relationally determined.

2. *Withdrawal of a "true partner."* What will be the effect of providing the critical subject with a partner who responds correctly and then withdrawing him? The critical subject started with a partner who responded correctly. The partner was a member of the majority who had been instructed to respond correctly and to "desert" to the majority in the middle of the experiment. This procedure permits the observation of the same subject in the course of the transition from one condition to another. The withdrawal of the partner produced a powerful and unexpected result. We had assumed that the critical subject, having gone through the experience of opposing the majority with a minimum of support, would maintain his independence when alone. Contrary to this expectation, we found that the experience of having had and then lost a partner restored the majority effect to its full force, the proportion of errors rising to 28.5 percent of all judgments, in contrast to the preceding level of 5.5 percent. Further experimentation is needed to establish whether the critical subjects were responding to the sheer fact of being alone, or to the fact that the partner abandoned them.

3. *Late arrival of a "true partner."* The critical subject started as a minority of 1 in the midst of a unanimous majority. Toward the conclusion of the experiment one member of the majority "broke" away and began announcing correct estimates. This procedure, which reverses the order of conditions of the preceding experiment, permits the observation of the transition from being alone to being a member of a pair against a majority. It is obvious that those critical subjects who were independent when alone

Table 3. Errors of critical subjects with unanimous majorities of different size

Size of Majority	Control	1	2	3	4	8	10–15
N	37	10	15	10	10	50	12
Mean number of errors . . .	0.08	0.33	1.53	4.0	4.20	3.84	3.75
Range of errors	0–2	0–1	0–5	1–12	0–11	0–11	0–10

would continue to be so when joined by a partner. The variation is therefore of significance primarily for those subjects who yielded during the first phase of the experiment. The appearance of the late partner exerts a freeing effect, reducing the level of yielding to 8.7 percent. Those who had previously yielded also became markedly more independent, but not completely so, continuing to yield more than previously independent subjects. The reports of the subjects do not cast much light on the factors responsible for the result. It is our impression that some subjects, having once committed themselves to yielding, find it difficult to change their direction completely. To do so is tantamount to a public admission that they had not acted rightly. They therefore follow to an extent the precarious course they had chosen in order to maintain an outward semblance of consistency and conviction.

4. *The presence of a "compromise partner."* The majority was consistently extremist, always matching the standard with the most unequal line. One instructed subject (who, as in the other variations, preceded the critical subject) also responded incorrectly, but his estimates were always intermediate between the truth and the majority position. The critical subject therefore faced an extremist majority whose unanimity was broken by one more moderately erring person. Under these conditions the frequency of errors was reduced but not significantly. However, the lack of unanimity determined in a strikingly consistent way the *direction* of the errors. The preponderance of the errors, 75.7 percent of the total, was moderate, whereas in a parallel experiment in which the majority was unanimously extremist (i.e., with the "compromise" partner excluded), the incidence of moderate errors was 42 percent of the total. As might be expected, in a unanimously moderate majority, the errors of the critical subjects were without exception moderate.

The Role of Majority Size

To gain further understanding of the majority effect, we varied the size of the majority in several different variations. The majorities, which were in each case unanimous, consisted of 2, 3, 4, 8, and 10–15 persons, respectively. In addition, we studied the limiting case in which the critical subject was opposed by one instructed subject. Table 3 contains the mean and the range of errors under each condition.

With the opposition reduced to 1, the majority effect all but disappeared. When the opposition proceeded from a group of 2, it produced a measurable though small distortion, the errors being 12.8 percent of the total number of estimates. The effect appeared in full force with a majority of 3. Larger majorities did not produce effects greater than a majority of 3.

The effect of a majority is often silent, revealing little of its operation to the subject, and often hiding it from the experimenter. To examine the range of effects it is capable of inducing, decisive variations of conditions are necessary. An indication of one effect is furnished by the following variation in which the conditions of the basic experiment were simply reversed. Here the majority, consisting of a group of 16, was naïve; in the midst of it we placed a single individual who responded wrongly according to instructions. Under these conditions the members of the naïve majority reacted to the lone dissenter with amusement. Contagious laughter spread through the group at the droll minority of 1. Of significance is the fact that the members lacked awareness that they drew their strength from the majority, and that their reactions would change radically if they faced the dissenter individually. These observations demonstrate the role of social support as a source of power and stability, in contrast to the preceding investigations which stressed the effects of social opposition. Both aspects must be explicitly considered in a unified formulation of the effects of group conditions on the formation and change of judgments.

The Role of the Stimulus-Situation

It is obviously not possible to divorce the quality and course of the group forces which act upon the individual from the specific stimulus-conditions. Of necessity the structure of the situation molds the group forces and determines their direction as well as their strength. Indeed, this was the reason that we took pains in the investigations described above to center the issue between the individual and the group around an elementary matter of fact. And there can be no doubt that the resulting reactions were directly a function of the contradiction between the observed relations and the majority position. These general considerations are sufficient to establish the need to vary the stimulus-conditions and to observe their effect on the resulting group forces.

Accordingly we have studied the effect of increasing and decreasing the discrepancy between the correct relation and the position of the majority, going beyond the basic experiment which contained discrepancies of a relatively moderate order. Our technique permits the easy variation of this factor, since we can vary at will the deviation of the majority from the correct relation. At this point we can only summarize the trend of the results which is entirely clear. The degree of independence increases with the distance of the majority from correctness. However, even glaring discrepancies (of the order of 3–6″) did not produce independence in all. While independence increases with the magnitude of contradiction, a certain proportion of individuals continues to yield under extreme conditions.

We have also varied systematically the structural clarity of the task, employing judgments based on mental standards. In agreement with other investigators, we find that the majority effect grows stronger as the situation diminishes in clarity. Concurrently, however, the disturbance of the subjects and the conflict-quality of the situation decrease markedly. We consider it of significance that the majority achieves its most pronounced effect when it acts most painlessly.

Summary

We have investigated the effects upon individuals of majority opinions when the latter were seen to be in a direction contrary to fact. By means of a simple technique we produced a radical divergence between a majority and a minority, and observed the ways in which individuals coped with the resulting difficulty. Despite the stress of the given conditions, a substantial proportion of individuals retained their independence throughout. At the same time a substantial minority yielded, modifying their judgments in accordance with the majority. Independence and yielding are a joint function of the following major factors: (1) The character of the stimulus situation. Variations in structural clarity have a decisive effect: with diminishing clarity of the stimulus-conditions the majority effect increases. (2) The character of the group forces. Individuals are highly sensitive to the structural qualities of group opposition. In particular, we demonstrated the great importance of the factor of unanimity. Also, the majority effect is a function of the size of group opposition. (3) The character of the individual. There were wide and, indeed, striking differences among individuals within the same experimental situation.

Exercises

1. How do you think you would have behaved in the situations that Asch devised? How would you have tried to account for your behavior when you were interviewed?

2. Do you think people ought to be exposed to such pressures? How could you reduce susceptibility to such pressures in yourself? How could you reduce it in others? What disadvantages might you incur from reducing susceptibility?

3. Can you suggest any strategies based on Asch's findings that you might use to get agreement if you were chairman of a committee?

Section Three

Message Systems and Sub-Systems

In the general introduction to this volume we pointed out that the purpose of communication is to alter the response probabilities of the receivers of our messages. Obviously, then, we need messages and we need channels through which to send our messages so that we may interact with our receiver. This section deals with messages, with systems, and with channels.

The Meadow essay deals with information systems and the languages employed in retrieving information. Many of his examples are drawn from library work, but the concepts he develops are widely applicable and provide a framework within which it is possible to discuss messages and language.

Hill provides a sensible and straightforward discussion of human language from the point of view of the modern linguist. Harrison discusses the nonverbal languages—an area that is attracting more and more interest with each passing year. The Lloyd and Warfel essay illustrates the importance of language in the business context and provides a frame of reference for the discussion of organizational communication.

Johnson, in a classic essay, comments on the teaching and learning of writing. He sheds valuable light on an often confused and confusing subject. The last article attempts to illustrate the interrelatedness and interdependencies of reading, writing, talking, and listening.

The Analysis of Information Systems

Charles T. Meadow

The types of problems posed by the population explosion are more than matched in impact and complexity by those posed by the information explosion. Both of these problems, in our view, may be more usefully attacked as communication problems. Here the techniques of information storage and retrieval are discussed. Though the emphasis of this selection is on retrieval, comments on retrieval are largely the direct derivatives of comments on storage, *and vice versa.*

The central problems of category systems are: whether they shall be flexible (and therefore ambiguous), or rigid (and therefore limited in usefulness in a rich and changing environment); and whether the categories shall be few and broad (and therefore inaccurate since they may include that which does not belong, though they are easy to handle), or numerous and narrow (and therefore inaccurate since they may exclude that which should be included).

Men cannot choose not to make errors—they can only choose which sort of error they wish to make.

1.1 Information Retrieval as a Communication Process

Information retrieval is the process of recovering information-bearing symbols from their storage places in response to requests from prospective users of the information or from librarians on the users' behalf. The basic thesis . . . is that information retrieval is part of a complex communication system existing between the authors of information-bearing documents and their readers. We treat the book, research paper, or other document as a message to be communicated from the author to the reader, usually via one or more communications centers. Although we often make reference to a library and to books or other "hard copy" documents, the principles espoused here apply as well to photographs or to systems in which all data are stored in a computer and no reference to external documents is involved.

Our primary concern is with the organization of information to facilitate its retrieval. As a preliminary to this material, we shall review some basic principles of the languages used in information retrieval, the creation of index records, and the retrieval of information from index files. We then proceed to the organization of information and, finally, to the processing of it. Our first concern is with the basic notion of information and of the information retrieval process.

1.1.1 Concepts of Information

One of the most intriguing aspects of information retrieval is that it deals, through a variety of tools, with only one substance or material—an abstraction called information—and we know so little about it. Shannon[2] provides a measure for information but does not define it. He does, however, point out that his concern is not with *meaning,* or the semantic aspects of information, but with the engineering problems of transmitting it. He states that

> The fundamental problem of communication is that of reproducing at one point either exactly or approximately a message selected at another point. Frequently the messages have *meaning;* that is, they refer to or are correlated according to some system with certain physical or conceptual entities. These semantic aspects of communication are irrelevant to the engineering problem.[3]

Warren Weaver,[4] although tending to agree, points out the important fact that accurate physical transmission is a requirement if the semantic meaning is to be communicated. Weaver, in fact, defines three levels of the communication problem: the *technical* problem of physical transmission, the *semantic* problem of conveying meaning by names of transmitted symbols, and the *effectiveness* problem of influencing the conduct of the receiver. The latter two aspects of communications are essentially those defined by S. I. Hayakawa[1] as the *informative* and *affective* functions of language. The word *affective,* according to Hayakawa, refers to the arousing of response, not to efficiency, effectiveness, or strength of the responses as might, he feels, be implied by the word *effective.* Nonetheless, both authors agree that one function of language is to influence behavior. Although information can be measured, in an engineering sense, and its problems and functions defined, we are still unable to describe it well analytically.

. . . We generally try to follow Weaver's resolution of communication into transmission, semantic, and effectiveness problems. We have no definition for information either, but we assume that, whatever it is, it is communicated only in terms of structured sets of symbols which are *representations* of information but are not the *same as* information. If the reader of a book feels he has found information therein, so be it.

The function of an information retrieval system (which might be no more than the reference librarian at the village library) is to locate and recover information from a store. To do so, the patron issues a request describing his wants in some way that may vary from, "I want to know Napoleon's birth date." to "I want a good mystery." Often, and this is our principal focus, the patron uses this request, or *query,* to locate and recover some string of symbols which might, by our two examples, range from a single number to a shelf of books. If the retrieved symbols add nothing to his store of knowledge, he may challenge their veracity or accuracy, this being his prerogative. On the basis of new information contained in the patron's rejection of the first retrieved message, the librarian can help him to perform another search and perhaps retrieve another, more palatable string of symbols. The patron's rejection, and the reason therefor, constitute effective use of language—its use to induce the librarian to make another search.

1.1.2 Transmission of Information

According to Shannon,[5] the communication process requires five elements: a *source,* or originator of a message; a *transmitter,* which usually modifies the form or coding of the message, enabling it to be sent out; a *channel,* the medium through which the message is conveyed and which may introduce noise into the system; a *receiver,* which reconverts the form of the message; and a *destination,* the recipient of the information. These are illustrated in Figure 1. An example of a communication system is a

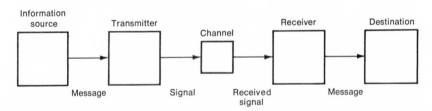

Figure 1. Schematic diagram of a general communication system (after Shannon[5])

man as a source, his speech organs as a transmitter, air as the channel over which sound waves are transmitted, the auditory system of another man's body as receiver, and the brain of the receiving person as destination.

Message Systems and Subsystems

Many systems actually involve a chain of transmissions, receipts, and retransmissions. A microphone is both a transmitter and receiver, receiving sound waves and transmitting electric power. Figure 2 illustrates how a

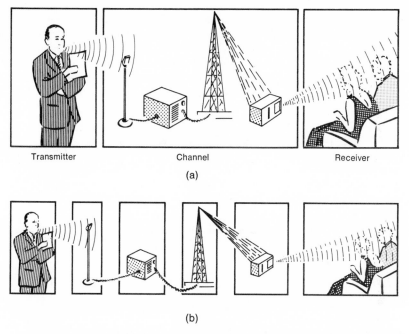

Transmitter   Channel   Receiver

(a)

(b)

Figure 2. The arbitrary nature of the transmitter-channel-receiver designation: (a) The studio announcer is the transmitter. The entire broadcasting process may be viewed as a channel and the listener at home, the receiver. (b) The announcer's vocal chords are the transmitter of air pressure variations, air the channel, the microphone a receiver of sound waves and a transmitter of electricity, and so on, until the listener's inner ear sends electrical signals to his brain.

conventional communication system can, almost arbitrarily, be subdivided into smaller, linked systems.

Because communication system elements can perform dual roles, we can visualize a system as consisting of a set of basic elements, each a generalized signal transducer which has an input, an output, and a functional role to play in converting the input to the output. This is the "black box" concept illustrated in Figure 3. The description fits a transmitter, receiving a signal from the source and converting it for dispatching through the channel. The channel performs a different conversion role; it physically displaces the signal in space and, although less important to this definition, often attenuates or weakens the signal. The receiver very often

Figure 3. Transducer

performs an inverse function to the transmitter. A radio receiver, for example, converts electromagnetic signals back into sound signals very similar to those originally spoken into the microphone. If we adopt this convention, the Shannon definition of communication amounts to a requirement for five basic, black-box elements in series, as shown in Figure 4, which is not dissimilar to Figure 1. An advantage of this notation is

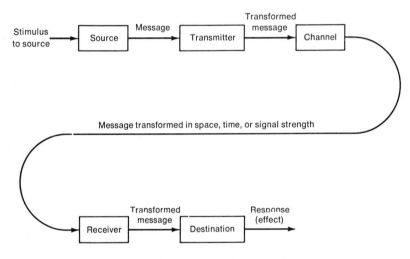

Figure 4. The communication process as a chain of transducers

that, rather than concerning ourselves with sources and destinations, we can treat both the input and output of any communication link as messages subject to some forms of transformation, and we need not be concerned with the identity of the message originator or ultimate reader. This represents only a symbolic departure from the Shannon definition for he goes on to talk of a source as a processor by which signals or symbol sequences are generated by selection from a finite set of possible symbols. This *process* may be represented by one of our black-box elements if we assume that the input is the set of possible signals, that the transducer performs the function of selecting one signal and rejecting all others, and that the output is the selected message.

No real communication can have taken place unless the transmitter and the receiver are making use of compatible codes or schema for

Message Systems and Subsystems

symbolic representations of information. Identical codes are not always a requirement, but communication cannot have taken place unless the destination is sent the codes it is prepared to recognize and act upon. We often find that when a bridge player has apparently failed to catch and properly respond to his partner's bidding signal the partners have learned their signals from different bridge books and are using the same symbol to mean two different things. Here, we are interjecting semantic information connotations into the question of physical communication; that is, the bid has been uttered and heard. For engineering purposes a message was sent and received and technical communication was accomplished. Semantically, the received message sounded reasonable—was a legal bid and not a nonsense signal—but the receiver did not recognize the meaning that the transmitter intended. Thus *semantic* communication was not accomplished but the transmitting partner was unaware of this. As a result, *effective* communication was not accomplished—the receiving partner did not respond as the transmitting partner expected.

The documents stored in a library are messages, originating in the brains of their authors, and transmitted through a long chain of transducers to the library. The catalog, or index, card prepared in the library on arrival of the document may be looked upon as a further encoding of the document. This new form is arrived at by having a librarian read (transmit to the brain) the message and recode it, classifying the subject content and recognizing the symbols that denote author, publisher, date, or title of the document. The recoded form is then stored in the library for the convenience of patrons. The patron comes in, sometimes for specific facts and sometimes for broad knowledge. In the first case he may be satisfied with a phrase from a single book. In second, he will want a variety of books on his subject. In either case it is his function to communicate his needs either directly to the librarian or to the card catalog or index file. Any fuzziness of definition of his subject can often be resolved in a conversation with the librarian. However, if communication is to be directly with the catalog, the user must be able to translate the language he normally uses to describe his subject into the language of the catalog. This is not so easy as it sounds, and it is especially important to realize that ability to state questions accurately to a card catalog is not necessarily correlated with performance ability in the subject discipline. A brilliant physicist is no more innately endowed with this sort of communications faculty than he is with the ability to communicate with his professional colleagues in Iceland, using their native language. The language of the library is a different language from everyday English, and skill with its use must be acquired.

1.1.3 The Library as a Switching Center

Large, true-life communication systems tend not to be just simple links from A to B or even from A_1 to A_2 to A_3 . . . to A_n. They often have node points where more than two lines meet. These are switching centers without which modern communication—telephone, telegraph, mail, or even network radio and television—would be impossible. A switching center essentially makes use of some attribute of an incoming message to determine the disposition of the message. In a simple, two-input, one-output switch the first message to arrive, over either channel, may capture the output line, and, if a second message arrives on the other line while the first is being sent, the second message may be lost. A more complex switch may require more than one message to make a decision. An example is a modern, stored-program communications multiplexer which can accept messages from any one of over a hundred input lines and use a computer program (itself having been entered into the computer as a message) to decide on priorities and dispositions. To help visualize the role of a library as a communication center, let us contrast its operation with another center for communication of documentary data, a post office. We find the following major points of difference:

1. The post office finds an explicit address on each item of mail (leaving out illegible addresses and other error conditions). Even "junk" mail is addressed to a street address, the name of the resident being redundant, except for a multiple dwelling or office for which the addition of an apartment number is sufficient. Books, on the other hand, are addressed to the library, not to the library's patrons.

2. A postal patron gets all mail addressed to him, and only such mail (again, leaving out deviant cases). He cannot be selective. He cannot cut off the flow of third class mail or refuse to accept bills. He cannot ask for more Christmas cards than are explicitly addressed to him. A library user not only has these selectivity powers, but he is actually required to exercise them if he is to receive any messages at all. Nothing is delivered by a library to a patron without some form of request by the patron, and this request must describe the nature of the material he wishes to receive. A library patron, then, uses his description of desired messages as an "address," requesting all documents that fall into a given, figurative pigeonhole to be given to him.

3. The post office is not very selective on its input. It prohibits certain materials (e.g., matches) in the mail and limits the size of parcel post packages. It bars obscene or seditious written material from the mails, but it does not rule on subject matter. Obscenity or treason, for example, are permissible as *subjects*. The ban is on writings for which these terms describe *properties*, not *subjects*. Libraries *may* also impose restrictions on the properties of books but *must*, to meet the requirements of their patrons, exercise control over the subject

matter. They must do, or try to do, just what the post office cannot do—try to find out what kind of messages their patrons would like to receive and see to it that these are the kinds of messages that are acquired.

4. Both must contend with ambiguity in addressing—the post office with poor or smudged writing, the library with poorly defined topics of interest in queries or subject matter of books received. The manner of resolving these problems is quite different. The post office can assume that an item of mail was directed to a specific person or address, even if a misspelling or digit inversion mars the accuracy of the address. The library faces a different problem. Neither the topic sought by the client nor the topic written about by the author necessarily fits into any unique, predefined pigeon-hole; that is, the "address" or subject category need not exist before receipt of the book at the library. It is an intellectual exercise to express a subject in terms of the library's language, the classification system.

5. Some of the library's search problems derive from the fact that it accumulates its input, while the post office, of course, passes its receipts along as quickly as it can. The growth of a collection intensifies the search problem. For example, if there is a pigeonhole for *biology* and one for *physics,* then *biophysics* can go in either category or a new pigeonhole can be created for it. As the volume of material on *biophysics* grows, some documents will be more "biological," some more "physical," and some will be misclassified. A cluster will develop, and although users will soon learn that all biophysical material is somewhere in the *physics-biology-biophysics* classes, there can be no guarantee which, if any, single subject will contain all the material. Both librarians and users will grow accustomed to this ambiguity. This is a natural trend. Certainly, the meanings of words in natural language tend to change over the years as once erroneous usages become proper because of repeated use. With no accumulation, even though the post office may make errors of interpretation, it is not likely to create adaptive processes by which early errors reinforce the tendency to repeat the errors and to endow these errors with authenticity through usage.

1.2 The Information Retrieval Process

In Figure 5 we show a highly oversimplified, schematic representation of the information retrieval process. The purpose of this diagram is to illustrate the organization of this book, not to attempt to represent all the many activities and interrelationships that contribute to the successful communication of information through the medium of a library.

We base our description on the flow of information into and within a library, and we continue to make reference to a library throughout the

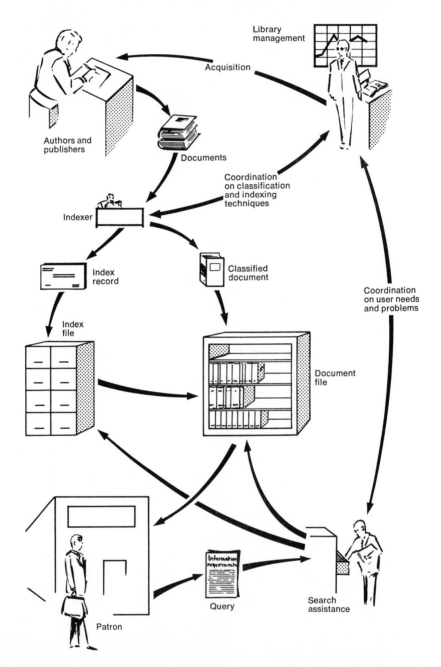

Figure 5. The information retrieval process

Message Systems and Subsystems

book. However, we mean to imply a library in the most general sense—an organized collection of documents and an organization to handle both documents and the information requests made to a collection. Thus an information system in which all "documents" are files stored within a computer falls under this definition. . . .

References

1. Hayakawa, S. I., *Language in Thought and Action,* Harcourt, Brace & World, New York, 1949, p. 82.
2. Shannon, Claude E., and Warren Weaver, *The Mathematical Theory of Communication,* The University of Illinois Press, Urbana, Illinois, 1959, p. 18 et seq.
3. *Ibid.,* p. 3.
4. *Ibid.,* p. 95.
5. *Ibid.,* p. 4.

2.1 Introduction

To retrieve desired information from any large collection of documents we require two things of that collection. First, the collection must be ordered so that when we know what we want we will know where to find it. Second, we must have a means of searching and matching, some way of recognizing whether or not any given document contains the information we want. Reading a document in its entirety is one approach to the latter requirement, but, in addition to its obvious deficiency from the point of view of time, it still does not guarantee the searcher that he will recognize the material he wants. Suppose, for example, he wants some tutorial material on data processing and he comes upon a book on computer programming. If he is totally ignorant of the field, it will not be obvious that the book at least partially answers his needs. To resolve both the time and the recognition problems, we use an *index,* or *catalog,* as a tool for locating desired information. In this sense an index or catalog is basically a list of the documents in a library which contains some descriptive material about document content and the location of the documents. We shall enlarge on and formalize this definition later. We call each entry in the index an *index record.* An *abstract,* or natural language *summary* or *condensation* of a document, performs some of the functions of an index record, and, in certain of its uses, can be considered a form thereof.

In the context of our analogy of information retrieval as a communication process both an index record and an abstract are messages. They are created by a specialist in indexing or abstracting, upon his receipt of a new document. Both are further transformations of the author's original mental concept which he transformed into the document. The usual purpose of creating an index record or abstract is to inform the reader about the document, not about the concept symbolized in the document. Although the document serves the end of informing its reader about a concept in the mind of the author, the index record or abstract informs its reader that a document is available on a given subject or with given characteristics. If the index record or abstract performs this duty then the reader will use it to decide whether he wishes to select the original document from a store of documents.

There are two major uses for index records and abstracts. In the first they are stored in a file called an *index file* which may be searched by a person looking for information. Here, indexes are used to help find information. A searcher uses the file to help him decide what documents he wants to retrieve and to tell him where these documents are. The second major use is to indicate what information is available in a library— a *holdings list* of all material on hand, or an *accessions list* which is disseminated to library users, and tells them about new material acquired by the library. In an index file search the prospective information user takes the initiative in seeking out information. An accessions list represents the library's initiative in telling its users about information of potential interest. In a *selective dissemination system* these approaches are combined. Here, the user tells the library of his general and continuing information needs. The library disseminates to each user only new acquisition data which fall in his self-defined area of interest. To do this, of course, the library must go through a search procedure but one in which document index records are used to search for user interest records which they satisfy.

An index has special language requirements. As a gross generality, an index record will simplify those attributes of a document it is describing, making the search of the index easier by reducing both the amount of material to be searched and complexity of the search process, thereby reducing the time required to perform a search. As we pointed out in Chapter 1, the use of this intermediate communication channel requires the use of a language or coding that is comprehensible to all parties to the communication, in this case the searcher, the cataloger or indexer, and the documents being searched for. This chapter is devoted to the languages used in this special communications situation.

In traditional library usage a *catalog* is,[17] "a list which records, describes, and indexes the resources of a collection. . . ." A catalog entry, such as the familiar catalog card, is made up of a number of elements descriptive of subject matter, publisher, physical size, and so on. Making up this entry is called *descriptive cataloging*. One element of a catalog entry is often a *classification code*. In conventional library work, in addition to serving as an aid to describing content of a book, this code is also used to determine placement of the document on the shelf. For this reason, only one classification code is affixed to a document. This does not imply, although it often results in the conclusion, that each document neatly fits into one and only one subject class. We shall consider this topic at greater length later in this chapter. In library usage, an *index* is often a file used to find information in another file, and does not necessarily contain much descriptive material about the document ultimately sought.

We prefer to generalize these concepts and to stress the similarity among *index, catalog,* and *classification,* rather than their differences. We use the term *index* to encompass both the meanings of *catalog* and *index* as given above. An index, then, contains some descriptive material about records or books in a file or library, and may give some information about their location. An index can refer, not just to the main document collection of the library, but to any collection of records within it, such as the card catalog itself. We shall use the term *index record, index of a document,* or *index* (when the context makes clear the difference) to refer to an individual record or entry in an index file. We shall treat the words *indexing* and *cataloging* as synonymous.

Classification, as we shall see, is treated in this book as one, out of many, ways of describing a document for use in an index. We do not accept that there exists a unique classification for each document, but we respect the operational problems of a library which make the use of a single code desirable. Classification, then, we treat as a part of the indexing or cataloging process.

2.2 Attributes of Index Languages

2.2.1 The General Nature of Index Languages

Almost all index languages in use are to some extent artificial. A natural language, although hard to define, is easy to illustrate. English, French, and German are natural languages. They are the languages that people "naturally" speak. Index languages are invented, not for general communication, but for a very special form of communication—that of enabling indexers and library searchers to communicate with each other and, in a sense, with the documents of the library. The particular role that the language is to play will vary with the library, the collection, and the users. Selection or design of an index language is probably the single most difficult step in designing an information retrieval system; in our opinion, the biggest single reason for this is our general inability to predict the performance of human beings when faced with a communication system different from that with which they have become familiar. Our approach here is to present some basic principles for the design and use of these languages, leaving it to the designer of an individual system to apply them to each local condition.

2.2.2 Index Language Requirements

Some of the attributes of any language in which an index is expressed are the following:

1. Index records usually are to be read by a human searcher at some point in his interrogation procedure. Hence, they must use a vocabulary and syntax that can be understood by the searcher. If the patrons of the library are the general public or any large, not specially trained group, this implies that the index language should approximate natural language, or be otherwise easily learned.

2. Some index files, and these are our primary concern here, are also intended for computer searching. This means that the format, syntax, and vocabulary of the index language must be comprehensible to a computer, just as they must be to men. Usually, this implies more rigidity in the language than is needed for a manual, or nonmechanized, system.

3. The records or messages written in index language must be sufficiently descriptive of the corresponding documents to provide for accurate retrieval, yet not so detailed and cluttered as to slow searching or index composition to an uneconomical rate. Descriptiveness implies not only degree of detail but also concentration on the "right" subject. The "right" subject of concentration for an index varies among user groups.

4. Some indexes are to be prepared by a computer and then are to be searched by man or machine or both. The language of a computer-prepared index is limited by the analytical capability that can be built into the index preparation program. This is not to say that a computer-prepared index must always use a rigid language, for the automatic abstracts produced by Savage et al.[15] are in natural language. But Savage used the exact language of the author. His program is able to select rich, descriptive sentences, if they exist, from the original text, to form the abstract, but the program cannot modify a sentence to make it a better descriptor of the document.

5. Because the individual index records are to be grouped into a file, they must use a format and a physical storage medium that eases file organization. For example, the three-by-five inch cards traditionally used for library catalogs contain information that follows a defined format which greatly speeds perusal of the card during a search. Figure 1 shows the format of an index card produced by the Library of Congress. As to the importance of the physical medium, it can readily be seen how the use of nonuniform card sizes or even use of lighter paper stock could slow the search process.

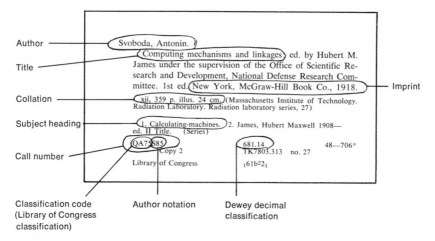

Author	Svoboda, Antonin.
Title	Computing mechanisms and linkages; ed. by Hubert M. James under the supervision of the Office of Scientific Research and Development, National Defense Research Committee. 1st ed. New York, McGraw-Hill Book Co., 1918.
Imprint	
Collation	xii, 359 p. illus. 24 cm. (Massachusetts Institute of Technology. Radiation Laboratory. Radiation laboratory series, 27)
Subject heading	1. Calculating-machines. 2. James, Hubert Maxwell 1908— ed. II Title. (Series)
Call number	QA75.S85 681.14 48—706° TK7803.313 no. 27 Copy 2 ₁61b²2₁ Library of Congress

Classification code
(Library of Congress
classification)   Author notation   Dewey decimal
                                                   classification

Figure 1. Library of Congress catalog card

6. Languages change, index languages among them. A properly designed index language must contain provisions for its own modification, as the language of the documents or of the users changes.

The foregoing list is in terms of results we would like to see from our index language. We shall proceed, through this and the next chapters, to develop a basis for selecting a language capable of giving the required results and for ways of using the language to achieve them.

2.2.3 The Structure of Index Languages

We are concerned with two major components of language—vocabulary and syntax. Indeed, because we are working only with written languages, we may treat these as sole components of a language. A *vocabulary* is the set of words that is used in a language. As applied to natural language, this is a fairly self-evident term. We shall apply it as well to index languages. The set of numeric codes of the Dewey Decimal Classification is, in our usage, a vocabulary for that index language. The set of headings used to describe businesses in the yellow pages of a telephone directory constitute a vocabulary which, although not the most precise language for describing businesses, is apparently quite effective. The vocabulary of an index language, then, is the set of words that is or may be used to describe a document in an index record.

The *syntax* of a language is the set of rules for combining elements of the vocabulary into language units with meanings not expressible by the basic vocabulary. We call these units *syntactic units*. A syntactic unit, typified by a natural language sentence, or the concatenation of a classification code and author code into a unique call number, is, then, a means of extending the descriptive capability of a vocabulary. If we admit, as nouns, *tree* and *water,* and as adjectives *green* and *blue,* we can use syntax to convey the images of *blue water* and *green trees,* which the basic vocabulary cannot convey. The word *syntax* is also used to refer to the particular construction of a sentence, phrase, or other syntactic unit.

In the artificial languages of indexing an authority for vocabulary and syntax is a vital part of the language. These languages derive their usefulness by being restrictive in usage and by expecting of their users fairly rigid conformance to formal definitions and syntactic rules. We generalize the word *dictionary* to include all lists books specifying or a vocabulary, rules of syntax, or general word relationships and include a dictionary as a vital element of an index language. Dictionaries are discussed in Section 2.6 where we further define this tool and diverge even more from the conventional meaning of the word.

We postulate that our readers will accept the expression *word,* as used in natural language, without formal definition. We define the expression *descriptor* to be a word in an index language. A descriptor may have semantically meaningful subdivisions, but it need not have. Most of the time it will imply a single word, number, or code, but, as we shall see later, it can include larger syntactic units as long as they are not subdivisible within the vocabulary of a given language. We define a *term* as a syntactic unit composed of descriptors in a language. In natural language a phrase or sentence falls under our definition of *term.* We define an *index phrase* as a set of index terms somehow linked together. Hence our phrase is analogous to the grouping of sentences into a paragraph or of phrases into a sentence. Note that in natural language there is little syntactic relationship between phrases and none formally defined between sentences, whereas there is a complex syntax among the words of a phrase or sentence. We shall see a similar phenomenon in index languages.

In natural language the word *term* can mean a single word or a phrase. We carry this ambiguity into our own usage because it is so common. More formally, we allow for the possibility that a term is composed of only a single descriptor, in which case we can use either word to describe it.

2.2.4 Measures of Index Language Effectiveness

There is no single scale on which languages can be compared in general. There are many, often not fully separable from one another. Furthermore, the importance of any given factor will vary considerably

Message Systems and Subsystems

with the particular use of the language. A crossword puzzle author makes use of certain redundancy characteristics of a language, and a specialized scientific writer may use a subset of a natural language, a jargon, to convey very precise meanings to other specialists. Index languages perform a special limited role; hence they are more amenable to an analysis of their effectiveness than are natural languages in general use. The particular value or relative importance of any factor remains a function of the individual application.

We use four language attributes as a basis for comparison: expressiveness, ambiguity, compactness, and cost. We caution the reader to be aware, in considering the definitions to follow, that these attributes are not independent or mutually exclusive. A language can be expressive, yet have much ambiguity. The compactness of the words in its vocabulary is not what determines its cost of usage.

Expressiveness is the ability of a language to identify a subject, to distinguish between fine differences in subjects, and to describe a subject to differing levels of detail. We are, of course, concerned with the potential of the language to be expressive and not with the skill of the user or the degree of skill involved. A language such as the Dewey Decimal Classification is not very expressive, whereas natural language is highly so.

Ambiguity, in the sense in which we use it, connotes both a word or syntactic unit having more than one meaning and a meaning that can have more than one symbolic representation in the vocabulary of a language. Ambiguity is caused by *synonyms* and *homographs*. Two words with the same meaning are synonyms. When one word has more than one meaning, it is called a homograph. In spoken language we have *homonyms*, which are words that sound the same but have different meanings. Synonymy and homography can exist in syntactic units larger than individual words. "My book is colored red" and "Red is the color of the book belonging to me" are, for all practical purposes, identical in meaning. The sentence "He covered the field" can refer to literature searching, crop dusting, or baseball, and is a full-sentence homograph. The extent to which synonyms and homographs can occur in a language is independent; that is, they neither exclude nor imply each other. Ambiguity is not necessarily an undesirable quality in language, for although it can blur meanings and cause misunderstanding its existence and recognition puts language users on guard that whether meanings are the same or different depends on context and user. A language without synonyms or homographs will require of its users a number of quite arbitrary decisions on word meanings.

Compactness refers to the physical size or length of an index term or record that is required to convey a certain amount of information. A highly compact language is in use by telegraph companies which permit a customer to select from among a set of standard messages, then transmit a message *number,* but deliver to the ultimate addressee the full, reconstituted message. This example also illustrates why we consider compactness —because the physical memory requirements for storing index data and the communication requirements for transmitting them can become significant in the design of an information retrieval system.

Cost refers to the cost of the decision-making process when an indexer or searcher is faced with the selection of one or more index terms to describe his material. Entering into cost are *training costs* to prepare people to use the language, *cost of dictionary preparation and maintenance,* and *cost of recovering from errors* in selecting terms, all in addition to the cost of the time actually spent indexing or preparing a query.

2.3 A Survey of Index Languages

This discussion follows, in general, the approach taken by Frederick Jonker in his paper entitled, *The Descriptive Continuum, A 'Generalized' Theory of Indexing.*[10] The reader is cautioned that a continuum is not restricted to a single dimension, and any attempt to oversimplify the relationship among index languages can result in confusion, if not bafflement.

The languages to be described range from the hierarchical classification structure, which is a set of descriptors in which the relationship of every word to every other word is precisely defined, to the key word languages where far more freedom of vocabulary usage exists, but where word relationships are not necessarily defined. Then a group of *syntactic languages* is described in which the language user is able to assemble sets of descriptors into terms or phrases, using various syntactic relationships to create semantic concepts not defined in terms of individual descriptors. Following this discussion, in Section 2.4, we turn to a more formal, logical analysis of index languages.

2.3.1 Hierarchical Classification

This is probably the most widely used type of index language. It is based on the assumption that subjects of interest can each be divided into more specific subjects, a process repeated as often as necessary until a structure, or hierarchy, is created to cover the domain of subjects expected to be received by, or requested of, the library. Each subdivision, at each level, is given a single descriptor. There is nothing unique about a hierarchy. The same document set, or library, even in combination with the same group of users, can be structured in many different ways. Even different branches of the same hierarchy may be subdivided differently or

to different depths. The principal value of this type of language is that
when a user is unsure of his search descriptors, or an indexer of his index
descriptors, it is easy for him to generalize or particularize from the point
at which he started, and it is easy for him to learn the language in which
he must phrase his message. Such a language structure is often illustrated
by use of "tree" or "pigeonhole" analogies, as shown in Figure 2.

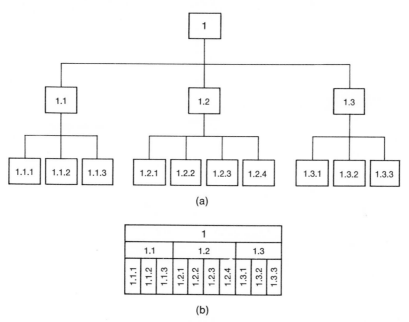

(a)

(b)

Figure 2. Representations of a hierarchical structure: (a) "Tree" representation of a
hierarchical index structure. (b) "Pigeonhole" representation of the same structure.

The vocabulary of a hierarchical language is quite simple, consisting
of a fixed* set of descriptors representing the allowable subjects. There is
usually no attempt to use mnemonic codes. Instead, highly structured
numeric or alpha-numeric codes are generally used. Many libraries employing a hierarchical index language do not use more than one code
number per document, although nothing in the language structure im-

---

* A language that never changes is difficult to conceive. When we use the
adjective *fixed* to apply to a vocabulary, we mean that the vocabulary is fixed at any
given time but that it can be changed, usually by a specially designated authority,
through a formal procedure. The change procedure may be artificially tedious in
order to discourage capricious changing.

poses this restriction. When so used, there is no need for phrases, or syntactic relationship between descriptors, because there is never more than one descriptor in a record. There is an interesting morphology, however, in that a descriptor at one level contains the symbols for all those generic to it, and this is the essence of a hierarchical language. For example, in the Dewey Decimal Classification[2] we find that an artificial earth satellite is classified by the code 629.138 82. This code contains within it, or implies the use of, the following additional descriptors which are higher in the hierarchy, hence more general:

600.	Technology (applied science)
620.	Engineering
629.	Other branches of engineering
629.13	Aeronautics
629.138	Uses of aircraft
629.138 8	Space flight (inertial navigation)

When we say "artificial earth satellite" in Dewey's language, we are also saying "aeronautics," and there is no way to avoid it. The advantages and disadvantages of this situation we leave until the next section.

In Section 2.2.2 we stressed the importance of being able to change an index language to keep pace with changes in users' language usage. Expanding the vocabulary of a hierarchical language is relatively easy, but changing the meaning of an existing descriptor can be very difficult. Expansion can be achieved by extending descriptor codes to the right, and defining the next lower order set of meanings. We might, for example, define 629.138 821 as "manned, artificial earth satellites," and 629.138 822 as "unmanned . . ." Alternatively, the subdivision could be by use, say, . . . 821 for earth reconnaissance . . . 822 for space reconnaissance . . . 823 for communications relay, . . . 824 for weapon carrying, and so forth. An important point is to (try to) keep the codes mutually exclusive. A reconnaissance satellite, for example, may be manned or unmanned. We should not, then, have as subdivisions of the code for artificial earth satellites

629.138 821	manned
822	unmanned
823	reconnaissance

because the third code does not exclude either of the first two. It would be possible to have

629.138 821	Earth reconnaissance satellites
821 1	-manned
821 2	-unmanned
822	Space reconnaissance satellites
822 1	-manned
822 2	-unmanned

The difficulty with this approach is that there is no single descriptor covering the subject of manned satellites, which points out a basic defect in this class of languages, that there are some concepts which either are not able to be stated with a single descriptor, or are not able to be separated from another concept. Yet one descriptor per document is all that is used in many systems. However the structure is changed or twisted, the concepts we wish to define in our example have two facets: use of the vehicle and nature of its crew, and no subdivision of a higher level code can resolve this split in such a way that a single code could distinguish between manned and unmanned vehicles, regardless of usage, or between usages, regardless of whether or not manned.

The problem of changing the *meaning* of an already established descriptor is that this can affect the meaning of other descriptors. If, for example, one were to modify the meaning of *aeronautics* in the Dewey Decimal System to include only flight based upon lift provided by the atmosphere, then *space flight* can no longer be a subordinate descriptor, and *aircraft* will have to be defined in such a way as to distinguish it from *space craft*. Then, *space flight* and *space craft* would have to be reinserted somewhere else in the hierarchy, possibly necessitating a change in the meaning of some other descriptor.

In summary, hierarchical languages are rigid in the sense of being hard to change except by expansion at the bottom. They are somewhat arbitrary in that the subsumption of one subject under another is fixed by the library, not by nature. Finally, they are very valuable, their very weaknesses being convertible into strengths from another point of view. Their rigidity makes them stable and makes it easier to train people to use them, but perhaps their most useful attribute is the ease with which a language user can state his subject more specifically or more generally by moving down or up the hierarchy. Even though subject subsumption may be arbitrary, the existence of a complete code structure assists the user to interpret it. Even if a searcher disagrees with the organization of the hierarchy, he can study it and learn to cope with it.

In addition to the Dewey Decimal Classification system already mentioned, the hierarchical systems in most common use are the Library of Congress system and the Universal Decimal Classification (UDC), a modification of the Dewey system in wide international use.

2.3.2 Subject Headings

A subject heading language is one that makes use of a fixed* number of subject classes, just as does hierarchical classification, but does not usually adopt a special code for its terms, and generally is used in such a

---

* See footnote of Section 2.3.1.

way as to permit more than one term to be assigned to the index of any given document. A subject heading language, however, has little if any structure or means of relating one term to another. This gives the designer a work-saving advantage. It is no longer necessary to create a structure into which all knowledge (or at least all that is expected at the designer's library) will fall. As a practical matter, subject headings tend to be made up to describe information received, not information expected to be received. The practical advantages of this feature can be enormous when an index language must be constructed from scratch, and little information is available on subject spread. The vocabulary of a subject heading language consists of natural language terms and phrases, but they are not made up of descriptors which are in themselves elements of the vocabulary. If, for example, *data processing* were a subject heading, it does not follow that *data* and *processing,* individually, would be legal descriptors. Thus, although subject headings are composed of natural language words, these words need not be descriptors in the index language. Because the subject headings are not built up from index language descriptors, we may call them descriptors, regardless of the length or composition, as measured in another language.

As a document collection grows, it sometimes becomes necessary to enlarge the subject heading language. Adding new terms to cover subjects not previously covered poses no problem, for there is no resultant change in existing descriptors. However, subject headings are often split, creating a new term to cover the new subject, and changing the meaning of the old term to exclude the subject area of the new term. Subject headings may also be subdivided to introduce some hierarchical structure into the language. As a general observation, subject headings have a tendency to increase their degree of structure over time, although no law governs this phenomenon. Because of their relative lack of structure, the subject headings are often listed for users in alphabetical order, and the existence of such a list is sometimes erroneously considered to be a necessary feature of the language. The order of listing of terms for language users has no particular bearing on the structure of the language. These two points—the tendency toward hierarchy and the habit of alphabetic listing—can be seen in comparing the old and new classification systems used by the Association for Computing Machinery for its publication *Computing Reviews.*[3]

Figure 3 shows the subject headings in use from the *Review's* inception in 1960 until the end of 1963. In 1964 a new classification was introduced which is shown in Figure 4. Note that Figure 3 has two levels of generality and that the terms are listed in alphabetical order by major heading. With the introduction of the new system came an additional level of generality and abandonment of alphabetic term listing. The new system could easily be called a hierarchical classification language, although it is somewhat lacking in depth.

Administration and Operation of
    Computer Centers
  General
  Organization
Analog Computers
  General
  Applications
  Equipment
Artificial Intelligence
  General
  Pattern and Speech Recognition
  Simulation of Human Activity
Automation and Process Control
  General
  Communications Systems
  Industrial Applications
  Theory
Business Data Processing
  General
  Auditing
  Insurance
  Inventory
  Payroll
  Programming Languages
Digital Computer Applications
  General
  Aeronautical Engineering and
    Space
  Astronomy, Astrophysics, and
    Astrodynamics
  Chemistry and Chemical
    Engineering
  Electronics and Electrical
    Engineering
  Health Sciences
  Logic and Fundamentals of
    Mathematics
  Machine Translation and
    Linguistics
  Mechanical Engineering
  Number Theory
  Physics
  Power Engineering

  Social Sciences
  Weather and Meteorology
  Miscellaneous
Digital Computer Components and
    Circuits
  General
  Storage
Digital Computer Programming
  General
  Algorithmic Languages
  Assembly Programs
  Automatic Programming
  Specific Algorithmic Languages
  Storage Allocation
  Theory of Programming
Digital Computer Systems
  General
  General Purpose
  Real Time Control
  Peripheral Equipment
Education and Computers
  General
  Digital
  University and Other Teaching
    Usage
  Techniques in Machine Teaching
History
  General
Information Storage and Retrieval
  General
Information Theory and Coding
  General
Logic, Logical Design, and Switching
    Theory
  General
  Formal Logic
  Logical Design and Switching
    Circuits
  Theory of Automata and Turing
    Machines
Managerial Applications
  General

Management Simulation and
  Games
Mathematical Methods
Mathematics
  General
  Analysis
Numerical Mathematics
  General
  Finite Differences
  Functional Approximation and
    Interpolation
  Integral Equations
  Linear Systems and Matrices
  Ordinary Differential Equations
  Numerical Integration

Partial Differential Equations
Tables and Specific Computations
Texts
Standards
  General
  Glossaries
  Terminology
Statistics and Probability
  General
  Monte Carlo Methods
  Programming
  Random Number Generation
Technological Effects and Cybernetics
  Sociological Effects

**Figure 4. Subject headings used by the Association for Computing Machinery since 1964
(source: Finerman and Revens,[3] *Communications of the ACM*)**

1. *General Topics and Education*
   1.0 General
   1.1 Texts; Handbooks
   1.2 History; Biographies
   1.3 Introductory and Survey
       Articles
   1.4 Glossaries
   1.5 Education
       1.50 General
       1.51 High School Courses
           and Programs
       1.52 University Courses and
           Programs
       1.53 Certification; Degrees;
           Diplomas
       1.59 Miscellaneous
   1.9 Miscellaneous
2. *Computing Milieu*
   2.0 General
   2.1 Philosophical and Social
       Implications
       2.10 General
       2.11 Economic and
           Sociological Effects
       2.12 The Public and
           Computers
       2.19 Miscellaneous

2.2 Professional Aspects
2.3 Legislation; Regulations
2.4 Administration of Computing
    Centers
    2.40 General
    2.41 Administrative Policies
    2.42 Personnel Training
    2.43 Operating Procedures
    2.44 Equipment Evaluation
    2.45 Surveys of Computing
        Centers
    2.49 Miscellaneous
2.9 Miscellaneous

3. *Applications*
   3.1 Natural Sciences
       3.10 General
       3.11 Astronomy; Space
       3.12 Biology
       3.13 Chemistry
       3.14 Earth Sciences
       3.15 Mathematics; Number
           Theory
       3.16 Meteorology
       3.17 Physics; Nuclear
           Sciences
       3.19 Miscellaneous

Message Systems and Subsystems

Subject headings, then, represent simply a loosening of the structure of a hierarchical language. Their use makes initial language design easier since there is less to predict, and makes future changes easier to implement because no elaborate structure need be perturbed by such a change. Their lack of structure makes them more difficult to learn and use.

2.3.3 Key Word Systems

Both the languages described thus far share the characteristic that the number of subjects that can be described by them is fixed and is equal to the number of defined terms. While a term in a hierarchy implies all terms above it, no variation or shading of the meaning of a term is possible. This is true even if the cataloging system permits use of more than one classification term per index record. Although the ACM does not do this, there is no reason why a document on the application of information theory (code number 5.6 in Figure 4) to linguistics (code 3.42) cannot be classified under both subjects. This technique is used by the Library of Congress which applies a set of subject headings as well as a hierarchical classification code to each document as shown in Figure 1. These terms do not modify each other, however. LC merely says that a book is on subject A, and also on subject B, and also on subject C. Language systems so organized are often called "pre-coordinated" systems, in that whatever semantically meaningful descriptor combinations are allowed have been made—the descriptors "coordinated" to form terms— by the language designers. We will generally avoid this usage because the descriptors that are coordinated into a term are not defined in the vocabulary of the language that results—hence are not truly descriptors. "Pre-coordinated" vocabularies, as we have said, leave gaps in their subject coverage and are slower to adapt to new subject matters. This is particularly true in libraries that must cover scientific literature wherein new concepts and terminology are constantly being introduced. To satisfy this need languages have been developed which permit their users to select several descriptors for an index, as many as are needed to describe a particular document. This family of languages is given many names but is most commonly called *coordinate* or *key word indexing*. A specific example of key word indexing is the Uniterm system, developed by Mortimer Taube et al.[16] Often we hear the word *descriptor* used to apply exclusively to a descriptor in this form of language.

These languages go part way toward allowing the use of concepts not specifically predefined, in that the vocabulary is large, consists of single words or short phrases, and encourages the use of many descriptors or terms per index to describe as many facets of the document as possible. Still, terms cannot be shown as modifying each other even if the indexer meant them to. *Brown* and *fox* are separate descriptors, and do not necessarily mean *brown fox*. Because there need be no structural relationship between terms, they can be added to or deleted from the vocabulary at will, making the language highly adaptive to subject matter changes.

One form of key word index language, which we call a *fixed vocabulary, key word language,* differs only slightly from the subject heading languages. The main differences are that key words are generally shorter than subject headings—usually a single word but possibly a short phrase—and the size of the total vocabulary, the number of possible terms which can be created, may be much larger than is common in subject heading languages. Like a subject heading language, the vocabulary is fixed. In such a language, if *information theory* and *linguistics* are both members of the vocabulary set, then a paper on information theory applied to linguistics would certainly be indexed by both descriptors. Significantly, however, the language has no way to tell us the connection between these descriptors. Literally, we must guess. Without a useful syntax, there is no difference between this languaage and a subject heading language, but the users of a language called a key word index will expect multiple descriptors, whereas users of a language called hierarchical classification will meekly make do without a complete description of documents in that language.

In spite of their lack of syntax key word languages do accomplish their purpose in being more adaptable to subject matter changes, and they do allow searchers to find documents more easily if the actual subject sought does not exactly coincide with a subject heading. Note, in the ACM languages, that a search for anything concerned with programming could be quite tedious to request, while the same request requires only one word if a key word index is used. Although there are headings that encompass *programming,* every computer application implies programming, although the word is not mentioned in all ACM headings, on *applications.* We do wish to emphasize, however, that the difference between subject heading and key word languages is relatively slight and, what is even more important, that the commonly used phrases "pre-coordinated" and "uncoordinated" refer to descriptors, not terms, as we have defined them. The pre-coordination is between individual words (descriptors) not between terms (combinations of descriptors). *Terms* in any language described so far can be concatenated freely into phrases which do not modify each other, but there is a restriction on term composition, wherein descriptors do modify each other.

An example of a fixed key word system is found in use by the Defense Documentation Center (formerly Armed Forces Technical Information Agency, or ASTIA). Their language has a vocabulary of about 7000 terms and descriptors listed in the *ASTIA Thesaurus,*[22] which are subject to occasional change. DDC's index language, a sample of which is shown in Figure 5, also makes use of a subject heading system. In this language, multiple subject headings, as well as multiple key words, may be applied to any index record. The *ASTIA Thesaurus* defines some hierarchy among descriptors. The National Library of Medicine[20] uses a similarly constructed language.

We made brief mention of the problem of the ambiguity, or uncertainty of meaning, caused by lack of a syntax for relating descriptors within terms. It is for this reason that we cannot distinguish between a

Figure 5. Sample from Defense Documentation Center Thesaurus[22]

Computers
(Computers & Data Systems)
Includes:
Calculating machines
Generic to:
Analog computers
Analog-digital computers
Bombing-digital computers
Digital computers
Digital differential analyzers
Fire control computers
Guided missile computers
Impact computers
Navigation computers
Parallax computers
Radar range computers
Special purpose computers
Torpedo data computers
Also see:
Data processing systems
Electronic accounting machines
Programming (computers)
Simulation

Computing gun sights use *Gun sights*

Concrete
(Structural Engineering)
Generic to:
Reinforced concrete
Also see:
Cements

Concrete surfacing use *Pavements*

Condensation
(Physical & Physicochemical
Concepts)
(Change of state from gas or
vapor to liquid or solid; also
meteorological phenomenon, ex-
cludes chemical reaction.)
Also see:
Atmospheric precipitation
Clouds

Condensation reactions
(Chemical Reactions)
Includes:
Reformatsky reactions
Specific to:
Chemical reactions
Generic to:
Friedel-Crafts reactions
Grignard reactions
Also see:
Diene synthesis
Grignard reactions

Condensation trails
(Meteorology & Climatology)
Includes:
Contrails
Exhaust trails
Vapor trails
Also see:
Wake

Condensers (Electrical) use
Capacitors

Condensers (liquefiers)
(Instrumentation)
Generic to:
Refrigerant condensers
Steam condensers

Condiments
(Food)
Includes:
Pepper
Seasonings
Spices
Specific to:
Food

Conditioned reflex
(Psychology & Psychometrics)
Includes:
Conditioned response

The Analysis of Information Systems

213

Specific to:
Behavior
Reflexes
Also see:
Adjustment (psychology)
Learning
Motor reactions

Conductivity (Electrical) use
Electrical conductance

Conductivity (Thermal) use *thermal conductivity*

Conduit pliers
(Industrial Equipment & Tools)
Specific to:
Pliers
Small tools
Also see:
Maintenance tools
Splicing tools

Conferences use *Symposia*

Confidence limits use *Statistical analysis*

blind Venetian and a venetian blind, without going, as does DDC, to a second, more generically oriented language to explain context. Here, we see the importance of recognizing the level of descriptor grouping to which syntax is applied, for if these descriptor pairs were subject headings there would be no confusion between them. Associating descriptors together into semantic units which give a misleading idea of document content is called *false coordination*.

Sets of key word index terms provide greater flexibility of subject description than do precoordinated terms, but this is still not sufficient in some environments to be adequately descriptive of document subject matter. Users of information sometimes want to search on the actual words that the author used, rather than having to use a set of predetermined words, approximately synonymous to the desired words, but which may not provide enough detail, and may be subject to misinterpretation. In this case an approach can be used wherein the indexer is instructed to select his index terms solely on the basis of importance in the context of an individual document and not on the basis of their occurrence on any approved vocabulary list or thesaurus. Except for word classes that might be excluded, such as conjunctions, prepositions, and numbers, the indexer is free to choose his own index vocabulary. Members of this family of index languages are called *free vocabulary* or *free key word languages*.

We have now discussed three language families which have in common the lack of a syntax for allowing terms to modify each other but which vary as to freedom of choice of terms, number of terms to use, and degree of definition of terms. In continuing our discussion of index languages we shall now turn our attention primarily toward syntax. The point was made at the beginning of this section that, although a language continuum might be said to exist, it does not follow that it is a one-dimensional continuum. The index language families to follow vary in both vocabulary and syntax.

Message Systems and Subsystems

2.3.4 Syntactic Languages

The simplest family of syntaxes is that in which a fixed number of descriptors is required to make up a term, and the exact role of each descriptor in the term is specified in advance. Probably the simplest of these languages we may call *tagged descriptors*. Here, a descriptor has affixed to it another descriptor to describe the first. The role of the affix might be to classify the basic descriptor, denoting it as a proper name, an attribute, or an activity. It might be used to group together a set of descriptors all implied by one subject of the document. If the document were about an inventor *and* his product, descriptors of the person and the device might be separately tagged, to avoid confusion on retrieval.

A more advanced syntactic language is one in which the various descriptors modify one another, greatly enlarging the number of distinct statements that can be made in the language. One example of such a syntax is a computer instruction which is represented in the computer as a binary number, the first part typically specifying an operation and the second part an address, or the location, of the operand. Both the instruction and address descriptors are expressed by using the same vocabulary— numbers—but by assigning different meanings to differently positioned numbers a language of great flexibility is created. Similarly, use of numbers alone as descriptors on a purchase order can enable the creation of terms describing a list of items to be purchased. The different roles of the numbers might be: *quantity, style, color, unit price, total price.* The structure of such a language is illustrated in Figure 6. More appropriate to indexing, terms may consist of a key word descriptor and an additional descriptor for the subject context of the key word, so that we might say:

> *Tank, weapon*
> *Tank, petroleum*
> *Train, transportation*
> *Train, education*

This permits the use of context to resolve ambiguity in artificial languages, just as is done in natural languages. Without the prior definition of the syntactic role to be played by each descriptor, the reader may assume that *train,* appearing next to *education,* means take the interpretation of *train* implied by the general subject *education,* but he cannot be sure. With the definition of role, he is assured that he has made the assumption intended by the author of the term. This does not rule out ambiguity—homograph problems can still occur. For example, the descriptor pair *ship, transportation* may described a vessel or an act of transporting. Ambiguities can be lessened by these means, however. Synonym problems also remain, for unless the vocabulary (not syntax) is restricted, *vessel* might be substituted for *ship,* compounding the search problem, yet adhering to the rule for term construction.

GADGET CORP.

ORDER FORM

Quantity	Style	Color	Unit Price	Price
3	104	6	10-12	30.36
12	347	58	9.00	108.00
			Total	138.36

Figure 6. A common form of artificial syntax

We may still consider ourselves within the same language family if we permit some variance in the number of descriptors of each type that may be present. A number of key words may be modified by a single subject descriptor, or a key word may be modified by more than one subject heading. The overriding consideration is that the role of any descriptor that does appear be precisely defined, and that each syntactic role have its own associated vocabulary. For example, we might use a term such as *train, coach; education* to denote two key words, both in the context of the same subject field.

The various roles played by descriptors in such languages may be called facets and, if so, we have described a language called *faceted indexing*[18] in which a variety of attributes, aspects, or facets of the subject are written into the index. The listing of title, author, and publisher on a library's index card is a form of faceted indexing. Here, it is position on the card that indicates the role of the facet. It could also be sequence, or relative position, as it is in the *tank* and *train* examples above. The term *faceted indexing* is more commonly used to describe methods of subject description than it is to describe document attribute indexing. There might be a code which identifies *steel* as a subject. But is this a special kind of steel? What aspect of steel is implied? Its manufacture? Its transportation? The raw materials used in its manufacture? These questions can be answered by appending modifiers to the subject term *steel* which might result in creation of an index term such as one of these:

Message Systems and Subsystems

steel, hardened, manufacture of
steel, as a component, use in automobiles

These resemble subject headings, but in a faceted language they are not made up in advance (not "precoordinated"). They are true terms constructed out of defined descriptors following a defined syntactic rule, such as: subject is followed by a restricting modifier, which is followed by a modifier descriptive of use or operation performed. Each facet may draw its descriptors from the same vocabulary. We might, for example, have the following terms:

glass, stained, design of
textiles, glass, sale of

Here, *glass* appears first as a basic subject, and then as a modifier. Where the vocabularies and roles are clearly defined, there would be no confusion caused by two uses of the same symbol.

In a faceted index term, then, each facet plays a specifically defined syntactic role, permitting the term to be readily parsed into its constituent descriptors. The descriptors, as do any descriptors that make up terms, have meaning themselves in the index language. It is possible to draw each descriptor from a different subset of the total vocabulary, which happens when one descriptor is verbal and another numeric.

Faceted indexing is not restricted to key word descriptors. Faceted hierarchical languages are possible also. For example, a single classification code could handle the first two descriptors in each of the "glass" examples above; that is, *stained glass* and *glass textiles* can each be defined by a single Dewey classification code.* The third facet, descriptive of process or action, could be described by another Dewey code or by a term from another classification language specifically designed for this purpose.

In natural language the parts of speech or elements of a sentence can be regarded as facets, each playing a different role in the composition of a vastly complicated syntactic unit—the sentence. Here, a combination of position and choice of vocabulary element is required to determine the role being played by individual words. The subject, verb, and object of a sentence are facets which are each representable only by limited grammatical forms. Prepositions and conjunctions are facets, playing special roles in sentence construction, but can occur in any major part of a sentence. There is a fundamental difference, however, between a natural language expression and one of the faceted expressions illustrated above. In the illustrated systems the precise role and relationships can be prescribed beforehand. In natural language we have no rigid set of rules which governs the relationship among words. We can have homographs and synonyms at the phrase level. There is not just one way to express a

* 748.5 and 677.54, respectively.

concept, and the same set of words can have different meanings depending upon the sentence that preceded them. Nonetheless, the descriptive power of natural language makes it sometimes advantageous for indexing use over the less ambiguous, but less descriptive, artificial languages.

One of the major reasons why natural language is not in common use as an index language is its difficulty of search. To tell if the last sentence contains the word *language* it is necessary to look at each word in sequence until either the term is found or the sentence ends. Searches of this length have not been an important difficulty of the other languages described thus far. The rise in popularity of *permuted indexing* has eased this situation, making limited natural language expressions easier to search. A permuted index resembles a concordance but, instead of giving only the location of word occurrence, it gives the surrounding context of each occurrence of each word, and is commonly known as key-word-in-context or KWIC indexing.[19] In practice the method is most often used with phrases, especially titles, selected out of the documents. The technique overcomes the problem of quickly determining the role of a word in a phrase, but this is done at the cost of memory or other space requirements. The sentence or phrase to be permuted is listed several times in alphabetical order by each word in the sentence (barring "common" words), retaining original word context. The sentence, "The black cat ran away," would be permuted as follows. First, reproduce the sentence once for each "noncommon" word:

The	**black**	cat	ran	away.
The	black	**cat**	ran	away.
The	black	cat	**ran**	away.
The	black	cat	ran	**away.**

Then, sort the sentences on the base word and rearrange as follows:

The	black	cat	ran	**away.**
	The	**black**	cat	ran away.
	The	black	**cat**	ran away.
	The	black	cat	**ran** away.

The center, boldface column is used for searching. These lines would be merged with the permutations of other sentences providing a single list, or file, to be used for all searches. In this way any word in any sentence can be quickly located by an alphabetic search, and this permits use of natural language abstracts—index phrases—to be used as searchable records. The surrounding context can be used to resolve many problems of semantic ambiguity. The difficulty lies in the total number of characters needed for the simplest sentence, and the fact that no single approach to phrase selection, such as use of title, is guaranteed to be as descriptive as a subject heading or key word system *might have been.* The method shares with any key word system, with or without syntax, the lack of a built-in technique for generalizing or particularizing searches. Use of short, natural language phrases we call *phrase indexing*. This should not be equated with KWIC indexing. KWIC is a technique that makes phrase indexing effective and economical.

Our final index language is the language of the document itself, the full, natural language. It is not feasible to use this language as an index without the aid of a computer because of the enormous volume of material to be searched or reorganized to permit searching at reasonable speeds. Exactly the same problem is faced as described for phrase indexing—that too many words have to be examined to find out if a given word occurs in the document. To permute in their entirety all documents in a library is not economically feasible today. If we assume that an average technical paper contains 5000 words, that half of these are common words, and that sentences average ten words in length, each document would generate 500 (sentences) $\times$ 10 (words per sentence) $\times$ 5 repetitions (one for each non-common word) = 25,000 words of storage required *per document*.* A technique devised at the University of Pittsburgh[11] is the preparation of a concordance and the use of it to locate the search terms. The concordance is merely a resequencing of the document by which words are listed alphabetically and the locations of their occurrence in the original text are given. The search logic can be the same, then, as for a key word system, but full context is retained. It would be possible to search for documents containing the word *set* with the word *theory* to be found within two words in either direction. This would enable the recovery of the subject of *set theory* (or *theory of sets*) without recovering all documents mentioning both the words *set* and *theory,* in any context.

2.4 The Logic of Indexing Languages

When we assign a descriptor to a document, we are making the statement that the document is a member of the set of documents described by that term. Similarly, when we admit a term to use in the vocabulary of an index language, we are assigning that term to a set of subjects, saying that all subjects in the set have the attribute that they are described by this term. In some languages, such as hierarchical classification, each set of subjects has only one descriptor, but more than one subject may share the same descriptor. In some a subject may belong to any number of descriptor sets. This tends to be true of the key word index languages. The convention of representing index terms as sets of elemental subjects, or sets of documents described, permits us to construct geometric analogies that are useful in studying index language structure. This

---

* The fact that some words are repeated in a sentence does not help. Each occurrence of each word generates a full repetition of its sentence.

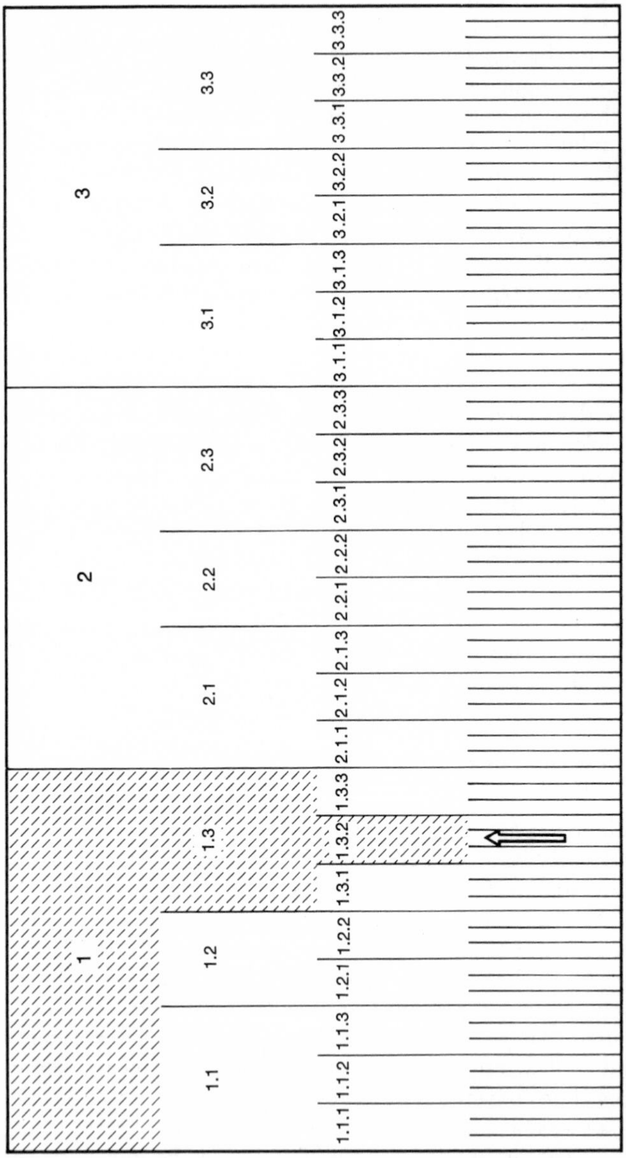

Figure 7. Hierarchical classification. In a hierarchical classification language, selection of any code or descriptor, such as 1.3.2 (arrow), places a lower bound on the region of subject space denoted and automatically selects all portions of the space above the bound, shown by the shaded area.

Message Systems and Subsystems

method of approach permits a more uniform view of all index languages and tends to subordinate the differences among them.

To represent an index language geometrically we assume that every point or small region of a portion of a plane represents a subject. The set of subjects represented by a term is then an area on this planar surface. The total portion of the surface considered, the complete set of subjects, is called *subject space*. In this conceptual framework an index language is a means of *partitioning subject space*.

A hierarchical language is representable by the configuration shown in Figure 7. This diagram is similar to that of Figure 2, but we have removed the dividing lines at top and bottom of the subject regions, and we can see how the selection of any single code (naming of a subdivision or pigeonhole) also implies the naming of all portions of the space in a direct line above the named region, but not below. The lateral subdivisions of the space are intended to be mutually exclusive, so that any stated subject falls cleanly in one and only one defined region.

A subject heading language is simpler but not so orderly. It is represented schematically in Figure 8 by a similar division of subject space

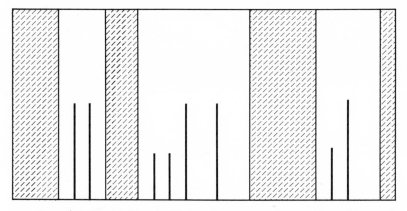

Figure 8. Subject headings. A subject heading language does not necessarily cover the entire space, makes no attempt at uniform "size" subdivisions, and may have a few levels of hierarchy. Shaded areas represent possible subjects not covered by this language.

into mutually exclusive regions, but with two differences. 1. No attempt is made to cover all of subject space, to have a descriptor for every possible subject. In the diagram, the shaded portions represent possible subjects that are not represented in the language. 2. While subdivision is possible, it is generally done only to a shallow and nonuniform extent.

Figure 9 illustrates the key word systems. The fixed-vocabulary key word systems, like subject heading languages, specify a partitioning of

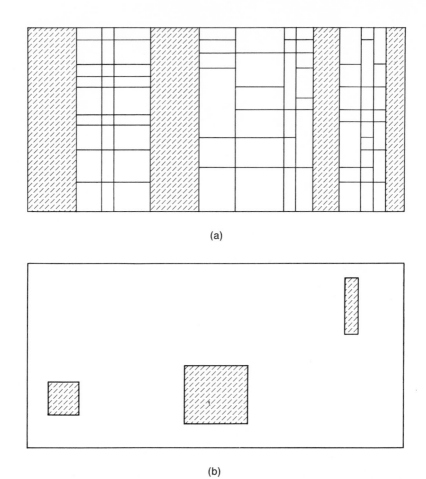

(a)

(b)

Figure 9. Key words. (*a*) Limited key words occupy predetermined areas of subject space. Not all the space need be covered by defined descriptors. (*b*) Free key word languages do not partition the space in advance of word use. Instead, because words can vary in meaning each time they are used, indexers are mapping out regions of subject space as they use words. In both illustrations the blacked-in areas represent a possible document description.

some, but not all, of subject space. Each rectangle in the nonshaded areas represents the set of subjects described by a key word. A free key word system shows no prior partitioning. Because neither the set of words (vocabulary) to be used nor the set of meanings of these words is specified in advance, the indexer is ruling out a region of subject space with each key word he uses and the extent of the region denoted by any given word may vary somewhat each time that word is used. Hence there is a risk of indexer and searcher ascribing different meanings to a term. This conforms with S. I. Hayakawa's[4] concept that word meanings are never fully determined in advance of utterance and that words never have exactly the same meaning twice.

To see clearly the difference between precoordinated languages and indexer-coordinated languages, we must realize that a region in subject space representing a concept need not be connected. It can consist of two or more small regions which do not overlap. However, a precoordinated language is one in which all the term regions that may be used to represent one document have been decided upon before use. An indexer-coordinated language permits the indexer to use small, disconnected "building blocks" to build a subject description out of a combination of predefined elements in a configuration that may never have been used before.

In the language structure illustrated in Figure 7, selection of a point in subject space exactly determines the region of subject space that will represent the document. In the language of Figure 9b, the indexer is free to select any set of regions he wants. The total region represented by this set (e.g., the set of three rectangles shown in black in the figure) need not have been predefined as a region, but its constituent elements (the individual blocks) have been predefined to some extent, although the exact coverage of subject space by a descriptor will vary with each use.

The languages which use facets or syntax are not so simple to represent geometrically. To attempt to do so, we introduce another representation, *Venn diagrams,* which graphically demonstrate certain logical relationships among sets. The technique is best explained by a simple example. In Figure 10a the left-hand circle represents all people in the United States. The right-hand circle represents all men in the world. The

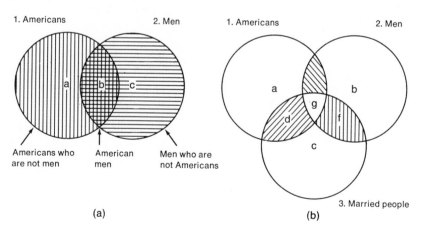

Figure 10. Venn diagrams. (a) The intersection of two sets or subjects. (b) The intersection of three sets or subjects.

intersection (darkly shaded area) represents people in the United States who are men. The lightly shaded areas, *a* and *c,* represent American non-men (women and children) and non-American men. If we introduce a third circle, married people, as shown in Figure 10*b*, we create the following regions: (*a*) Americans who are not men or married, (*b*) men who are not Americans and not married, (*c*) married people who are not American and not men (non-American, married women), (*d*) American married women, (*e*) American unmarried men, (*f*) non-American married men, (*g*) married American men. The region (*a-b-d-e-f-g*) represents all people who are Americans or men, regardless of marital status.

To represent an index with a Venn diagram we must define the area we are to cover as the subject area that is, or could be, implied by the use of a term. Even though descriptors in a limited key word system may be so defined that no synonyms are permitted, any given subject may have more than one appropriate key word. We may, for example, represent *steel* and *manufacturing* as intersecting circles. The intersection cannot be equated to the natural language expression *manufacturing of steel,* but it includes this expression. The intersection covers all commonality of meaning between these words, including the use of steel in manufacturing something —say, steel tools used to manufacture wood products. In a key word language without syntax the intersection of *steel, automobile,* and *manufacturing* includes use of steel in manufacturing automobiles, use of automobiles in manufacturing steel, and manufacturing of steel for use in automobiles.

It is important to note that when an indexer writes down a set of key words he does not imply just the intersection of their subject areas. He is simply stating that the document is about A, is also about B, is also about C, and so on. A document could be about automobiles and about manufacturing. Both these words would be key words. The same key words would result if the document were about automobile manufacturing. In terms of a Venn diagram a key word index expresses the union·of the terms stated. In Figure 10*a* the union of *American* and *men* is region a plus region b plus region c—it consists of anyone who is an American, a man, or both. The symbol for the union of subjects *a* and *b* is $a \cup b$ or $a + b$.

The faceted index term is represented by the *intersection* of its constituent descriptors. Figure 11*a* shows a Venn diagram representing the key word implication of *steel, automobile,* and *manufacturing,* the union of these sets. Figure 11*b* shows a representation of the same descriptors if formed into a syntactic unit: *Manufacturing of steel automobiles.* We are not interested in the entire intersection of *steel* and *automobiles.* The syntax of the term implies a narrower use of *steel* (as a product) than would normally be assumed by its use in a key word index, and a narrower use of *automobile* (as a manufactured product). The representation of the term *manufacturing of steel automobiles* is the small, double-hatched area

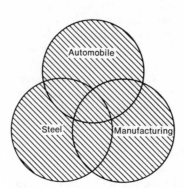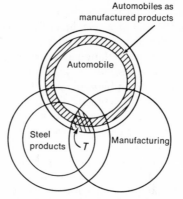

Figure 11. Key words and faceted index representations. (a) The union of three descriptors of a key word index. Any point within the shaded area may be within the subject of the document. (b) The faceted index term, *manufacturing of steel automobiles*, is represented by the intersection of three terms. Only points in the small shaded area are in the subject of the document.

marked T, in Figure 11*b*. The reader can easily discern other meaningful subjects that could be formed out of the basic three descriptors and their implied roles. The logic of the Figure 11*b* applies to all forms of faceted or syntactic languages, from the simplest tagging of a key word up to a natural language. The reader must reason by analogy for the more complex languages, for diagrams cannot easily represent more complex sentences involving conditional statements or the use of general context, rather than a single adjective, to modify meaning. The reader must also be aware that although natural language offers the capability for great precision of description not all authors take advantage of it and not all natural language statements are necessarily small regions in subject space.

2.5 A Comparative Analysis of Index Languages

In Section 2.3 we stated that language structure is (at least) two-dimensional, varying in both syntax and vocabulary. In Section 2.2 we introduced four measures of language performance: expressiveness, ambiguity, compactness, and cost. In this section we compare the languages of Section 2.3 on these measures. Before proceeding, we wish to emphasize that probably the most important points that can be made about the parameters of language are that language can be a highly complex structure, not at all easy to measure or even study, and that hasty generalization based on small or restricted samples may be highly misleading. Language use is a manifestation of human behavior, the oversimplification of which is always hazardous.

So far in this chapter we have simply tacked the syntactic languages at the end of a one-dimensional continuum based on vocabulary variability. Let us now reconsider the two-dimensional aspect of language. In our progression of languages vocabulary ranged from a rigid set of mutually exclusive descriptors, as in hierarchical classification, to a freely variable, but more ambiguous, set of descriptors in a free key word language. Within the syntactic languages we also saw the phenomenon that the greater the freedom of choice of vocabulary, the more ambiguity there was in the language, and we found that syntax helps both to overcome this problem and to increase expressiveness.

We may apply a scale to both vocabulary and syntax to measure their variability, or freedom of choice by the user. A hierarchical classification language has no syntax to combine descriptors into terms. It has relatively little freedom of choice of descriptors in the sense that there will be only a few descriptors considered appropriate in classifying a document. A free key word language, although still having no syntax, offers a great freedom of choice of descriptors to express any single concept. The nonsyntactic languages, of course, offer no syntax variation. The simple syntactic languages, in which we might use two facets in an index term, offer a small amount of choice in organizing terms, and the languages with complex syntax, such as natural language, offer a wide choice, even with the same key vocabulary terms, in how to express a concept. A language that is highly variable will have less rigid rules of word meaning and syntactic construction. Indexers will have more freedom of expression, which opens the possibility both of greater expressiveness and greater ambiguity. A less variable language will have fewer word meanings allowed and fewer grammatical constructions. Although potentially less ambiguous, it will probably also be less expressive.

Figure 12 shows these language measures as axes of a graph. Distance away from the origin, in either case, represents increasing variability in word meanings or syntactic usage. Although we cannot make actual measurements on these scales, we have laid out the progression of languages described in Section 3. The graph shows the nonsyntactic languages with increasing variability of vocabulary. The languages are hierarchical classification, subject headings, and the key word systems. Then the syntactic languages—tagged descriptors, faceted terms, phrases, and full, natural language are shown, with a great increase in syntax variability but little additional increase in vocabulary variability. If we then draw a curve all around this line, we have very probably enclosed all the points in this plane representing useful languages, for it is difficult to conceive of a language with, say, a rich, variable vocabulary but no syntax at all or a complex syntax with only a small, rigid vocabulary. We mean by this illustration only to exclude extreme language forms from consideration; we do not imply that a plotting board could be used to judge a language's performance.

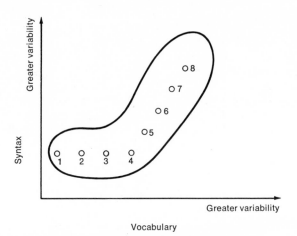

Figure 12. Useful range of languages: (1) hierarchical classification, (2) subject headings, (3) fixed key words, (4) free key words, (5) tagged descriptors, (6) faceted terms, (7) phrases, (8) natural language.

We shall now consider each of the major languages previously described as measured on each of the four performance scales. Clearly, "measure" must be interpreted broadly. Our approach is to present a rating, showing only the rank ordering of languages on a measurement scale of each attribute.

2.5.1 Expressiveness

Although not strictly a logical requirement, hierarchical languages generally purport to cover all of subject space, even if only by use of the descriptor *other*. Subject heading and fixed key word languages do not try for full coverage. They concentrate only on those regions in which documents are expected to fall, their designers knowing that omissions can easily be rectified. Free key word languages make no attempt to anticipate subject coverage but can accommodate any subject coverage requirement as it arises. None of these languages, however, can necessarily provide the degree of precision or generality desired at any given time. The syntactic languages have whatever subject coverage is defined for their vocabularies and then provide both for increasing the extent of coverage and for discriminating ability through combinations of descriptors. There is no predefinition of the set of all possible terms, those syntactic units assembled by the indexer from descriptors. This omission permits errors or poor expressions to be caused by improper association of otherwise proper descriptors; the problem of poor usage of language. We see, then, that the syntactic languages, although offering more expressiveness, are also more prone to creating ambiguous terms. Figure 13 illustrates the ordering of languages on the scale of expressiveness.

The Analysis of Information Systems   227

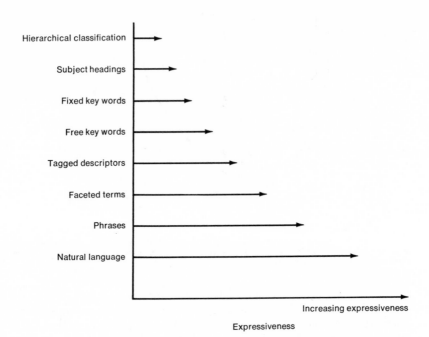

Figure 13. Relative language expressiveness

2.5.2 Ambiguity

By definition synonyms do not exist in a hierarchical language, and by convention they do not exist in subject heading or fixed key word languages. In any of these languages near-synonyms are possible, since it is always a highly subjective matter whether or not two descriptors are synonyms. Synonyms are controlled in these languages by use of dictionaries, with careful definition of terms in use. A free key word language makes control of synonyms very difficult. In syntactic languages there are more ways in which the same concept can be expressed by different symbols. This is certainly true in natural language, but it is less of a problem in languages with a more rigid syntax.

There are some similarities in the conditions underlying the occurrence of homographs and synonyms. The restricted vocabulary languages generally make the control of homographs easy, whereas a free vocabulary makes control almost impossible. Use of syntax eases the problem sometimes, for the syntax enables the specification of context needed to resolve the homographs. There can be full phrase or sentence homographs (see Section 2.2.4), but this is quite rare.

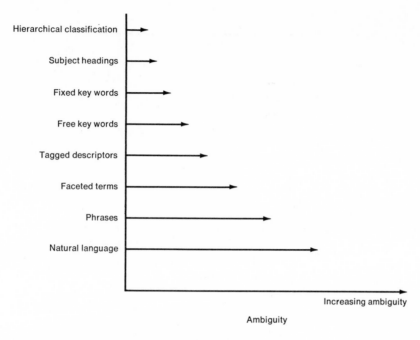

Figure 14. Relative potential ambiguity of languages

These forms of ambiguity are independent of each other. One does not cause the other and one does not alleviate the other. Their control is through the establishment and maintenance of authority, represented, in our usage, as a dictionary. Hence the actual degree of ambiguity is as much a function of the dictionary as it is of the basic structure of the language. Figure 14, then, shows an ordering of languages on this criterion, based not only on structure but on actual manner of use as well.

2.5.3 Compactness

There is successively less information per term in each language from hierarchical to free key words, because of the amount of information contained in the language structure from which the term was selected. In the syntactic languages, as syntax approaches the complexity and variability of natural language, the amount of information per term begins to increase. A term in these cases may be a natural language phrase or sentence, but the amount of space required to store an index term begins to increase in the syntactic languages, making them less compact. *The number of index terms* used in a record shows an exactly opposite behavior

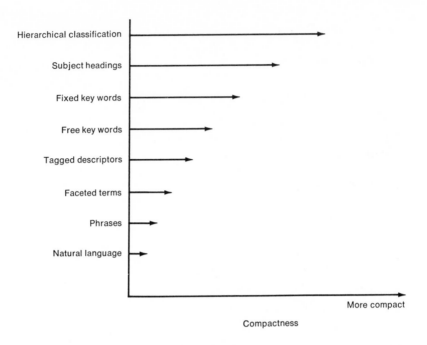

Figure 15. Relative language compactness

to that of information content. For example, whereas hierarchical languages usually use only one term, subject headings may use one to three or four terms; fixed key word languages, such as ASTIA's,[22] may use 5 to 10 descriptors, and free key word languages such as that devised by B. K. Dennis[1] of the General Electric Company may use as many as 10 to 20. Use of rigid syntax will reduce the number of terms selected, but, as syntax becomes more flexible, the length of terms will increase. This relationship suggests that *good indexing* calls for about the same amount of information (net length of index record), regardless of the language used to express it. The emphasis on good indexing arises because poor quality indexing shows wide fluctuation in number of terms used,[9] tending either toward a "shotgun" approach or one of oversimplifying the index. Relative measurements of compactness are illustrated in Figure 15.

2.5.4 Cost of Term Selection

This very crucial factor is among the most difficult to measure. Entering into a cost estimate are time required to index, training required for the indexers (which might be regarded as time expended before

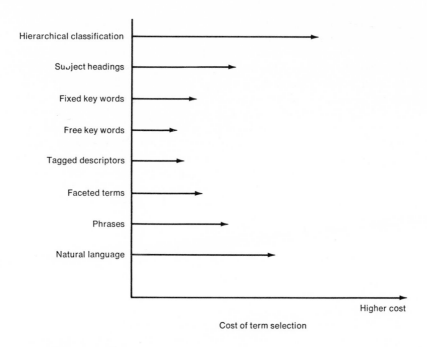

Hierarchical classification	
Suʊject headings	
Fixed key words	
Free key words	
Tagged descriptors	
Faceted terms	
Phrases	
Natural language	

Higher cost

Cost of term selection

Figure 16. Relative cost per term of term selection

indexing), and risk (the cost or effect of indexing error). Based on these criteria, we feel that hierarchical classification is the most costly per term selected and that cost per term decreases as we move through the progression of nonsyntactic languages, rising again in the syntactic languages, as shown in Figure 16. Our reasoning is as follows. In hierarchical classification the indexer must not only find the appropriate branch of the classification structure, but must determine the appropriate level at which to stop. This requires a good understanding of both the document and the code structure. The problem is slightly simpler with subject headings because there are fewer levels to choose from, and, as we get to key words, the problem becomes closer to one of selecting important words on the basis of their grammatical roles or frequency of repetition rather than comprehension of the text. Also, nonhierarchical languages use more terms, with the very important result that the indexer can worry less about mistakes and about resolving uncertainties. With a key word language, he can select all terms which appear appropriate rather than try to pick the single best one. This not only speeds selection of individual terms but reduces risk or cost of error. Syntactic languages are not necessarily easier to use than hierarchical, but they often offer alternative ways to express essentially the same concept, again reducing the amount of time that must be spent to select a single, "right" approach.

Using these assumptions, we find that cost per term follows the same pattern as term length. This leads to the not-unexpected conclusion that more information requires more cost to provide it, and, because a fairly constant amount of information seems to be desired in an index, the further conclusion may be drawn that the total cost of producing an index record will hold roughly constant over the various languages if all are employed with equal skill. This conclusion is to some extent supported by a study performed by Cleverdon[13] utilizing four different languages to index a set of documents. The costs in his experiment were controlled by limiting indexing time. Retrieval capabilities were found to be rather close, key words being rated somewhat higher than the hierarchical, subject heading, or faceted languages.

2.6 Dictionaries

When a language is complex enough to permit synonyms and homographs, the need for a dictionary, or language authority, to resolve these ambiguities is apparent. Even without these problems, a simple list of the "legal" descriptors in a language can be of help to the indexer or searcher in composing an index record or query. Such a list can also serve as a quality control device since it will contain the approved spelling of terms. We assign the name *dictionary* to all authority lists that specify the membership, spelling, usage, or meaning of the elements of a vocabulary. Included in our concept of dictionary are the usual meanings of *thesaurus, classification schedule, synonymy, glossary,* etc. Each of these can be considered a language authority and gives word meanings, in one form or another, and word relationships. Our reason for departing from standard terminology, as it has been previously, is to unify the meanings for the designers of a data processing system who will find relatively little difference of form or logic in the design and use of such files.

2.6.1 The Need for a Dictionary

Before examining dictionary functions in detail, let us define the context of this discussion. We are not discussing the science of lexicography in general. The compilers and publishers of a dictionary of natural language for wide general use face problems and count on solutions not met in an information retrieval system. For example, a conventional lexicographer considers himself a historian or reporter, and must expend considerable cost and energy to survey actual language usages. He cannot, or will not, establish usage by decree, which would take much less effort.

In his role as a reporter he need not try to "clean up" the language, to guard against dissimilar words merging their meanings, new words being created which mean the same as existing words, or the same word acquiring more than one meaning, but these are problems for the index language lexicographer, whose job it is to help his readers discriminate between terms and to reduce ambiguity in the languages. The index language lexicographer, then, cannot simply report on usage. He must guide or dictate usage. We are concerned with the role of a dictionary in an information retrieval system, assisting both indexers and library searchers in using and manipulating the library's index language. In particular, information retrieval systems have the following problems which require a dictionary-like tool, one which explains or defines word usage.

1. *Synonyms and homographs.* One of the principal problems of language usage is that of discriminating between similar words or similar ideas. Confusion over word meanings can be resolved by appeal to an authority if all language users agree on the same authority.

2. *Search for appropriate words.* Regardless of whether synonyms and homographs exist in a language, a language user will often find himself in the situation in which he is unsure of the words to use to describe some concept. In this case he needs the same tool required to resolve synonym-homograph problems—a list of the vocabulary of the language and some definition of the meaning of each word. In other words, even if two words do not have exactly the same definition, as long as there is any possible commonality of meaning, there needs to be an explanation of the difference.

3. *Record authoritative decisions on usage.* This differs only slightly from the first two problems. It refers to the need for, or utility of, a single, final authority, accessible to all system users, for all vocabulary usage rules and decisions. Since the index language is not normally the same as the natural language spoken by the system users there may be some difficulty when first learning the language until they fully understand that the retrieval system has its own language whose designers have the right to make their own rulings on word usage. Such problems can arise where inexperienced users insist on employing words in the sense normally used by them, perhaps the jargon of their profession, without recognizing that the library, as a different culture, may have a different jargon. A user, either indexer or searcher, can request that a dictionary change be made but, before a change is made, he must and can recognize the rulings currently in force. The dictionary, in perhaps its most important role, is a vehicle for communication among all language users.

4. *Error control*. Among the most maddening problems of any data processing system is that of violation of input specifications, minor errors in the data to be processed. To a computer *McNamara* and *MacNamara, New York* and *NewYork, mathematics* and *mathmatics* are six *different* symbols. Unless great pains are taken, a computer program does not attempt to tell how alike the pairs are; it merely notes that they are not equal. A human reader can easily make these spelling errors, but he can immediately and easily notice the similarity in the word pairs and equate them. He may be a trifle irritated if a request for information on *NewYork* fails to recover anything because the library's *official* spelling is *New York*. Yet *NewYork* could as easily be a misspelling of *Newark* or *Newport* as *New York*. Even more likely to occur are confusions such as that between *Silver Spring*, Maryland, and *Silver Springs*, Florida, or *radium* and *radian*. The expense of a computer search of an index file makes it highly desirable to detect such errors as early in the program as possible, and to reject questions containing illegal words, words that definitely could not be found even if the search were to continue. The detection and rejection of words not in the approved vocabulary is another reason for needing a dictionary of the index language. We must be careful not to misconstrue a need for rigid control over input as implying that the dictionary is so rigid it cannot be changed. A word may be absent from the dictionary (hence rejected as an input term) either because it is a misspelling or because it is a genuinely new word in the language. In either case it should be brought to the attention of someone who is capable enough, and authorized, to decide which condition holds and who will either correct the spelling or take action to have the new word admitted to the approved vocabulary list.

2.6.2 The Role of a Dictionary

In listing the requirements of a dictionary, we have come close to specifying what it must look like or do. Yet, largely because of the semantic confusion about what a dictionary is (or what a thesaurus, etc., is), it is well to develop a formal definition, insofar as this is possible. The difficulty we shall experience in trying to define the word *dictionary* is akin to that a dictionary editor will have in defining *any* word.

The most critical point to consider is whether a dictionary can "define" words at all or the extent to which "meaning" can be conveyed from one person to another through written or spoken language rather than through perception of the thing denoted by the word. To begin this discussion, let us look at the problems of compiling a dictionary of a natural language. The following quotations are from S. I. Hayakawa; all italics are his.

It is an almost universal belief that every word has a correct meaning, that we learn these meanings principally from teachers and grammarians (except that most of the time we don't bother to, so that we ordinarily speak 'sloppy English'), and that dictionaries and grammars are the supreme authority in matters of meaning and usage. Few people ask by what authority the writers of dictionaries and grammars say what they say.[5]

The writer of a dictionary is a historian, not a lawgiver.[6]

. . . one of the premises upon which modern linguistic thought is based: namely, that *no word ever has exactly the same meaning twice.*[7]

To say dogmatically that we know what a word means *in advance of its utterance* is nonsense. All we can know in advance is *approximately* what it will mean.[8]

If we accept Hayakawa's arguments, as we do, then we must accept that a dictionary cannot be entirely self-contained, cannot define each word of an entire vocabulary solely in terms of that vocabulary. This would appear to be completely at variance with our stated requirements for a dictionary except for the word *approximately* in the last sentence quoted from Hayakawa. Unfortunately, although index languages and their dictionaries have the appearance of great precision of definition, mainly because of the imperious manner with which word meanings are handed down, the expressiveness of such languages can suffer accordingly. In return for rigid dictionary definitions which a computer can use with a not too difficult interpretive program, we give up much expressiveness, and our precisely written definitions are only approximately representative of the ideas they are supposed to convey. We must accept, then, that we will accomplish no miracles in compiling a dictionary to meet our previously stated requirements, especially that of serving as an absolute authority. The dictionary will unhesitatingly and with great authority hand down decisions which are necessarily imprecise. We are not going to get something for nothing.

Now we can go on to show some ways of constructing dictionaries that meet our requirements, but which are all subject to the qualifying remarks just concluded.

A dictionary that will prevent misuse of words is a virtual impossibility but, as we described under the heading of *Error Control,* a dictionary can be used to catch all attempts at using new words, and these words can be referred to the lexical authority for his decision as to whether they should be allowed to become vocabulary descriptors or be kept out of the language. He can "define" the new word his own way and, by the two acts of ruling on admissibility and making a formal definition, he can exercise a degree of control over an index language that is impossible in the case of general use of natural language. The dictionary authority cannot prevent gross usage errors. If a searcher writes an erroneous descriptor which happens to be part of the language, it is enormously difficult to detect the error in most cases, dependent as it is on interpretation of context and recognition that some usages are prohibited in some contexts. For example, the word *London* is a reasonable descriptor in many index languages but, if used in the context of *U.S. Presidential Elections* in the 1930's, it could be an erroneous spelling of *Landon,* the Republican candidate in 1936. While a dictionary may not be able to change *London* to *Landon,* a more probable descriptor in this context, it may be able to reject *London* as being unrelated to the subject matter, and could easily suggest that an error has occurred by the simple device of not showing any connection between the word *London* and the subject of *U.S. Elections.*

However tight the control of the lexical authority over the dictionary, he must recognize that languages change, and he must, like the lexicographer of natural language, yield to consistent pressure from language users for change in word meanings. A distinct advantage of index language lexicographers over their conventional brethren is the ready capability of an information retrieval system to keep records of itself, one such being the record of word use rates. Changes in these rates are indicative of language areas needing change. Perhaps words are falling into disuse and might be proscribed from the dictionary, or some words may be getting such heavy use that their definition should be narrowed by creating new words to describe portions of the subject originally described by the single term. Compare this latter situation with the discussion in Section 2.3.1 of expanding a hierarchic code.

Let us now review the kinds of definition that might be used. The word *definition* needs definition first. In our usage, *a definition simply gives the relationship between the word defined and another word or set of words, which need not be in the same language.* We may say that

> *red* is the quality in common among an American
> Beauty rose, a strawberry, the setting sun, and human blood.
> *ran* is the past tense of *run.*
> *plume* is the French term for the English word, *pen.*

Occasionally another relationship is stated in a dictionary and that is the location of some information pertaining to the word being defined, such as

> *New York:* see page 16 (or disk 3, track 12)

The kinds of relationships usually expressed in a dictionary are

| equality | *plume* (in French) $=$ *pen* (in English) |
| | *ran* $=$ the past tense of *run* |

class inclusion:	*aeronautics* is a subdivision or subclass of *engineering*
class membership:	*New York* is an individual representative of the class, *city*
attribute:	*red* is an attribute of a *strawberry*
location:	*New York* (information about it) is on page 6 *Calculator*: see (the place where) *computer* (is defined)
conditional relationship, e.g., conditional equality:	*Lead:* 1. physics, a metal, atomic number 82. 2. nautical, a device used for measuring depth of water. 3. printing, a device for making space between lines of type.

A form of conditional relationship is a statistical relationship where no more tie between words is indicated than that they often occur together in the same document or sentence.

A tool which performs one or more of these definition services becomes an integral part of the language.

2.6.3 Types of Dictionary

The most commonly met dictionary in conventional usage is, of course, one which provides a natural language definition for each entry. Such a dictionary is very convenient to use because it gives ample opportunity for explanation of context, for examples of usage, and even for pictures of an object being defined. Thus, the lexicographer has a reasonable degree of latitude in drawing distinctions between words and contexts. This is not a particularly useful dictionary for a computer because of the difficulty of programmed interpretation of the text of the definition. It lacks one of the desirable attributes of an index language, stated in Section 2.2, that the language be comprehensible to a processor. The following list describes varieties of dictionaries that are in actual use, either in an information retrieval system or for general language use. We have included the latter both for the sake of completeness and because, even in a restricted vocabulary system, users will probably make use of dictionaries of the general language, by habit, to help resolve index language problems. We adopt the convention that the entry is the word being defined and the definition, regardless of whether or not the dictionary provides a "definition" in the usual sense, is whatever the dictionary tells about the entry. An argument, in our terminology, differs from an entry in that an argument is the word used for searching, and possibly will not be found in the dictionary.

1. *The one-for-one synonym dictionary.* Although not very common, this form of dictionary has the great advantage of simplicity and clearcut, unambiguous definitions. For each entry there is a one-term definition whose meaning is construed to be identical to that of the entry. More than one entry can have the same definition, permitting the accommodation of alternate spellings as well as different word forms. In a language that permits synonyms it is necessary to make some provision for relating a word to its synonyms. This may be done when the word has been used in an index record and is being entered into an index file, or when it is going to be used in a query. At one or both of these times each word must be converted into a form representative of all its synonyms to permit matching. The definition in this case can as well be a number as a natural language word. A number is more compact, hence more conservative of computer memory. A dictionary such as that described here was used by the U.S. Air Force.[21] A somewhat simplified form is illustrated in Figure 17.

Entry	Numeric Code	
Book	1*	
Calculator	2‡	* These pairings follow the usage of this book, that is, *book-document*, but the words paired are not generally used as exact synonyms.
Catalogue	3*	
Cataloguer	4	
Computer	2‡	
Descriptor	5*	
Document	1*	
Index	3*	† All vocabulary words must be in this list, whether or not there are synonyms.
Indexer	4	
Processor	2‡	
Query	6*	‡ Any number of entries can be equated to the same value.
Search	6*	
Term	7†	
Word	5*	

Figure 17. One-for-one synonym dictionary

2. *The multiple-relation dictionary.* This name we give to a variety of dictionaries which, like the one-for-one synonym dictionary, have definitions composed of descriptors or terms, but may have more than one term in the definition; the definition terms may bear any of several relationships to the entry. The most common relationships are: synonymity, inclusion, subordination, and the conditional forms of these. A relationship of near equality is often used, more frequently expressed as "See also," instructing the reader to try all terms in the definition under this heading with the assumption that at least one of them is approximately equal to the entry in the context under consideration. Such a dictionary

is the ASTIA Thesaurus illustrated in Figure 5. This dictionary form provides a human reader with the best features of both hierarchical classification and fixed key words. The language has structure, concepts can be expressed at various levels of generality, fine distinctions between subjects can be made; yet the language can easily be changed. It is most interesting to note that the flexibility derives almost entirely from one fact—that no code number is assigned to a "node" point of the hierarchy. Hence a change in the hierarchic structure does not produce a change in a string of related codes as is the case in a true hierarchical language. This is shown in Figure 18 where the code first used for analog computers (code 123.1) acquires a new, incompatible meaning as the dictionary is reorganized. This causes difficulties in searching previously indexed material.

Computers	123
Generic to	
Analog computers	123.1
Digital computers	123.2
Electrical accounting machines	123.3
Electrical calculators	123.4

    a. Portion of a possible entry and definition in a multiple-relation dictionary. In the column at right possible hierarchical codes are shown.

Computers	123
Generic to	
Electrical and electromechanical calculators	123.1
Electronic computers	123.2
Electronic computers	123.2
Generic to	
Analog computers	123.21
Digital computers	123.22
Electrical and electromechanical calculators	123.1
Generic to	
Electrical accounting machines	123.11
Electrical calculators	123.12

    b. Example of how the definition in the first example might be revised to show an additional level of generality.

Figure 18. Changing an index language structure

3. *The language-to-language dictionary.* Common in general language use, and becoming common in data processing, is a dictionary that provides a definition whose vocabulary is drawn from a different natural language than that of the entry. In form such dictionaries range from one-for-one synonymies to those having full text definitions, permitting phrases as well as words as entries. An interesting example is the diction-

ary developed by IBM for its Automatic Language Processor.[12] This machine has the feature that it will find the longest dictionary entry that will match a string of input words, thereby providing for idiomatic translation. For example, an input expression such as *il y a* ("There is," in French) would be translated, *as an expression,* into *there is* in English, and not word-by-word into *it* (or *he) there has.* Naturally, the machine is built on the assumption that idioms will be entered into the dictionary in the first place. If the full expression cannot be matched with an existing entry, then small portions will be tried until the string is reduced to *il,* a common word almost certain to be an entry in any French dictionary. If an input word is found which has no match (e.g., a proper name) the machine will break it down letter by letter and either reproduce the original form of the word or transliterate, if appropriate.

4. *Natural language definition.* We have already described this dictionary, at the beginning of this section, and have given the reasons against its use in a data processing system.

5. *Thesaurus.* The thesaurus, invented by Peter Mark Roget,[14] groups words together according to the subject concept to which they are related. It has two kinds of entries, the term of descriptor word, for which a location is given where the word appears again in context, and the concept word, the definition of which provides a contextual frame of reference in which the relationships of terms to the concept are explained. Concepts are organized on a hierarchic basis. The term *thesaurus* is sometimes used to describe what we have called a multiple-relation dictionary. We have no quarrel with this usage for it corresponds to our definition of thesaurus if we recognize Roget's concepts as descriptors at a high generic level.

6. *Classification schedule.* A dictionary that gives natural language definitions for hierarchical classification codes is often called a classification schedule. It differs in only one respect from a natural language dictionary. The entries are numbers or subject titles, and, being members of the vocabulary of an index language, are in a different language than the definitions, which are natural language expressions. There may be cross references in the definition, but rarely will a word or term used to define an entry be, in turn, an entry itself. Thus, if a reader has difficulty understanding a definition, he will get little help from the schedule. The first volume of the Dewey Decimal Classification is such a schedule, some sample entries from which appear in Section 2.3.1.

7. *Location tables.* To round out the review of dictionary types we include this one which provides no semantic information about an entry but in all other respects resembles a dictionary. The "definition" here is a

symbol giving the location of information about the entry. An index to a book is an example.

2.6.4 A Dictionary Example

The Dewey Decimal Classification[2] (DDC) is one of the best known and, with the Library of Congress classification system, one of the most frequently used classifications in the United States. A variant of it, the Universal Decimal Classification, is in common use in Europe. We shall describe a *classification schedule* which, recall, is subsumed under our definition of *dictionary*.

Volume I of the DDC, subtitled "Tables," lists the vocabulary in numeric order. It includes a language translation of each descriptor into an English phrase or title. In a different typography from that of the titles are *scope notes*, natural language comments, not part of the translation of the meaning of the numeric descriptor, which assist the reader in selecting the most appropriate term. For example, descriptor code number 551.594 means *weather belts*, and has subordinated to it *Tropical, Subtropical, Temperate, Cold,* and *Polar* belts, codes 551.594 2–6. Each of these terms has an explanatory, or scope, note, such as

> *Tropical Belts*
> No cool season; mean temperature of coldest month above 64.4° F
> *Subtropical Belts*
> Arid or semiarid climate; mean temperature above 68° F for 4–11 months, 50°–68° F for 1–8 months

In yet another typography are the "see" references which direct the reader to other descriptors with similar or related meanings. We stress the typography because we have, in effect, three lists, or files, in one, each identified by the use of different type faces. . . .

Volume II of the DDC is called the "Index." It contains an alphabetic listing of English language terms and gives the classification code or codes pertinent to that term. This permits a reader to locate the general subject area in which may be found some detailed subject, such as *epiglottis.* The code 611.22 is defined in a scope note in Volume I under the general heading, *Larynx,* as consisting of "laryngal cartilages, glottis, muscles of larynx." Starting with *epiglottis,* and being unfamiliar with anatomy, would leave the indexer or searcher with a formidable problem of locating the correct subject heading in the volume alone. Reference to the index, however, gives the following:

> *Epiglottis*
> diseases medicine   611.22
> human anatomy   616.22
> human physiology   612.78
> surgical treatment   617.533

Thus, although *epiglottis* is not a descriptor in the language, the translated title of a descriptor, nor even a word appearing in the title of a descriptor, its proper position in the hierarchy can still be determined. Returning to the ACM classification, we can see that the older form used the alphabetic index approach—the listing of terms in an order that makes it relatively easy to find a subject heading—and the new form uses the hierarchy approach—presenting headings in hierarchical order, but with order among highest level terms being completely arbitrary. There is nothing "natural" about either of these orders. Subjects could as well be ordered by frequency of use or by order of their occurrence in some special field (e.g., data on commodities could be indexed according to role in the basic industry-to-consumer chain of events, such as mining, raw-materials processing, manufacturing, distribution, retailing, consumer utilization of a product).

References

1. Dennis, B. K., *High Speed Literature Searching on an IBM 704*, General Electric Co., Evendale, Ohio.
2. Dewey, Melvil, *Dewey Decimal Classification and Relative Index*, Forest Press, Lake Placid Club, Essex County, New York, 1959.
3. Finerman, Aron, and Lee Revens, "Revision of the Classification System," *Computing Reviews*, Association for Computing Machinery, 4, 6 (1963), 309–311.
4. Hayakawa, S. I., *Language in Thought and Action*, Harcourt, Brace & World, New York, 1949, p. 61.
5. *Ibid.*, p. 54.
6. *Ibid.*, p. 55.
7. *Ibid.*, p. 60.
8. *Ibid.*, p. 61.
9. Jacoby, J., and V. Slamecka, *Indexer Consistency under Minimal Conditions*, Documentation, Inc., Bethesda, Maryland, November 1962, p. 19.
10. Jonker, Frederick, *The Descriptive Continuum, A "Generalized" Theory of Indexing*, Documentation, Inc., Washington, D.C., 1957.
11. Kehl, William B., John F. Horty, Charles R. T. Bacon, and Davis S. Mitchell, "An Information Retrieval Language for Legal Studies," *Communications of the Association for Computing Machinery*, 4, 9 (1961), 380–389.
12. King, Gilbert W., "Table Look-up Procedures in Languages Processing, Part 1 The Raw Text," *IBM Journal of Research and Development*, 5, 2 (1961), 86–92.
13. Lancaster, F. W., and J. Mills, "Testing Indexes and Index Language Devices: The ASLIB Cranfield Project," *American Documentation*, 15, 1 (1964), 4–13.

14. Roget, P. M., *Thesaurus of Words and Phrases,* Grosset & Dunlap, New York, 1947, Preface to First Edition.
15. Savage, T. R., H. C. Fallon, and M. E. Saxon, *ACSI-Matic Auto-Abstracting Project,* Interim Report, International Business Machines Corp., Yorktown Heights, New York, 1959.
16. Taube, Mortimer, C. D. Gull, and Irma S. Wachtel, "Unit Terms in Coordinate Indexing," *American Documentation,* III, 4 (1952), 213–218.
17. Thompson, Elizabeth H., Ed., *A.L.A. Glossary of Library Terms,* American Library Association, Chicago, 1943.
18. Vickery, B. C., *On Retrieval Systems Theory,* Butterworth & Co., London, 1961, p. 33.
19. ————, *General Information Manual, Keyword in Context (KWIC) Indexing,* International Business Machines Corp., White Plains, New York, 1962.
20. ————, *Medical Subject Headings,* Third Edition, National Library of Medicine, Washington, D.C., 1963.
21. ————, *Programming Manual, Volume III, Unformatted File System,* International Business Machines Corp., Rockville, Maryland, 1961.
22. ————, *Thesaurus of ASTIA Descriptors,* Second Edition, Armed Forces Technical Information Agency, Arlington, Virginia, December 1962.

Exercises

1. Meadow's discussion of Shannon's model and the communication process omits consideration of "noise." First write a definition of "noise." Then modify Meadow's discussion to take noise into account. What modifications did you make in your definition?

2. Compare Meadow's fifth point of difference between libraries and post offices with March and Simon's conception of reification in organizations.

3. What are the differences and similarities between a grocery list and a catalog, using Meadow's definition of a catalog? Is a catalog an inventory? Do inventory control procedures apply to some information retrieval situations? Which situations? How?

4. Why are libraries changing from the Dewey Decimal Classification System to the Library of Congress System? What difference does this shift make to your local druggist, shoe-store man, or filling-station attendant? What difference does it make to you?

5. Is it possible to describe uniquely a unique document in "natural" language? Why or why not? Is this capacity or incapacity changed by shifting to some "artificial" language? Why or why not?

6. Does your library have a copy of *Indexes and Indexing* by Robert L. Collison? Who published it? When was it published? Write a description of the process by which you retrieved the information or failed to retrieve it.

7. Consider the statement: All learning is the acquisition of classificatory systems. Do you agree? Why or why not?

8. Make a tabular array of the various index language families and their characteristics. Which family seems to possess the greatest number of characteristics listed? Is this a reasonable way to decide which is the superior language? Why or why not? How does your tabular array compare with Figures 12 through 16?

9. Consider the statement: Error is only variability of which we do not approve. Would Meadow agree, do you think? If not, would it be possible to define error in terms of variability in a way you think he might approve?

What Is Language?

Archibald A. Hill

The more you know about the various codes used in communicating, the more effective you will be as a communicator. The most commonly used code is language, and this essay is a sensible and straightforward attempt to define language and to provide a rationale for studying it. The areas covered in this essay may be profitably contrasted with those covered by Lloyd and Warfel.

Some Basic Assumptions

The subject of linguistics presents an initial difficulty because the word which designates it is unfamiliar. The word can easily be defined as the scientific analysis of language, but it is doubtful if such a definition is meaningful to anyone who lacks familiarity with this kind of analytic activity. It is far better to begin by defining language, since language is

From *Introduction to Linguistic Structures*, pp. 1–12, by Archibald A. Hill. © 1958 by Harcourt, Brace & World, Inc. and reprinted with their permission.

closer to the reader's experience. Yet even the definition of language presents unsuspected difficulties and needs preliminary discussion before it is attempted directly.

If a group of educated speakers are asked to define the language they are using, the reply will probably be "All the words and sentences used to express our thoughts." The definition is satisfactory in everyday situations, since long practice has made plain what is meant, and consequently most hearers know how to respond accurately. But for all that, the definition is not sufficiently accurate to be the basis for analysis. Terms like "words and sentences," which seem transparent to a speaker of a Western language, would be more misleading than enlightening if applied to some languages. Moreover, there are phenomena similar to language which this definition does not identify. Most important, the definition identifies language activity by thought. Language activity can be observed, and is therefore subject to verification. Thought can be observed only by subjective introspection, and so is not subject to verification. Language activity is therefore more knowable, thought less knowable. Obviously a definition must define the less knowable by the more knowable if it is to cast light. In what follows, such a definition will be attempted. There must first be a warning, the need for which will be clearer as we advance. A definition is not a description. A definition gives only those characteristics which have diagnostic value for recognition. A description attempts to give all characteristics, preferably in the order of their importance. A definition necessarily leaves out much and may make use of relatively trivial characteristics, but it is not to be condemned for that reason.

Most professional students of language proceed from a few assumptions, one of which is that the fundamental forms of language activity are the sequences of sounds made by human lips, tongues, and vocal cords—the phenomena usually distinguished by the narrower name of "speech." Though this first assumption may seem like a truism, it is important, since many who accept it verbally still act as if they did not believe it. Some few even deny it. There are only two reasons for questioning the assumption. Writing has great permanence and great prestige. Further, the basis of our education is training in the manipulation of written symbols of ever-increasing complexity. Highly literate people, and those who would like to be literate, are therefore apt to think of writing as the real center of language and of speech as peripheral and derived—often badly—from the written forms.

There are a number of facts which should settle this question of priority. First, speech reaches back to the origins of human society; writing has a history of only about seven thousand years.[1] Also, no contemporary

---

[1] The great antiquity of language, as compared with writing, is a reasonable assumption, but it is often presented without evidence. To arrive at the conclusion that language is older than writing, linguists and anthropologists start from the

community of men is without language, even though it is probably still true that most of the world's several thousand language communities remain in the preliterate stage, without benefit of alphabet or even picture symbol. Individual members of literate communities, furthermore, learn their language some years before they learn to read or write it; and adults, even adults who are professional writers, carry on a good deal more speech activity in daily living than activity involving writing. The final fact is that all writing systems are essentially representations of the forms of speech, rather than representations of ideas or objects in the nonlinguistic world. There are exceptions to this statement, like the Arabic numbers which work independently of the words for numbers in the Western languages. The exceptions, however, are in a minority disproportionate to the majority of symbols which always indicate the forms of language. The point can be driven home by a pair of simple examples. The symbol for *one* in Japanese writing is a single stroke, that for *two* two strokes, and so on. It might be thought that such a symbol has no relation to the Japanese word for *one* (*ichi*) but represents instead the nonlinguistic idea of "oneness." Actually the occurrence of the single stroke is correlated with the occurrence of the word. It occurs not only in the number but also in such forms as *ichiji, primary*. The Japanese symbol, therefore, has a quite different range from the letter sequence *one* of English, which is not used in the dissimilar word *primary*. The one-stroke symbol corresponds with the occurrence of the Japanese word *ichi,* proving that the one-stroke symbol is a representation of the word (though an understandably pictorial one), and not a direct representation of the idea of oneness.

Written symbols can be understood, furthermore, insofar as they fit into a linguistic structure, even when they refer to nothing in the nonlinguistic world. Thus, if an English text should have the sentence "He *sprashes* it," the second word could immediately be recognized as a verb in the third person singular and as a sequence of sounds quite in accord with English structural habits, though it represents nothing in the outside world at all. For the purposes of this book, therefore, the linguist's assump-

---

observed fact that in modern communities, all organized cooperative activity rests firmly and necessarily on language as the means of controlling and directing interaction. This being so in all observed communities, it is assumed by archaeological anthropologists that when remains of past communities show material evidence of social organization, these remains are those of communities which possessed language. Communities which show such evidences of social organization also show artifacts or other evidences which are much older than the remains of any communities which show evidences of even primitive systems of writing. It is possible that early human communities possessed some other form of highly organized communication, such as the gesture language which has been occasionally proposed since the days of Locke—cf. Max Müller, *Lectures on the Science of Language* (London, 1862), p. 31. But though possible, such a nonvocal symbol system is unlikely. Language is now a universal activity; it is an extra and unnecessary hypothesis to suppose something else.

Message Systems and Subsystems

tion that language is a set of sounds will be adopted. It is no contradiction of this assumption that the sounds can be secondarily translated into visual marks, grooves on a wax disk, electrical impulses, or finger movements.

Linguists assume that the description and analysis of language must begin with description of the sounds and their patterning and that description of meaning must be put off until the first task is done. Such an attitude is often misunderstood to be a denial of meaning, but this is not true. The linguist's desire to put off analysis of meaning is no more than an application of the principle of working from the more knowable to the less knowable, and though linguistics has not as yet had very striking results in semantic analysis, it can be hoped that the next few decades will see results of real value in semantics.

The Defining Characteristics of Language

Working with the assumptions given above, linguists can offer a set of five defining characteristics which serve to set off language from other forms of symbolic behavior and to establish language as a purely human activity. Often animal communication will have one or more of these five characteristics, but never all of them.

First, language, as has been said, is a set of sounds. This is perhaps the least important characteristic, since the communication of mammals and birds is also a set of sounds. On the other hand, the system of communication which is in some ways most strikingly like language, that of bees, is a set of body movements, not sounds. It would be easy, further, to imagine a language based on something else than sound, but no human language is so constructed. Even the manual language of the deaf is derived from the pre-existent spoken language of the community.

Second, the connection between the sounds, or sequences of sounds, and objects of the outside world is arbitrary and unpredictable. That is to say, a visitor from Mars would be unable to predict that in London a given animal is connected with the sound sequence written *dog*, in Paris with the sequence *chien*, in Madrid with *perro*. The arbitrary quality of language symbols is not infrequently denied, for a number of reasons. Sometimes the denial is based on nothing more than the notion that the forms of one's native language are so inevitably right that they must be instinctive for all proper men. Sometimes the denial is more subtle. It is often maintained that all language, even though now largely arbitrary, must once have been a systematic imitation of objects by means of sound. It is true that there are some imitative words in all languages, but they are at best a limited part of the vocabulary. It is easy to imitate the noise of a barking dog, for instance, but difficult if not impossible to imitate a noiseless object, such as a rainbow. Though imitative words show similarity in many languages, absolute identity is rare. A dog goes "bow-wow" in English, but in related languages he often goes "wow-wow" or "bow-bow." The imitative words do not, after all, entirely escape from the general arbitrariness of language. The imitative origin of language appears, therefore, at worst unlikely and at best unprovable. The same injunction holds for theories of language origin which speculate that it is an imitation of facial or other gestures.

If it is assumed that language is arbitrary, what is meant by the statement? Just that the sounds of speech and their connection with entities of experience are passed on to all members of any community by older members of that community. Therefore, a human being cut off from contact with a speech community can never learn to talk as that community does, and cut off from all speech communities never learns to talk at all. In essence, to say that language is arbitrary is merely to say that it is social. This is perhaps the most important statement that can be made about language.

In contrast, much of animal communication is instinctive rather than social. That is to say, all cats mew and purr, and would do so even if they were cut off from all communication with other cats. On the other hand, some animal communication seems to share the social nature of human speech and is therefore learned activity. A striking example is the barking of dogs, which is characteristic only of the domesticated animal, not of dogs in the wild state. Similarly, the honey dances of bees may not be altogether without an arbitrary element. It is also likely that when more is known of the cries and chatterings of the great apes in the wild state, a considerable social element in their communication may be found. Nor should it be thought that all human communication is social. A part of our communication consists of instinctive reactions which accompany language, like the trembling of fear or the suffusion of blood which accompanies anger. Yet even in the nonlinguistic accompaniments of speech, the tones of voice and the gestures, it is now clear that there is more of arbitrary and socially learned behavior than had at one time been supposed.

Third, language is systematic. I cannot hope to make this statement completely clear at this point, since the whole of this book is devoted to an exposition of the system of language. However, some observations may now be made about the system of language. As in any system, language entities are arranged in recurrent designs, so that if a part of the design is seen, predictions can be made about the whole of it, as a triangle can be drawn if one side and two angles are given. Suppose there is an incomplete sentence like "John —s Mary an —." A good deal about what must fill the two blanks is obvious. The first must be a verb, the second a noun. Furthermore, not all verbs will go in the first blank, since it requires a verb whose third person singular is spelled with —*s* and which can take two objects (that is, not such a verb as *look* or *see*). Nor will all nouns fit in the second place, since an initial vowel is required, and the noun must be one which takes an article. There is no difficulty in deciding that the sentence could be either "John gives Mary an apple" or "John hands Mary an aspirin," but not "John **gaves* Mary an **book*."[2]

Another observation that can be made about language systems is that every occurrence of language is a substitution frame. Any sentence is a series of entities, for each of which a whole group of other entities can be substituted without changing the frame. Thus the sentence "John gives Mary an apple" is such a substitution frame. For *John* there can be replacements like *he, Jack, William, the man, her husband,* or many others. For the verb, entities like *buys, takes, offers,* as well as the alternatives *hands* or *gives,* may be used. This characteristic of extensive substitutability for all parts of any language utterance is of some importance in that it enables us to say that parrots, no matter how startlingly human their utterances may be, are not carrying on language activity. A parakeet may produce the sentence "Birds can't talk!" with human pitch, voice tones, and nearly perfect sounds. But the bird never says "Dogs can't talk!" or "Birds can't write!" His utterance is a unit, not a multiple substitution frame.

Still another characteristic of language systems is that the entities of language are grouped into classes, always simpler, more predictable, and more sharply separated than the infinite variety of objects in the world. For instance, a whole series of objects is grouped under the single word *chair,* and *chair* is put into the large class of nouns. In dealing with objects in the outside world it may be difficult to decide whether something is a chair, a stool, or merely a rock. In language, we think of nouns and verbs as quite separate and are apt to say that the one class represents things, the other events. But in the outside world, as the physicists tell us, it is often hard to decide whether an object is best described as thing or as event.

To return once more to the defining characteristics of language, the fourth characteristic is that it is a set of symbols. That is to say, language has meaning. In this form the statement is a platitude and does not distinguish language from other activities which are also symbolic. The nature of language symbols turns out to be rather different from the symbols of other types of communication. The simplest nonlinguistic symbol can be defined as a substitute stimulus. Pavlov's famous dogs, fed at the sound of a bell, eventually began to drool at the sound of the bell even when no food was present. The dogs were responding to a substitute stimulus. Nonlinguistic symbols can also be substitute responses, and these can also be

[2] An asterisk placed before a form means that it is believed to be impossible.

taught to animals. A dog who learns to "speak" at the sight of food has learned such a substitute response. In human speech, however, one of the most striking facts is that we can talk about things which are not present, and we can talk about things which ordinarily produce a strong physical reaction without experiencing that reaction. For instance, I can talk about apples even though there are none in the room, and I can talk about them without always making my mouth water, even when I am hungry. This type of language, which occurs without an immediately present stimulus or response, is called "displaced speech," and it is obviously of great importance. It is what enables man to know something of the past and of the world beyond the limited range of his vision and hearing at a given moment.

The crucial fact in producing this almost miraculous and purely human effect seems to be that a given language entity can be both substitute stimulus and substitute response, and can also be a stimulus for further language responses or a response to other language stimuli. I can talk about apples when they are absent because "something reminds me of them." That is, I can make language responses to what is before me, and these language responses can stimulate the further response *apple* without any direct physical stimulus to my vision, touch, or smell. *Apple* can call forth still further language entities, like *pear* or *banana,* in an endless chain; these entities are also both stimuli and responses. When human speakers do this, they are setting up what philosophers call a "universe of discourse." The ability to make connected discourse within the symbol system is what enables men to talk at length, and profitably, about things they have never seen. By means of language men make elaborate models of distant experience and eventually test their accuracy by acting upon them. All that is known of animal communication leads to the supposition that precisely what is absent from it is the kind of symbolic activity here described, symbolic activity connected not merely with experience but with all parts of the symbol system itself. We believe, in short, that animals are incapable of displaced speech.

The paragraphs above are rather general, so that a concrete example may be helpful. Let us suppose that two speakers of English are together in a room. One of them is cold. A direct response for him would be to close the window.

Instead of this he can use the substitute response, which is also substitute stimulus: "John, please close the window for me." John can either close the window or reply with a further substitute: "Just a minute. Wait until I finish this page." Such a reply may produce acceptance or may lead to a discussion of John's procrastinating character, of the fact that his parents did not discipline him properly in youth and that modern young people are generally rebellious and unmannerly. To all of this John may reply that modern times are marked by progress and the disappearance of old taboos. In the meantime the window may have been quietly closed, or completely forgotten in the warmth of discussion. What is important is that each speaker has begun reacting, not to the immediate situation, but to the other speaker's language and to his own. And in so doing, each has been building a model of general social conditions, of wide scope and ultimately of some value, even in a random and unchecked conversation of the sort described.

We are now ready to turn to the last defining characteristic of language, the fact that it is complete. By this is meant that whenever a human language has been accurately observed, it has been found to be so elaborated that its speakers can make a linguistic response to any experience they may undergo. This complex elaboration is such a regular characteristic of all languages, even those of the simplest societies, that linguists have long ago accepted it as a universal characteristic. Nevertheless, in early books about language, and in the descriptions by linguistically untrained travelers today, there are statements that tribe X has a language with only two or three hundred words in it, forcing the tribe to eke out its vocabulary by gesture.[3] Linguists maintain that all such statements are the product of lack of knowledge, and are false. Skepticism about such statements is borne out by the fact that in all instances where it was possible to check on tribe X, its language proved to be complete as usual, whereupon the statement was transferred to tribe Y, whose language was as yet unknown. The statement that human language is complete once again serves to distinguish it from animal activity. In the communication of bees, for instance, the subjects of systematic discourse are severely limited. Bees cannot, apparently, make an utterance equivalent to "The beekeeper is coming."

The statement that human language is always complete should not be interpreted to mean that every language has a word for everything. Obviously the ancient Greeks had no words for automobiles or atom

[3] A typical recent statement of this sort was reported by Leonard Bloomfield in "Secondary and Tertiary Responses to Language," *Language*, Vol. 20 (1944), p. 49 n.

"A physician, of good general background and education, who had been hunting in the north woods, told me that the Chippewa language contains only a few hundred words. Upon question, he said that he got this information from his guide, a Chippewa Indian. When I tried to state the diagnostic setting, the physician, our host, briefly and with signs of displeasure repeated his statement and then turned his back to me. A third person, observing this discourtesy, explained that I had some experience of the language in question. This information had no effect."

For a good general account of the completeness of primitive languages and the use of gesture as a substitute among mutually unintelligible language groups, consult Ralph L. Beals and Harry Hoijer, *An Introduction to Anthropology* (New York: The Macmillan Co., 1956), pp. 508–511.

bombs, and probably the modern Yahgan of Tierra del Fuego lack them as well. The completeness of language lies rather in the fact that a speaker of ancient Greek would have been perfectly capable of describing an automobile had he seen one, and further that had automobiles become important in ancient Greece, the speakers of Greek would have been perfectly capable of coining a word for them. It is a characteristic of vocabulary that, except in languages which have gone out of use, it is always expansible, in spite of the fact that resistance to new forms may frequently appear. Since language enables the user to make appropriate responses to all things and since vocabulary is thus characteristically "open," differences in vocabulary between two languages are not an accurate measure of the difference in efficiency or excellence of the two tongues. The fact that Eskimo does not have as highly developed a vocabulary of philosophy as does German merely indicates that the Eskimos are less interested in philosophy; on the other hand, Eskimo has a highly developed vocabulary for various kinds of snow, indicating that snow is important in Eskimo society. The completeness of human language and the openness of vocabulary make a groundless chimera of the occasionally expressed fear that a language might so degenerate as to become useless.

We can now attempt a definition of language, though the definition will be cumbersome. Language is the primary and most highly elaborated form of human symbolic activity. Its symbols are made up of sounds produced by the vocal apparatus, and they are arranged in classes and patterns which make up a complex and symmetrical structure. The entities of language are symbols, that is, they have meaning, but the connection between symbol and thing is arbitrary and socially controlled. The symbols of language are simultaneously substitute stimuli and substitute responses and can call forth further stimuli and responses, so that discourse becomes independent of an immediate physical stimulus. The entities and structure of language are always so elaborated as to give the speaker the possibility of making a linguistic response to any experience. Most of the above can be paraphrased by saying that every language is a model of a culture and its adjustment to the world.

Language and the Study of Its Nature

Since language is something that we habitually take for granted, it may not be clear, even after this discussion, why language and, even more, the study of language are important. Primarily they are important because language is a solely human activity, which separates man from other living beings. But though this may be readily granted, it is not always realized how fundamentally language is a defining characteristic of man. Even among students of man it is probably more common to define him as "the tool-making animal" than as "the talking animal." But it is quite possible that tool making is less crucially human than talking is. For one thing, it is natural that an archaeologist's attention should turn toward tools, which can be dug up, rather than toward language, which cannot. For another, it is not always easy to recognize how fundamental language is, even in our own society. There are individuals who lead nearly normal lives in spite of being deprived of speech, so that it may be argued that speech —admittedly the fundamental form of language—is a dispensable form of activity. Yet such speechless individuals always develop some form of substitute language, and all such substitutes presuppose the individual's membership in a society fully provided with speech. There are many things, such as wearing neckties, making movies, or cooking, which only human beings do. But many of these are not universal among men, and all of them are secondary. As for tool making, this activity is universally human, but it is in some sense shared with the higher primates. When, however, it is argued that tool making involves more than the use of a convenient stick or stone and is the purposeful molding of an object for future use, it would seem that the tool maker is an individual capable of displaced speech and of shaping his activity in accord with a symbolic model. In other words, as soon as man is defined as a maker of tools whose use lies in the future, we presuppose the existence of language. Therefore linguists, and many anthropologists, believe that language is the phenomenon most basic in human society. Historical anthropologists assume that when humanoid remains are found in a situation indicating an organized community, they are necessarily remains of a group possessed of language. If, then, it is language more than anything else we can observe which makes us men, it is ultimately the study of language which is most likely to throw light on the essential humanness of human beings. I wish at this point, however, to make a specific disclaimer. There are characteristics inaccessible to science which also distinguish man; the science of language is not concerned with these and should under no circumstances be understood as denying them. On the other hand, the existence of spiritual qualities ought equally to be understood as not being a bar to the study of those things which can be investigated by science.

If scientific study of language can throw light on human qualities and activities, there is no direction in which there is greater likelihood of illumination than in the investigation of thought, whether that investigation be understood as a part of psychology or a part of logic. It was said earlier that linguists do not deny the existence or importance of mind. The American linguist insists that language entities cannot be profitably investigated in terms of the mental concepts or thoughts back of them, but this insistence ought always to be understood as carrying with it the corollary that mental concepts can be profitably investigated in terms of the language entities which are so largely instrumental in their formation. It has also been said that language is basic to society. It is therefore probable that increased knowledge of language will mean increased knowledge of society. The promise is already recognized and has already borne fruit, since anthropologists have made brilliant use of linguistic insights. Less broad than thought and society, another area in which linguistic knowledge is beginning to prove useful is in the study of literature, if for no other reason than that literature is an art constructed in language. Similarly, the practical activity of language instruction, whether that of a foreign or the native tongue, can profit by knowledge of the nature of the material which is to be imparted.

I have up to now spoken of the importance of language study from the broad aspect of human knowledge; for the individual student the impact of language study is different. The native language provides its speakers an ever-present and deeply habituated instrument by which they measure and control experience. All adults have had a long indoctrination in the attitude that language is both a transparent glass through which we see the world and a tool by which we mold it. Therefore the first stages of study of language for the sake of knowledge rather than with a practical aim are apt to be disquieting, or even to seem useless. A somewhat parallel case can be drawn from optics. We think of our eyes as instruments which transmit the "real" appearance of objects directly to our minds. It is often disturbing to realize that our eyes necessarily influence the appearance of objects and that a surface which appears flat to us can scarcely appear so to the nearly spherical eye of a fly. Yet to say that language study is apt to be difficult or disquieting is not the same thing as to say that it is of no value to the individual. An important aim of education is the adjustment of the individual to the world in which he has to live, and linguistic knowledge is a help toward that end. The individual's understanding of reality is increased if he can learn to distinguish the ways in which the structure of his language may influence his perception of reality. Study of language is one of the best ways in which a narrow belief in the rightness of one's own ways of doing things, and the wrongness of every other way, can be broken down. It is instructive to find that some languages, even among the European group, are not felt to be inadequate because they do not distinguish between fingers and toes by separate vocabulary items. The knowledge that there are languages which have no tenses at all and others which attach tenses to their nouns is a good introduction to the myriad ways in which men channel the basic human needs, experiences, and activities which indeed remain much the same throughout the world. A student trained in language is aware, on the practical level, of language pitfalls. A very little training may prepare him for failure of communication when an Englishman and an American talk about *corn*. More sophistication is needed for dealing with the situation reported by Bloomfield in which an Englishman misunderstood his American pronunciation of

Comedy Theatre as a request for a nonexistent *Carmody Theatre*.[4] In all such instances, the student trained in language will deal with the inevitable failure of understanding in realistic terms, without wasting time in denouncing one group or the other for not knowing its own language. And similarly, he is prepared to deal with the difficulties of a foreign language on a more realistic level than by supposing that there is a one-to-one correspondence between its forms and those of English.

By now, I hope that some meaning has been given to the definition of linguistics as the scientific study of language. Linguistics has for its goal the understanding of language, and it is secure in the belief that such understanding will increase human knowledge. It strives to present a picture of language as complete as possible, as consistent as possible, and as simple as possible, again secure in the belief that if these conditions are fulfilled it will be as truly and revealingly a science as is chemistry or astronomy. This . . . is an attempt to take the reader through some of the first steps in this young science. It is hoped that he may gradually come to accept a scientific attitude in a kind of activity where most people, even those thoroughly educated, have not tried to be scientific, and where some, indeed, have resisted the suggestion that they should be. The first stages of investigation and statement may seem to be disturbing and even to introduce confusion where none existed before, but as the design of language and its analysis unfold, clarity emerges, and with it the security of understanding.

Exercises

1. Compare Hill's list of the defining characteristics of language with Meadow's. Discuss.

2. "Language is observable and measurable thought." Would Hill agree with this statement? Why or why not? Do you? Why or why not?

[4] *Language* (New York: Holt, 1933), p. 81.

Nonverbal Communication: Explorations into Time, Space, Action, and Object

Randall Harrison

Every message must have an originator or source. Every message must also be received by someone or some group, have some sort of content, and be put into code. The code to which we direct most of our attention is language—both spoken and written. However, another code does exist. This other code, the nonverbal, has been studied relatively little, and many of us use it almost unconsciously. The nonverbal code consists of such things as gestures, facial expressions, and our use of time and space. The Harrison essay provides a conceptual framework and a set of terms helpful when working with nonverbal communication; this essay is included in the belief that we need to concern ourselves with every aspect of communication if we want to persuade people to respond in the way we desire. Also, the essay expands on and supplements what is said in other selections in the book. For example, much of our image of the world (discussed by Boulding) is formed by nonverbal means, and the way that we present ourselves to others (described by Goffman) is often nonverbal.

Many verbal expressions point to the importance of nonverbal communication. We say, for instance, "actions speak louder than words," or "one picture is worth a thousand words."

In spite of these familiar clichés, nonverbal communication remains an underdeveloped area of study. It sprawls like a huge, mysterious continent, intriguing but impenetrable. The photographer, the artist, the motion picture and TV man, all draw on its riches. Yet these practitioners frequently fear to explore too far, lest they destroy its magic spell.

The behavioral scientist, fearless in the face of magic, now forages into the nonverbal more and more. But often the game he pursues is of only incidental interest to the communicator. He does return, however,

This is an original essay prepared for the first edition of this book. All rights reserved. Permission to reprint must be obtained from the author and the publisher. Dr. Harrison is an Associate Professor in the Department of Communication at Michigan State University.

Message Systems and Subsystems

spinning fascinating tales about the tangled jungles of meaning, the submerged swamps of unconscious symbolism, and the rich but unmarked wilderness of communication potential.

Is it possible to bring order to this mysterious region? Is it possible to point out some trails to the communicator who wishes to find a short-cut to his goal and to share in the riches this area promises?

Let us try. The maps are still crude, not unlike those used by Magellan when he set out to explore the world. But some work has been done; previous adventurers have given us some guidance.

Even before we unfurl the maps of the early explorers, however, let us try a small excursion into the nonverbal, a test-run to see how well equipped you are for the journey ahead. Look at Figure 1. What is going on here?

Look first at the verbal level. Both men are saying the word "right." Are they both saying it in the same way? No? In how many ways do their "rights" differ?

Most people will note that the man on the left, Mr. *A,* is asking a question; his voice will rise while Mr. *B*'s will not. Which "right" is louder? Most people would say Mr. *B*'s. Why? Because it's bigger? Why should bigness be equated with loudness?

Look next at the nonverbal level. Various people project different stories into this simple scene. The differences will tell quite a bit about your personality. But equally important, most people from your culture will come to certain common conclusions. Do you, for instance, have a meaning for a hand-shake? Not all cultures do.

Now let's look at some of the subtler visual cues in Figure 1. Who is more powerful? More aggressive? How do you know that? Who is more trustworthy? More honest? What makes you think so? Who is more competent? More intelligent? Who is more friendly? If this is a business transaction, who is going to come out ahead?

With your hand or a sheet of paper, cover the lower left corner of the picture until you cannot see Mr. *A*'s left hand. Does the picture without that corner have the same meaning as with it? Why?

What has been going on here? What have you learned from this simple experiment?

At least three lessons might be drawn:

1. A good deal of nonverbal communication goes on around us.
2. This nonverbal communication is important; we make decisions based on it.
3. Frequently, nonverbal communication is at a low awareness level; we may not realize that we are sending or receiving.

Do you agree with these points? Let's re-check the evidence.

Figure 1

In this particular picture, relatively little information is transmitted in the verbal band; a great deal is transmitted in the nonverbal band. The proportion of information in each band varies, of course, with the communication situation. A textbook may include little nonverbal communication, while a sports event, a ballet, or a silent motion picture may be highly nonverbal. Interestingly enough, it has been estimated that in face-to-face communication no more than 35 percent of the social meaning is carried in the verbal messages.

What kinds of decisions have you made based on nonverbal cues? If you found differences in power, trustworthiness, and competence, you made some quite important decisions. Research indicates that these may be some of the key dimensions of source credibility, which in turn is believed to be a vital element of persuasiveness. In short, whether you are persuaded or not may rest on nonverbal cues.

Equally important, you may have a hard time putting your finger on what these cues are. What, for instance, communicates "power"? A jutting jaw? A straight-shouldered posture? Down-turned eyebrows? A straight arm instead of a curved arm in a hand-shake? What communicates low intelligence? A large nose and close-set eyes? A small forehead? An upper lip that protrudes beyond the lower lip?

If this were a real-life situation, Mr. *A* and Mr. *B* would probably be quite unaware of the nonverbal messages they are sending. If you were a receiver of those messages, you probably would be unaware that you were receiving and using them. Unless we stop the action and force ourselves to think about it, we are not likely to attend to many of the specific cues that lead to our feelings or hunches about a person or a situation.

With the lessons from this trial-run in mind, let us now unroll the mappings of the nonverbal made by previous explorers.

Previous Mappings of the Nonverbal

Any area of potential knowledge can be mapped in several ways, just as we can draw a variety of maps of the United States. We could have a political map that showed only state boundaries and major cities. We could have a highway map, a weather map, a map showing altitude above sea level, and so on.

Maps of intellectual areas are useful in much the way maps of physical regions are useful. They help the intellectual traveler identify major divisions and points of key interest. They help him see differences and similarities between various regions. They keep him from getting lost; from thinking he's in one area when he's actually in another. Finally, and especially important for progress, they allow other investigators to follow the path of the original mapper, expanding and improving his work.

The intellectual explorer makes a map that is useful to him. In charting the nonverbal, different boundaries have seemed useful to different investigators. Some of those who use the term "nonverbal" are likely to include everything except the spoken and written word. The meaning of the term would then encompass, for these users of it, messages obtained by touch and smell. Thus, the use of perfume might be considered nonverbal communication.

Even this distinction is not as clear-cut as it might seem, however. Some writers observe that the written and spoken word are not completely exempted from the nonverbal world. When we choose large type instead of small type, italics instead of regular, Old English type instead of modern, we are making communication decisions that might be considered nonverbal. The size of the words in Figure 1 might be considered nonverbal. Similarly, there are certain aspects of speech such as intonation, rhythm, and speed which seem to lie on the fringes of traditional linguistic mappings.

Some explorers prefer to draw the boundary around visual communication instead of nonverbal communication. This would cut off perfumery at one end and clearly include the selection and layout of type in printing at the other end. Perhaps one of the oldest ways to cut up this area is to speak of audio-visual communication. This includes the spoken word but tends to exclude the printed word.

Two of the most active explorers within the nonverbal boundaries have been Jurgen Ruesch and Weldon Kees. Ruesch is a professor of psychiatry at the University of California School of Medicine while Kees is a poet, critic, and film producer.

In their book, *Nonverbal Communication,* they divide the world of nonverbal into three parts: sign language, action language, and object language.

Sign language is in use when a gesture, such as the hitchhiker's thumbing, replaces words, numbers, or punctuation. The individual makes the gesture for the purpose of communicating.

Action language includes all bodily movements that communicate, but are not primarily meant to communicate. For instance, a young man wolfing down his food communicates something about his hunger, and perhaps about his upbringing. He does not eat that way primarily to communicate, however; he eats that way to satisfy his hunger quickly. Nevertheless, his actions are messages available for decoding by any observer.

Object language includes the display of material things, including the human body and its clothing. For Ruesch and Kees, object language includes both the intentional and the unintentional. Some objects, for instance an engagement ring or a display model, are meant to communicate. Other objects, such as the furniture in a room, may be made and arranged for some utilitarian purpose, but may also communicate much about the person who lives there.

Ruesch and Kees suggest that one way to draw the boundary between verbal and nonverbal is to apply the concepts of analogic and digital codification. Recent work with computers has stimulated thinking about the coding, transmission, storage, and manipulation of information. Essentially, there are two types of computers, the digital and the analogic. In the analogic code, some similarity exists between the code element and the aspect of the world being represented. Examples would be pictures, maps, and model trains. Digital codes, such as numbers and letters, tend on the other hand to be sharply different from the things represented. For the practicing communicator, each of these codes has certain advantages in transmitting information. Ruesch and Kees point particularly to the way the two codes complement each other in spatial and temporal characteristics.

Edward Hall, in his book *The Silent Language,* marks space and time as two special areas of nonverbal communication worth studying in their own right. As Hall puts it, "time talks" and "space speaks." In the American culture, for instance, punctuality communicates respect while tardiness is an insult. (It says, "I don't think you're important; your time's not worth much.") In some other cultures, however, to arrive exactly on time is an insult. (It says, "You are such an unimportant fellow that you can arrange your affairs very easily; you really have nothing else to do.") Rather, an appropriate amount of tardiness is expected.

Similarly, the use of space can communicate. In our culture, when we talk to another person we stand about an arm's length apart. If you see two individuals standing closer, you are likely to conclude they are lovers or that they are plotting a conspiracy. You can demonstrate this to yourself quite easily. The next time you are chatting with someone, slowly move in. You'll find they will quite unconsciously withdraw to maintain the right distance. In some cultures, the accepted interpersonal distance is smaller. When people from different countries interact, you may find misunderstandings arise because they cannot find a distance that is mutually comfortable. As someone advances on you, you may feel, "He's pushy and overbearing," or "He's falling all over me." On the other hand, if someone withdraws, you may feel, "He's avoiding me; he's trying to hide something," or, "He doesn't like me."

While time and space are two important areas of communication for Hall, he would go on to codify all of what he calls the "primary message systems." Hall, an anthropologist, sees culture as communication, and he would apply to culture the approaches that have been so successful in descriptive linguistics. Spoken language is analyzed in terms of phonemes, morphemes, and syntax. Hall suggests that culture might be examined in somewhat comparable categories that he calls isolates, sets, and patterns.

Perhaps the most ambitious attempt at mapping part of the non-verbal area can be found in "kinesics," the study of communication through bodily movements. Ray L. Birdwhistell is the founder of this research.[1] Drawing on the mapping methods of linguistics, Birdwhistell developed a notational system that enabled him to make very precise, second-by-second recordings of bodily movements. In analyzing his data, he speaks of the kine and the kinemorph, concepts similar to the phone and the morpheme in linguistics.

Birdwhistell finds that, in the gestural language, very small shifts may make a big difference. He discovered, for instance, that in raising the eyebrows perhaps 23 different positions are seen as having separate meaning. Interestingly enough, from his early studies, it appears that men can produce these different positions at will more easily than women can.

Birdwhistell also finds that the eye-area and the hand are particularly important for communication in our culture. Among the Japanese, the German, and the Bombay Indians, these areas seem less important.

Kinesics has opened the possibility of examining the relationship between communication bands. Birdwhistell notes that television an-

[1] Ray L. Birdwhistell, "Background to Kinesics," *ETC.: A Review of General Semantics,* Vol. 13 (1955), pp. 10–18.

nouncers can sometimes be seen contradicting in gesture what they are saying in words. When this happens to an announcer, or an actor, it is frequently amusing, but this type of interband conflict in other communication situations can lead to tragedy.

Recently Birdwhistell has been working with psychiatrists exploring the origins of mental disturbances such as schizophrenia. One hypothesis is that schizophrenia arises when an individual has been placed constantly in what Gregory Bateson calls "the double bind." This means the person gets two conflicting orders at the same time; he cannot obey one without disobeying the other. Birdwhistell's work indicates that one or both of these conflicting orders may flow in through the nonverbal band.

While kinesics is perhaps the best mapped area of nonverbal communication so far, other areas are getting increasing attention. At Michigan State University, we have recently focused on the pictorial code. Much, of course, has been written in this area by artists, designers, and experts in aesthetics, but so far the maps do not agree very well. Different people going into this area see different things as being important.

We have begun by breaking down the code, using such categories as the pict, the pictoform, the pictomorph, the pictophrase, and so on. In Figure 2 are six simple face pictomorphs.

Do you have a meaning for each expression? What are your meanings? What cues are you using to arrive at these meanings?

These simple figures give us a chance to demonstrate one more aspect of nonverbal communication. Let's imagine that each of these little fellows is saying, "That's great!" Is there any difference when *A* says it and when *D* says it?

| A | B | C | D | E | F |

Figure 2

Any message can be broken down into two parts: the content and the instructions on how to interpret that content. The source is likely to communicate his own evaluation of the content, his interest, his excitement, his intentions. Implicitly or explicitly, he tells the receiver how to react to the content. This part has been called meta-communication. The nonverbal band can carry content or instructions, but it seems to have a particularly important role in meta-communication. It allows the instructions to arrive at the same time as the content and, as in the above case, it tells us whether the message is sincere or sarcastic.

Looking to the future, we can expect more and better mappings of nonverbal areas. We can already see, however, that at least four major areas are important; time, space, action, and object. These are related to each other as shown in Figure 3.

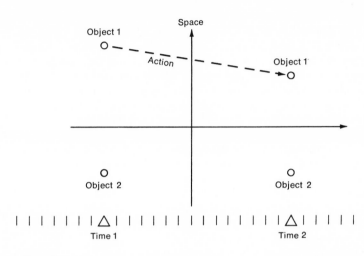

Figure 3

Time and space provide the major dimensions. Actions occur in time and objects occur in space. Actions and objects are related since actions occur through the movements of objects. In Figure 3, object 1 moves closer to object 2, from time 1 to time 2. The dotted line represents action.

Finally, we need to note that we can represent time, space, action, and object at various levels of abstraction. If you are object 1 and a friend is object 2, we have an event in real life. If you and your friend wish to tell me about this event and perform it again, we have a re-enactment. This might be live, or we might do it in a motion picture. If you wish to show me what happened in a photograph or a drawing we have a portrayal. (Figure 3 is a diagrammatic sketch, or one kind of a portrayal.) Finally, you may wish to tell me about the event only in words, or even in numbers. Here we have a description.

You will note that as we moved from event to re-enactment portrayal to description, we moved from analogic to digital coding. As we move each step, we lose some aspects of the original event, but we also gain some communication advantages. I cannot put you and your friend in this book; I *can* put Figure 3 in.

Now then! Studying a map is all well and good, but that alone does not get a traveler to his destination. The practical communicator has a right to ask: How does this help me get where I want to be? First, we need to make sure he knows where he wants to be.

Communicator Goals

The competent communicator usually wants certain things to happen to the information he sends out. He may want selection, comprehension, acceptance, recall, and use. These are his communication goals. Often he wants all these goals. Sometimes, he places more emphasis on one than on the others. If he is in entertainment, he may stress selection. If he is in education, he may point toward comprehension and recall. If he is interested in persuasion, he may concentrate on acceptance.

Each of these goals has subgoals. Selection, for instance, may involve attention and interest. The communicator wants his message selected over competing messages, and within the message he wants certain information attended to more than other information. He wants continued selection, or attention.

Comprehension includes meaning and understanding. The communicator wants some meaning response elicited, and he hopes it is a shared meaning, i.e., that there is understanding.

Acceptance includes belief and attitude. In other words, is the information true, and is it good for me? Finally, most communicators hope that the information they send out will be recalled and used at the appropriate time.

Given this array of goals, what routes are most likely to lead there? How can nonverbal communication help or hinder?

Selection

Selection is likely to increase as the perceived rewards of a message increase and the perceived costs go down. Nonverbal techniques are frequently used to boost rewards and slice costs. Time, space, object, and action all play a part in determining what will be selected. Similarly, the abstracting process that goes on in analogical codification can play a role. Let's see how this works.

The communicator can frequently control the timing of his message. Where he can, he will try to have the message land on target when the audience is most likely to select it, when the rewards are highest and the costs lowest. To help this process along, he may provide lead time; he may give his audience advance warning that a message is coming. If an audience is expecting a message at a given time, punctuality becomes an issue. A late message—whether a term paper, a business report, or a press release

—is likely to have undesirable consequences for the communicator. Tardiness is likely to communicate, in our culture, low regard for the audience and for the message. Selection can sometimes be increased, of course, by communications off schedule. Delay may build anticipation and suspense. A call at "odd hours," late at night or early in the morning, may suggest urgency and importance. If the message is not worth the anticipation and urgency, however, the communicator may get initial selection but cut his chances of being accepted, or ever selected again.

Within a message, the communicator also makes decisions about timing. Pacing of information and message elements may make the difference between an exciting and a boring communiqué, between interest and disinterest. Similarly, duration of a message may influence selection. As the length increases, cost goes up and selection may drop.

Here the communicator may have to choose between selection and some other goal such as comprehension. Fortunately, using the nonverbal band can sometimes increase both selection and comprehension. A multi-band presentation may provide redundancy that will bring the audience to the desired comprehension level faster. In other words, a ten-minute motion picture might do the job of a twenty-minute speech.

The multi-band presentation may eliminate competing messages even where it does not introduce redundancy. The man listening to an after-dinner speech may be watching the pretty waitresses; the man watching a film has this opportunity removed. (He may, of course, find other pursuits, such as dozing.)

The communicator seeks monochronism, which is a fancy way of saying "one thing at a time." He wants his audience's full attention, and in interpersonal communication, he usually feels complimented when he gets it. He's likely to feel that his message is going to get the attention it deserves when the man behind the desk calls his secretary on the intercom and says, "I'll accept no calls, Miss Smith, we don't want to be disturbed."

Finally, multi-band presentations provide a channel for meta-communication. As one band provides information, another band provides instructions for interpretation: "This is important, this is rewarding, this is for you." The simultaneous transmission of information and instructions seems more likely to hold attention than a message that alternates content and comment.

Within the visual band, space and object play a vital role in selection. One frequent way to boost selection is to increase size. As size increases, the object, whether headline type or motion picture image, becomes more easy to see; effort drops and selection should increase.

But beyond a certain point, an increase in size can no longer reduce effort, although it may increase rewards. The oversized object has a novelty value that may be rewarding in itself. Similarly, the oversmall object may be selected for its novelty.

Just as the communicator wants monochronism, or isolation in time, he may want isolation in space. The liberal use of white space may make a printed message stand out, while a spacious office may be the fitting setting for an important man.

Considering people as objects that may be arranged in space, the communicator may wish to give attention to the placement of his audience. A conference where everyone faces the speaker's platform suggests one kind of information flow, while a circular seating arrangement around a conference table suggests another. The effective communicator may also pre-arrange his own selection of messages. He may place overcommunicators in the silent corners up front in a classroom, or at his elbows at a conference table, where they can be overlooked. He may place some more reticent communicator in a hot spot where he will be encouraged to speak.

Similarly, many men give attention to the seating arrangement in their offices. At one time, the executive communicated to the visitor only from behind his mammoth desk. Today, coffee tables and easy chairs are becoming an increasingly common feature of executive decor.

Finally, selection may be influenced by the type of codification used. Traditionally, cartoons and photographs are more popular in readership studies than printed material. This may be because of their novelty. It may be because they promise more reward for less effort.

For example, the use of pictures is believed to increase the popularity of the total publication. There are many examples, however, of a cartoon or photo being so popular that it reduced the attention given to surrounding printed material.

In general, it might seem that people like to be eye-witnesses at real events. As we move from re-enactment, to portrayal, and thence to description, selection should drop off. Frequently, however, as the communicator re-codes an event he condenses and sharpens it, so that unimportant elements are dropped and pertinent elements are pointed up. The skillful communicator is ever seeking the proper level of code, one that gives him all he needs and yet eliminates the extraneous.

Comprehension

Selection is the first step in comprehension; the message that is not attended to cannot be understood. Comprehension may, however, also influence selection. Both that which is completely understood and that which cannot be understood are likely to be bypassed.

Timing is important in comprehension since a pace that is either too fast or too slow will lose the audience. Modern teaching programs offer an excellent example of a way of placing the control of pacing in the hands of the audience; the students progress only when they have comprehended.

In other communication situations, the communicator will have to devise other ways of checking his audience's comprehension. In speaking to an individual or a group, the communicator may increase his effectiveness by being a good receiver of nonverbal messages. While one man is speaking, it is impolite for another to interrupt verbally, but the receiver is very likely to be sending nonverbal messages in the form of perplexed frowns, nods of agreement, smiles of understanding, and so on.

It is frequently assumed that comprehension can be increased by moving from a digital to an analogic code. If we wish someone to understand an event, a re-enactment may provide more complete information than a three-dimensional model. The model, in turn, may allow certain kinds of comparisons that could not be gleaned from a photograph. And the photograph or drawing may offer information not easily available in a written description.

This assumes that we want the receiver to understand the complete event. Frequently, however, the communicator wishes to point up some principle within the event, or some relationship among a number of events. Here, it is again important to move to the best level of codification for the abstraction desired. "Best" is defined, of course, in terms of the receiver.

Analogic codes tend to be more expensive to prepare and use. Thus, the communicator may need to balance the level of comprehension he'll settle for against the cost of reaching this level.

Acceptance

In courtrooms, we rule out hearsay evidence; we want only eye-witnesses. We also say, "Seeing is believing." If the communicator is concerned about being believed, he may try moving his receiver closer to the event by live demonstration, by newsreel, or by photograph. He may also invoke expert testimony from unimpeachable sources.

The receiver can evaluate any piece of information in terms of its fidelity and its authenticity. Fidelity is based on completeness; how much of the original event do I have here to look at? Authenticity relates to validity, and takes into account the amount of tampering or restructuring that may have taken place.

In general, films and photographs appear to have more fidelity and authenticity than verbal messages. We know, however, that films and photographs can deceive in many ways. First of all, the scene can be staged; it may not be a real event. Here the receiver may use nonverbal cues to decide on authenticity. The sharp, slick photograph, while having high fidelity, may be rejected as unauthentic. Meanwhile, the blurred, low fidelity picture may have the candid or newsreel quality that stamps it with authenticity.

Even when the event has not been staged, distortions can creep into a picture. The public has become aware in recent years of the composite photograph in which pictures of two individuals, taken separately, are re-photographed into one print so it appears that the two are friendly. Through re-touching and a variety of photographic techniques, authenticity may be reduced.

Still photographs, even when they have not been tampered with, may lead to false impressions. For example, a rare event recorded in a photograph may be taken as the typical. Thus, anti-American propaganda may use actual photographs of violence and crime with the implication that this is the everyday norm. Similarly, a picture taken many years ago may be mistakenly assumed to represent conditions today.

With motion pictures, of course, editing can re-arrange events so that totally different impressions are left with the viewer. By manipulating time, causal relationships can be made to emerge. Most commercial films are not shot in sequence. Rather, similar scenes are shot at the same time and then re-arranged into the desired order in editing.

In interpersonal communication, nonverbal cues are frequently monitored to determine the authenticity of verbal statements. Partly this is because the sender may not realize he is sending nonverbal messages, and he might not be able to stop even if he knew. Thus, the blush or the frown is likely to be taken as more reliable than accompanying verbal reassurances.

Belief, as we have used the term, is only one step in acceptance. The communicator may want his audience not only to say, "That's true," but in addition, "I like it that way," or "I agree with you."

Much has been written about belief and attitude change, but let us take just two simple notions about attitude change and see how nonverbal communication fits in. One method we might call "sugar-coating." The other we can call, "I'm-your-buddy." Both are based on the theory that the attitude toward the information in a message may improve if the receiver, in the first case, likes the message treatment and, in the second case, likes the guy who sent it.

"Sugar-coating" can be done in purely verbal messages, but frequently the nonverbal band is brought into play. Color, pictures, cartoons, three dimensions, even music can be used. While these treatment devices can make a message more appetizing, they are not without danger. Sometimes the content gets lost in the sugar and the audience eats the coating but not the pill.

In the "I'm-your-buddy" approach, steps are taken to build up the source, his friendliness, his expertise, his power—all the qualities that make him a person you'd want to agree with. Many nonverbal cues contribute to these impressions, such as a man's dress, his letterhead, his office, his facial expressions, and so on. In less personal communication situations, inferences may be made about the source on the basis of the quality of his message treatment, whether, for instance, he uses high-grade or low-grade paper, multi-color or single color, pictures or type only, motion pictures or film strips.

Here again the more expensive is not necessarily the best. The natty congressman who drives around Washington in a limousine may switch to folksy clothes and an old jalopy when he tours his district talking to voters. Similarly, a lavish promotional piece put out by a government agency or a charitable organization can backfire. The receivers may resent the group's spending money on the publication instead of on its task; funds may be cut instead of increased.

Recall

Once you've gotten information into your receiver's head, how do you get it out again? How do you increase the chances that he will recall pertinent information at the appropriate time? Information is likely to be recalled if it is distinctive and if it is organized in such a way that it is available. For distinctiveness, we emphasize cue clarity. For organization, we look at cue association.

The verbal cue "d-o-g" is distinctively different from the cue "c-o-w." The two words both have three letters and a common middle letter. But the differences in the first and last letters make it easy for us to discriminate between them.

If we move to a more analogic codification of the same two objects, whether in picture, model, or actual animal, we will find a great many more differences. The size, shape, and such physical features as horns, teeth, and tails, distinguish one animal from the other. Greater cue clarity exists.

While nonverbal codes are often used to increase cue clarity, they can also be used to build cue association so that an individual can more easily pull the right response out of his reservoir of knowledge. We learn verbal chains of association when we memorize a rhyme such as, "Columbus sailed the ocean blue . . ." This may be the most efficient way to remember the digital response, "1492." If, however, we want to remember the path of the voyage, a visual map may be more helpful than a verbal description or a numerical notation of longitudes and latitudes.

Space is perhaps used most frequently among the nonverbal mnemonic devices. We arrange objects or cues into spatial patterns and recall individual elements by remembering what was located around them. Interestingly enough, people seem to differ in their ability to use visual mnemonic devices; they are more helpful to some than to others.

Efficiency of recall may increase if we pair verbal with nonverbal stimuli (that is, use multi-bands). In learning a foreign language, for instance, seeing an object while hearing its name is more effective than seeing the English word and then the foreign word. With multi-bands we have been able to pair stimulus and response more closely in time and thereby improve learning.

A variety of nonverbal cues can be used to change the learning curve. If for instance, you memorize ten items in sequence, you will find a gentle U-curve of recall. You will remember the first and last items best, the middle items least. But if you make the fifth item distinctive in some way, you will find an upswing in your memory curve at that point. To make the fifth item distinctive, change its color, add a sound, introduce a picture, or provide some other convenient nonverbal cue. A string around your finger is one type of nonverbal reminder. There are obviously many other nonverbal techniques that can aid recall.

Use

The final test of communication effectiveness is whether the receiver uses the information he has obtained. In most academic settings, the first use of information is in a test. A student wants to be able to make verbal responses to verbal questions.

In many communication situations, however, the communicator wants more than a verbal response; he seeks some overt action. If you want a man to fly an airplane, you are not satisfied if he can only tell you how it's done. This may be a first step, but the real test is in getting the plane off the ground and back safely. In other words, as you move to seeking nonverbal responses, you may want to move to the nonverbal stimuli that will trigger those responses in the actual use situation.

In interpersonal communication, whether a person uses his information or not may depend on the group sanctions and expectations that he observes. Frequently these sanctions and expectations are communicated nonverbally. For example, an individual may see a wide variety of behavior on television. He has this information and presumably could use it. If he starts to use it, however, and it is not approved by his group, he will get nonverbal messages telling him so. His friends will look startled, they'll frown, glare, and possibly add specific verbal communications if he persists in his behavior.

A Final Word

In what we have said, we have implied that you can be more effective if you harness the nonverbal into your communication strategy. A final word needs to be said about communication efficiency—the price you are willing to pay for effectiveness.

Sometimes nonverbal communication is more expensive than verbal communication. This cost arises from three sources. It may come from the intrinsic costliness of nonverbal materials. It may come from a lack of knowledge about alternatives. It may come from poor planning. Many kinds of nonverbal communication are costly because they require expensive materials and the time and talent of skilled creators. A publication with pictures is likely to cost more than one without. A motion picture is more expensive to produce than a pamphlet.

However, not all nonverbal techniques are expensive. Some cost very little; some indeed are worth the price of many words. The proper timing of a message or an effective seating arrangement at a conference may cost only a little thought on the part of the communicator.

As you become aware of nonverbal techniques and increase your skill in their use, they take less effort, and in this sense are less costly. As you work, your repertoire of alternatives expands and you are also better able to predict which alternative will get the desired result.

Perhaps the greatest stumbling block in the path of the unskilled communicator, however, results from poor planning. Usually, he does not allow early enough for the incorporation of nonverbal communication into his strategy. Early incorporation is important for two reasons. Certain kinds of nonverbal materials take more lead time to produce than verbal materials. Even more important, however, the nonverbal dimensions can play a vital part in shaping the verbal dimensions of the message. The two should work together, each drawing on its strengths to complement the other and multiply the total impact. All too often, the verbal component is decided upon first. The nonverbal elements are attached last, and they never quite mesh; they detract as much as they add.

Since so much nonverbal communication flows at a low level of awareness, both for the source and the receiver, the alert communicator may want to build into his message framework check-points when he can stop and think about the nonverbal effectiveness of his communication.

Exercises

1. Is the general position of Goffman compatible with Harrison's?

2. Write a paper pulling together what the various authors in this book of readings have said about the importance of the source's intent. What about the intents of the receivers?

3. Discuss the difference between games like football and baseball and games like chess and bridge, in terms of the nonverbal behaviors of the players.

The Language of Business

Donald J. Lloyd
Harry R. Warfel

Although they appear in different sections of our book, this selection, the one by March and Simon, and the one by Katz and Kahn deal with the same set of questions and problems. Lloyd and Warfel, in this selection, write on language communication. Like March and Simon, as well as Katz and Kahn, they are interested in the effects of communication within an organizational structure. The difference among the articles is one of emphasis.

No matter what career a young person in school or college chooses for himself today, he can be sure that one part of his career will choose him. Set his sights as low or as high as he will—day labor, semiskilled or skilled labor, white-collar work (clerical or executive), teaching, art, writing, music, law, medicine, engineering, science, social work, national defense, government—it does not matter. Sooner or later the American business system touches every man and woman, and each has to deal with it. Even early marriage no longer removes women from contact with business, for in the management of family finances women control most of the spending for consumer goods. Many married women hold jobs until they have children, and again between children. Women retire as mothers in their forties and turn to outside work to fill their lives; chances are that they will outlive their husbands by seven years, during which they have to manage their own affairs. No matter what we do or how we live, we spend a good part of our lives doing business.

This is an era in which business means organization—the organization of people, machines, materials, and finances toward one end, one purpose. That end is efficiency, doing the work as quickly, cheaply, and effectively as it can be done. Almost two hundred million people now live well on a continent that once barely supported four or five million Indians in hardship and peril. Most Americans live in cities which can exist only because life in cities is highly organized; it is not magic that brings the people to their jobs in the morning and home at night, that stocks the stores with food and clothing, provides the coal, oil, gas, and electricity for heating the houses and cooking the food. It is organization. Every day the ordinary American is affected by dozens of organized activities that have been developed from very small beginnings over the last three centuries, each one there and functioning as long as it is efficient and because it is efficient. Let it lose its efficiency, and it is soon disintegrated and swamped by some other organization that is more efficient.

The whole business runs on money. What is bought is bought with money and what is sold is sold for money, whether it is a piece of land, something grown, mined, or manufactured, or the services of someone's hands or brains. Artists paint for money, writers write for money, doctors doctor for money, soldiers fight for money, churches tithe for money, charities solicit money, governments tax for money. Everybody takes his pay and turns around and pays again. Money is the blood of the system. You might dream of a self-sufficient life, like Thoreau's at Walden Pond, growing your own food and making your own clothes; but somehow it seems a fuller, richer life to get into the flow of money deep enough to get by, and take money into your hand and pay it out like the others. And so you get a job and take your check like the rest. The money depends on business, not merely what we think of as buying and selling, but business as a way of life.

Business touches us all. If you have anything to do that is like anything done in business, it is done best the business way. If you write, you write fast and well with a typewriter—the basic business machine. If you count many small and simple figures, you do it best with an adding machine; if you count in large, complicated figures, you do it with Univac or something like it. If you handle money, as in a charity or a tax office, you do it the business way with business machines. If you handle people, as in a university or an army camp, you use personal records and an IBM machine; you "streamline your procedures" to increase efficiency and save money. You mechanize, mechanize, mechanize, whether with self-opening doors or with self-loading ships, self-operating elevators or self-tripping timers. You may not call in the businessman in person except for his advice, but you carry on the most humane and humanitarian activities most efficiently and most cheaply his way. You save your own hands and brains for what is important for you to get done, whether it is putting out a college yearbook, searching for a rich man to endow an art museum, or computing the statistics on a polio serum administered to second-graders in school.

If money is the lifeblood of business, the nerve is language. Every business suffers in one way or another from disease in this nerve. Every corporation, no matter how successful it seems, confesses itself to be in trouble in its communication in one of three aspects. One of these is passing the word from top to bottom and bottom to top. A person afflicted in the same way would be slow to feel pain in his hand and slow to pull his hand away. The second is passing the word among units at the same level —from person to person, office to office, from branch to branch. A person afflicted in this way would not be able to let his right hand know what his left hand does. And the third is passing the word from the organization to the outsiders—to other organizations and to the public. A person afflicted in this way would strangle on his own words, with intelligence shining in his eyes and a stammer coming from his mouth. A person afflicted in all these ways would be a spastic, and a community of such persons would be a mental hospital. Business has outgrown its nervous system—communication. Business is still growing, and is looking rather desperately for ways of improving the flow of information without which it cannot thrive.

Thus the administrator, sitting in his office, writes a memorandum that flutters from desk to desk among his subordinates, signifying nothing. The research laboratory submits reports that only the person who wrote them can understand. In a public utility an order goes out setting up a new procedure; on the basis of that order, five different powerhouses set up five different procedures. Thus in the Army Ordnance Corps one department consigns to the junkpile surplus switches which another department has on order and cannot get. Automobile dealers report defective brakes on a new car and continue to correct the same defect on the next year's model. A union goes out on strike to correct an abuse which has kept its men sullen for years but never was mentioned to top management by the personnel director. Thus American business in general has had to confess failure in its fantastically expensive effort to "sell" the "business point of view" to the American public. Thus the U.S. submarine service enters World War II with torpedoes that submariners know won't track down a target and won't explode if they do. "Now hear this—" says the loudspeaker. Is anybody listening? No. Nobody listening.

However bad this news is to the nation at large (the mere thought of its cost in money is appalling), it can be good news to the intelligent student in college. If communication depends on language, then a failure in communication is a failure in the use of language. Somebody doesn't get the word. The student in college is in a good position because he is in a position to learn. The college may or may not be able to teach him the knowledge that is important in his field, and that knowledge may or may not still be worth something when he gets out. The college can give him something that will stay with him the rest of his life, whatever he does and wherever he goes—a command of his language. Then when he speaks or writes he communicates what he has to say in such a way that it is heeded. Then he will be of value to business, and it will have a place for him. Business is the interaction of human beings; the means of their interaction is language. If the college student will put his mind to it, he can develop a control of English that will serve him well in business.

The language used in business depends very much on what it is used for: who originates the communication, what it is about, and whom it goes to. There is of course a kind of communication which is largely mechanized and consists of the forms that accompany people and things through the organization, such as orders, invoices, and trace slips of various kinds for things; time cards and personnel records for people. If we think of a corporation as a living body, then this is the "autonomic nervous system" which keeps the heart beating and the lungs pulsing even while the conscious mind sleeps. Girls with machines take care of most of it; machines will soon handle all of it.

Then there is the communication that passes upward from small shot to big shot, from workman to foreman, from foreman to manager, from manager to superintendent, and so on up. This is like the sensory nervous system in a living body that tells the brain what the limbs are feeling and how they are doing. It is a flow of information, often from the less articulate to the more articulate, and usually from the more specialized person to the less specialized. The person who originates it is concerned with a specific problem which may be a small thing in itself but is what occupies his time. It often passes through very sluggish channels, partly because the person who originates it is inept at saying what he means and partly because each person who gets it has many things to think about. It could be the report of a testing laboratory on a product or material the company is thinking of buying. It could be an appeal for promotion. It could be a summary of a recommended change in method, a report by a salesman or a sales manager. Its direction is upward, from the less important person to the more important.

Inability to do the writing for this kind of communication can nip a promising career before it starts. Like most upward communication, it must be formal, relatively impersonal, and relatively respectful. By formal we mean that it imitates the tone which has been established in the organization for this kind of message. It must be clear, brief, factual, and definite. It ought to be honest in what it says, and what it says ought to be on the subject. If the writer has any side remarks to make on the way the company is run, he should save them for his wife. Upward messages should be written in the consciousness that they will fall in with other communications of the same kind from other persons or units on the same level. The writer probably knows more about this particular matter than the reader; he should make a point of telling the reader what will get the point across. Where he cannot avoid the jargon of the expert, he should translate it. If graphs, charts, or pictures will make the point easier to grasp, he should include them. "Brief me," says the boss. Well, brief him. If you do this job well, you may move up with your message to that heaven of all specialists—a job where you no longer do the work but direct the people who do it.

Flowing from the top down, from big shot to small shot, is the communication that gets things done. It is like the efferent nerves in a living body that move the limbs at the command of the brain. This flow of command moves generally from the more articulate to the less articulate; the person who originates it usually has more education, more experience, and more varied experience than the person who receives it. It seems easy—just tell them what to do and let them do it. But the transmission line is like a funnel; more can get in at the top than can get out at the bottom. The matter varies. It could be a simple order to start up the machines. It could be a directive to do a certain task in a certain way, but the directive may vary from assigning a man to his job for the day to setting a policy for a department, branch, or agency. This kind of communication must bring about exactly the kind of action that the originator intends and not something else.

Inability to do this writing can keep an otherwise competent man in minor positions throughout his life. The writing that goes up can assume that the reader is able to handle the language of the educated and can appraise the message on the basis of a more general grasp of the situation than the writer has. The writing that goes down must assume that the reader, whatever his special competence may be, knows less about the whole situation than the writer, often has less education, and needs to be addressed in simpler English. The writer must not only have a general knowledge of people; he must know specifically what he can say to each person or group of persons and how he can say it. If he wants a specific electrical device designed, he does not necessarily have to know much about electricity, but he does have to know the crotchets of electricians. He must put his instructions in their terms, or they will come up with something he can't use. If he is setting a sales policy, he must know his salesmen and how to address them. If he is changing the workload for the men on the assembly line, he must make clear that he is not attempting a "speed-up," or he will spend some uncomfortable time with the shop stewards while the line sits idle. He must put his directives in terms of the men they go to, or they will be non-directives.

This kind of downward communication has more to do with a young man or woman starting out on a career than you might think, for there is a line of promotion in large organizations in what we may call "staff" work. The head of an office or of a concern does not sit down at a typewriter and peck out his instructions. He dictates them and turns them over to his staff, a group of people he has drawn together because they are capable. They know him and what he wants, and they know how to get it done. An executive in a large organization does not move alone through his business day. No matter how much he likes to "get out into the works and talk to the boys," he is always at least within telephone call of his staff, who are his real eyes and ears. Chief among these is his secretary, usually a woman but not always, who sets up his schedule, filters calls and callers to him, buys his tickets and makes his reservations, sees that a car meets him at the station and takes him back to it, and incidentally writes his letters and speeches from his instructions. Backing her up are his assistants to whom he delegates anything they can handle. She, too, may have her assistants. Competent people for these jobs are so rare that executives scrabble for them, bribe and steal them from each other. A person with a delicate sense of language, who can phrase instructions and orders so that the receiver knows what is expected of him and can act on it, can move in the shadow of the executive and build up experience for his own advancement.

It was probably while the secretary was sick that the general editor of one of the dictionaries we have discussed sat down and typed out an order which was posted on a photostatting machine. The machine had just been introduced to eliminate the typing of passages which illustrate the uses of words. It photographed them on 3 x 5 paper. The memo went something like this:

NOTICE TO EDITORIAL AND CLERICAL PERSONNEL

1. The operation and utilization of this machine shall be under the cognizance of the supervisor of clerical personnel.
2. Utilization of this machine for company business shall take precedence over non-editorial purposes.
3. Editorial and clerical personnel having matter of their own to photograph will consult the supervisor of clerical personnel. . . .

And so on, through about twelve points. Visitors being shown through the plant did not usually have time to read to the bottom. Possibly the editor was depending on the high educational and intellectual level of his employees, but the point of the memo was quite simple and could have been simply expressed:

1. The head clerk is in charge of this machine.
2. It is here for company business but employees may use it for their own work when it is idle.
3. If you have anything to photograph, arrange it with the head clerk, and she will see that it gets done.

Within any organization there is also sideways or horizontal communication, which goes on between persons or units working together on common problems, though on different aspects of them. Rank or status is not much involved; the persons are pretty much on a level. They may work side by side at a machine; they may be in charge of comparable offices, laboratories, departments, or branches. The company expects them to co-operate; as the little boy said, "Nobody talk big, nobody talk little, everybody talk medium." Each person involved is a specialist who knows his own job but often little about the others. The communication is thus normally from the specialist to an outsider who is a specialist in another field. Examples would be departments of Design and Engineering. Design works out a model which Engineering has to put into production, preferably without buying a plantful of new machine tools. Engineering defines the limits of its equipment; Design goes over the model and brings the parts within the range of the machines. In the same way production, packaging, and shipping departments have to work together.

This sideways writing is a real test of skill. It varies as the people vary, but it always involves explanation. Since no one can order anyone else to do anything, the writer has to make clear what is to be done, why it has to be done, what the issues are, and which are important. He has to let it be known that the necessities are not personal; it is the nature of the work or the material or the equipment that dictates what has to be done. He has to indicate he is not trying to run the other fellow's job, that he has tried everything possible to keep difficulties down, and that he is open to suggestions. Often the matter is extremely technical, but it must be sufficiently translated so that the specialist who has to pick it up from there knows what is involved. The person who has bolstered his technical education with a mastery of the language has an edge over the specialist who has not.

Finally there is the communication that passes from the organization as a whole to the outside—that vast area of contacts now known as "public relations." Here the organization faces its suppliers, its employees, its customers, and the community at large. Here, like a nervous lover, the organization tries to establish an image of itself that will be attractive, that will have dignity, and that will win and keep friends. To this end it builds an attractive plant—or at least an attractive façade—with a green lawn and a fountain, if possible, with ducks in it. It sets up impressive front offices in which an atmosphere of dignified calm approaches rigor mortis. It hires specialists in packaging to package its products, artists to design its letterheads, and public-relations men to make sure that it supports the right charity drives, athletic teams and leagues, and other community enterprises, so as to join the effort without seeming to take it over. It tries to be lovely to look at, friendly to live with, easy to do business with. To this end it organizes its communication.

An organization presenting a unified face to the world cannot set up a single office to handle the matter and let every other employee be as hairy-chested as he likes. Its contacts with the public occur at all levels and at every point. Telephones jingle on every desk. Letters come and go from every office dealing with purchases, production, sales, adjustments, and the thousand issues that come up in any complicated endeavor. It soon becomes obvious which people in which offices can be trusted to write letters. They are not specialists in letter writing but persons who know the work and understand the problems and can interpret to others in some kind of gracious way. These chances of any employee to be, for a moment, a representative of the whole outfit come as unexpectedly and as often as spring rainfall, and each is a small opportunity to grow a little bigger in stature and influence in the enterprise.

Possibly the touchiest of all the outside relations of a big organization is with its own personnel. Each employee has only one foot planted in the business; the other is outside groping around for something solid to stand on. Each person is seeking something for himself—a job with another concern, a better job where he is, more pay, more dignity, more status, a better living, or a better way of life. The personnel department must see that he finds what he seeks within the organization, if it can be provided. Most of the labor force has a dual loyalty—to its union as well as to the company; an employee is most productive when he can feel that these two loyalties are pulling together toward a common end. If the two are divided and resisting each other, then each employee is split right down the middle; if he is forced to a choice, he will go with the union. Therefore, the people in charge of personnel must approach the staff as outsiders and must understand the needs and drives of men and women at work.

Several things of importance are here for the young person looking for a career. Personnel relations—often miscalled "personnel management" —is a growing field in large organizations as more and more concerns discover that friction between a man and his job is a costly waste. Personnel relations is a practical art for which some people are gifted and some are not, and those most likely not to be gifted have trained too narrowly for specialized work and have slighted literature, art, psychology, and social studies in their education. This cuts two ways. It is no great blow to be shut off from work in the personnel department itself on account of a barbarously narrow training in engineering, chemistry, or business administration. It is a blow to be cut off from advancement because a narrow interest in a specialty has unfitted you for a supervisory post. A concern that will hire you to do a job for which you are trained would prefer to have you grow up, out, and away from that job, but personnel studies demonstrate fairly well that if you promote a specialist to manager you may ruin a specialist and not get a manager. It is easy to develop some breadth of outlook in school or college, but hard to develop it in the day-to-day pressure of a job; if you cannot develop it, you stay in the same bottom job where you began—at close to the same pay. Industry is full of arrogant young technicians and disgruntled older ones, still sweating it out where they began.

The public relations of a large organization involve all its contacts with its customers and the public at large. The customers are hidden until they are discovered in the public at large, so that the simplest form of public relations is the avoidance of unnecessary friction. The picture editor of a newspaper made this point clear. He listened to an exasperated desk man explain to a woman by telephone that her tip on an accident had come in too late to win a prize; somebody beat her to it. "Madam," he said, "you did not get in first; you do not get the money, and that's that!" He banged the receiver. "Do you know who you were talking to?" said the editor. "Oh, some dame. . . ." "For your information," said the editor, "that was a *former* reader of the *Times.*" Every concern has some employees who should be locked away from telephones and typewriters; they have to be very good at their specialized work to stay on.

The "institutional" side of public relations is the creation of the image of a concern which it wants to present to the public—usually the image of a good citizen. It is as if you added up all the people in the organization as citizens concerned with health, schools, recreation, government, and public welfare generally, and take over as an organization a concern for their concerns. A big organization has a great deal of weight; its citizenship is a matter of delicate negotiations, careful scrutiny of projects and appeals for money and services, and constant watchfulness for the effect of rejection or approval. It commits a little and then a little more, and then, when the project is obviously going to be a success and everyone connected with it is going to look good, the company plunges and puts it over.

Closely allied to this institutional public relations is advertising of the product, which can range all the way from the sleazy come-on of a streetcorner pitchman to the sober statement in a medical journal of the properties of a drug. This is the only kind of public relations that all the people in the enterprise do not participate in. It is a specialist job. In spite of the number of experts involved in it and the money spent on it, advertising is not yet well understood. We can see that in the mass it does influence people and it does move goods. What ad in which medium is best for each item is hard to say; as a result, advertising is wasteful, like a blind man sowing clover seed by hand on a windy day. It seems to cry out for some of the citizenship in institutional promotion. Not surprisingly in its vast range from responsibility to empty dishonesty, advertising reflects the morals of the multitude that engages in it. The fact that the same concern can advertise the same drug with the cynicism of the pitchman and the scrupulousness of the scientist certainly raises some questions of ethics; and we may well wonder as consumers what image of us lives in the murky minds of the advertising experts. Still, it is a specialist job, and the young person whose writing will help or hinder his career in fields that are mainly not writing need only know that it is part of the public relations of business, a part that will not involve him except as captive audience.

We may now look at a typical corporation and see the place of written communication in it. This is a corporation, located in southern California, which manufactures civilian and military airplanes. It is a growing concern with large contracts for airliners and larger contracts for jet bombers and fighters.

This aircraft company is typical; we mention it not because it is special—which it is—but because it represents present-day business. We could take an automobile factory with its ceaseless inflow of materials and outflow of finished cars and trucks, or a building contractor with its giant trenchers, bulldozers, and earthmovers to prepare the ground and its army of skilled and unskilled workers who may put housing for thirty thousand people in a cornfield, build factories for them to work in, or thrust a shimmering tower of glass and aluminum toward the sky. We could take a steel company with its iron and coal mines, ships and trains to carry the ore, blast furnaces and foundaries, fabricating plants making partly finished bolts, sheets, and slabs of steel of special formulas for everything from needles to machine tools. We could take an oil company with its wells, refineries, and chemical plants, its gas stations and tire factories. We could take a university of fifteen to fifty thousand students, with its libraries, classrooms, laboratories, atom smashers, and even farms and airports. We could take a shipyard, a government bureau, a philanthropic foundation like the Carnegie or Ford, a branch of the Armed Forces, a labor union. It is the same story in each: elaborate organization of diverse elements to accomplish a common set of purposes, and an elaborate spread into sidelines unexpected by the founders of the enterprise. Modern organizations are like many of the people in them: they didn't plan to end up where they are or doing what they do.

Except for a battleship, the big modern bombing aircraft is about the largest and most complicated machine built by man. In the ten years since World War II came to an end, each military aircraft has become about ten times as complicated as the World War II model; it is bigger, faster, heavier, and more costly to build and to maintain, since ten more years of experience has gone into the design and building of it. Yet each one—Sabre-jet, helicopter, and Strato-bomber—is obsolete when it goes into production; the day and almost the date when it will go out of production can pretty well be guessed in advance. The paper work involved for each one, gathered together, would make a pile almost as high as the plane itself. Because of the interdependence of every element on every other element in a plane, each must be planned with respect to the others; each has its number and paper to correspond to that number in the records. Somewhere there is an exact description and probably an exchange of notes or letters in which its shape and function were worked out. Because an aircraft is seldom "frozen" during production, newly designed elements are slipped in here and there, until the last completed plane of a specific model bears little resemblance to the pilot design for which the production line was originally set up. Complication on complication, the modern aircraft in itself is no greater marvel than the intricate modern organization that produces it.

The Language of Business 281

To see the place of language in aircraft production, let us divide the whole enterprise into two parts, external and internal. Between the company and outsiders there is a host of contacts: purchase, sales, and maintenance, among others. The company must buy what it needs—in part, raw materials; in part, semifinished materials like sheet aluminum and preformed girder stock; and, in part, finished components like instruments and control mechanisms. It must also buy tools and machinery and sometimes whole factories. A modern company depends so much on its suppliers that it looks on purchasing as a form of public relations; it must be a good, reliable, honest buyer, exactly describing its needs and responding to suggestions for substitutes or improvements. Second, it must sell its products, and in the air world this means selling to persons using many languages, not only English, German, French, and Spanish but Arabic, Chinese, Japanese, Amharic, Hebrew, and several others. Third, it must keep its products in the air as long as the owners want to fly them. Purchasers of the old Ford Trimotor still feel that it is the best cargo-carrying aircraft for short hops over rough terrain, still use it, and still write in from Cleveland, Ohio; Brazil; and perhaps even New Guinea for parts. Yet Ford went out of production on this plane many years ago. Battered old Lend-lease craft from World War II still lumber over distant continents and seas with Ethiopians, British Indians, and Chinese pilots, not to mention the British, French, Americans, Germans, and Italians who still make a living with them. The maintenance department must respond to inquiries couched in many languages and must offer the sum of the company's experience with its planes translated into the same languages. Technicians who can translate—let alone give clear instructions in English—seldom hunt long for a job. Every need anyone feels in regard to purchase, sales, or maintenance is expressed in writing and must be dealt with in writing.

A company building large passenger and transport planes for civilian use, and the same planes plus fighters and bombers for the military, does not ordinarily do business with individuals either in buying or selling. It deals mainly with other large organizations like itself and with governments. It does not have full control over its own actions; it cannot get high and mighty and say, "Take it or leave it." It does not even have full control over its own correspondence. It has to be multilingual. If it is addressed in French, it replies in French, not English. More difficult than this, it has to observe protocol; that is, it has to address each system in terms of the system, and each person in the other system in terms of his place in it. It has to have an internal system of its own which it can equate to the other, so that in a touchy case it can assign a vice-president to reply to letters from a vice-president, or ask its own very top man to communicate with a general, an admiral, or a Minister of Foreign Affairs. In most cases, before these very high-level heads are permitted to bump together, a crisscross of low and middle-level correspondence has cleared the ground and defined the issues to be settled.

Ordinarily, when two business systems have to deal with each other, they fit together pretty well because they understand each other—both are in business to make a profit. There is a natural symbiotic relationship between them; one thrives with the other. But when a concern does business with government, one does not necessarily thrive with the other, for only one is concerned with profits. When the product is matériel for war, the other agency—the government—is committed to waste. It cannot set out to fly its aircraft as long and as cheaply as it can; it has to have the craft capable of the highest speeds, the longest flights, and the most integral efficiency. To be caught with the second best can mean death, not merely to men and women but to the nation itself. The end and aim of all the aircraft is destruction—if it does not ride to flaming disaster in the sky, it rots to surplus and the junkyard, while other, newer, better aircraft take its place. Thus the government which is pinning the very life of the nation on its purchases must interfere in the corporation at every level; and in every contact or conflict the government has the final word. It lays down the specifications, inspects the work, guards the production and its secrets, and tests the product. Every communication that passes between the company and the government must be "according to regulation," often secret, often on forms provided by the government, and always through channels determined by law.

Every internal element in the corporation is under the eye of the Armed Forces and must justify its actions to the government. We may distinguish four of these elements: Research, Design, Production, and Testing. Research has its eye on the future: impossible speeds, fantastic heights, unimaginable destruction. It must determine the effect of cosmic rays on high-altitude flight; it must fling shuddering experimental airframes against the leaden wall of air. It must discover the potential and limitations of the human body in flight, and devise ways to bring its crew to earth alive with or without the plane it flies in. Design, working a little closer to today, must translate present knowledge into blueprints for tomorrow's flight. Production must convert yesterday's blueprints into today's power plants, armament, controls, and airframes. Testing must torture production models beyond any stresses produced in flight, so that flyers can sit their seats in confidence as they ride the skies. Each department must be in constant communication with the other, with the cold eye of the military overlooking all. The flow of reports, instructions, requests, and answers is colossal; there must be a record of everything, and every record must be as clear as it can be made.

A modern aircraft is a complex product of many men and many minds, each a specialist at his own task. It involves mechanics, hydraulics, electronics, ballistics, physics, chemistry, geography, meterology, astronomy, physiology, psychology, and even psychiatrics and medicine. There must be communication between these specialties; each must in some way reach out to comprehend others. But through channels only, and to control the channels the aircraft industry has "security"—a means of making sure that no one man knows more than he needs to know in order to do his work. The highest security involving experimental and classified materials is itself a secret matter.

Plant security goes by levels: one man may have security clearance for his own department only, another for several departments, and another for the entire plant, depending upon his responsibilities. A man's clearance is indicated by a security card and by a badge with a color bar which shows whether he is salaried or "on the clock"; he may have two badges, one for where he belongs normally and the other for where he is permitted to move around. Thus in the plant no man looks first at a stranger's face; he glances at the badge to check status and security clearance. Some groups have clearance that admits them to just about everything: supervisors, engineers, schedulers, etc., and the technical writers. These have to cross all specialties and nose into everything.

The supervisors and the technical writers are important in industry today, and they will be more important in the industrial world which will face young men and women now in college. In a specialist world they are generalists; they cut across trades, professions, and disciplines. They have to have that keen understanding of human beings which is native to a few people, but which comes to most of us as the result of study and reading—reading of literature, history, philosophy, psychology, sociology—and of an acquaintance with the arts. They have to have alert open minds, quick understanding, and broad interests. They have to be able to move in on a specialty and master it in the jargon of the specialists, then turn around and express in ordinary English the gist of what they have learned. Supervisors become more important as industry becomes more highly organized, and the technical writers become more important as the products of industry become more complicated, as doorbells, automobiles, washing machines, ships, and aircraft become more complex and involve more diverse components. Each of these constructions must have its instruction manual —a clear guide to dismantling it, fixing it, and putting it back together. This is the real McCoy among "How-to-do-it" books, and technical writers are the cream of the "How-to-do-it" experts.

We may follow a technical writer through a small part of his day to see how he fits into the industrial picture. He approaches a line of partially finished airframes to check on one little thing. In the belly of a fighter plane is a set of holes into which supports may be screwed for carrying loads—an extra fuel tank, a rocket-launcher, a parachute drop. Over each hole a small plate is fastened with screws to maintain the smooth skin of the plane in the stream of air. This plate goes with the plane everywhere; when it is not covering the hole, it is fastened to a frame member inside with the same screws. The question is where.

The technical writer knows from the blueprints, but he has to put the location in the manual, and he wants to see how to get at it. He crawls into the fuselage beside a riveter who glances at his badge and then gets back to work because the badge is ambiguous; the wearer could be anybody or nobody, but he has overall clearance. The writer looks for the screw holes, but he does not find them. He introduces himself and asks; the riveter does not know: he rivets for a living. The writer asks the lead-man, the foreman, the superintendent. Nobody knows. He sighs and goes back to the blueprints. The blueprints have been revised by Engineering Orders; as each production change is introduced, it is recorded in an E. O. bearing a change-letter, A, B, C, etc., then AB, AC, AD. These nearly completed airframes are up to their sixtieth production change: there may be twenty more before the first ship is completed. He begins with the sixtieth set and works back through them, looking for the location of the storage holes for the cover plates. At fifteen he finds them. Somebody failed to carry them over to sixteen, and they dropped from the record. Now they will have to be put back in. He makes a note for the draftsmen and goes back to his job of writing the manual: "These cover plates must be stored with their screws . . ."

Obviously it is not the main job of the technical writer to keep some mechanic on Okinawa from standing around with a set of cover plates in his hand, wondering what to do with them. His task is writing the manual. He has to be free to nose into the whole written story of the air-craft, and free to question any of the technicians who have designed it and put it together. He is a gatherer of relevant information, and a trans-lator; what he learns must go into the book in common English that can be understood by any craftsman. He works a little sadly because of the production changes. The technical writers begin to lay out the manual according to a standard form when the plans are delivered and when the first airframe begins to take shape on the line. Almost immediately, as Design begins to feed in the latest developments of Research, the pro-duction changes start to come through. Components change—a new air-speed indicator, a new shape for the tail surfaces, a new pilot-ejection mechanism. Finished work has to be pulled out of completed units. The writing staff works on, keeping up as long as it can, but sooner or later it must stop—in order to have the manual completed when the planes are ready for delivery at, say, eighty production changes. The staff gives up at the fortieth or fiftieth, conscious that part of its work, at least, will be obsolete before it is done, and that the manual will have to be followed by a supplement of corrections.

Who are these technical writers? Where did they learn their trade? Like many people in modern industry, doing work that often did not even exist when they were in school or college, they "drifted into it." A former pilot who tried school teaching, office work, and selling before he drifted back into the building of the planes. An electronics specialist whose gift for making complicated things clear pulled him off the bench and into the office, a college instructor who took one last look at an English class and went out looking for a job, a mechanical engineer, a salesman—almost anybody with an intellectual bent and an inquiring mind and with that one necessary quality in modern business organizations, the habit of reading widely and writing constantly with craft and care. No illiterate specialists these, but citizens of the air world and of the universal Republic of Letters.

Let one of them speak for himself. "When I came into this business, everything was hydraulics, and hydraulics are complicated. Now we still have hydraulic mechanisms all through the plane, but they're triggered by electronics. The planes go so fast that human reflexes are too slow: electronics respond instantly and correct themselves. At the speeds these planes fly, the forces are so great that you have to have power controls. Power controls have no 'feel'; they're as dead as an electric light switch. So you have to build machines that put the feel back in. All this machinery adds weight, so you have to miniaturize—cut everything down in size, make it smaller, lighter. Then you have to protect the pilot. These jets are sturdier than piston planes, because they're simpler, in a way. They'll take a lot of pounding. Even so, they put a terrible strain on the pilot, on his blood and his guts.

"The human brain is a very complicated instrument in a fragile body, and you have to do what you can to bring each one back. So the next step is still ahead of us: replace the pilot with a mechanical brain that is expendable. You don't have to bring it back. That means guided missiles. We're not building them now, but we've got to. That brings in the physicist and the meteorologist. Will the machine work the same at ground level as at forty thousand feet? Will it take in weather information and correct itself according to the winds, moisture conditions, and icing the way a pilot does? The hydraulics man says, 'I don't know anything about electronics; that's his business.' The electronics man says, 'I don't know anything about meteorology.' The meteorologist says, 'I'm a weather man. I just feed the information to the fly boys and let them figure out what to do with it.' Somebody has to learn hydraulics, learn electronics, and then go on and learn meteorology and any other -ology that comes into it. I think it's the most exciting thing I ever got into, and I can't see where it's going to stop.

"And that isn't all. Every business is up against the same thing. Look at your washing machines—they run themselves. Your flatirons keep their own heat wherever you want it. Look at your television. Radio was complicated enough; now you've got television, and color is coming in. A black and white tube costs twenty dollars, say—a color tube about a hundred and seventy-five. Look at your automobiles, with automatic transmissions, power steering, power brakes, power seats, and automatic dimmers. Ships with automatic pilots, trains that stop if they run a block signal, lawn mowers that hunt around for the long grass to cut. We've got big computers here, but when we have anything really complicated to figure out, we send it to places like MIT, Wayne, and Harvard, where they've really got machines that think, big enough to fill up a whole building. Even looking at where we are today, it's hard to see where we're going to be tomorrow.

"And we do it all with language. If you tie up our communications, we're sunk. Everything stops until you get it going again. And you can't leave language to the other fellow. You've got to do it yourself. Everybody's got to do it.

"Another problem I can foresee is that I see more and more terms being used which I never heard of, for example *enthalpy* ('heat content'). Pretty soon I can see where only engineers of like interest will be able to communicate with each other; and if my argument is correct, then in the near future it would appear that engineering progress is going to rely entirely on the technical writer or editor or abstract writer to translate many of the highly scientific pieces of writing into something comprehensible to interested parties in other allied fields."

The technical writer, like the supervisor, is not a special breed of person. He is the ordinary business person with ordinary writing responsibilities lifted to the nth degree. He is one who patiently cultivated his ability to take in information from writing and put it out again in writing while he was learning his own specialty, whatever it was. Most cultivators of language tend to be lovers of words; they like the feel and savor of words. The technical writer, like the poet, is a patternmaker more than a mere wordlover. He uses various technical vocabularies, but they are known in advance to his readers. He does not look for ways to get around using a single term for an object like a condenser, a rheostat, a turbine, or an afterburner. That is its name, and he sticks with it. He tries for a plain style, though not necessarily a simple one, for he has to deal with an organized complex of things in an organized complex of language that fits it. His tools are the commonest patterns of the common speech, and the inflections and structure-words that build those patterns. Anyone can see his problems who has tried to put together a knocked-down cabinet or build a boat from a kit, and has had trouble figuring out from the instructions which parts go together first. The technical writer must show how to find out which mechanism has failed, how to get into it, how to detach it, how to find the trouble, and how to fix it. Then he has to tell how to work the unit back into place, how to connect it, and how to ease it back into operation again. To do all this, he has to play with the sentence so that it tells in order what has to be done in order.

The technical writer has to weigh the values of the most familiar words, so that he does not use one when he means another. Let us say that two relays, *A* and *B*, operate simultaneously. The chances are that his readers will not recognize the word *simultaneously* in print: he must be sure that a tired airman working with stiff fingers on a cold desert base will make no mistake. Should he say, "If the coil of relay A is energized, the coil of relay B is energized," and add, "at the same time"? Or should he say, "When the coil of relay A . . ."? Or would it be better to say, "As the coil of relay A is energized, the coil of relay B is energized at the same time"? Both *if* and *when* are ambiguous; they may set up the wrong notion too well for "at the same time" to correct it. He may "try it out on the dog," as they say, by handing it to one of the boys on the line to read. He feels some urgency because if those two relays are hooked up wrong, an aircraft representing a million dollars or more of the taxpayers' money may go up in smoke.

The technical writer must sharpen his ear for the common speech, that part of the language that is understood by everybody, educated and uneducated, from any part of the nation. *Carry* in the South may mean "take," as in *I carried my girl to the movies* or *Carry me back to Old Virginny*. In the North it may mean "lift and bear from one place to another," or "support." Can he stay within a range of meanings that is shared by both? He must, to avoid mistakes. He must watch pronouns. A sergeant told a private, "This is a hand grenade. You just pull this pin and throw it. Go ahead and try it." An explosion injured both men. The private asked, "What happened? I threw the pin just like you said." The technical writer must especially watch the names of the various parts and elements. Nomenclature is very important. The same name must be used throughout the entire manual; otherwise complete confusion results. Many times there is a close similarity between names; for example: *secondary relay, secondary bus relay, secondary bus control relay, secondary bus power relay*, and so on. The technical writer must consider the physical movements involved in the work; he cannot define a procedure that only a contortionist midget with four hands could carry out.

Every advance in technology and in business methods increases the burden on language in business and the responsibility of those who use it. Automation in manufacture replaces muscles with brains; every workman becomes a supervisor; every supervisor, a director. The human element is reduced in quantity and increased in quality; the marvel of humanity is that it rises by sharpened use of language to meet every need. Any person who takes a responsible position in the world of modern business moves away from direct contact with things into the management of men and women whose actions he must direct by language.

A business executive addressing an "Industrial Liaison Symposium" at MIT stated the case for technical writing in terms of cold cash: "The technical report—as a means of transmitting information internally or to the public—is an increasingly important item in company operations. To maintain the competitive advantage derived from competent technical reporting, management should recognize, encourage, and plan for the writing activity at all levels, from that of the individual engineers through the various stages of review and editing to printing in effective format."

The business of writing for business is everybody's business. Business writing must be clear, factual, honest, and accurate. Only the advertiser can play fast and loose with language, hinting at love that will come if you use a certain toothpaste, calling on "medical science" to justify smoking a certain cigarette, wearing a certain girdle, washing with a particular soap. Every other kind of business writing must honor the facts, or business cannot run. Language is the nervous system of all organizations; it cannot be handled too well. Like all other uses of language, writing for business must be prepared for; at the moment of writing you have to go forward on what you know. If your writing fails, the failure is only the end-product of all you have done or not done, through all your life, to communicate with other people in terms that they can understand. The place to start is where you are, reading the books and magazines that the educated read, and writing at every odd moment for that most critical eye— your own. Then you will meet the tests of your career, serene and ready to bring all your powers to bear.

Exercises

1. What justification can you think of for using language that is deliberately obscure or ambiguous? Is this justification called "diplomacy"?

2. Respond to the assertion: The business of business is buying and selling.

3. What role did Lloyd and Warfel see for the technical writer in business? What do the people presently performing the functions that Lloyd and Warfel mention call themselves?

Punctuation

Eric Partridge

When attacking questions about punctuation, Partridge exemplifies the attitude and approach of the modern linguist. Partridge states that "correct punctuation" is the kind presently valued most highly by that segment of the population with whom you are dealing or with whom you wish to identify. The specialist is sometimes technical in his talk with nonspecialists in order to remind his listeners that he *is* a specialist. He wishes to establish his particular qualifications and to identify himself with other specialists, and he does so by using discourse (including punctuation) commonly held to be the mark of specialists. (Note that, of course, Partridge's own punctuation style is British.)

Introductory

§ 1: A Few Opinions

All the parts of Syntaxe have already beene declared. There resteth one generall affection of the whole, disposed thorow every member thereof, as the bloud is thorow the body; and consisteth in the breathing, when we pronounce any *Sentence;* For, whereas our breath is by nature so short, that we cannot continue without a stay to speake long together; it was thought necessarie, as well for the speakers ease, as for the plainer deliverance of the things spoken, to invent this meanes, whereby men, pausing a pretty while, the whole speech might never the worse be understood. *The English Grammar made by Ben Jonson,* written ca. 1617, published in 1640

Points, serving for the better Understanding of Words, are either *Primary, or Secundary.*

Primary Points, which shew their Tone, Sound and Pauses, are eight: four simple and more common; Period, [.] Colon, [:] Semicolon, [;] Comma, [,] and four mixt and less frequent.........................
The mixt Points, are *Erotesis* [?] *Ecphonesis;* [!] *Parenthesis,* ( ) *Parathesis:* [] which have always some simple Point, exprest or understood, in them . . . .
Secundary Points, now shewing Tone, Sound, or Pause, are *four:* Apostrophus, ['] Eclipsis, [–] or [– –] Dieresis, [..] and Hyphen, [-] or ["]. CHARLES BUTLER, *The English Grammar,* 1633

Great care ought to be had in writing, for the due observing of points: for, the neglect thereof will pervert the sence. RICHARD HODGES, *The English Primrose,* 1644

Pointing is the disposal of speech into certain members for more articulate and distinct reading and circumstantiating of writs and papers.

From Eric Partridge, *You Have a Point There* (London: Hamish Hamilton, Ltd., 1953), pp. 3–13. Reprinted by permission of Hamish Hamilton, Ltd.

Message Systems and Subsystems

It rests wholly and solely on concordance, and necessitates a knowledge of grammar. ROBERT MONTEITH, *The True and Genuine Art of Pointing,* 1704

I know, there are some *Persons* who affect to *despise* it, and treat this whole Subject with the utmost *Contempt,* as a Trifle far below their Notice, and a Formality unworthy of *their* Regard: They do not hold it difficult, but *despicable;* and neglect it, as being *above* it.

Yet many learned Men have been highly sensible of its Use; and some ingenious and elegant Writers have condescended to point their Works with Care; and very eminent Scholars have not disdained to teach the Method of doing it with Propriety. JAMES BURROW, *An Essay on the Use of Pointing,* 1771

The pauses which mark the sense, and for this reason are denominated *sentential,* are the same in verse as in prose. They are marked by the usual stops, a comma, a semicolon, a colon, or a period, as the sense requires. NOAH WEBSTER, *Dissertations on the English Language,* 1789

Punctuation is the art of dividing a written composition into sentences, or parts of sentences, by points or stops, for the purpose of marking the different pauses which the sense, and an accurate pronunciation require. LINDLEY MURRAY, *English Grammar,* 1794

The sense, or meaning, of the words is very much dependent upon the points which are used along with the words. WILLIAM COBBETT, *A Grammar of the English Language,* 1819

It has already been frequently shown by writers on the subject that our punctuation-marks do not indicate the most suitable places for pauses in reading aloud; the voice of an intelligent reader ignores some of the textual pointing and introduces breaks at places other than those where there are points. The pointing of matter 'to be sung or said' is, in fact, a subject apart. With regard to constructional pointing it may be urged that in reality it rests on sense and meaning, since grammar is the analysis of the forms in which rational expression is made. We think, however, that all the complexities and divergences and confusions of grammatical pointing arose just because it was not in constant and direct touch with meaning. A PRACTICAL PRINTER, *A Manual of Punctuation,* 1859

Of all the subjects which engage the attention of the compositor, none proves a greater stumbling-block, or is so much a matter of uncertainty and doubt, especially to the mere tyro, as the Art of Punctuation. This arises partly from the necessarily somewhat inexact nature of the art itself, but far more from ignorance of the principles on which its rules ought to be founded, and the illogical construction of the sentences with which the printer has sometimes to deal.   Henry Beadnell (some forty years a Printer's Reader), *Spelling and Punctuation*, 1880

Modern printers make an effort to be guided by logic or grammar alone; it is impossible for them to succeed entirely; but any one who will look at an Elizabethan book with the original stopping will see how far they have moved: the old stopping was frankly to guide the voice in reading aloud, while the modern is mainly to guide the mind in seeing through the grammatical construction.

A perfect system of punctuation, then, that would be exact and uniform, would require separate rhetorical and logical notations . . . Such a system is not to be desired.   H. W. & F. G. Fowler, *The King's English*, 1906

When punctuation was first employed, it was in the role of the handmaid of prose; later the handmaid was transformed by the pedants into a harsh-faced chaperone, pervertedly ingenious in the contriving of stiff regulations and starched rules of decorum; now, happily, she is content to act as an auxiliary to the writer and as a guide to the reader.   Harold Herd, *Everybody's Guide to Punctuation*, 1925

Intellectually, stops matter a great deal. If you are getting your commas, semi-colons, and full stops wrong, it means that you are not getting your thoughts right, and your mind is muddled.   William Temple, Archbishop of York, as reported in *The Observer*, 23 October 1938

We ought to deplore the growing tendency to use only full stops and commas. Punctuation is an invaluable aid to clear writing, and I suggest that far too little importance is attached to it by many journalists.

Frank Whitaker, in an address to the Institute of Journalists: reproduced in *The J.I.J.*, January 1939

Mr Partridge's account of punctuation shows by its wealth of possible effects that punctuation can be made a part of the art of writing— instead of the simple, almost mechanical routine that American schools recommend.   W. Cabell Greet, in his gloss at 'Punctuation' in *Usage and Abusage*, American edition, 1942

We indicate time by means of stops known as punctuation marks. These marks also help to make the sense clear, to show the expression, and to avoid confusion in reading.   L. A. G. Strong, *An Informal English Grammar*, 1943

A thoughtful reading of § 1 will have shown that already in the 17th Century the principal points were being used. It will not have shown that they arose late in the 16th Century and that we owe them to the ingenuity of Aldus Manutius, the distinguished Italian printer (Aldo Manuzio: 1450–1515) whose 'Aldine' Press operated at Venice.

Before him, punctuation had been virtually confined to the period or full stop and, in several countries, to the question mark. Before that, punctuation was unknown. But, as we are not concerned with the history of the subject, I refer the curious to T. F. and M. F. A. Husband's *Punctuation,* 1905, or to the briefer, yet adequate, treatment in Reginald Skelton's *Modern English Punctuation,* revised edition, 1949.

As § 1 shows, there have been two systems of punctuation: the rhetorical or dramatic or elocutionary, seen at its height in Elizabethan and Jacobean plays, but after the 17th Century very rarely used; and the grammatical or constructional or logical, which has always predominated in prose and has predominated in verse since ca. 1660. On the subject of dramatic punctuation, the standard work is Percy Simpson's *Shakespearean Punctuation,* 1911.

But to insist upon the dichotomy *dramatic-grammatical* would be both pedantic and inept. For much of the time, as is inevitable, the two coincide: a speaker tends to pause wherever either logic or grammar makes a pause; and even the most 'logical' or 'grammatical' of punctuators tends, when he is writing dialogue, to point what is clearly an elocutionary or dramatic pause, as in 'He speaks often of freedom. But, he takes good care to avoid going to prison for the cause of freedom', where the comma represents a dramatic pause. (In dialogue, however, the sensible way to indicate that pause would be to italicize 'But', not to punctuate it with a comma.)

The elocutionary element occurs again in the second of these two sentences: 'He intended to finish the task, but then he fell ill' and 'He fell ill; but then, he was always falling ill' and 'He fell ill, but *then* he was always falling ill'. In the first sentence, *then* means 'at that point of time'; in the third, *then* means 'at, or during, that period'; in the second, however, *then* has no temporal meaning. 'He fell ill; but then, he was always falling ill' could have been written '. . .; but he was *always* falling ill'. With *then,* the sentence is much more colloquial and idiomatic; here, *then* is hardly less interjectional than *alas* is in 'He fell ill; but *alas!* he was always falling ill'. However elocutionary *then* may be, the comma is demanded by logic: the omission of this comma would not only create ambiguity, it would positively falsify the intended meaning.

In short, English—or, if you prefer, British and American—punctuation is predominantly constructional or grammatical or logical, yet it has what is in some ways a non-logical, non-grammatical element, necessitated by the part played in speech by intonation and pause and in writing (or printing) by emphasis.

Even that modification slightly exaggerates the importance of logic and the power of grammar. In punctuation, grammar represents parliament, or whatever the elected body happens to be called: logic represents King or President: but the greatest power of all is vested in the people or, rather, in the more intelligent people—in good sense rather than in mere commonsense. Commonsense can and often does produce a humdrum, barely adequate, wholly unimaginative punctuation: good sense (another name for wisdom) can and sometimes does produce a punctuation that is much superior to the barely adequate.

One could write a monograph upon the psychological principles of punctuation. That monograph would form an exercise in psychology and occupy an honourable place on the shelves of a psychologist's library; it would hardly benefit the writer, the journalist, the student; and to the pupil, as to the ordinary person who rarely writes anything other than a frequent cheque or an infrequent letter, it would, so far from being a help, be a hindrance.

The most abysmal low-brow, like the dizziest high-brow, needs punctuation in order to make his meaning clear. The good journalist and the conscientious writer (whether of essays at school or of larger works elsewhere) will find, if he has not already found, that punctuation forms an integral part of composition and an invaluable assistance to both the public expression and perhaps even the private formulation of lucid thinking.

Punctuation too often ranks as an adjunct. In the fact, it should rank as a component. It is not something that one applies as an ornament, for it is part of the structure; so much a part that, without it, the structure would be meaningless—except after an exhausting examination.

Period or Full Stop

The stop that comes at the end of a sentence or of any other complete statement has been called *point*, elliptical for *full* (or *perfect*) *point*; *full* (or *complete*) *pause*; *full stop*; *period*. The second is obsolete; the first, obsolescent. Of the other two, *period* and *full stop*, the former is preferred by most scholars and printers, the latter by most other people. Nobody will go to heaven for using *period*, nor to hell for using *full stop*.

A *period* is so named because it comes at the end of a period, strictly of a periodic sentence, but now loosely apprehended as any sentence, even if it consists of only one word, e.g. 'Yes', elliptical for 'Yes, that is so', 'Yes, I will', etc. Compare the modern catchword 'Period': indicating the end, not only of a statement, a telegram, a letter, but also of a holiday, an indulgence, a permission, and so forth. Compare also Chaucer's 'And there a point, for ended is my tale'.

Full stop virtually explains itself: a full stop, like a full or perfect point, is obviously not an imperfect point or stop, whether as brief as a comma or as clear-cut as a semicolon or as disruptive as a dash or as smooth as a pair of parentheses or as culturedly poised as a colon: here ends the statement, here ends the sentence. The etymology of *period* is helpful, as etymology so often is. *Period*, French *période*, Latin *periodus*, Greek *periodos* (*peri*, around + *hodos*, a way, a road), means literally a going round, hence a rounding off, especially as applied to time, more especially still the time represented by a breathing. At the end of a breathing, a sentence, a statement, one pauses to take breath, either because one must or because it is convenient to do so. This explains why the elocutionary term *pause* and, for the full stop, *full pause* were formerly used as synonymous with (*full*) *point* or (*full*) *stop*.

The one indispensable stop is the full stop. In most simple sentences —those containing one verb—this stop suffices. In the following examples, only an over-punctuator would increase the punctuation:

> He went home early that day.
> He could hardly have done anything else.
> He knew all about it.
> Quite unconcernedly she continued her knitting.
> She said No.

Many compound and some complex sentences require nothing but a full stop. A consideration of the following examples will show the kind of compound sentence where this is permissible and, indeed, correct:

> He went home early that day and got the chores finished by seven o'clock.
> He went home early that day in order to do a number of small things that could not very well be left until the next morning.
> He went home early that day and finished his chores before he went to bed.
> He did not get home early that day because he had been delayed in town.
> He did not get home early that day because he had been delayed in town by a friend he had not met for quite twenty years.
> When I saw him I departed as soon as ever I could.

The factor common to all these sentences is continuity of subject.

Take that last sentence:

> When I saw him I departed as soon as I could.

If we changed it to

> When I saw him he ran away,

we should not be wrong; some elegant writers, however, would put a comma after 'him'. An abrupt change of subject usually demands a comma, especially if the conjunction happens to be 'but' or 'however' or 'for' or 'since'. For instance,

> I looked hard at him but he took no notice of me

would be improved thus:

> I looked hard at him, but he took no notice of me.

That, however, is to anticipate.

Beginners, especially children, overdo the period, inasmuch as they seem to think that no other stop exists. This is what the Fowler brothers call 'the spot-plague'. Few practised writers would commit themselves to such simplicity as this:

> My father drove to the town yesterday. He had to go there because he needed flour and salt and sugar for the house and equipment for the farm and some special food for some hens that seemed to be off their food for some reason or other. When he reached town he went straight to the store and got what he needed before he went to arrange with the agent for agricultural machinery for the delivery of a new tractor and certain repairs to be done to the harvester. But he did find the time for a cup of I don't know whether it was tea or coffee. The poor man felt so thirsty that he thought that his throat had been cut or so he told my mother when he finally got back home after dusk. She said that he ought to have had a square meal because it didn't do him any good to go for so long on such a tiring day without food. But he said he had been so busy and so anxious not to overlook anything that he wasn't even aware that time was passing so rapidly and that if he wasn't careful he would be caught in the dark.

Nevertheless, the lack of all punctuation other than that of the full stops is much less tedious in such a passage, where, in fact, the unrelieved full stop is shown at full stretch and almost at its best, than in the following:—

He was a good man. He was a brave man. He was also a very kind man. He had a very kind wife. She was not brave but she was certainly very good. He and she formed an almost ideal couple. At least I think so. You may think differently. I shouldn't blame you if you did. They were very popular with everyone in the district. It was a large district. And so their popularity meant a good deal both to themselves and to the district. There exist few people like them. Perhaps I should say 'live' instead of 'exist.' But I must return to my subject. This couple lived in that district for eighty years. They lived there from birth to death. That is a long time. I mean eighty years is a long time. But perhaps I am boring you. I must stop. You won't speak to me again if I don't stop now. So I do at last stop.

The educated will say, But nobody writes like that. The trouble is that a vast number of people write exactly like that: and some of them, if not well-educated and cultured, are certainly not illiterate; a few pass for (and, in the sobering fact, are) averagely educated persons. If anyone objects, But that is a matter of style, not a matter of education, some such reply as the following could be made:

Punctuation is not something apart from style, which, after all, means no more than the way in which a person writes, whether badly or well; punctuation does form part of English in its practical aspects, a part far more important than most of us realize. The ability to write at least a letter is extremely important; and if you think that you can write an even passable letter without knowing how to use one and preferably two other stops (comma and semicolon), you are making a grave mistake. To go further: if you think you can write a good business report or an essay or an article, without knowing also how to employ at least two of the remaining stops—the colon, the dash, and parentheses—then you are probably over-estimating your own abilities as a writer and the intelligence of your readers.

Punctuation is not something that, like a best suit of clothes, you put on for special occasions. Punctuation is not something you add to writing, even the humblest: it forms an inescapable part of writing. To change the metaphor, punctuation might be compared to the railway line along which the train (composition, style, writing) must travel if it isn't to run away with its driver (the writer of even a note to the butcher).

To revert to the period or full stop. It ends a sentence, i.e. a statement, i.e. the expression of a self-contained or complete thought. So, of course, does a question mark or an exclamation mark. . . .

Then there is the non-constructional, non-syntactical use of the period in, for instance, 'i.e.' and 'e.g.' and 'Prof.': that is, in abbreviation. . . .

But there remain several uses relevant to the present chapter. Examine the following sentences:

She did not dislike him. Far from it.

He acted as though he were an all-powerful dictator. Not that he ever would be one.

You could hardly have been there. Of course not.

'Far from it' and 'Of course not' are neither complete thoughts nor even sentences. They form a kind of shorthand for 'She liked him very much' and 'Of course you could not have been there'. 'Not that he ever would be one' may be a complete sentence, although some grammarians contend that sentences of this sort are imperfect; it certainly is not a complete, self-contained thought, for strictly it belongs to 'He acted as though he were an all-powerful dictator'. Many writers would prefer the single sentence, 'He acted as though he were an all-powerful dictator—not that he would ever be one'. . . . Perhaps a better example is this:

He said that he intended to commit suicide. As if he would.

There, 'As if he would' represents 'Yet he intended to do nothing of the sort'.[1]

Of this kind of imperfect sentence there is a variation, equivalent to an intermediate stage, for in addition to

The angry man protested. Vehemently.

we have

The angry man protested. Protested vehemently.

'Protested vehemently' merely omits the subject, presumably 'He'. . . .

An Anomaly. There is one conclusion that is left unconcluded. After one's signature at the end of a letter (or note) one omits the period; even in

Your loving
Ann Smith
(not much longer to be Smith)

—for a period is felt to be pedantic.

Exercises

1. If you had been compiling this book, would you have left the introductory quotations from archaic sources as a part of this selection? Why or why not?

[1] A more forceful writer would probably have punctuated 'As if he would' thus: 'As if he would!' The dot-obsessed would have written: 'As if he would . . .'

2. Do you think Meadow would agree with Partridge about the importance of punctuation? Do you think Meadow might call "punctuation" by another name? If so, what would that name be and why would he use it?

3. Would you agree that every punctuation point has one set of proper uses and that these proper uses never overlap?

You Can't Write Writing

Wendell Johnson

Johnson's essay discusses the quality of responses to writing efforts. If you are satisfied with the results you are achieving with your writing, you will probably read the article, nod agreeably, murmur "Of course," and turn to another problem. But if you are not fully satisfied with the results you are obtaining, or if you are seriously interested in the further study of written communication, you would do well to take to heart Johnson's words: A communicator must know his subject matter and receiver. An artist, for example, cannot demonstrate his technique without putting color on his brush and creating a painting; a writer cannot write significantly without concern for the content of his message and for the reader to whom it is directed.

The late Clarence Darrow, while speaking one day to a group of professors of English and others of kindred inclination, either raised or dismissed the basic problem with which his listeners were concerned by asking, "Even if you do learn to speak correct English, who are you going to talk it to?"

What Mr. Darrow was contending can be summarized in the statement that the effective use of the English language is more important than the "correct" use of it, and that if you can speak English "correctly," but not effectively, it does not matter very much "who you talk it to." I agreed that day, ten years ago, with Mr. Darrow's contention, and I still do, but whereas ten years ago his remarks served to dismiss for me the problem of the teaching of English, they serve now, in a new context of experience,

Wendell Johnson, "You Can't Write Writing," *ETC.*, I, No. 1 (August 1943), 25–32; reprinted in S. I. Hayakawa (ed.), *Language, Meaning, and Maturity* (New York: Harper & Row, Publishers, 1954), and in S. I. Hayakawa (ed.), *The Use and Misuse of Language* (Greenwich, Conn.: Fawcett World Library, 1962). Copyright 1943, 1954, and 1962 by International Society for General Semantics.

to raise that problem to a position of peculiar educational and social significance. For, like many others, I have come to take a serious view of the apparently astonishing discrepancy between the opportunity and responsibility of the teachers of English and the actual contributions which they appear to make to the efficiency and well-being of individuals and of society.

The point of view which I have to present with regard to this problem has gradually developed during the decade that I have spent, sitting near the end of the educational conveyer belt, helping to put certain finishing touches on the human products of the scholastic mill. This is a way of saying that my experience has been chiefly with graduate students. When they arrive in the graduate college they have had, as a minimum, sixteen years of formal education. During practically every one of those sixteen (or more) years they have undergone some kind of training specifically designed to enhance their skill in the use of the English language. In spite of this, there falls upon me, as upon other directors of masters' and doctors' dissertations, the task of teaching graduate students how to write clear and meaningful and adequately organized English.

What are the linguistic shortcomings that the teachers of English seem unable to correct? Or do they in some measure nurture them? First of all, it is to be made clear that grammatical errors are not particularly serious. Whether or not they find anyone to "talk it to," the majority of graduate students have been taught most of the rudiments of "correct" English. In fact, it appears that the teachers of English teach English so poorly largely because they teach grammar so well. They seem to confuse or identify the teaching of grammar with the teaching of writing. In any event what they have failed to teach my graduate students about writing is not grammar. It is skill in achieving factually meaningful statements, and skill in organizing statements into an order consistent with the purposes for which the statements are made. The students have not been taught how adequately to achieve either precision or systematic arrangement in the written representation of facts. This can be stated in another and more significant way of saying that they have not been taught how to use language for the purpose of making highly reliable maps of the terrain of experience.

These students exemplify the simple fact that although one may have learned how to write with mechanical correctness, one may still have to learn how to write with significance and validity. One of my friends, who is a particularly astute investigator of the psychology of reading, has stated essentially the same problem by saying that the one place in which a child is not likely to learn to read is the reading class, for the simple reason that one cannot read reading. One can only read history or geometry or biology, etc. If the child reads such material in the reading class, then it is difficult to see how the reading class differs appreciably from the classes in history, geometry, and other subjects. If the child does not read such material in the reading class, then the reading class must differ from these others, but in a puzzling way, for it may be that the reading teacher is actually making the amazing effort to get the child to read reading.

In the teaching of writing, or any other of the language skills, the same problem appears. One cannot write writing, any more than one can read reading. One can only write, just as one can only read, history, or geography, or physiology, or some other such subject about which writing can be done. One can, of course, write about writing, but what one writes about writing will have little, if any, significance, except insofar as one writes about writing about something else. We have to deal here with a very general, and a very crucial, problem. What is true of reading and writing is true, also, of speaking. It holds for any kind of symbolizing. Just as one cannot, with significance, read reading, or write writing, or speak speaking, except insofar as one reads about something, or writes about something, or speaks about something, so one cannot, with significance, symbolize symbolizing in general except insofar as one symbolizes the symbolizing of something.

It seems clear to me, as I attempt to analyze the writing difficulties of graduate students, and as I ponder over my own experiences as a student of English, that these considerations, sketched immediately above, are crucial. The teacher of English appears to attempt to place the emphasis upon writing, rather than upon writing-about-something-for-someone. From this it follows quite inevitably that the student of English fails in large measure to learn the nature or the significance of clarity or precision and of organization in the written representation of facts.

He learns grammatical correctness reasonably well, because that is emphasized. But so long as the student's primary anxieties are made to revolve around the task of learning to spell, punctuate, and observe the rules of syntax, he is not likely to become keenly conscious of the fact that when he writes he is, above all, communicating. If he is to learn to communicate effectively, he must realize that his first obligation to his reader is not to be grammatically fashionable, but to be clear and coherent. One does not just communicate; one communicates something to someone. And the something communicated is not the words used in the communication, but whatever those words represent. Moreover, the degree to which there is communication depends precisely upon the degree to which the words represent the same thing for the receiver or reader that they do for the sender or writer. And the degree to which they do is an index of the clarity of the communication or written statement. Thus, clarity can be *measured*, not just "felt" or "appreciated," but measured, in terms of the ascertainable agreement between writer and reader, and among various readers, as to precisely what the words of the writer represent.

My graduate students have not been taught this. They write as if they had been trained to observe a principle of *caveat lector*. Such a principle, strange as it may seem, is championed, in one form or another, by certain teachers of English. Mr. Cleanth Brooks, Jr., writing on the subject of communication in poetry in the journal, *American Prefaces*, in 1940, expresses this curious point of view in these words:

> The theory of communication throws the burden of proof on the poet, overwhelmingly and at once—the reader tells the poet: here I am; it's your job to get it across to me—when he ought to be assuming the burden of proof himself. Now the modern poet has thrown the weight of responsibility on the reader.

I have quoted Mr. Brooks because he has succeeded in stating with unusual conciseness this strange notion that the writer is properly under no obligation to be communicative. I do not wish, on the other hand, to be understood as saying that a reader has no obligation to try to meet a genuinely original (and therefore difficult) writer halfway, for obviously many writers and poets, dissatisfied with the clichés of their time and trying to create new ways of feeling (i.e., to recanalize the reader's semantic reactions), must necessarily rely upon the reader's willingness to accept a revised vocabulary of an unfamiliar set of symbols. But this is a problem only in extremely advanced levels of artistic composition. In undergraduate instruction, even to imply that a writer has no obligations to his readers is to become, whether one wishes to or not, an advocate of obfuscation.

Such advocates of obfuscation apparently teach fairly well, if it is they who have instructed my graduate students. They have never learned, so far as I can see, to take the reader seriously into consideration. They do not, to be sure, artfully avoid clarity; they artlessly fail to achieve it. The contention that in writing they are communicating, that they are addressing a reader, simply strikes them as a novel point of view. They do not rebel against it; many of them just don't understand it.

This basic notion of communication, however, is not extraordinarily difficult to explain, and as it begins to sink in, and when the students have seen a few demonstrations, not of the reading or criticizing of communications, but of the *process* of communicating by means of writing, they are at least prepared to understand that there are techniques of clarity. Moreover, they are able to understand that these techniques have something to do with effectiveness in writing—unless one means by writing a gyring and gimbling in the wabe of literary slithy toves, or unless one believes the excuse offered by frustrated literary midwives: namely, the "only-God-can-make-a-tree" theory that effectiveness cannot be taught at all. But this definition of "writing" and this theory of "effectiveness" have practically nothing to do with the kind of writing that involves communication. For communication is achieved by virtue of clarity, as this is defined in terms of agreement between writer and reader, or among various readers, as to what the writer is referring to. The ability to achieve clarity in this sense, and thus communicative effectiveness, is a tree that others besides God can make, at least in a rough fashion.

This discussion is not designed to take the place of a textbook for the teaching of effective communicative writings, but it is offered in the hope that a brief statement of a few simple principles upon which such writing is based might serve at least to raise the question as to why these principles are not more adequately taught by English instructors.

The first of these principles has already been given in the statement that clearness depends upon, and can be measured in terms of, the degree of agreement between the writer and his readers as to what the words of the writer represent. Simply by striving for a high degree of such agreement, the writer discovers, in some measure, his ingenuity in achieving it. He discovers the usefulness of conditional and quantifying terms, the confusion created by leaving out significantly differentiating details, the degree to which the meaning of a term varies from context to context, and the kinds of differences he must allow for among his readers' habits of interpreting words. He learns to rely less on the dictionary and more on the linguistic habits of the people for whom he writes. He discovers that literary posing, pleasurable as it may be, usually can be enjoyed only at the expense of effective communication—that Chesterton's paradoxes or Paul de Kruif's chronic astonishment are more titillating than informative. He discovers that there are various levels of abstraction, and that if he goes systematically from lower to higher levels he can use so-called abstract words and still be reasonably clear.

Above all, perhaps, he discovers the basic significance of order, or relations, or structure, or organization. This matter of structural relationships has wide ramifications, and no writer ever exhausts it, but the student quickly grasps some of its more obvious aspects, if he is striving for agreement between himself and his reader. It does not take him long to understand that the organization of what he writes should correspond to the organization of what he is writing about if the reader is to follow him readily. The graduate students with whom I work frequently have difficulty organizing their descriptions of experimental techniques or procedures, and I have found that it is more helpful to refer them to a cookbook than to a textbook on composition. By examining a cookbook they see at once that the organization of a description of procedure is determined simply by the order of the events that make up the procedure. First you do a, and then b, and then c, and you write it in that order because you do it in that order. This simple principle of order is fundamental in practically all descriptive, narrative, and expository writing, and it is obvious to anyone who is attempting to be considerate of the reader.

One might suppose that graduate students would know this, but in spite of the years they have spent in English courses most of them seem not to have learned much about it. The more significant fact is that, as a rule, they learn quite readily to apply this simple principle, once it is clearly explained and demonstrated to them. In this case, certainly, one can make a tree that either God or the English teachers forgot to make.

One aspect of organization that seems to have eluded practically all graduate students is that involved in the making of transitions. Even those who have been taught how to lay beads in a row have not been taught how to string them. Just as the order of what one writes is determined by the order of the parts or events involved in what one is writing about, so the ways in which transitions are made in the writing are determined by the ways in which the parts or events are related in the realities one is describing, narrating, or explaining. The ability to move from one sentence or paragraph or chapter to the next, in such a way as to blend them into a unified whole, is largely dependent upon an understanding of the reasons for going from one to the next, of why one statement should follow another instead of the reverse, of why one should say, "It follows, then," rather than "But." And these reasons are found in the character of the relations existing among the details of that about which the writing is being done. This becomes obvious to one who is not trying to write writing, but who is attempting, rather, to write-about-something-for-someone.

Another principle underlying communicative writing is that clarity is a prerequisite to validity. It is to be considered that statements that flow beautifully and are grammatically superb may be, also, utterly devoid of factual meaning, or meaningful but vague, or precise but invalid. For writing to be effective, in the sense in which I am using this term, it may or may not be grammatically correct, but it must be both clear and valid. It can be clear without having validity, but if it is unclear its validity cannot well be determined. It must, then, first of all, be clear; it must be that before the question of its validity can even be raised. We ask the writer, "What do you mean?" before we ask, "How do you know?" Until we reach agreement as to precisely what he is writing about, we cannot possibly reach agreement as to whether, or in what degree, his statements are true.

Only to the extent that the various readers of a statement agree as to the specific conditions or observations required for ascertaining its validity can the question of its validity have meaning. And the extent to which the readers of the statement agree on these conditions is, of course, indicative of the extent to which the statement is clear. If a statement is such that its readers do not agree at all as to how it might be verified or refuted, the statement may be "beautiful" or "rich in meaning" or grammatically irreproachable, but it is also, from the point of view of scientific courses such as I am teaching, nonsense. It cannot be demonstrated to be valid or invalid, and is meaningful, therefore, to its author, possibly to his English teacher, and perhaps to his psychiatrist.

My graduate students have not learned this, either. They show this in a particularly disturbing manner when they first attempt to state the topics or problems they propose to investigate in undertaking their theses. They quite characteristically propose problems which preclude the possibility of clear discussion. They propose questions for investigation, for which they desire to obtain precise answers, but which are so stated as to be unanswerable. Apparently they have never been taught that one cannot get a precise answer to a vague question—that the terminology of the question limits the clarity and thus the validity of the answer. Many students are so befuddled on this point that they do not recognize any relation at all between clarity and validity. They actually assume, for example, that they can ask, "What causes personality maladjustments?" without specifying what they mean by "causes," or by "personality," or by "maladjustments," or what observations one is to make in order to comply with their definition of "what." Many of them appear to have been taught that to eliminate the vagueness of a question or statement is to destroy its "richness of meaning"—that for a statement to be "full of meaning" it must not mean anything in particular!

Even though they have been so taught, and come, therefore, to the graduate college quite untrained in the writing of valid statements, they can be taught, to a considerable degree, to gauge the validity of what they write. They can be trained to do this by being trained, first, to write clearly. For when a statement is made clearly—when there is reasonable agreement among its readers as to what it represents in the realm of fact— its validity can be judged, or a procedure for determining its degree of validity can be devised.

In summary, then, what graduate students, as I know them, have been well taught—and what, in my judgment, their English instructor should have been able to teach them, because the students do learn readily —is the ability to write a clear, organized, unified, and valid document. They have been made familiar with grammar, for the most part, and they have picked up a few tricks of literary flavoring. The grammar can be used to advantage; most of the literary condiments have to be chucked.

There appear to be three main reasons for the English instructors' failure. The first is that they do not appear to utilize to any considerable extent the principle of teaching by example. They tell the student how to write and how not to have written, but they don't, as a rule, do any actual writing for him or with him. They show him examples of what has been written, but no examples of something being written.

To try to learn to write by reading literature that has already been written and thoroughly jelled, instead of by observing the actual writing of literature, is much like trying to learn to bake a cake by eating one, instead of by watching the baker. One should teach by example, and what the teachers of English forget is that there are no examples of writing in the grammar book or the anthology; there are only generalized blueprints of statements yet unwritten and examples of something already written—cakes that were baked yesterday. The teacher herself has to provide the examples of writing to demonstrate the process. She must bake the cake of written English, not merely eat the cake that Hawthorne baked, as she stands before the class.

The second, and a more grave, reason for their failure is that they appear to place the emphasis on "writing," rather than on writing-about-something-for-someone. You cannot write writing. Or, at least if you do, you are not likely to learn how to write with clarity and validity, because they are not important to one who merely writes writing. Unless the emphasis is placed upon writing as a form of communication and directed very definitely, therefore, to an actual, live reader, the importance of clarity, organization, and validity is not likely to become very apparent. Their importance becomes obvious, and the means of achieving them suggest themselves more or less readily, the moment one begins seriously to write about-something-for-someone.

The third and final point in this "diagnosis" of English instruction is that teachers of English, with apparently only a few exceptions, cling tenaciously to two strange theories. The first is that writing is an art, and the second is that it cannot be taught. What they seem to mean when they say that writing is an art is that writing does not have to say anything—except to the reader who has "appreciation"—that writing is at its best when it is a form of expression *qua* expression.

In teaching the student to write, if one takes this view of "writing as an art," there is no point—in fact, there is a strong argument to the contrary—in training the student to express himself clearly or with validity. For truth that is "not art" would be of no value, and if art that is clear is regarded as a contradiction in terms (and it seems to be so regarded by some), there would remain only truth that is vague as the ideal of the teachers of English whom we are here discussing. But in communicative writing, truth is never vague, for unless a statement is clear, the degree to which it is true cannot be determined. All of which goes far to explain how students can reach the graduate college without learning how to produce effective communicative writing.

The explanation is extended when we recall the other theory, so popular among some teachers of English, that real effectiveness in writing, since it is an "art," cannot be taught at all. Only God can make a tree; the teacher of English can only water the tree with verbal dew in the hope of keeping it green, and even the value of doing that is debatable. Teachers frequently boast of having "discovered" a writer; it seems that this in itself is regarded as no mean accomplishment. It is also to be noted that writers are sometimes said to have been "influenced" by a teacher. But when a teacher has "discovered" a writer and "influenced" him, he cannot further add to what the genes have done, nor detract from what the fates will do. Presumably, then, he doesn't try. And this pedagogical swooning by the teachers of English, on the theory that you can't make a silk purse out of a sow's ear, results in their making a great many sows' ears out of silk purses. It is not a question of the truth or falsity of their theory that effective writing cannot be taught, although this theory is probably not as largely true as many teachers of English suppose. The significant point is that the theory makes for unimaginative and lackadaisical teaching. Even God's trees might benefit from some systematic pruning and spraying.

My own narrow concern with all this lies in the fact that the ineffectiveness of the English instruction in our schools makes for a serious difficulty in the graduate college in all its branches. But the problem has an importance far more vast than this fact could ever give to it. For the ability of the individual, and of groups of individuals, to use language clearly and with validity is basic to personal efficiency and general development—it is basic to sanity itself—and it is fundamental to intelligent social organization and to the adequate management of national and international problems. The teachers of English in our schools and universities have been and are being entrusted with the heavy responsibility of training the members of our society in the effective communicative use of our language. It is not a responsibility that they can meet appropriately merely by teaching the formalism of grammar, or superciliously disclaim by asserting that effective writing is an art and cannot be taught.

Effective writing is a human necessity in anything resembling a democratic culture, and this becomes increasingly true as the culture becomes increasingly complex. If the effective use of language cannot be taught, or if it is not to be taught to a far greater extent than it has been, we may well have occasion to despair of the grand experiment dreamed by Voltaire, championed by Washington and Franklin, and cherished by the American people through many generations. And if we must despair of that, then truly, even if you do learn to speak correct English, it may well not seem to matter very much "who you talk it to." For when the people cannot adequately speak or write their language, there arise strong men to speak and write it for them—and "at" them.

The issues of which I write are by no means to be regarded as academic issues. We are a symbolic class of life. To say that we are human is to say, above all and with incalculable significance, that our problems, as individuals, as groups, and as a world culture, are symbolic problems. They are problems that center around the symbols of government, the symbols of finance and general economy, of social status, of power and prestige, of class and race. They are the problems involved in the great institutionalized symbol systems of the Church, the Law, the State. They are problems of meaning, of evaluation, or orientation, processes which, on human levels, are predominantly symbolic in character. It is not the vestige of some forebear's whim that the whole structure of our educational system is founded squarely on the three R's, for reading, writing, and the use of numbers are forms of behavior in the absence of which *human* society would disintegrate and vanish. The degree to which these forms of behavior are cultivated and made adequate determines, more than does anything else, the degree to which a symbolic class of life may escape the threat of self-destruction and achieve cultural maturity. Our maladjustment, no less than our genius, as individuals and as groups, lies in our way of responding to and with symbols.

The place of the teacher of English in the structure of a symbolic society is, thus and indeed, not one to be occupied by petulant little men engrossed in verbal "fancy work." It is not too much to say that our possibilities for progress are determined, and limited, by those who instruct us in the use of our language. This view is as disheartening, perhaps, as it is challenging, but the more challenging it is to some, the less disheartening it need be to others.

Exercises

1. Rank in order the authors in the "Message Systems" section of this readings book on prescriptiveness/permissiveness. Where does Johnson fall? Are the ranked authors equally spaced along the ranking dimension, in your judgment? How would you display graphically the intervals between ranks?

2. Johnson talks about structural relations. What does punctuation have to do with these?

3. Does Johnson suggest sacrificing all rules except that of effectiveness?

Communication: Practical Interdependencies in Writing, Reading, Talking, and Listening

J. H. Campbell
Hal W. Hepler

Introduction

We write so that you may read. We talk so that others may listen. When we do these things, we make estimates of the probable behavior of our readers and listeners. Because you are our readers, these estimates have to do with the range and diversity of your behavior repertory. Have you ever tried to write about something you thought complex and important? If you have, you have experienced the same concerns and uncertainties that beset us as we write for you now.

A letter to a loved one in whose love you feel secure is not what we are talking about. Perhaps a letter to a loved one in whose love you do *not* feel secure would be a closer approximation. But even in this latter instance, you probably feel that you have a fairly good idea of who this person is and what many of his or her characteristics are. Your knowledge of him or her is, probably, at first hand. But our knowledge of you is only inferential and statistical. Your knowledge is limited, too, whenever you write for a mass audience. Even if you are not writing a textbook for college undergraduates, you can still find a large number of similarities between our concerns and many of the concerns that you have in your everyday communications.

We will now try to tell you what and how we thought about you. Often, you are expected to draw your own inferences about what authors or speakers thought about you, or else you are expected to remain unaware of the opportunity to draw inferences.

You, our readers, are probably enrolled in a college course and are required to read our book. Therefore you may wish to predict what the instructor of the course will find in this written message to ask you about in order to infer from your response whether or not you have read the message. In most instances, your interpretation will have to have a resemblance, at least, to the interpretation the instructor has formed. That is reasonable, since he will have been providing you with a context for your interpretation. This context may consist of his written and spoken evaluations of your own written and spoken messages, as well as his lectures and remarks, which are designed to give you some notion of what he considers appropriate criteria for interpreting messages in general and these essays in particular. But you may not appreciate the existence of that context. We have some idea of what some of the contexts may be like within which interpretations of this written message are likely to be made. But we have no way of knowing exactly which of them is in use by a particular reader's instructor or by a particular reader. We do have some statistical distributions in mind that may help us, and we'll try to talk about those a bit later. Right now we'd like to go on with our analysis of what we think you may be like.

We have some notion of the age range into which most of our readers are likely to fall. And we have a notion of the age range into which most of the readers who are most important to us are likely to fall. This latter group consists of the readers who decide whether or not they will use this book as a text in their courses and, therefore, whether they will require it of their students. They are our most important readers for at least one very good reason. If they are not satisfied that there is something of value in this book that is usefully made available to their students by having them read the book, then the larger numbers of people whom we would like to have read and interpret the book will never have an opportunity to do so. A faculty member traditionally acts like a gatekeeper for most of his students.[1]

The two age ranges overlap only slightly, if at all. More important than the difference in age is the difference in experience. For example, we are confident that relatively few members of the first group will have as many earned academic degrees as those in the second group. And this difference in degrees held is direct evidence of experiential differences.

If we must get the book adopted in order for it to be read, then the strategy of composition will undoubtedly contain components that have more to do with those who make adoption decisions than with those who are, in some sense, the final consumers of the book.

Do you begin to get some feeling for the extent to which communication is necessarily complicated? The situation partially analyzed above, in which our desire to "reach" one audience requires us to "reach" another, is, perhaps, a little like wishing your best girl "good evening" under the eyes and ears of her mother. At any rate, this situation is not unique, nor even unusual. It is the general case in most communication situations.

---

[1] Compare "gatekeeper" with "uncertainty absorber" in the March and Simon essay in this volume.

What do we like to listen to? What do we like to read? People tend to listen to people whose speech patterns conform to those patterns the listener thinks "appropriate." People tend to read that which is written in ways that conform to those ways the reader thinks "appropriate."

Before further examining this complex of dimensions called "appropriateness," we need to look at some other, equally complex, dimensions. There is, of course, the dimension of time and energy commitment. When the need is strong enough, a human being will undertake the grievous task of mastering that multiplicity of special terminologies (jargon) control of which is the *sine qua non* of the Ph. D. or M. D.

Learning to control these terminologies may include the frustrating task of learning the "language" of human behavior or the incredibly complicated language of the genetic code controlling growth in the human organism. If the need and desire are great enough, the message—from a man's way of using facial expression, posture, and gesture to indicate his internal emotional states to the indeterminate probability shifts of genetic material within the cells of a growing organism—will be, somehow and at whatever cost, decoded and interpreted. So, when need and desire are maximum, the time and energy commitment is maximum.

A puzzle is left us by the semantics of "work" in Newtonian physics. If you push against a boulder all day you will be tired, and you will have expended energy, but no "work" will have been done if the boulder has not moved. If need and desire are strong enough, people will continue to exert themselves for a considerable time without direct evidence of achievement. Such persistence may be seen in the adherence of a bureaucrat to a particular procedure when he can see it is outmoded.

Reading can be like pushing against a boulder, and comprehension like work. You can read without comprehending just as you can push without working. But the need to know and the desire to learn, if sufficiently great, can generate a sufficient commitment to the task of comprehending the phenomenon, whether it be words on paper or the dance of the double helix.

Reading

Reading is done by the brain and not by the eyes. Eyes are only an input-output device, although, of all the input-output devices attached to the brain, they are the most intimately attached. Reading at great speed seems to be mostly a matter of using an adequate sampling procedure. If a sampling procedure is not the exact analogue, neither is the steady wheel-to-pavement contact of the automobile tire traveling down the road at high speed. Be careful: avoid thinking that all there is to reading rapidly and with comprehension and retention is "skimming." It is much more nearly the problem of intelligently designing a sampling procedure. It is a matter of knowing what to look for. And *that* has to do with the power and elegance with which you think rather than with how you read (move your eyes across the pages).

The faster you read, the more adept you become at assessing the necessity for reading a particular message at all. The more you have read, the more complex and useful are your interpretations of what you are reading, because of the extension of your information store and the resultant increase in your capacity to synthesize.[2]

A few people read a lot. College students think they read a lot. One estimate is that college students read, on the average, fifty books a year. That sounds like a lot, doesn't it? But let's look at it a bit more closely. If we assume, for the sake of the argument, that the average college students reads at about 400 words per minute, and that the average book is 300 pages long with an average of 300 words per page, then college students spend only about 3⅔ hours per *week* reading.

When we say "read a lot," we mean two hours per day or more. And people who read that much tend to read faster than 400 words per minute. Let's just turn the calculations around. Let's assume only a modest increase in the reading rate—to, say, 500 words per minute. And let's assume our criterion minimum amount of time spent reading per day—two hours—as the average. In a year our reader will have read 242⅔ of the "standard" books used in the previous calculation. That is almost five times the reading consumption of the average college student, according to these figures.

If you are reading some 22,000,000 words per year, what does that imply about your discriminatory powers? We think it implies that they, of necessity, become honed to a finer edge. Why? If you spend ten minutes pondering and meditating on a 200-word paragraph, you have used up the time in which you might otherwise have "read" 5,000 words. Awareness of this fact, of the cost in lost opportunity of meditation, causes the reader to exercise more care in the selection of those paragraphs on which he will ponder. Or, at the least, it will heighten his resistance to indiscriminate pondering.

Don't forget that the rates at which individuals process information are variable. There is some reason to suppose that the greater the store of integrated prior inputs you have accumulated *and integrated,* the larger the number of inputs you can handle per unit of time, or the fewer units of time you will need in order to handle a set of inputs.[3]

[2] See H. M. Schroder, M. S. Driver, and S. Streufert, *Human Information Processing* (New York: Holt, Rinehart and Winston, Inc., 1967).

[3] See especially chapters 3 and 4 in Schroder et al, *Human Information Processing.*

Then, too, there is something we shall call the social-psychological context. One of the more important parts of this context might be the extent to which the reader is confident of his assessment of the goals and motivations of the writer. Again, this is a matter of interpretation.

Writing

One reason writing may be so painful is that we predict our readers' reactions as we write. This places us in a situation analogous to that of a speaker. But the analogy breaks down because few of us are as confident of our ability to predict accurately the reactions of some individual or group of people to what we write as we are of our ability to "read" the responses they make to us if we are speaking face to face, no matter how lacking in confidence we may be in the latter situation.

Writing rates, expressed in words per minute or pages per hour, are as various as the tricks we play on ourselves to get ourselves started writing. We would be willing to guess that every 250 words of final copy costs about one man hour. That hour does not include preparing to write, whatever that may involve. All that is included is the drafting of the original and one careful revision, plus the usual copy-editing and proof-reading.

It is interesting to note that, if our estimates are anywhere near being accurate, our heavy reader annually consumes the output of 88,000 writer hours. That's the annual output of approximately 50 to 100 writers.

Many people write for you, and they are aware that they are competing for your attention. No only are they competing with each other, but, even more important, they are competing with all the other possible input sources in your environment. This is true for anyone who emits a message.

Listening

We listen all the time. We sleep with our eyes closed, but we can be awakened by a change in the sound pattern that exceeds some built-in rate-of-change threshold or warning level. True, we can be awakened by a sudden change in the light intensity of the room in which we sleep. But there is no lid to shutter the ear. There may be a reduced sensitivity of the central nervous system that inhibits the processing of data from other parts of the body, but the ear continues to operate with less mechanical blockage than the eye while the mind rests.

Though work has been done with such things as compressed speech, for the most part we tend to speak at rates between 140 and 180 words per minute.[4] Though there may be some sense in which a man "hears more than is spoken" (as well as reading more than is written), here we are interested only in the sense in which you cannot listen faster than someone speaks. You can, however, process inputs faster than someone else can provide them if he is operating only in the speech output mode. Remember that if it is possible to process inputs to the central nervous system from the eyes at the rate of 400 or more words per minute, and a speaker provides you with only 150 words per minute, you will obviously have some processing capacity left over. (We make the assumption, for the sake of only the present argument, that one spoken word equals one written word.)

What will be done with this surplus processing capacity? First of all, it is probably misleading to refer to it as "surplus." Our environments are rich enough so that we almost always have something for our minds to do. So something else *will* be done with that processing capacity of 250 or more words per minute. Very often, especially since only a minor part of anyone's language-processing capacity is in use to handle your spoken inputs, he is no longer attending to your inputs at all. And that is most particularly true when he is able to predict what you will say next with either very high or very low confidence. If he predicts with high confidence he becomes bored. If he predicts with low confidence he is made tired and anxious by this uncertainty. We have all had trouble staying awake in college classes for both of these reasons.

Listening, then, requires a greater discipline on the part of the listener than does reading, simply because there is such an apparent mismatch between the input volume variety and the input capacity of the listener. If this greater discipline is not available, then the listener must be powerfully motivated. Motivation and discipline, in this sense, are inversely related.

Speaking

Some psychologists have suggested that there may be physical bases for the behavioral states we call "emotions." A boy running through a graveyard at night would produce, by the act of running, shifts in the chemical makeup of his body, especially the blood tissue, that would heighten his subjective awareness of his overall state. Put more simply, the first person affected by any behavior is he who exhibits it.

By the same token, he who is first affected by a verbal behavior is he who utters it. And herein lies one of the major control or discipline

[4] See Herbert L. Friedman and Raymond L. Johnson, "Compressed Speech: Correlates of Listening Ability," *The Journal of Communication* 18 (September 1968). (This whole issue of the *Journal* is devoted to the subject of compressed speech.)

requirements of speaking. The situation seems especially clearcut when we consider what may happen during the production of a comedy. The cast of a comic play may try to "break each other up." That is, they will try to cause each other to lose that poise, control, or discipline that permits us to make each other laugh. This need for control is often revealed when we are telling jokes to each other. The man who cannot "get out" the punch line to a joke he is telling needs a considerable store of tolerance in his audience if he hopes to hold their attention. Actors do break up, not only in high school auditoriums but also on nationwide television programs. Joke tellers sometimes dissolve, well before the punch line, into helpless wheezes of laughter. On the more serious side, every man recalls how he talked himself into readiness for a boyhood fist fight.

Besides this self-impacting character of speech, there is the use of speech as an IFF (Identification, Friend or Foe) device. This involves the use of special codes. Codes and languages are defined as consisting of a set of symbols and a set of rules for displaying or arraying those symbols. Many would add to this a set of rules by which symbols or arrays of symbols can come to have meaning for the arrayers. In any case, the code is deliberately designed to serve as a quick and easy indicator of social, moral, and ethical values. Language has a *shibboleth*[5] function, which is most noticeable in the spoken languages simply because the written languages have become so thoroughly standardized because of mandatory public education and the mass media. Spoken language is similarly standardized, but perhaps not to the same degree.

Besides, the IFF function, which is often an organizational or social economy, offers some interpersonal economy. Many codes designed for the sake of facilitating some task performance use more or less standard symbols. They merely eliminate the socioeconomic status markers from the symbol set and relax the rules of combination and association that have similar marker functions. Such language is called "telegraphic" because the telegraph was one of the first public communication systems in which, for many reasons, there was a high payoff for economy in coding.

Reading and Listening

These activities are usually thought of as the province of the receiver of messages rather than the province of the originator. However, as we are at pains to point out, we are all both sources and receivers of communications. It is evident that reading and listening are intimately concerned with one another. Certainly the ability to listen comes before the ability to read for all of us. The world is full of people who can listen but who cannot read. Perhaps a majority of the adults of the world are illiterate. In

[5] *Judges* XII: 4–6.

the United States, because of its very high literacy rate, we tend to overlook this.

One way to think about reading and listening is to consider ourselves as processors of information derived from messages that occur in a number of modes. Many of these modes have been detailed earlier in this essay and discussed at other places in the present volume. We talk and listen before we read and write. Yet we often find ourselves combining the modes. Children and learners often read aloud to themselves. Even after they have become expert readers, many people find that they change the written words into spoken words at a subconscious level.

Reading is a combination of the visual and the auditory. Another example of the cross checking that goes on between message system modes is that of the student who may not be satisfied that his instructor is really listening to him unless the instructor is looking at the student. The reverse is, of course, also true. Many of us can recall the type of student who assures his professor that he is indeed listening to the lecture even though his eyes are closed. Few are willing to accept in others the capacity of handling multi-mode inputs. Many have the idea that "you can only pay attention to one thing at a time." Yet many people seem to be able to read while listening to the radio, and many writers seem to be able to compose while listening to music.

Some have suggested that men prefer the spoken mode when they are primarily concerned with interpersonal relationships and the written mode when they are concerned primarily with content. This view is typified in the old saying, "Do right and fear no man, don't write and fear no woman." We suggest that there is a complex relationship among the following:

1. the receiver's capacity to discriminate among cues in written message situations as compared to his capacity to discriminate in spoken non-face-to-face message situations as compared to his capacity to discriminate in spoken face-to-face message situations;
2. the extent to which the source is constrained by some set of conventions regarding his choice of content and format;
3. the confidence the source has in his own discriminatory capacities;
4. the source's awareness of these and other relevant characteristics of the receiver;
5. the receiver's awareness of the source's awareness.

There are many more dimensions to this relationship constructed along the lines of the above.

Writing and Speaking

Many of the same arguments and points made with regard to reading and listening may be made with reference to writing and talking.

But we now have to deal with the decisions taken by the source end of the communication process (remembering always that the source is also receiver, and the receiver is also source, simultaneously in face-to-face situations, at least).

The source's task, like the receiver's, is the collection, categorization, storing, and retrieval of information. It is in connection with this task that the source makes decisions about his communication behavior. Some types of information the source would like to have are the same as the types the receiver would like to have. In the context of prolonged face-to-face communication, the source-receiver dichotomy is useless. Writing about the source and receiver separately (as we do here) is most useful in thinking about the mass media. That is, the separation seems to be most useful in thinking about communication situations that involve one-to-many or few-to-the-many messages.

In the face-to-face situation, as well as in the mass media situations, information has to be collected in terms of some statistical model. To oversimplify, we might say to ourselves in the face-to-face situation, "Well, I know Charlie is generally conservative, but in the present circumstances his self-acknowledged great desire for a particular goal *is probably going to increase his propensity for risk taking.*" The italicized part of the preceding sentence is, in the crude, implicit definition used here, the statistical-inferential part of the expression. We could argue that the prior part of the sentence is statistical-inferential in its bases and only seems assertive-declarative. We would rather, for the purpose of the present argument, conceive that the prior part expresses some belief without reference to any evidential basis or to any probabilistic validity assessment.

To return to our oversimplification, if you were in the situation in which we presently find ourselves, you might express some of your notions about your audience as follows: "The probability is quite high that a large majority of our readers are between the ages of 18 and 21. Since lower division (freshman and sophomore) classes tend to be larger, the mean age of all readers is probably closer to 18 than to 21. According to information about the adoptions of the first edition of this book, these students are not discriminable in terms of the regions of the United States in which they attend college. A minority of readers will be in the upper division and some will be in graduate school. There will be a small minority of readers consisting of faculty who have read the book to make a decision regarding its possible adoption in a course. (In some ways, remember, these are our most important readers because of their gatekeeper function.) Too, the lower division courses in which the book is used are probably required courses for some curricula, while the upper division and graduate courses are more likely to be elective courses. We know that on many campuses, certainly our own, there is a definite difference in the attitudes and expectations with which faculty and students alike approach an elective course and those with which they approach a required course. If we select some dimensions such as expected interest in the text, type of examination procedure, and the like, we might hypothesize that the mean of measurements along these dimensions might be lower for groups entering required lower-division undergraduate courses than for groups of students not entering such courses." All of these statements are of the statistical-inferential variety, or, as is sometimes said, they conform to and are derived from the hypothetico-deductive system of inquiry.

One reason why many prefer to "read" from written copy when they are using one or another of the so-called mass media (we call them "so-called" because they can only be used by the few to communicate to the many) is that the generation of a statistical model of the audience to permit prediction of audience response is expensive and risky. One who takes responsibility for the emission of a message wants the prior judgment of others regarding the probability of responses of various kinds to what he is doing. When a television program is broadcast "live," it quite often means that the show has been recorded on video tape a few hours earlier and that there has been no rehearsal or replaying of the program. Any untoward incidents or unacceptable words will be deleted either by cutting the tape or by "bleeping" out the unwanted words. The question, of course, is who decides what is to be deleted? And according to what criteria is the decision made?

At any rate, the choice between speaking and "reading" (speaking aloud a written message) is based upon estimates of the probable importance of the probable consequences (responses) to the message situation. Rapidity of adjustment (response) to the consequences is often considered easiest in the face-to-face situation and often has a mitigating effect upon consequences. We are usually willing, then, to take the greater risks attendant on spontaneous generation of spoken messages in the face-to-face situation, where we can adjust more quickly. At other times we prefer the reduced risks involved in written messages. In the mass media situation, as we have defined it, we find people becoming increasingly unwilling to be spontaneous and unrehearsed—especially if the stakes are high.

Exercises

1. It might be instructive to take a survey of the reading habits of the people in your class. How many books are read each year? How many of these are *not* required reading?

2. We discussed "telegraphic" codes and language that indicates social, moral, and ethical values. Cite and discuss examples of these.

3. How could the credibility of a speaker (see Hovland, Janis, and Kelley in this volume) affect the disparity between the source's emission of spoken words and the receiver's ability to process inputs?

4. How many variables can you list that might determine what messages you decide to send? This should, we think, be a big list.

Bibliography

Allport, Floyd H., *Theories of Perception and the Concept of Structure*. New York: John Wiley & Sons, Inc., 1955.

Anderson, Wallace L., and Norman C. Stageberg (eds.), *Introductory Readings on Language*. New York: Holt, Rinehart and Winston, Inc., 1962.

Baker, Sheridan, *The Practical Stylist*. New York: Thomas Y. Crowell Co., 1962.

Beardslee, David C., and Michael Wertheimer, *Readings in Perception*. Princeton, N.J.: D. Van Nostrand Co., Inc., 1958.

Bennis, Warren G., Kenneth D. Benne, and Robert Chin, *The Planning of Change: Readings in the Behavioral Sciences*. New York: Holt, Rinehart and Winston, Inc., 1962.

Berelson, Bernard, *Content Analysis in Communication Research*. Glencoe, Ill.: Free Press of Glencoe, Inc., 1952.

Berelson, Bernard, and Gary A. Steiner, *Human Behavior: An Inventory of Scientific Findings*. New York: Harcourt, Brace & World, Inc., 1964.

Berlo, David K., *The Process of Communication*. New York: Holt, Rinehart and Winston, Inc., 1960.

Bettinghaus, Erwin P., *Persuasive Communication*. New York: Holt, Rinehart and Winston, Inc., 1968.

Bion, W. R., *Experiences in Groups*. New York: Basic Books, Inc., 1961.

Birdwhistell, Ray L., *Introduction in Kinesics: An Annotation System for Analysis of Body Motion and Gesture*. Washington, D.C.: Foreign Service Institute, Department of State, 1952.

Blake, Robert R., and Glenn V. Ramsey (eds.), *Perception: An Approach to Personality*. New York: Ronald Press Co., 1951.

Bram, Joseph, *Language and Society*. New York: Random House, Inc., 1955.

Broadbent, D. E., *Perception and Communication*. New York: Pergamon Press, Inc., 1958.

Brown, Roger, *Words and Things*. Glencoe, Ill.: Free Press of Glencoe, Inc., 1958.

Bruner, Jerome S., Jacqueline J. Goodnow, and George A. Austin, *A Study of Thinking*. New York: Science Editions, 1962.

Carpenter, E., and M. McLuhan (eds.), *Explorations in Communication*. Boston: Beacon Press, 1960.

Cartwright, Dorwin, and Alvin Zander (eds.), *Group Dynamics: Research and Theory*, 2nd ed. Evanston, Ill.: Row, Peterson & Co., 1960.

Chase, Stuart, *The Tyranny of Words*. New York: Harcourt, Brace & Co., 1938.

Cherry, Colin, *On Human Communications*. New York: Science Editions, 1961.

Church, Joseph, *Language and the Discovery of Reality: A Developmental Psychology of Cognition*. New York: Random House, Inc., 1961.

Fine, B. J., "Conclusion-Drawing, Communicator Credibility, and Anxiety as Factors in Opinion Change," *Journal of Abnormal and Social Psychology*, 54:369–374 (1957).

Fogel, Lawrence J., *Human Information Processing*. Englewood Cliffs, N.J.: Prentice-Hall, Inc., 1967.

Greenberg, Joseph H. (ed.), *Universals of Language*. Cambridge, Mass.: The M.I.T. Press, 1963.

Hall, Edward T., *The Hidden Dimension*. New York: Doubleday and Co., Inc., 1966.

Hall, Edward T., *The Silent Language*. Garden City, N.Y.: Doubleday & Co., Inc., 1959.

Hall, Robert A., Jr., *Leave Your Language Alone!* Ithaca, N.Y.: Linguistica, 1950.

Haney, William V., *Communication: Patterns and Incidents*. Homewood, Ill.: Richard D. Irwin, Inc., 1960.

Hare, A. Paul, Edgar F. Bargatta, and Robert F. Bales (eds.), *Small Groups: Studies in Social Interaction*. New York: Alfred A. Knopf, Inc., 1955.

Harvey, O. J., and Jeanne Rutherford, "Gradual and Absolute Approaches to Attitude Change," *Sociometry,* 21:61–68 (1958).

Hayakawa, S. I., *Language in Thought and Action*. New York: Harcourt, Brace & World, Inc., 1964.

Hebb, D. O., *Organization of Behavior*. New York: John Wiley & Sons, Inc., 1949.

Heider, Fritz, *The Psychology of Interpersonal Relations*. New York: John Wiley & Sons, Inc., 1958.

Hilgard, Ernest, *Theories of Learning*. New York: Appleton-Century-Crofts, Inc., 1956.

Hoggart, Richard, *The Uses of Literacy*. Boston: Beacon Press, Inc., 1961.

Homans, George Caspar, *Social Behavior: Its Elementary Forms*. New York: Harcourt, Brace & World, Inc., 1961.

Hovland, Carl I., *The Order of Presentation in Persuasion*. New Haven, Conn.: Yale University Press, 1959.

Hovland, Carl I., and Irving L. Janis (eds.), *Personality and Persuasibility*. New Haven, Conn.: Yale University Press, 1957.

Hovland, Carl I., and H. A. Pritzker, "Extent of Opinion Change as a Function of Amount of Change Advocated," *Journal of Abnormal and Social Psychology,* 54:257–261 (1957).

Huff, Darrell, *How to Lie with Statistics*. New York: W. W. Norton & Co., Inc., 1954.

Janis, I. L., and S. Feshback, "Effects of Fear-Arousing Communications," *Journal of Abnormal and Social Psychology,* 48:78–92 (1953).

Jespersen, Otto, *Growth and Structure of the English Language*. Garden City, N.Y.: Doubleday & Co., Inc., 1955.

Johnson, Wendell, *People in Quandaries: The Semantics of Personal Adjustment*. New York: Harper & Row, Publishers, Inc., 1946.

Katz, E., and Paul F. Lazarsfeld, *Personal Influence: The Part Played by People in the Flow of Mass Communication*. Glencoe, Ill.: Free Press of Glencoe, Inc., 1955.

Kiesler, C., Barry Collins, and Norman Miller, *Attitude Change.* New York: John Wiley and Sons, Inc., 1969.

Klapper, Joseph T., *The Effects of Mass Communication*. Glencoe, Ill.: Free Press of Glencoe, Inc., 1960.

Kohler, Wolfgang, *Gestalt Psychology*. New York: Liveright Publishing Corp., 1947.

Lado, Robert, *Linguistics across Cultures*. Ann Arbor: University of Michigan Press, 1957.

Lehmann, Winfred P., *Historical Linguistics: An Introduction*. New York: Holt, Rinehart and Winston, Inc., 1962.

Lindzey, Gardner (ed.), *Assessment of Human Motives*. New York: Grove Press, Inc., 1960.

Lindzey, Gardner (ed.), *Handbook of Social Psychology*. Cambridge, Mass.: Addison-Wesley Publishing Co., Inc., 1954.

Matson, Floyd W., *The Broken Image*. Garden City, New York: Anchor Books, Doubleday and Company, Inc., 1966.

Matson, F. W., and A. Montague (eds.), *The Human Dialogue: Perspectives on Communication*. New York: Free Press, 1967.

Maurer, David W., *The Big Con*. Rev. Signet ed., P-2212. New York: New American Library of World Literature, Inc.

Miller, George A., *Language and Communication*. New York: McGraw-Hill Book Co., Inc., 1951.

Miller, George A., Eugene Galanter, and Karl H. Pribam, *Plans and the Structure of Behavior*. New York: Holt, Rinehart and Winston, Inc., 1960.

Miller, G. R., *Speech Communication: A Behavioral Approach*. New York: The Bobbs-Merrill Co., Inc., 1966.

Mowrer, O. Hobart, *Learning Theory and the Symbolic Processes*. New York: John Wiley & Sons, Inc., 1960.

Newcomb, Theodore M., *The Acquaintance Process*. New York: Holt, Rinehart and Winston, Inc., 1961.

Nida, Eugene A., *Linguistic Interludes*. Glendale, Calif.: Summer Institute of Linguistics, Inc., 1947.

Olmstead, Michael S., *The Small Group*. New York: Random House, Inc., 1959.

Orr, David B. (ed.), "Special Issue on Compressed Speech," *The Journal of Communication*, 18:3 (Sept. 1968).

Osgood, C. E., and T. A. Sebeok, *Psycholinguistics: A Survey of Theory and Research Problems*. Bloomington, Indiana: Indiana University Press, 1965.

Penfield, Wilder, and Lamar Roberts, *Speech and Brain-Mechanisms*. Princeton, N.J.: Princeton University Press, 1959.

Riesman, David, *The Lonely Crowd*. New Haven, Conn.: Yale University Press, 1950.

Rose, Arnold (ed.), *Human Behavior and Social Processes*. Boston: Houghton Mifflin Co., 1962.

Ruesch, Jurgen, and Gregory Bateson, *Communication: The Social Matrix of Psychiatry*. New York: W. W. Norton & Co., Inc., 1951.

Ruesch, Jurgen, and Weldon Kees, *Nonverbal Communication*. Berkeley: University of California Press, 1956.

Samstag, Nicholas, *Persuasion for Profit.* Norman: University of Oklahoma Press, 1958.

Saporta, Sol (ed.), *Psycholinguistics: A Book of Readings.* New York: Holt, Rinehart and Winston, Inc., 1961.

Schramm, Wilbur (ed.), *The Process and Effects of Mass Communication.* Urbana: University of Illinois Press, 1954.

Schramm, Wilbur (ed.), *The Science of Human Communication.* New York: Basic Books, Inc., 1963.

Schroder, H. M., M. Driver, and S. Streufert, *Human Information Processing.* New York: Holt, Rinehart, and Winston, Inc., 1967.

Shannon, Claude E., and Warren Weaver, *The Mathematical Theory of Communication.* Urbana: University of Illinois Press, 1962.

Smith, A. G., *Communication and Status: The Dynamics of a Research Center.* Eugene, Oregon: Center for the Advanced Study of Educational Administration, University of Oregon, 1966.

Smith, A. G. (ed.), *Communication and Culture.* New York: Holt, Rinehart and Winston, Inc., 1966.

Smith, Bruce Lannes, Harold D. Lasswell, and Ralph D. Casey, *Propaganda, Communication, and Public Opinion.* Princeton, N.J.: Princeton University Press, 1946.

Snow, C. P., *Science and Government.* Cambridge, Mass.: Harvard University Press, 1961.

Sorenson, Theodore C., *Decision-Making in the White House: The Olive Branch or the Arrows.* New York: Columbia University Press, 1963.

Strunk, William, Jr., and E. B. White, *The Elements of Style.* New York: Macmillan Co., 1959.

Thayer, Lee O., *Administrative Communication.* Homewood, Illinois: Richard D. Irwin, Inc., 1968.

Thayer, Lee O. (ed.), *Communication: Concepts and Perspectives.* Washington: Spartan Books, 1967.

Thayer, Lee O. (ed.), *Communication: Theory and Research.* Springfield, Illinois: Charles C Thomas, 1967.

Thayer, Lee O., *Communication and Communication Systems.* Homewood, Illinois: Richard D. Irwin, Inc., 1968.

Waterman, John T., *Perspectives in Linguistics: An Account of the Background of Modern Linguistics.* Chicago: University of Chicago Press, 1963.

Watzlawick, Paul, J. H. Beavin, and D. D. Jackson, *Pragmatics of Human Communication.* New York: W. W. Norton and Co., 1967.

Weaver, Warren, *Lady Luck: The Theory of Probability.* Garden City, N.Y.: Doubleday & Co., Inc., 1963.

Weeks, Francis William (ed.), *Readings in Communication from* Fortune. New York: Holt, Rinehart and Winston, Inc., 1961.

Weiss, Walter, and B. J. Fine, "Opinion Change as a Function of Some Intrapersonal Attitudes of the Communicatees," *Journal of Abnormal and Social Psychology,* 51:246–253 (1955).

Whorf, Benjamin Lee, *Language, Thought, and Reality*. Cambridge, Mass.: The M.I.T. Press, 1956.

Whyte, William H., Jr., *Is Anybody Listening?* New York: Simon and Schuster, Inc., 1952.

Wiener, Norbert, *The Human Use of Human Beings*. Garden City, N.Y.: Doubleday & Co., Inc., 1956.